I Don't Have A Clue How To Live This Life

..... and I would bet that you don't either!

Ken Jones

Howe Town Publishing

Contents

Introduction

After numerous years of this miserable existence that we call our reality, I have come to an awareness that I do not have a clue how to live this life. Regardless of who we may be, where we are from, or where we may find ourselves in life at the moment, all of us retain a deep inner assumption that something is missing—that there must be more.

We crave more. We desire more. We want more. And not so much in terms of quantity, but of quality. More meaningful, more purposeful, and more fulfilling. But no matter where we turn, no matter how hard we may try, no matter how deep we look, we always seem to find ourselves back in that same empty place, never having unraveled the quagmire of our lives. And each time we find ourselves in that empty place yet once again, it is only more dejected and confused than we were before.

This is my life and has been my life for the past forty plus years. One could easily say that this is who I was, or functionally still may be to some extent. However, those who do know me would surely acknowledge that a significant change has occurred recently in my life, causing me to become noticeably different. And while a complete shift in my direction has overtaken me, I still find myself having the same mindfulness that I don't have a clue how to live this life, albeit for much different reasons now.

The truth is that you are probably very much just like me, probably more so than you might want to admit—at least at this point. And probably more so than you will care to admit by the time you reach the end of this book. As I begin writing this book, I am a middle-aged man living what most people peering in from the outside would call a 'good life'.

From the inside – I have acquired a completely different perspective, one of a life which has been an utterly misguided disaster. A life of erroneous choices, wrong paths, and futile resistance. A life of insecurity and doubt. A life of abuse and destruction, both to myself and others. A life full of questions, many of which still remain unanswered.

A man constantly looking back trying to figure out how and where it all went wrong. A man left wondering how a world filled with so much potential and opportunity could only lead to never-ending pain and devastation. A man left questioning the possibility of any logical reasoning for his existence at all. A man who does not see himself as a man at all, but as that little boy of his past who's only desire was to be wanted.

While I may not be the next cover model for GQ Magazine, I would like to think that my looks would not make you nauseous either. I am of average height at 5 foot 11 inches. I have never been overweight and would call my build athletic or slim. I have brown hair and hazel eyes and have no outstanding features on my face or body that would make me easily distinguishable. If I were to walk down any given street, on any given day, I would easily blend in with everyone else. I am what you would call an 'Average Joe'.

I am also not a writer per se, nor have I ever had the desire to write a book until recently. I do not have a doctorate degree in counseling, psychology, or any other field for that matter. I do not have a pastoral degree, nor have I ever attended seminary. Again, I am an Average Joe!

I came from what most people would call 'the wrong side of the tracks', a neighborhood which was less than desirable to say the least. A neighborhood that people do not choose to live in, but most always find themselves in due to some type of financial crisis. Our neighborhood wasn't actually that bad, albeit in the perception of a teenage boy. However, it was not the environment that most adults would intentionally choose to raise their children in.

When I was a young boy, we lived in a part of town that was populated by lower middle-class people—okay, maybe lower, lower middle class. Most all of the homes were small in size, lacking any aesthetical features. Most all of the homes were one-story. Most all of the homes were poorly maintained. And . . . most all of the homes were single-parent homes. That was my home as well, with a single mom trying to raise four kids, just trying to get by and survive. We will touch more on this in later chapters.

So, I am an Average Joe, with average looks, raised in a broken family. I managed to dig my way out of the slums and find a path that would eventually lead me to the more desirable west side of town and now have what most would consider the good life. Sounds like an American success story, right? **Wrong!**

Success is a matter of perception. What one person views as a success can and will be seen as an absolute failure by another. And just as well, while reaching a specified target or goal may be viewed as a success, the processes or path taken to reach that target or goal may have been disastrous, leaving chaos and havoc in its wake. The target or goal may have been achieved, but at what cost to yourself and to others.

A few years ago, God came into my life in a very strong and confrontive way and woke me up (think Moses and the burning bush with God's presence, just without Moses and the bush - or the fire). Yes, it truly was that powerful. God showed me that the way I had been living my life – everything that I had been doing which I had come to understand as the good Christian way to live life, and everything that I had come to accept as the way to live this life – was completely wrong.

God showed me how I had been misled, lied to, and deceived by this worldly system and Satan, who is the father of lies. And then God showed me how we should be living this life, how He wants me to live my life, and how He intended for me to live my life. By nothing but the pure grace and love of Jesus Christ, God stepped into my life and said, *"Enough is enough. It's time to start paying attention."*

As you will see throughout the course of this book, God had been trying to get my attention for many years. However, I had become so entrenched in the self-life that I was completely unaware that God was even there. I had become so focused on the ways of this world and trying to adapt and fit in as a means of survival that I had long since forgotten how to be me, let alone who me was – and was simply trying to be the me that I thought everyone else wanted me to be, or that I needed to be for everyone else.

I am one of the lucky ones though, and I am hoping and praying that since you have picked up this book, you will be too. I have written this book because I was just like you – I was a lost soul who thought he had it all figured out. I then became a Christian and was attending church weekly and believed that I was doing what I needed to do, or what God wanted me to do. I was a so called 'good person', or so I thought – at least I tried to be. I thought I had life all figured out . . . once again.

Then, after God opened my eyes and allowed me to see the Light, the Truths, and His true desires, I knew right away that there were millions of Average Joes (and Janes) out there just like me, who needed to hear and know the Truth. I also realized that what we have come to perceive as the truth – our reality – is nothing more than lies and deception meant to keep us from seeing life as it was truly meant to be lived.

This book is my perspective of life, and the events which have transpired throughout my life. It is the story of a boy who does exactly what we all try to do in this life – adapt and survive. It is the story of a life filled with pain and loneliness brought on by the drugs, sex, violence, death, and countless acts of harm against others, all while living out a life of self-indulgence and pleasure. It is the story of how God came into the life of a young boy who was destined for never-ending misery and destruction and then showed that boy what he was truly created to be and the fulfilling life that he was meant to live.

Your past may not be the exact same as mine was, but since you are more than likely just like me in one way or another, your future can be the same as mine. Your perspective will most certainly be different than mine as well. You may even find yourself having difficulty in making an early association with my character at this point, thus debating whether you should read on or not. However, you very well may be one of the lucky ones too, and reading on may just open your eyes to the numerous tendencies and flaws which we have in our perspectives, which limit and restrict our view of reality, and also inhibit who we become as well as any possibility of reaching our true potential.

God loves you as if you were the only person on this earth! You do matter to God, and He has been and is always willing to fight for you, just as He did for me. That statement is simply validated by the fact that God has allowed a way for this book to get into your hands. It did not happen merely by accident or chance!

God has given each of us a 'purpose' for our lives, whether we have realized that yet or not. God has recently shown me what the 'purpose' in my life is, which I will detail more throughout the book. My simple and concise purpose statement is *'to simplify the complicated.'* This book has been written with that purpose in mind, in a very simplistic and understandable way, thus enabling the reader to easily understand and comprehend God's true Word, His true desires and plans for us, with a straightforward and understandable meaning of the Scriptures and the Word which God has given all of us to live by.

While some may quickly say – *"I already know Scripture and God's Word"*, and therefore believe nothing further can be gained, I would challenge you to read on as we will also come to learn how God's Word, God's true intention for our lives, as well as the ways in which we view God, have all been skewed just as our perspectives have.

I invite you into my life, my stories, and my experiences – some having never been revealed to anyone prior to this book. There may be some portions of this book that become difficult to grasp using our modern-day understanding and perspective. I ask that you set aside those preconceived beliefs and ideas for now and proceed with an open mind and heart. You may just learn something. After all, that is why you picked up this book, is it not? That is why you read, is it not? So that you may learn something new.

Life does not have to be hard or complicated—we just like to make it that way. Religion does not have to be hard or complicated—we just like to make it that way. And God does not have to be hard or complicated—we just like to make Him that way!

"Because the knowledge of the secrets of the kingdom of heaven has been given to you, but not to them. Whoever has will be given more, and they will have an abundance. Whoever does not have, even what they have will be taken from them"
Matthew 13:11-12

Preface

I t is just another Thursday morning . . . or is it Wednesday? How quickly I forget. It's 5 a.m. and another day is opening just as they all do. The same routine, the same steps, the same scenery, the same boring outlook in a world which promises me nothing—over and over again. Hopelessly lost somewhere in the middle of this week, I force myself to pick up and carry on. Not even halfway to the weekend I am already completely drained of anything that I may have possessed just a few days ago which perhaps was good or hopeful. I am no longer excited about or looking forward to anything or anyone. My only desire is to make it through yet another agonizing day, another week . . . and to just survive.

My mind, my heart, and my soul all retract inward for yet another attempt at self-preservation. *Is this all there is?* The same old monotonous existence which plays itself out in an ever-so-painful way? The abuse, the misery, the suffering. The emptiness, the loneliness, the abandonment. Being beaten down, weary, and utterly worn out. Unable to grab even the smallest slice of enjoyment or happiness, let alone a moment of peace or serenity. And even the very few moments of joy or pleasure that we do allow ourselves are never fulfilling as they are all counterfeit at best. We are simply teasing ourselves with something or someone which we know, all too well, will only leave us even more broken and empty than before.

There has to be more. Someone, please, tell me there is. There has to be a more meaningful and satisfying reason for our existence than this pathetic life that pummels us each and every day.

But then, just as always, I pick myself up and unwillingly force myself back out into the world for yet another round of torture and abuse. Why? Because I have too. I have obligations. I have commitments. I have bills to pay. I have a family depending on me. I have an image to uphold, and I must continue to play out the role of me. The role that was created for me, and that was created by me. The role that I despise with everything in me.

Chapter 1

The Question

It was late fall, early winter in 1993. It was a cold Midwestern night, and I believe we already had snow on the ground. I laid in bed that night, completely naked and fully exposed to the beautiful young woman that I had recently started dating several months before. The night was playing out as it usually did, and just as I had hoped it would. However, I had no fathomable idea that what would transpire that night would change my life forever and lead me down a road of complete confusion, with so many unanswered questions. It would eventually take me to a place deep within my soul, leaving me totally exposed and vulnerable, just as I was on this night. It would show me the phony facade of the world that we live in, as well as reveal to me the counterfeit that I had become. It would discredit all the knowledge that I had come to believe as being accurate and true, leaving me to question everyone and everything, including myself and all of my own thoughts.

The **it**, was one question. One simple question that turned my whole world upside down. One question from a beautiful, harmless young woman. One question with no ill intent or detriment intended. One question – five simple words that would have an impact on my life greater than I could have ever imagined. Five simple words that would turn my entire life upside down and eventually provide the answer to all the questions that unbeknownst to me I had been so desperately seeking since my childhood.

I was born and raised in Omaha, Nebraska. Some refer to it as the Biggest Small Town, while others call it the Smallest Big Town. I, however, usually called it a bunch of other things, none of which are worth repeating. I had never been very fond of my hometown, but like it or not, it would become the backdrop for most of my younger years.

Winters in Nebraska can be brutal at times. Some years you can get snow as early as September and it will stay on the ground all the way through May. Other years you may not see any snow. However, every year it would always get cold. Bone chilling cold. Nebraska seems to be situated in the perfect spot in the middle of the country where it always gets the brunt force of the weather systems coming down out of Canada during the winter. It wasn't always the freezing temperatures that got to you during winter, it was the wind. Thirty, forty and even fifty mile per hour winds are not uncommon with these systems, and when coupled with temperatures below freezing, and sometimes below zero, staying warm was not an easy task.

I had graduated High School in Omaha and then bounced around doing a couple different jobs in that area as I was not sure what I wanted to do with my life. My father lived in Colorado and had for the last eighteen years after he had left my mother. My father had been a pilot for a period of time back in his younger days and suggested that I move out to Colorado to check out a flight school, and possibly enroll, with the goal of becoming a commercial airline pilot. I finally did make the move, enrolled in the flight school, spent the next three years getting my licenses and certifications . . . and then moved back to Omaha where I got another job as a chef.

I had my usual long day at work as the Head Chef at a local restaurant on that cold day in 1993. I opened the kitchen at about 5 a.m. Received deliveries. Got the staff going on that day's prep work. Had a meeting with the general manager. Paperwork, ordering, scheduling, and other mundane tasks. And then cooked the orders for the lunch crowd. I would then handle any other issues that came up throughout the day, clean the kitchen up, and hopefully be done by 5 p.m. This was a normal day, and on this particular day in 1993 I believe I left work between 4 and 5 p.m.

The beautiful young woman that laid beside me on that cold night attended a local medical school and was soon to graduate. She would attend school all day and then would spend all evening with me as we had been hitting it off pretty well since we started dating. We met several months prior to this day in a very unexpected way.

She had a sister, Sandi, who worked as a waitress. I had known Sandi for many years as she had worked with me at other restaurants and now worked with me at the restaurant where I was the chef. Sandi was always very nice and friendly, and we would occasionally chat about menial things throughout the day. Sandi would occasionally say to me *"I have a sister that I am going to hook you up with."* That went on for what seemed to be a couple of years, and I would always shrug it off. I had little-to-no interest in a blind date with someone I had never even seen a picture of or knew anything about. And I certainly was not looking for any type of commitment.

One Sunday afternoon several months before, as we were finishing up with the breakfast/lunch crowd, Sandi came up to me and said *"Hey, do you want to go out for drinks with my sister and me after work?"* Sandi was married, and I knew her husband as well. Sandi was also a model on the side, and was attractive herself, so I figured there was a good chance that her sister may also be attractive. Something got the curiosity in me going, and I said *"Sure, why not?"*

We all met later that evening at a small local pub in an older part of town. When I arrived, I saw Sandi and her husband sitting at the bar with another gal which was her sister. The only thing I could see, or notice, was her long blondish hair and her long legs that went on forever. Suddenly, I began to have thoughts that I may not be good enough for this. I was in over my head and would surely be exposed for what I truly was. Fortunately, I was a 'type A' kind of guy. I always had, or at least showed, confidence on the outside, even if I wasn't feeling it on the inside and had to fake it. I walked over and greeted Sandi and her husband, and was introduced to her sister, Robin.

We sat around the bar for a few hours. I honestly can't remember how long we were there as I was so intoxicated by the beautiful young woman sitting next to me. I don't exactly recall what we did when we left the bar either. However, I can tell you that as most people do nowadays, we did not go home and have sex. While I was a type A kind of guy, I had been going through many changes in my life at that point and was trying to view women differently than I had in the past. I was beginning to see them for the people they were and not just an object to satisfy my sexual desires. Or I was at least trying to anyways – change doesn't happen overnight. So, at some point that night, we parted ways.

I chased after Robin almost daily. She was the only thing that I could think about, day and night. As you will discover in later chapters, my reasoning wasn't always the best, and despite my newly acquired view of respect I was usually only thinking about one thing. I was in my early twenties, had a good job, had a nice sports car, and spent my free time partying. I just needed a pretty girl to complete the package and satisfy all my needs. Robin managed to see something in me that she liked as well, and we started dating and seeing each other on a regular basis. I am not sure what it was though. To this day I give her a hard time and tell her that the only reason she had interest in me was because she just wanted to drive my sports car.

Back to that cold night in 1993 – I left work around 4 or 5 p.m. Robin finished up school and came over to my place as she had been doing a lot lately. A long-time buddy and I shared a house together. We had rented a one-story home in the middle of town, which had a completely finished basement. My buddy lived on the main floor, and I lived in the basement. We were both single and had good jobs. He held the same position that I did, but for a different restaurant, so our work hours were almost always the same. We would both be up and out of the house early, work all day, and then stay up late at night, usually drinking and having friends over. This wouldn't happen every night but was a common theme several nights of the week and especially on weekends. We pretty much ran our own little part of the world. We called all of the shots at work and did whatever we wanted to do in the evenings.

Before too long, Robin began to spend the nights at my place, and we began to get intimate. I am sure that if I knew then what I do now, I would have realized that Robin, as the female gender does, was looking at our relationship differently than I was, and she was likely being more logical and thinking long-term. I still had my head where it always was, in the here-and-now. I would have also realized that although Robin seemed to be this perfect, innocent, pure woman, she did not come without baggage either.

I know now through having a daughter of my own that women, or girls, seek and need affirmation and love from their father, and if they are unable to get that from their father, for whatever reason, they will seek it elsewhere. More often than not, that ends with them finding an abusive boyfriend/husband, resulting in divorce, and at times something much worse.

That was not me, however. My life had been nothing but a series of traumatic events that led me to be so intently focused on just surviving that I didn't have the ability to see or understand any issues that others may be dealing with. Every thought I had, every action that I took, every decision that I made, was with the sole purpose of survival, or making my life better for me.

This was the early to mid '90s, and waterbeds were popular back then. I loved mine, and the thing I loved most was that mine had a heater attached to it. I could turn the heater on before going to bed, set it to the desired temperature, and the bed would be all warm and toasty throughout the night. I think Robin liked it more than I did.

As we laid there completely naked in my waterbed on that cold night, Robin was laying her head on my chest as she usually did. I was probably thinking about the super- hot, sexy girl lying next to me, and what we were about to do. She was obviously thinking about other things, which is almost always the case with women and men as well. Neither one of us were talking or doing anything, just lying there enjoying each other. Then out of nowhere, Robin lifted up her head, stared right into my eyes, and announced, *"I have to ask you a question."*

Oh man, here we go! The alarms start going off in my head. What could it be? Is she going to find out about my past, the things I have done? Is this it? Is this the end of something that seemed so good that would last forever? I had a lot of questions of my own running through my head, trying to prepare for the worst-case scenario and mentally readying myself with any explanation that would keep her in my bed and in my life.

After that, she paused for a few seconds, then uttered the question as I was holding my breath, hoping that the world didn't end right then and there.

"Do you believe in God?"

I had to stop and process that for a second. I told myself that it could not be that simple. It had to be a trick question! Was that it? That was the question? I looked at her and said, *"What?"*

She asked me again, *"Do you believe in God?"*

I kind of laughed and said, *"That's an easy one"*, although she probably had no idea that I was comparing it to all of the other possible questions going through my head at that time. I looked back into her eyes and said *"Yes, I believe in God."*

That was the end of the questioning, and we had no further discussion. I don't remember what we did the rest of the night, but you can probably guess. What I didn't realize at that moment was how significant that one question was, and how that one question, and the answer, would forever change my life. I would not realize the impact of that night for many years to come, or how the answer to that question would unravel everything in my world, while at the same time lead me to a destination that would make everything so perfectly clear.

Robin never brought the question up again, and never tried to push any religion on me, which only made me ponder the reasoning behind the question even more as time went on. It took many years for me to fully understand why she didn't press the issue, especially if it was so important to her. I would eventually come not only to know, but truly understand the reason for her question, and why she didn't need any further explanation at that point in our lives.

You see, I did believe in God, or at least that there was a God. However, I did not know anything about God, let alone Jesus, even though I had been introduced to religion in my early childhood years. I had never given a minute's thought to God, religion, or how either may affect or impact my life or the world that I lived in up to this point.

Robin and I got married several months later in 1994. Over the following years we had four children – three boys and one girl. Robin obviously had her roots grounded in God's word and was obedient in honoring God. She by no means was what we used to call a 'preachers' daughter', but she knew who she served, and that would never change. I truly believe now that God put Robin into my life for a specific reason, because she was exactly what and who I needed.

However, before we can get into the details of our lives together, and what has transpired over the years, we must understand where I came from and what shaped me into who I was.

"And I will put enmity between you and the woman, and between your seed and her seed; He shall bruise your head, and you shall bruise His heel" Genesis 3:15

Chapter 2

In the Beginning

I was born in the late '60's. The United States government was desperately trying to find a way out of Vietnam, and a war that had divided our country in more ways than one can explain. The Baby Boomers, as we would soon come to know them, were at that time rising up against the legalistic views of their parents and busting loose in a completely opposite direction. The early '70s would lead to continually rising inflation year after year and is now known as The Great Inflation decade with devastating double-digit inflation. By 1980 inflation rates had hit a high of 14%. Mortgage rates began the decade around 7% and eventually climbed to an all-time high of 16% in the early 1980's, making it all but impossible to purchase a home. President Richard Nixon became the only President to this date to resign his office, as a result of the Watergate scandal. Vice President Gerald Ford succeeded Nixon and held the office of President for two years until being beaten by Jimmy Carter during the election. Ford was the only person to hold both the office of Vice President and President, without having been elected to either position. In 1974, Carter would assume control of a country that was socially divided, beaten up, in financial despair, and was in the middle of an energy crisis. What a great time to be a young kid, growing up in America.

My mother and father were married at the time, and it was the picture of a normal family upbringing, or so I thought. My parents had four children, of which I was the second. I had a brother who was two years older, a sister who was two years younger, and then another brother who was four years younger. We lived in an average size home in an average part of town, that my father's parents had either purchased or helped to purchase (Grandpa was the President of a local bank).

Life seemed good as a little runt running around without a care in the world. However, I have very few memories of those days anymore, and the one's that I do have do not seem to be very good, with one exception. I often wonder if I just really did not have anything special or dramatic happen in my younger years, or if I have just chosen to so deeply push those memories down that they are now impossible to drag out.

My Grandparents on my father's side lived about six blocks down the street from us, and they were an integral part of my childhood. My grandfather was the President of a local bank, which really meant nothing to me as a child. All I knew was that he was a firm, honest, sincere man. He was capable of showing you love and attention, but that was usually Grandma's job. Mmmmm, Grandma. Now there are some of the best memories that I have as a young child. Grandma was always there, to teach us, love us, care for us, and try to give us new experiences. Grandma was like the mother that you wish you always had. In grandma's arms and embrace you felt a warm secure feeling that nothing else could compare to. You knew you were safe. You knew you were loved unconditionally. Grandma was the first person that I can remember who showed me what a Bible was and actually read to me from the Bible. I miss her so much. Even though I was only able to spend limited time with her, every memory that I have of her is one of my most cherished.

Grandma passed away in 1980. My Grandparents had a two-story home, and their bedroom was on the second floor. Grandma came down the stairs after waking that final morning and felt pain in her chest which caused her to sit down on the floor. Within moments she had a ruptured aneurysm, and her heart basically exploded. I was too young to realize the extent of this loss at the time, but it still pains me today. Things were never the same after that day, and trips to my grandparents' house completely disappeared.

It took me most of my adult life to realize it, but the day that my grandma died was the day that I lost something, something that I would spend every moment of my life trying to replace. Love and affection. Grandma was the only person in my life that had ever shown me true, unbiased, unconditional love and affection.

My Grandparents were what you would call 'simple folks'. They could afford the luxuries that life had to offer at that time but chose not to. My grandma still washed clothes by hand on an old washboard and then hung them out to dry on the clothesline. They had a small AM radio that they occasionally listened too for news. In the corner of their living room was a cabinet style television with doors on the front that closed and made it look just like another piece of furniture. I can recall seeing the inside, or the TV, only once. My grandfather was the only one who would watch the TV, and then only on Sunday night for an hour or so, when the show 60 Minutes came on, and the occasional Lawrence Welk show. They had only one car, which I would speculate was five to six years old. It was a 4-door sedan. Nothing fancy. No bells or whistles. No upgrades. Just the basic car to get grandpa back and forth to work. Grandpa was the only one who ever drove that car. Not that grandma couldn't drive, she was more than capable, but I guess that is just the way things were in those days. The car was rarely ever used except for grandpa going to work and the occasional trip to the grocery store.

On the rare occasion, my Grandparents would take us kids out for an adventure in that bare-bone's car. Those were special days, and ones that I will never forget. We would pack up the car with a special picnic lunch that grandma had made and head out – always away from town. We would drive out to the country. Nothing too far, just far enough that we felt as if we were all alone. Just us and the beautiful, peaceful countryside. On one trip I remember driving out to some wide-open field and picking blueberries with grandma all day. On other trips we would go to a small lake and fish for bluegill. Grandpa was the one who taught me how to fish, and how to do it on my own, even at a young age.

They had lived through The Great Depression and had fought their way back to having a nice home, a comfortable savings, and a nice life. However, as with all of us, the events and experiences that we go through in our lives shape the way that we view life, and who we become. Author and Businessman W. Clement Stone provided the famous quote *"You are a product of your environment."*[1]

Even though my grandfather was the President of a local bank, my Grandparents had been so affected and traumatized by the events of The Great Depression that even into the 1980's, fifty years later, they still refused keep any money in a bank in any way. When my grandmother passed away, her two children which were my father and his sister, quickly came from out of town and rummaged through the home for anything of value and then became estranged to each other as they fought for whatever they could get their hands on. Maybe they didn't have the same memories that I had. Maybe they hadn't seen the love that I had. Maybe they had lost touch with what was important. I couldn't understand their greed and self-centeredness. It was found that my Grandparents had kept all their savings in cash, everywhere in their home. Large denomination bills were found stacked and lined in dresser drawers, books, cabinets, mattresses, and anywhere else you could imagine.

My grandfather soon could not live with being in that empty house alone, so he packed up and moved into a high rise assisted living facility. Within a couple years my grandfather passed away as well. I am not sure of the exact cause of his death, but I would bet that it was due to a broken heart. My Grandparents had been married for over fifty years, and my grandma was his first and only love.

My Grandparents on my mother's side had been divorced, and that grand-father lived out of town. My Grandmother lived in the same town that we did, but she too passed away when I was very young, and I have no memories of her. My mother had two sisters and a couple Aunts who lived in town as well. They had all been married once and were all divorced. Not one of them had remarried either. I have no fond memories of my mother's side of the family as a little boy growing up, and mostly only remember that after my parents divorced, we would spend most holidays with my mother's side of the family, which seemed like a gathering of angry, bitter women. Each of my mother's sisters had two children who were close in age to my siblings and I. Ironically, my mother and her two sisters who appeared to have a hatred for men, had all boys for children, with the exception of my younger sister. My sister became the center of attention at the family gatherings, and the boys were shooed off to do boy things. It was not a good environment for a young boy to grow up in. A young boy who inherently needs the love and affirmation of a father, and to know that he is loved and wanted by his parents.

I do not have much background on my mother's side of the family, or their upbringing as those Grandparents did not exist in my life, and it was not some-thing that my mother chose to pass on. I came to know that my mother's father, my grandfather, had a brother whose son went on to become a famous rock star. His name is Peter Frampton. He became one of the top rock stars in the 1960's and 1970's, playing with the bands *The Herd* and *Humble Pie*. Peter later went on to a very successful solo career in the early 1970's and had his most successful album released in 1976, titled *Frampton Comes Alive*[2], which has become one of the bestselling live albums of all time. A 2012 article in Rolling Stone Magazine stated, *"He owned the year 1976 like nobody else in rock."*[3]

I never met Peter personally but did become a fan of his music and his style of play. I was a bit young for hard rock when he was at his best. However, I am in my mid-fifties now, and Peter has taken back to playing again. He has recently released a couple new albums and is even touring again. The thought has crossed my mind a time or two to go to one of his shows. Maybe looking for that connection. Maybe hoping that I will find something that I never had. Maybe hoping that it will give me some sense of family again. But.... I never do.

I also know that my mother and her two sisters were raised in a Catholic family, and that all three sisters attended a Catholic school. This might explain why they chose not to remarry, but I cannot say for sure. It very much explained or helped me to understand their perception of life, the family unit, and us children. But their views on life, what they had learned from their parents and how to raise kids, especially boys, left me empty and searching for that love and connection that I had been deprived of.

I stated earlier that God has opened my eyes to many things over the past couple of years, in many ways. One thing God has given me lately is a passion for reading. I would say that my true passion in reading is the desire to learn more, to learn more about God, what God truly desires, and what it is that He is asking of me through my creation. *What is my purpose? Why am I here? What is the reasoning for my life?*

There are no simple answers to these questions, but to find the answers you first must go backwards and understand who you are, and what makes you who you are. I have always tried to bury and hide who I was for several reasons. The first being that it hurt. It hurts to go back and relive, even if only in my mind, a childhood of feeling that you were in this world all on your own, as a child, with no one that cares. The second reason being that my later teenage years are something that I am not proud of and am rather ashamed of to say the least. The mention of just a few of these things in later chapters will be the first time that I have revealed them to anyone since those dark days of my past, and it is with great reluctance that I do so knowing that my wife and grown children will see a side of me that they have never seen before. A side of me that I have done everything within my power to ensure never surfaced again.

However, to go forward, you must first go back. And that which lies ahead, is much greater than the iniquity and pain of the past.

I never liked to read. That was an unmistakable fact. Painful, boring. I would actually have to sit still for an extended length of time and focus. I think I have read maybe three books my entire life prior to my recent years, and two of those three were most likely MAD magazine (a childhood humor magazine started in 1952).

Several months ago, my pastor and I were having a casual conversation about life and its related struggles. At the end of the conversation, he said that he knew exactly what I needed and gave me a book to read. The thoughts of pain and torture came to the forefront of my mind. I took the book anyways, which I took home and placed on my end table in the living room. I had no plans on opening it any time soon.

About three weeks later, I woke up that morning and felt a sudden urge to grab the book. I figured I would skim through the first page or two at least. I started to read the book – and couldn't put it down. It was so liberating. It was as if the book had been written just for me, and every sentence was specific and relevant to my life and my experiences.

That book led to another book, which led to another, and so on. I am now on my 9th book in the last few months and still craving more. The book that my pastor gave me was *Wild at Heart*[4] written by bestselling author and counselor John Eldredge.

I would highly recommend Eldredge's book for any man today, and especially for younger men or teenagers. It provides a great understanding and basis for who we are as men, and why we were created to be the way that we are.

Eldredge states:

> *"A boy learns who he is and what he's got from a man, or the company of men. He cannot learn it any other place. He cannot learn it from other boys, and he cannot learn it from the world of women." John goes on to say "The plan from the beginning of time was that the father would lay the foundation for a young boys heart, and pass on to him that essential knowledge and confidence in his strength....... Above all, he would answer the question for his son and give him his name."*[5]

That is the point when I realized that the all-female, men bashing environment that was my so-called family, had actually been a culture that would effeminate, or attempt to demasculinize the little boys that they had been tasked to raise. In all fairness to my mother, her sisters, and the other women in their family, it may not have been and was likely not intentional. However, the consequences and outcome would be the same.

"let the wise listen and add to their learning, and let the discerning get guidance....... The fear of the Lord is the beginning of knowledge, but fools despise wisdom and instruction." Proverbs 1:5,7

Chapter 3

The Fallout

My parents divorced when I was about ten years old. I can only speculate as to the reasoning for their separation but would assume that my father no longer saw enjoyment and pleasure in the choices which he had once made. He had also failed to foresee the responsibilities and obligations that came with those choices. My father left my mother and his four children to chase after another woman – who was younger, thinner, and some might say more attractive. Once again, he had done the same in pursuing my mother, by leaving another woman and his two children with her, to chase after his own selfish desires and pleasures. I really do not have any quality memories of my father before he left. And I surely do not recall him spending time with me or my siblings or taking any interest in us at all. I certainly did not feel like I was loved as a child, and did not have that feeling of safety and security that every child should inherently feel. From a very young age I felt as if I was alone, and on my own.

I am married now myself, which we will dive in to in later chapters, and was curious about the divorce rates in our current society, as well as if and how that number may have changed since the 1970's. I spent several hours researching this topic on the internet, only to end up more confused and having more questions than when I began. The Internet offers us an abundance of information on any subject matter that we may wish to dive into, which is readily available for our consumption within just a few clicks. It is but one of the many benefits of the technological advances of the modern age. However, nothing in this world is given for free. Everything has a cost, in one form or another, whether it be up front or one that is incurred over time, and most often unbeknownst to the one incurring said costs. These costs that we pay for Internet information come in a multitude of ways which I am sure many other books have been written about. One of the costs that we incur with this ease of access is in the information that we receive which is almost always contradictory to numerous other sources that can be found in the same location, and many times is outright false, or inaccurate. While the intention for the Internet was positive, striving for growth and advancement of our society and culture, the system itself is flawed and creates nothing but confusion at its best.

We hear a common saying in society now-a-days that nearly 50% of marriages end up in divorce. WOW!! That is a shocking number, and one to cause great concern. I don't know many people that would willingly go out and start a new business or invest their hard-earned money if they knew that they had a 50% chance of loss or failure.

The truth is that divorce statistics are highly skewed and flawed. The CDC (Centers for Disease Control and Prevention) offers statistics that show a divorce rate of 2.4 per 1,000 people in data from 2022. The problem with the CDC study is that their data is polled from only women, and only from a polling of forty-five states. The biggest issue with the CDC study is the calculation method used to determine this number, known as the 'flow in, flow out' method. For example – If fifty couples get married in a year, and fifty couples get divorced in that same year – the divorce rate is 100%. The study does not account for people that were already married prior to that year.

The most accurate and correct information and study that I could find in relation to divorce statistics was from The National Center for Family and Marriage Research at Bowling Green State University[1]. This study shows that the divorce rate for the United States was at 14.6 per 1,000 in 2022. Quite a difference from the CDC rate of 2.4. The study also shows that divorce rates have been on the decline since the early 1980's and are close to what they were in 1970 at 14.9 per 1,000. The most shocking data comes between 1970 and 1979, when divorce rates spiked and reached their peak at 22.6 per 1,000. That is more than a 150% increase in divorces....... in less than ten years. Even more shocking is that divorce rates increase dramatically for second and third marriages during those times. What happened to us in the 1970's?

I find it no coincidence that several significant events took place during this time period in the '70's, which had a major impact on how we viewed each other as people, and how we viewed the family unit as a whole.

The Women's Liberation Movement began in the late 1960s and carried on through the 1980s.The WLM was a group of radical feminists and activists that supported and encouraged the independence, freedom and equality of women. The WLM was responsible for bringing about many changes in our society including the legalization of abortion and starting what we commonly know now as daycare centers.

Many men in our country were also just returning home from a war. A war which they did not choose to start or fight in. A war in which they were not supported or backed by the country that sent them to fight. A war in which many men were just trying to survive. And upon returning home most all these men were not welcomed with open arms – they were immediately thrown into another war with the people of their own country who now saw them as murderers, rapists, and pure evil. Their welcome home parade was a shunning from society, and it became next to impossible for these men to have anything of a normal life from that point on.

Shortly after my father left in the late '70's, my mother was on her own to try and figure out how to raise four kids, with no support. My mother made it a well-known issue that my father never paid child support, and that he did nothing to help care or provide for us kids. My mother never tried to hide these things from us either. She would always make sure we were aware of his shortcomings and that we knew how worthless our father was.

We ended up having to move out of our house and find another place to live after my parents divorced, which my mother could not afford on her own. We spent the next few years staying with friends and bouncing around from place to place. I think I have subconsciously blocked out many of the places we had to stay, but I do recall at one time living in the back of an empty office building which was basically just open office spaces, with no kitchen, and a very basic bathroom having only a toilet and a sink. I do not recall going to school during these times either, which would have been difficult as we never stayed in one place too long, and most places where we did stay were either on the other side of town, or in another state.

In the early 1980's my mother was eventually able to purchase a home for us. I am not sure how she did this, but I am sure it was not on her own. It was a much smaller house, in a less than desirable neighborhood, but we now had a home of our own. It was the home that I would spend my teenage years in, and the neighborhood that would become my new environment. Finally, some stability. A yard of our own to play in. New friends to run around with. A sense of peace, and that everything was going to be okay. Little did I know that this new fortress of solitude would be the environment that would cultivate me into a barbaric heathen.

Giving it Her Best Effort

I was in the sixth grade when we moved into that new house. I use the word 'new', as it was new for us, but certainly not a newly built home. The house was at least forty years old. I would spend one last year in grade school, and then be off to a new school, Lewis & Clark Junior High.

Lewis & Clark was several miles away from the neighborhood that we lived in, so we had to be bussed to school. Every morning the large yellow school bus would come down the street and pick us up as we stood on the corner waiting for its arrival. Then, it would drop us back at the same corner after school, and we would walk home from there. Almost overnight, with one flip of the calendar, I would go from knowing only the kids in my small neighborhood and small grade school, who were much like me, to being intermixed with kids from all across town who were being bussed in as well. I would soon be exposed to a whole new world whether I was ready or not – and had no awareness of what awaited me.

Mom was raised a Catholic. My father was a Lutheran. By no means were either of them what you would call religious though. When my father was around, I do recall occasionally going to the Lutheran church and being in the children's Sunday School while our parents went to service. This only happened on rare occasions though which leads me to believe that my father dictated any religious structure that there may have been in our family at that time. When he was no longer in the picture, Mom began taking us to mass on Sundays at her Catholic church. I think this is where I first learned about Jesus and began to hear more scripture. We would then go to church every Sunday, sit in the pew with Mom, go through the ritualistic chants and recitals, and then go home. To this day I still have no idea how anyone that does not know God is supposed to learn more about God or come to know God through these practices. If anything, the Catholic church just made me not want to go to church. Agonizing and painful! But mom tried.

At the start of Junior High School, I would like to think I was still Grandma's innocent little boy. I really had not been exposed to much outside of the few blocks around my home and certainly had no thought or intent of doing rebellious things. My new school had a reputation though, and not a good one. There was a nickname for our school, and everyone knew it. It was called "*Lewy Jewy, the whore house on the hill*". Lewis & Clark sat in the middle of town, high upon a hill. The school had everything, good and bad. It was an inter-racial mix of kids from all walks of life. Rich, poor, and middle class. Blacks, Whites, Asians, and every other race as well. My eyes and mind were suddenly exposed to countless experiences that I had no foreknowledge or concept of. I was a young boy with no inherent morals or values, just waiting for a role model to lead me. And then there it was – it was as if the entire world had opened up its doors to me and said – *Here I am!*

Times were rough for our family when I started Junior High. Mom had to work multiple jobs just to support and feed us kids. That meant that I would only see her early in the morning just before I left for the school bus and then would likely not see her again till late at night when she came home. Mom would occasionally have someone come by to watch us kids after school, more so for my little sister and brother. This meant that my older brother and I would almost always run off and do whatever we wanted too. You have to remember that this was the 1980's. Life was different back then. Kids actually went outside and played. Kids rode their bikes. Kids played ball. Kids ran around everywhere, without any real worries. Kids stayed out till dark without any concern from their parents. The saying back in that day was – *Just be home when the streetlights come on.* That meant that it was now getting dark, and it was time to head home. We didn't have cell phones, so our parents didn't always know where we were, or what we were doing. We just had to be home by dark.

I am entering my early teenage years at this point. I have my bicycle, and a baseball glove. The baseball glove was a Christmas present from my grandpa. The bike....... well, I think I 'borrowed' that from some kid across town who just left it sitting in the wrong place. Other than my clothes, those are my only worldly possessions. The clothes that I do have are not much either. Every year just before the school season would start, Parents would take their kids out to get school supplies and new clothes. Every kid wants to show up on the first day and look sharp. For us it was hand-me-downs. Clothes that my older brother had outgrown. And if we were lucky, Mom might have some money to take us to the Goodwill and buy other people's used clothes. People were very judgmental back in the '80's, just as much as they are today. People would look at you, the way you were dressed, the shoes you wore, your hair and hygiene, and would then form a lasting opinion about you within the first few minutes. Junior High School was no different.

As with most all schools now, and back then, the school was divided into cliques, or certain groups/classes of people. Who you were, how you dressed, and what you did influenced what group you fell in to. The big three were the jocks, the preppies, and the stoners. They made up roughly 90% of the school. Then there were the losers, the egg heads, and the Asians. The Asians were kind of a separate group of their own, mostly by their choice.

The United States had recently come out of the Vietnam war. During this time many families from Cambodia, Laos and Vietnam were given sanctuary in the United States. And since they were similar in many ways, they mostly associated with themselves. The losers were the kids that everyone else determined that they were too good for. Kids that were most always from lower class families and stricken by poverty. I was a border line loser but managed to find my way into another group. This was mostly due to my need to be wanted, and the fact that even the losers didn't associate with other losers. The egg heads were the brainy kids. The kids that were way smarter than everyone else and only focused on academics.

The Big Three – These groups consisted of the majority of the kids in the school.

- • - The Jocks – Jocks were the kids that were involved in a sport, most likely on one of the school teams. They were athletic, clean cut, and most always in very good shape. They always had nice clothes and a clean sharp look. The kind of kid that you want your son or daughter to date.

- • - The Preppies – Preppies were the rich kids. New clothes all the time. Penny loafers, argyle socks, Izod shirts. Snobby, stuck-up rich kids who were too good for anyone else. They always had the latest and greatest styles and gadgets, and mommy and daddy would most always buy them anything they wanted.

- - The Stoners – Stoners were the kids...... well, you guessed it, that were more than likely doing drugs. They wore the concert T-shirts, old jeans and many even had the billfold in their back pocket with a chain attached to their belt loop. Stoners didn't care what you thought about them, and stoners were almost always the first to break the rules. Stoners would try anything, go anywhere, and do whatever they felt like (or didn't feel like) doing.

I could have very easily been a 'Loser' had I just kept to myself. I had the look and certainly had no one pushing me to be better. I needed to belong to something though. I needed a family, a group, people to care about who I was. People to give me a sense of being wanted. I wasn't good at any sport, or so I thought, so being a jock was out of the question. My family had no money so I couldn't even attempt to look the part of a preppy. I wasn't Asian, and I wasn't extremely smart. That left me only one choice – *A Stoner*. I easily mixed in with the stoners and found myself some new friends.

Mom kept working multiple jobs and kept trying her best to keep us kids alive. To say that we didn't have much is an understatement. Breakfast was always a cold bowl of cereal – if we had milk. Lunch was a school lunch in the cafeteria because we qualified for the free lunch program. Dinners, well, that was hit and miss. When we did have dinners it most always was just enough to make the hunger go away. But mom kept working and kept trying to do her best to provide for us, and to just survive. Mom had very little time, if any, to devote to us kids.

For a small period in my life, Mom tried to become involved with what I did and tried to get me involved in 'healthy' activities. I liked baseball, a lot. It was the only sport that I could relate too. I was fast, and had quick reflexes, which made the game easy for me. Football was out of the question due to my size, and the fact that I feared the contact and getting hurt, although that would soon change as well. I am sure there were many other sports that were available at that time, but due to our family dynamic, baseball and football were my only options. In an effort to keep me occupied, Mom then signed me up for little league baseball, which I would play for the next few years.

As I previously stated, things were different back in the '80's. Unlike today, you didn't just sign up for a sport and then get to play. We had to 'try out'. Try-outs were a 'qualifying' to see if you were good enough to play. All of the kids that signed up to play would show up at Try-outs, which were held just before the season started. They would have several coaches there who would throw pitches to you as you attempted to bat, hit balls to the infielders and see how good your arm was in throwing to first base, and hit fly balls to the outfielders to see if they could catch. It was really the first time that I had to prove myself, and to say that I was nervous is an understatement. Despite the nerves and the intimidation of the other kids who had been playing ball for years, I made the team. The position that I played was 2nd base and Short-stop. I had a decent arm and was pretty quick and agile. I did not know it at the time, but I also had a good ability to see the big picture and notice the little details which helped. At second base and short-stop, I could see the signs that the catcher was giving to the pitcher and could see the little adjustments that the catcher would make in his stance. I also studied all of the opposing players, learning their stances and abilities and quickly learned to recognize where the ball was likely to go if it was hit and could start heading for that area before the pitch even crossed the plate.

Most all practices and games were held at a school field that was about two miles from my house. I would ride my bike to and from practice several times a week, and to games about once a week. Mom came to a few games when she could and would sit in the stands and watch. Mom was not the kind of mom that would get loud and cheer, she just watched. However, mom was one of the only moms there. Most all of the other kids had their dads there.

At some point I also wanted to get involved with The Boy Scouts. I do not recall if this was by my choice, or mom's choice though. The Boy Scouts of America was a much different organization back then as well. It actually was just about the boys, and men who wanted to mentor and help young boys become men of their own. Not the politically correct, gender-neutral organization that it is today. It is a sad fact that what once began as an organization to provide role models to young men and teach/train them how to become leaders of their own has now caved to the worldly views of a society which given enough time will find anything to be acceptable. One of the greatest needs in our world today is for men, real men, with solid morals and values who would stand up and fight for those beliefs while teaching and training other young men to be accountable and responsible as well.

I registered for the Boy Scouts and joined local Troop #597. We would meet in the basement of a church that was about six blocks from my house, one night a week. Our troop was more active than most, doing regular outdoor activities, and going on a camping trip one weekend every month. Yes, every month of the year. (Recall the previous chapter and my comments on the Nebraska winters.) We went on camping trips during those harsh winter months as well.

I remember one specific trip in the middle of winter. It was extremely cold that year, and we spent a great deal of time debating whether or not to go. Eventually we did go, and it was miserable. The temperature had to be near zero (Fahrenheit). I tried endlessly to go to sleep that first night in the tent but was unable too. I eventually got up and made my way out to the fire to warm up - and found almost the entire Troop there trying to stay warm. An hour later it started to snow.

It was not the 'glamping' (glamour camping) of nowadays either. Each kid had his own backpack, his own sleeping bag, and his own cooking gear. The Troop provided the tents that we would set up and sleep in, usually with two kids per tent. Part of our trips would include the planning of all our meals, and then the scouts would actually go to the store and purchase the food for those meals as well. We would then meet at the local church parking lot on Friday night and drive out to a camp site, most times within sixty miles of town, and then come home Sunday afternoon. These camping trips, as well as Boy Scouts in general, taught me how to survive when things got tough and uncomfortable.

Looking back now, I can see that I was once again most likely searching for that family and connection that I did not have. Looking to be recognized. Looking to be acknowledged. Looking to be loved. I learned a lot while in the Boy Scouts over the years. I earned many merit badges, worked my way up through the ranks, and achieved the highest rank of Eagle Scout, along with being 'tapped out' into the Order of The Arrow. I am sure the skills that I learned through all of the merit badges, all of the meetings, all of the campouts, as well as the ranks that I achieved, helped give me the confidence that I could survive on my own, and someday be my own man.

Of all the experiences in Boy Scouts that I encountered, two stick with me to this day. Two men in the Troop that I feel had an indirect impact on my life, my beliefs, and who I became. Mr. Palmer and Mr. Brown. Neither man was an actual Troop leader. They both had a son in the troop and were actively involved in every meeting and trip that the Troop had. They assisted the Troop leaders with teaching, training, and mentoring the boys. They were both firm in their beliefs and values and were always quick and ready to affirm or correct a scout when needed. They both knew how to teach and pass on knowledge in a very patient way, and they knew how to correct or discipline a scout when it was needed as well....... with their heart. If either of the men caught you doing something that you were not supposed to, and then disciplined you, you felt bad not because you had been caught, but because you had let them down. Our world today, and specifically our young men, needs more Mr. Palmers and Mr. Browns. Our boys of this generation are being led, or not being led, by the so-called men who are resolutely wrapped up in their own lives and careers, or who have evolved into complete pushovers as they have become emasculated by the feminine movement occurring in our lives today.

The entire Western society that we have become today gripes and complains endlessly about how weak men have become, while at the same time further ridiculing these men and trampling them down for being inadequate. Simultaneously, women are striving increasingly more to become dominant and powerful, and the men who actually are men are doing nothing to train, raise, or mentor young boys on how to become a strong and self-confident man.

We, as the men and women of the society that we live in today, have become a direct result of the feelings, actions, emotions and behaviors of our parents and those that came before us. Therefore, it only takes common sense to see that our children, and their future lives, will be a direct result of our feelings, actions, emotions and behaviors as well. Everything that we do today will shape the world and the future for our little ones. Every choice, every action, every behavior – and even more devastatingly, every lack of one as well.

A common saying amongst management experts today applies perfectly to most all of our modern-day societal issues, and the environments which we have created on our own:

"Your system is perfectly designed to yield the result that you are getting."

The results, or effects, of our society today are due to the system that we have perfectly designed ourselves!

Mom never attended the scout meetings, which did not surprise me as there was no need, and truth be told I did not want her too. On occasion, Mom would attend some of the camping trips though. Yep, my mom out camping with a bunch of little boys, and several grown men. Why she did it I will never know. It was not like she assisted in the teaching or training of any of the boys. She didn't help with any of the cooking either. I am not sure what she did on those trips, but she was the only mother who ever went. I could say that maybe she went for other reasons...... maybe the men. I don't know for sure. But for now, I will keep the image in my head that she tried.

That was the extent of mom 'trying' in my life and from that point on I seemed to be pretty much on my own. Mom seemed to focus any attention on her little girl, my sister, after that. My older brother and I were left to ourselves, and any time or attention that mom had went to my sister, or mom's 'baby', my little brother. This was most likely the point in my life where I learned, or came to believe, that I had to stand and fight for myself and anything that I wanted out of life would only come from me getting it or taking it.

"Train up a child in the way he should go, And even when he is old he will not depart from it" Proverbs 22:6 ASV

Chapter 4

The 1980s

I t was 1982 and I had just won the lottery. Well, it sure seemed like the lottery to me. One of my new friends from Junior High, who just happened to live about eight blocks from me, just got a new Atari video game system for Christmas. This was the jackpot. None of my other friends, or any one I knew for that matter, had anything so cool. We were all poor, and from poor families. But not Steve.

Steve's parents weren't rich, but his parents were still married, and they both had good jobs. Steve's mom was the head of some department at a local hospital. I don't recall if she was a doctor or a nurse, but that didn't matter. Steve's dad was more 'blue collar'. He had a mechanical job with the local newspaper where he was a supervisor over all of the printing equipment. Newspapers were the big thing back then, almost everyone had the 'paper' delivered to their house almost every day. We didn't have the internet, and we didn't have cell phones. We did have television but did not have cable TV yet. There was a total of four TV channels that one could watch -the three major networks, and then PBS. Nothing but news and soap-operas. Nothing that a kid would care to watch, and surely not something that could be an artificial babysitter as is so common in our world today.

But now we had an Atari. Video games that we could play on the television set. Steve had been given the main console along with three games – Pong, Asteroids, and Space Invaders. I would often spend the night at Steve's house on the weekends and we would play video games till three in the morning. Kids now days would laugh at what we perceived as entertaining. Staring at a black background screen while having the ability to control the white graphic pixels, in a challenge that would barely be intriguing for a kindergartner today.

Steve and I became best friends. It was not long before we grew disinterested with the Atari and its simplicity and began to sneak out of his house at night on the weekends. Initially, we had no plans when doing so. No preset goals or intentions. We just wanted to see what the forbidden world of darkness looked like, and experience some of it ourselves. At first it was just going up to the 7-11 convenience store on the corner and hanging out. We would buy Slurpee's, hang out, and play on the only pinball machine within miles.

The Dark Side

As summer came around and we were out of school, we began to sneak out more often, sometimes almost every night. And we then began to concoct intentions for our escapes as well. Our first venture into the criminal underworld began on trash night. On a certain night every week, people would take their trash bags out to the curb to be picked up by the city trash company the next morning. We lived close to a busier street in town, and Steve and I would wait till there was no traffic and then would line the trash bags up across the street blocking all the lanes.

Again, things were different back then. The only people that were out at that time of night were people working night jobs, criminals, and the Police. We would line enough bags up so that a car could not get through them, and then we would hide in the bushes on the side of someone's house and watch as the contents of each bag was soon blasted over the entire street. We were kids and it was the 1980's, it did not take much to amuse us. Kids back then learned to entertain themselves with whatever they could make use of as we did not have all of the gadgets and distractions that children have today.

Trash night became a ritual for us, and eventually word got around to the Police who were now aware of what we were doing, where we were doing it and on what night it was being done. The Police began to keep an eye out for us and try to catch us in the act. The first couple of weeks we were able to successfully get the bags out without getting caught. A few weeks later as we hid and waited behind the bushes, a cop car came down the street and stopped just before the bags. The officer had no clue where we were, as we watched him pick up all of the bags and move them back to the curb. A couple weeks after that, just as we were finishing placing the last bag on to the street, a cop car came into sight. The officer had caught view of us and the chase was on.

I felt bad for the cop, in a humorous way. He didn't stand a chance. We knew every house, yard, fence, alley, and shortcut in every part of that neighborhood. Running through yards, jumping fences, and cutting through alleys, we ran for what would have been several blocks before the cop finally gave up. We were too far gone for him to catch.

A Bunch of Punks

We figured we should probably give the trash thing a rest for a while and went back to hanging out at the 7-11. Slurpee's, pinball......... and what...... punk rockers?? HOLD ON!

Steve was a lot like me in the fact that we were so called Stoners. However, Steve was a fighter. His dad was built like a German weightlifter, and his uncle was in to martial arts. Although Steve was still a teenager, he was very muscular and was not afraid of anyone, and he let that be known. As we sat outside of the 7-11 with our Slurpee's one Saturday night, a car full of punk rockers pulled up blaring the sounds of Billy Idol and *Rebel Yell*[1]. Spiked hair, leather jackets with metal spikes, face piercings, black combat boots, and the dark black makeup.

This was not happening! This was our neighborhood, and we were sure that no one from our neighborhood was a punk rocker. It only took the exchange of a couple looks and it was on. Next thing I know, one of the punk rockers is opening the trunk of the car and pulling out a really long, thick chain, and begins swinging it around as he comes towards us. Steve took the challenge, as if someone had just invited him to breakfast, and headed straight for him with a 'why-not' attitude. My head was spinning with adrenaline, fear, and questions. I had never been in a fight before, and I surely never had anyone teach me how to fight or defend myself. But I knew two things, based on recent life experiences; I could do more than I thought I could, and buddies always have each other's backs. Steve was already in the fight, so my choice had already been made for me. I had to be committed and have his back, or I would lose any hope of ever having friends again.

The two other guys in the car started coming for me. Fortunately, fighting was a different back then as well. It was more 'respectable' in a sense. One guy would fight one guy, and whoever came out on top was the better. There was no 'jumping' of one guy, or having multiple guys beat another down. At least not in our world. There is no pride or sense of achievement, and it says nothing about you as a man, when it takes you AND your friends to overcome one other person.

If two guys wanted to fight one guy, the second guy would have to wait, and then could fight him if he came out on top. That was the case with my two guys. I went at it with the first guy for some time and beat him to the ground. Bloody and bruised, he gave in and realized his loss. Lucky for me neither of the two guys had any weapons, however, I looked over and Steve was still trying to dodge the thick heavy chain flying through the air and creating sparks as it hit the concrete pavement. The second guy started to come my way, but with a little less vigor than at first. Maybe I could fight?

Second guy, same result. Covered in blood, laying on the ground and barely moving. My struggles were over for the near future. I wanted to help Steve, but *"that's against the rules of fight club"*[2]. My only job at this point was to make sure that no one else tried to jump in on Steve and help the punk rocker. Steve managed to find an opening and tackled the guy to the ground.

Steve was involved in a sport at school, if you could call it that. Steve was on the wrestling team, and just so happened to be one of the best in the state. Naturally, that was Steve's first line of defense, take him to the ground. Once they were on the ground it was all but over. Steve's brute force, and likely his training from his dad and his uncle kicked in and the guy got the beating of his life.

The neighborhood was ours once again, and we went back to Slurpee's and pinball. Both Steve and I looked thru the large glass storefront window to see the store clerk who was working that night just standing there watching the whole debacle unfold. He hadn't called the police. He was just casually watching the show. He lifted up one hand, gave us a thumbs up, and with an endorsing grin said, *"Good job guys"*, and went back to work.

My confidence in my abilities soared after that night, and I had learned a valuable lesson – I can defend myself; I can go after the things that I want, and I don't have to do it in fear. Steve and I had many other ventures in to the dark underworld over that summer. We were pretty basic kids with basic desires at that point though, and they most always revolved around girls, jumping the fence at the city pool to go late night swimming, or the trip to 7-11.

The New Mayor

Several weeks later we heard a rumor going around school that our new city Mayor was an alcoholic. Kind of a strange rumor to being floating around a junior high school – except for the fact that the mayor's son was our age and went to the same school that we did. The rumor had it that he kept a large storage of liquor in his detached garage. We knew the mayor's son, at least who he was, and we also knew that they lived less than a mile away from Steve's house.

The temptation and the challenge overwhelmed us, so Steve and I set a plan in motion to relieve the mayor of some of his inhibitions. We snuck out of Steve's house again one Saturday night and made our way through the dark alleys and streets until we arrived at the mayor's house.

Most homes in this neighborhood were much older and had been built in the early 1900s but had recently been bought up by the upper-class elites, transforming the area into a sought-after part of town. Warren Buffett, who was one of the richest men in America at that time, lived just a few blocks away. I had no clue who Warren Buffett was at the time, and the only concept of money that I had was that I didn't have any.

As was the case with most homes built in the early 1900s, there was not a garage attached to the house. People did not have cars back then, and garages became an afterthought in the 1930s and '40s when the automobile revolution began to take hold. As people began to buy cars, they saw the need for a place to store them, out of the elements. It became commonplace for most of these homes to have a separate detached garage added at the back of the house, along the alleyway. These garages were much smaller than the garages we are familiar with nowadays, as the cars were much smaller as well. Most of these garages could barely hold one older vehicle and are incapable of holding a modern-day automobile. Therefore, most all of these garages are now simply used for the storage of personal items and not cars.

This was true with our newly elected city boss as well. A detached garage filled with boxes, papers, junk........ and alcohol. Steve and I found the mayor's house and made our way around back, down the dark alley and around to the garage. My heart was racing. This was big, probably the biggest thing we had ever done. Surely, if we got caught, the consequences would be severe as well. Those thoughts didn't deter us though, and we made our way in.

The entire back wall of the garage looked like an old run-down liquor store. More booze than I had ever seen in my life. And every kind that you could think of. Steve and I had brought large extra thick garbage bags to carry our loot home in (I know, but it was all that we could find at the time). We each filled two bags with as much as we could carry and made our way out. We headed back down the alley and made it a couple blocks over when we saw headlights coming around a corner.

It is now about 3am, and you have to recall what I said before – the only people out at this time of night are people who work the late shift, criminals, and cops. We were obviously the criminals, and this was not a part of town with businesses. Steve and I quickly recognized the look of a cop car and dumped our bags into some bushes in someone's yard and kept walking. As the car got closer it slowed down just before reaching us, and a beaming spotlight illuminated both Steve and me. We had been caught, or so one might think.

Almost instantly, both Steve and I bolted across the street, through yards, and over fences in what seemed like a never-ending chase. There was not as much crime back then as there is now, so there were not as many cops out either. This helped our cause as the one officer would not have any assistance for at least five to ten minutes, and by then we would be long gone. Steve and I made it out of the neighborhood and back to safety where we hid out and waited a while for things to blow over. Just before dawn we went back to see if our loot was still in the bushes, and it was. We carried all four bags back home and now hid them in the garage at my house. Wine, vodka, bourbon, scotch and many other intoxicants that I had never heard of. We now had all the makings for the perfect party, and what would be the start of our drinking problems.

Later that summer Steve and I snuck out of his house again late at night and made our way up to the 7-11. As we stood outside of the store with our Slurpee's, fixating through the glass storefront window on a guy who was dominating the pinball machine, a truck had pulled up behind us in the parking lot. Our attention and focus on the exceptional performance of the pinball wizard caused us not to notice the truck until it was too late, and a large man grabbed Steve by the back of the neck and threw him in the truck. I froze and was unsure what to do. The truck swiftly pulled out of the parking lot and was gone.

It was Steve's dad. He had woken up in the middle of the night and found that we had ventured off. I was left standing there in front of the store feeling guilty that Steve had been caught, and I knew he would not get off lightly. Steve later told me that his dad gave him a pretty good beating for that night, and that I was no longer allowed over. I would have to look for trouble elsewhere, on my own.

Steve and I were still friends, but our nightly gallivanting came to an end. I moved on and found other so-called friends, and even more trouble. I had no direction, no guidance, and surely no discipline in my life. At that time in the '80's, it was not hard for a teenager to get cigarettes, alcohol, or just about any drug that you could imagine. Pornography had now become new thing in my life as well thanks to the magazines that were so easily viewable on the shelves at the 7-11, or any other convenience store. I didn't even know what the word pornography was at the time, let alone how to spell it. I just knew that there were pictures of very sexy women who were almost completely naked on the inside of each magazine – right next to that alluring pinball machine.

Our Desires

One of the strongest and most deadly qualities that a teenage boy has is curiosity. We are adventurists and explorers by nature. As very little boys, we build forts, we love to play outdoors in the wild, and we seek and desire to storm the castle and save the princess from the evil villain. We play Cowboys and Indians and always want to be the Cowboy. We love the challenge. We love the adversity. We love the quest. We love the battle, and the uncertainty placed before us, with the never-ending question *Am I man enough to do it?*

We seek and yearn for the opportunities and chances to prove our manhood, no matter how misguided they may be. These yearnings and desires do not fade away as we grow older - the passions that we choose to chase and conquer just

change over time. The one perpetual longing, however, that stays with the boy
till his death is................ The Princess.

A boy is just a boy, and a man is just a man, until he has a woman in his life. She
becomes our reasoning for everything. With her we now have purpose. We have
a reason to fight the fights that we do. We have a reason to take on the challenges
that we do. Life now seems to make sense as everything we do; we do with her
as the justification. Whether it be right or wrong, we justify our actions, logical
or illogical, with our attempt at proving something to her. She has now become
our validation. This misguided passion and desire has been inherent to us since
the creation of the world, and Adam and Eve.

With the endless number of magazines that were available to my rebellious
eye, I now saw that there was a completely different side of the world; one that
was soft and gentle, one that could offer me the attention and love that I so
desperately required. This side was so alluring, so beautiful, so seducing. It gave
me feelings that I had never experienced before. It made me want to do things
that I have never thought of or desired to do before. I then began to pay more
attention to girls and purposely pursued them in a lustful way.

At this point in my life, I had also taken to smoking cigarettes as I thought
it made me look more cool. Drinking beer with the buddies was a norm, which
eventually became intertwined with smoking pot. Heck, I was a Stoner, right?
I had to smoke pot! The pot, or marijuana, quickly turned into other drugs, as
is the case with all of our addictions as a little is simply never enough.

"Discipline your children, for in that there is hope; do not be a willing party to their
death."
Proverbs 19:18

Chapter 5

Freedom

The mid '80's meant a lot of big changes in my life. I would turn sixteen – I could now legally drive a car and get a job, and I was now moving on to High School. I still lived in the same house and many things remained unchanged, however. I still had the same friends, and was still running around doing whatever I wanted, whenever I wanted too. Things in life were becoming more expensive though. The alcohol, the drugs, and the cigarettes which I had become dependent upon required money, money that I did not have. The vices that I had unwisely added to my life made me feel good - or at least made me not feel anything. And I had to find a way to pay for them.

In the 1980's, a person was not legally able to get a job until they were sixteen years of age. There were a few smaller farm jobs, like detasseling corn, that kids under the age of sixteen could do, but these were usually just over the summer months. For me though, the opportunities were endless in my neighborhood. I wasn't afraid of work, and with my lack of money throughout my entire life, I had become very creative in finding ways to get what I did not have. Another common job for kids under the age of sixteen at that time was that of a paper boy. As the internet had not been invented yet, newspapers were the standard form of information for most people back then and the news companies needed someone to deliver the papers to all of the houses, on a daily basis. This was a menial job, and it didn't pay much, so it was most always taken on by younger kids after school. That was my first so-called job. Every day during the week I would go to a drop spot where the newspaper company dropped bundles of newspapers for carriers like me to deliver on my route. I would then fold each paper into a roll, wrap a rubber band around it, and stuff it in my large bag that was provided for carrying sometimes hundreds of newspapers. Then I was off to my route, my area of roughly six square blocks that I had to deliver them too. During the week, the newspapers were smaller and lighter in size, and I would most always ride my bike which made life easier. Saturday's paper was also small in size but had to be delivered first thing in the morning which meant getting up at about 5am.

Every job in life has a downside, no matter how good or easy that job may seem. That one thing that you just absolutely hate about your job. For me, it was Sundays. The Sunday newspaper was a beast. This was the paper that everyone wanted. When a person purchased a subscription for the local newspaper there were three different options: They could get the paper delivered seven days a week, they could get Saturday and Sundays paper only, or they could get just the Sunday paper. The Sunday paper was massive and could not be rolled or folded. The Sunday paper always came with a large amount of 'stuff in' advertisements from local retailers as well. I had a fairly decent size route with roughly ninety to one-hundred homes. And since the Sunday paper was so large and heavy, there was no possible way that I could carry all of those papers in my bag or carry the bag on my shoulders. And taking the bike was certainly out of the question. Some kids had a makeshift wagon they would use to pull the papers to their route. Others had parents that would drive them around on Sundays. I had neither and always had to make multiple trips back and forth to the drop spot to get all of my Sunday papers delivered. But it was a job, and I was making money.

Soon after, I learned that I could mow yards for people in the neighborhood during the warmer months and then shovel the snow from their driveways in the winter. This was a game-changer for me as I could make $10-$15 per house, and

I only had to do the work one day a week. We already had a little push mower that I could use, all I would have to do is buy a gas can and keep it filled. I was off and running in my new career and felt like a king with the money that I was making. I began to look for other ways that I could make extra money as well and was not afraid to try anything.

I started my first 'real' job the day I turned sixteen. I couldn't wait to work in the real world. I had been applying for jobs just prior to my sixteenth birthday and got hired by Kentucky Fried Chicken as a cook. My first scheduled day of work was on my sixteenth birthday. This job was quite a few miles away from home, too far to walk, so I had to take the city bus at first. Not long after starting that job I was over at my old friend Steve's house. His parents had recently moved out of the metro area and purchased a small acreage just north of town. Steve and I still hung out occasionally, but I still wasn't allowed to spend the night at his house. Steve's dad said that he wanted to talk to me and began to walk me out to an old run-down barn on the property. I was shaking in my shoes. I figured that it was my turn for the beating that Steve got that night we were caught sneaking out, and there was no way out of it. I was out in the country with nowhere to run. Nobody would hear me scream. I guess there was just no way around it. I may have feared Steve's dad, mostly due to his size and firm disposition, but I also respected him as well for the consistent and reliable man that he was.

This may be shocking to some readers, but again, things were a lot different back then. Kids were actually held accountable for their actions, and were actually disciplined, which most always meant dad taking off his belt and giving you a pretty good whipping. It also was not unusual for another adult to discipline you either, especially if you did not have a father figure in your life. And no, it was not child abuse, it was love and the raising of a child just as God had intended. If more of our kids were disciplined nowadays as we were back then, we wouldn't have half of the problems that we do in our society.

Steve's dad walked me into the barn and took me to the far back corner which was dark and filled with cobwebs. He grabs the cover of a canvas tarp and yanks it back with one quick jerking motion to reveal a small car. Steve's dad then looks at me and said - *"You need a car. For fifty bucks it's yours!"* My heart sank to that old dirt floor in shock and amazement, and I had no idea what to say. Nobody had ever given me anything in my life, and nobody had ever cared about me or what I had or didn't have. How could this large, scary man that I had feared for years, have love for me in this moment and care for me as if I was his own? I managed to gather myself and respectfully accept his offer.

The car was a complete piece of junk, but it ran. It was a 1974 Chevy Vega, red in color, with a 4-cylinder motor and a 4-speed manual transmission. The ignition had been removed so you could not use a key to start it. I would have to pop the hood and bypass (or jump) the starter solenoid with a screwdriver to get it started. The shifter arms in the transmission were bent slightly, and if I went over a big enough bump, the transmission would be stuck in whatever gear that I was in at that time until I crawled underneath the car and popped the rods back into neutral. The '74 Vega had an aluminum block engine which got very hot, very quickly. The gaskets on the aluminum motor were leaking pretty good, which didn't help matters, so I would go through about a quart of oil a week. Fifty bucks sounds like a pretty fair price now, huh? I didn't care. It was a car, and it was now mine. I finally had my freedom. My independence. And I could go wherever I wanted. Little did I know how much that small car would just accelerate the poor choices that I made, and the troubles that I got myself in to.

About that time, I was also moving up to High School. I thought the jump to Junior High was an eye opener, but the move to High School would show me an even bigger world, one in which I would learn that it was every man for himself and do what you have to do to survive. The High School that I attended was Central High School which was located in downtown Omaha. It was the largest and oldest High School in the state, and just like the Junior High, it had every kid from every walk of life.

The building of the High School was originally built in the late 1800's, and then rebuilt in the early 1900's. The four-story square building had four equal sides, with a large courtyard in the middle area. The building was massive and impressive, but for a new sophomore it was a nightmare finding your way around to your classes on different sides and different floors. There was a common nickname for all sophomores at Central High. They were called 'door stop', and for good reason. Each interior hallway of the building had classrooms on each side of the hallway. In the middle of each side were the staircases that rose up to all four floors, and each would have a landing area, or open common area that would lead you down the hallway to the classrooms on that floor. At each side of the landing was a set of doorways, containing four doors that would be propped open in between classes allowing students to easily pass from class to class, and then closed when the classes started as to keep any excessive noise from the common areas out. When the doors were propped open, each door would lock, or hold, against a small door stop that was mounted on to the floor. And since there were four doors on each side that ran the width of the opening, this meant that several of the door stops sat out in the middle of the walkway. Sophomores were not accustomed to such a thing being in their way, and would constantly trip over the door stops.

As with most High Schools, sophomores are at the bottom of the hierarchy and must once again find their way to fit in or find themselves as an outcast. I had my small group of friends from before, that were now also at Central High, but now we were in a much larger school with much larger factions and we stood no chance on our own. My two best friends at that time were Bryan and Jerry. Steve now went to a different school since they had moved out to the acreage north of town.

Brian was a tall, skinny kid and was an oddball just like me. Bryan's nickname was 'Shaggy' as he looked just like Shaggy from the cartoon Scooby-Doo. Jerry was short, and quite pudgy. Bryan and Jerry were just like the other kids back then and were just trying to fit in somewhere. Bryan's parents were still married, both had good jobs, and they lived in a decent middle-class part of town. Brian could have been so much more had he chosen too, but I think that he just wanted to have friends, and most others were very judgmental of the way he looked. Jerry, and his younger brother, lived with their dad just a few blocks from my house. I never knew why his mom was not in the picture, but more than likely it was due to divorce which was the common theme in my neighborhood. Jerry's dad had a good job, but it is hard keeping an eye on two kids while you are working a full-time job to get by. Jerry too, was an outcast. Chubby kids in those days were looked down on by just about everyone, so Jerry found it hard to fit in as well.

Me, I didn't care what Bryan and Jerry looked like, people were people. And I was probably just looking for attention from anyone that I could get it from. Bryan and Jerry were friendly, and we got along good, so we became friends. I think that Bryan and Jerry decided to become friends with me because of my *'I don't give a shit'* attitude. I was pretty easy going and not much bothered me. I was a risk taker and always willing to do whatever, whenever. I had become confident in who I was and was not afraid of a fight. I had been having to fight for everything my whole life so far. Brian and Jerry weren't like this at all. It was new to them, and something that they desired and saw as appealing.

Over the next couple years Bryan and Jerry continued to follow my lead. My path and desires had not changed, and I was still drinking and doing drugs and looking for that one girl. Or at least that one girl for now. High School became boring, and I did not see the point or reasoning behind sitting in a classroom for eight hours every day. I began to skip classes and then started skipping the full day of school. Nobody knew however, and those that did know did not care. My mom would not find out for weeks as back then the school did not call your parents when you didn't show up, they would just mail out a letter. We also soon realized that the school reported attendance to the main office based off of your attendance for your homeroom class, which was basically the first class of the day. Therefore, if we just showed up for our homeroom class, we would be reported to the main office as having 'attended' school that day. We would show up for homeroom, and then leave school just after it was over, which was only about twenty minutes later.

The times that I did stay for the whole day usually didn't go well. I didn't want to be there, and my attitude showed it. I hated it more and more every day, and I began to hate the posers who were putting on the artificial image trying to be something that they weren't to gain the attention of others. The whole system, and all of the kids that were entrenched in it, had become a giant cult that was idolizing the views of its leaders. And for those who did not succumb to the cultivation, they became outcasts and were widely known as such by both the students and teachers. I was a rebel. I did not conform to authority, especially authority given in a dictatorial way. I wanted to be my own man, and be the one to decide my direction and future. I had better ideas, and ideas that would make me in to a far better man than this system could. I had new friends, I had a car, and I really didn't care what anyone thought about me. Or at least that is the image that I portrayed.

Stoners disliked the Preppies the most. We would literally chase them down, no matter where we were, and rip their penny loafer shoes off their feet. Why? I have no clue. It was just something that we did. Maybe to assert some sort of dominance, I guess. Not long after turning sixteen I acquired a new level of friends. I was nothing of the stoner life compared to these guys. They were all about partying, with anyone, anything, and at any time. I soon got introduced to other drugs, much bigger parties, and ...... along with that came the girls who were drunk or under some other type of influence as well.

There was one guy in our neighborhood that everyone knew. They called him 'Suicide Mike'. Mike was much older than most everyone else and had his own house. A large two-story house with a basement. It was the party house, and the place that everyone would hang out at. Mike got his nickname because he was crazy. He would do anything, like he was on a suicide mission. I'm not so sure it was Mike as much as it was the drugs.

It did not matter when you went over to Mike's house, there were always people there. You could stay as long as you wanted too as well. There was always plenty of alcohol, as well as drugs in one form or another, so there were always plenty of kids hanging out, doing things that they shouldn't be doing.

I remember one particular weekend at Mike's house. As usual, there was a huge party. People overflowed out of the house and into the front and back yard. It went on all night. My older brother was best friends with Mike so I could pretty much stay there as long as I wanted too. Back then, having an older brother or sister was, in a sense, your ticket to a world that you would otherwise not have access too. You were now allowed to be there simply because you were the younger brother of someone who was already a part of the group. And the more highly regarded that someone was, in my case my older brother, the better you got treated. My older brother was second only to Mike, so I got treated like the son of a King. I had full access to any part of the house, at any time, without question. I would never be disrespected or pushed around by any of the guys as they knew this would be a direct offense against those in charge. And the girls would all show me attention in hopes that they could be a part of the hierarchy as well.

Well, I got really drunk, or high, or both that night and was half passed out on the couch in the living room. Three girls, who were also drunk, had casually taken all of my clothes off and were beginning to use my body as a play toy. I was buck naked right there in front of everyone. I kind of freaked out and jumped up running out of the house as they were starting to do things that I was not used too. I so wanted to be with girls, and wanted to have that feeling, but I didn't want it in front of an entire crowd. But that was Mike's house – you could have and do whatever you wanted, whenever you wanted.

This new experience opened my mind to the possibilities and adventures that I could take advantage of at Mike's house. There were always girls, they were always under the influence, and there were plenty of rooms in the house to be alone in and try new things. Many parties came and went over the next few years, as well as countless girls, and a different experience with each and every one of them. I honestly can't recall the name of even one, and I'm not sure that I even cared at the time.

The Next Level

Over the next few years, my experiences with the drugs, the alcohol, and the girls increased greatly. The pot, the pills, the coke, and who knows what else. I probably took stuff that I wasn't even aware what it was at the time. And beer was just an appetizer that led to Jack Daniels and whiskey. I quickly realized that the girls at this level were different. They were not as appealing as the girls that I had seen in the magazines. They were not as soft. They were rough and hardcore. Many of them came from the same background that I had and were already hardened and obstinate in their attempt at survival. Some of these girls were more rough than the guys – they would slit your throat and leave you laying in a ditch just to get what they wanted. I soon began to see them in a different light, and thereafter only saw them for one thing.

There were many parties, at many different places, where many things happened with many girls, and to this day I am completely unaware of who they were. Again, things were much different back then. Not that it is excusable, but this in a time before AIDS and many of the STD's that are so common today. One would be on a suicide mission themselves if they did these things in today's world.

In the world that I came from, having anything more than a blue-collar job was not even a thought. You learned early on to get good with your hands. Almost everyone I knew was mechanically inclined and could fix almost anything.

By the time most of us were legally able to drive a car, we had already completely torn apart and rebuilt one, or several.

And thanks to the education that was handed down to me by my older brother and Suicide Mike, I had the skills that allowed me to be dropped off anywhere in the city, and then remove any needed part from another car, inside or out, within ten minutes. This came in very handy as car parts were not a luxury that we could afford.

Cars became our lives back then, as did drag racing. The quarter mile. Who was the fastest. There were several known 'strips', or sections of road that we used for racing on the outskirts of town. The two most popular were Abbott Drive and McKinley St. Both were on the north side of town, and both were in Industrial areas so there was almost no traffic at night. Everyone just knew that on Friday and Saturday nights, once the sun went down, there would always be racing.

Hundreds of cars would gather to watch. There would be people everywhere, most of whom were teenagers. The four deadliest things to mix together at any one time are alcohol, drugs, girls......... and testosterone. And there was always plenty of each to go around, which almost always led to multiple fights, some of which became deadly.

Anyone could race if they were willing to put some money on the line. Most did, and most races were not very stimulating. But then there was Marvin. Marvin had a 1984 Chevy Monte Carlo SS. The car was two years old and probably had a total of fifty miles on it – one quarter mile at a time. Marvin bought the car brand new off the showroom floor in 1984 and then took it straight to Charley's Speed Shop in Blair, Nebraska. I could spend the next two chapters telling you everything they did to that car. But for ease in understanding, I will just say that they made that car for one thing and one thing only – to be the fastest car around.

Marvin would bring the car out every weekend but would only race when there was serious money on the line. The cost of the racing fuel and the nitrous oxide for just one race alone were more than most people were usually willing to wager. Word got around about Marvin and his SS, and soon after people would come from out of town and out of state to try and take him down. I saw that car race maybe ten times over the years, and never saw it even come close to losing.

Marvin was a bit older than most of the crowd that hung out on the strips. Marvin was a Vietnam vet and had been paralyzed from the waist down. (I can see your mind going already – yes, he drove the car in the races. He had it customized so that he could do so.) And as with most people who are at the top of what they do, everyone always wanted to be around Marvin. I soon found myself a part of Marvin's crowd through another friend who was closer to him. Before long I was hanging out at Marvin's house, which then showed me another segment of this dark world that I did not know existed until then.

As with many Vietnam vets, Marvin was also into motorcycles. Harley Davidsons to be specific. And since Marvin was well known for being the fastest racer around, he attracted the attention of many others as well. At some point, Marvin had become friends with some Hells Angels and would regularly hang out and party with them. And simply by association, I was now a part of that crowd as well. A young and eager kid, willing to do anything to simply survive. – hanging out with the most notorious outlaw biker gang, that is infamously known for being willing and able to set their own rules.

The parties and crowds that I had been a part of before suddenly looked more like a twelve-year-olds birthday gathering. The crimes and assaults that I had done in the past were also child's play in comparison. While I will not go into detail about any specific events for various reasons, I will say that this period in my life forever changed my view of mankind and hardened me to the point that I did not think was possible to come back from.

I had many friends who lost their lives over that period of time, and saw others completely waste their lives away. One particular friend was Tom. We used to hang out at the corner arcade and play video games. This was in the 1980's as well, and most of the popular video games that we know today had just come out in the arcade. We would go to the arcade and play them for hours. Tom decided to try LSD (Lysergic acid diethylamide) one day. He was never the same again. The acid fried his brain so badly that Tom literally walked around all day from that point on as if he was playing a game of Space Invaders. I had other friends who overdosed as well, more than once, and also had close friends who had been shot, some not surviving.

I had beaten people up, badly, for very little reason at all. I had lied, cheated, stole and robbed people and places. I had done just about anything that you could imagine, short of killing or raping someone. I had been stabbed, shot at on more than one occasion, arrested, and had found myself in situations that I did not think I would make it out of alive.

This was the life I had chosen. This was whom I had wanted to be my so-called family. And I had been so drawn in that I couldn't even see the toll that it was taking on everyone else, let alone myself. And I hadn't even reached the age of twenty yet.

Boys Left to Themselves

On one random Saturday night, three boys jumped into the cab of a pick-up truck and ventured about town seeking a night full of drinking and partying. The first stop was a small corner liquor store where they knew that the guy behind the counter would sell them alcohol. A case of beer and a few bottles of Jack Daniels, and the boys were off to find the pleasures that awaited them. They made a few stops here and there at houses where they were likely to find a party in progress.

There were always parties going on. Someone's parents were always out of town. Or as was the case most of the time, the parents were at home and actually encouraged the party. The mentality of many parents back then was that they would rather have their child get drunk and do drugs at home in an environment that they could control opposed to not knowing what they were doing, or who they were doing it with. Many parents encouraged it, supported it, and even contributed to it. What in the world were they thinking? Absolutely mind boggling.

The parties would always have plenty of alcohol and just about any drug that you may desire. However, the parties promised one thing to those boys – Girls. Girls who would be intoxicated and easy. Girls that you didn't have to get to know or put any effort in to.

Several parties and hours later, the boys found themselves cruising the streets of the town in that pick-up truck once again. The night is nearing an end, but the boys resist the closing of the day. They stop at a pay phone and make a call to a girl that lived near-by and then head to pick her up. The girl packs herself into the cab of the truck with the three boys and they drive off to a vacant parking lot where they settle into a dark back corner. There is plenty of alcohol left and the drinking continues.

Over the next several hours each of the boys has his way with the girl in the bed of the truck while the other two await their turn inside the cab. The girl willingly gets passed around while the boys use every part of her body for their pleasure. Then, they call it a night and head home.

Nobody died. No tragic car accident. No bloody battle that would leave visible scars for life. Nothing that would be mourned as if any damage caused would be clearly evident to others. Just another Saturday night for these teenagers – where the scars and the wounds cannot be seen, only to be buried deeply within who they will become. Just a typical Saturday night for these boys, which would play out many more times in the years to come.

It pains me greatly to admit that one of those boys was me. This was my life as I would come to know it, and one that I had begun to crave and desire. A life that would leave its mark with a multitude of inner wounds and scars that would go unaddressed and unhealed for many years to come.

The Change

Almost always, when you are hell bent on heading down a certain path, something jumps up to really make you second guess the route you were so determined to take. For me, at this point in time, it was a girl. I was hell bent on leaving school, dropping out to pursue my ideas of success and re-inventing the world. Then the girl walks in, and all of your plans immediately get erased.

This girl and I hit it off pretty quickly. We were inseparable. I did not know it's affects at the time, but she had way too much trauma in her life which would inevitably lead to her own self destruction, while leaving casualties in the wake of every path she crossed. I just happened to be the first on a long list of men and women that she had been predestined to cause chaos and destruction in the lives of.

Due to the damage that was caused, as well as those involved, I will not directly name the girl in this book. We will just call her Pam. Pam came from a severely broken family. Both of her parents were drug addicts, and her father was currently serving time in prison. She lived with her grandma, who was the complete opposite of my grandma. Her grandma would spoil her and give her whatever she wanted. There had never been consequences or discipline in her life, and she learned at a very young age that she could lie her way out of anything. Pam knew how to get what she wanted, from whomever she wanted, and she had learned to use that methodology to work her way through life, as well as through others. I knew nothing about 'warning signs' or 'red flags' back then as there had never been a father figure in my life to make me aware of these cautions. I had to learn the hard way, which for me was to dive right in.

Pam and I became really close, which kept me showing up to school. One day Pam and I were walking up one of the stairways from class to class. We had to have been between the second and third floors when out of nowhere this guy calls Pam a B*@"". The guy was Brad. I knew him, somewhat. Brad was a wannabe preppy. He came from a middle-class family that didn't have a lot of money, but he so badly wanted to fit in with the clean-cut preppies.

We were in the middle landing area between two floors, along with about twenty other kids who were traversing to their next class. I heard the comment that Brad made and stopped dead in my tracks. I stuck my right arm out in front of Pam and guided her behind me in a protective way. Then I broke through the crowd and grabbed Brad by his shirt and slammed him up against the outer wall. Brad had several friends with him, but I wasn't concerned. Again, back then it was one-on-one, but even if they did decide to have a moment of bravery, I wasn't worried as I felt that I could take all of them in this small space. No one else stepped up, Brad and I tussled, making our way across the landing toward the inner stair railings. I picked Brad up and had him halfway over the railing just as a teacher came down the stairs and broke everything up. Brad quickly realized that he had just been only seconds away from plummeting two stories down, and what would have likely been his demise. This was not the end though. Brad knew it, and I knew it. Word travels fast in a school, even a large school like ours. I had a couple of classes later that day that some of Brad's friends were also in, and through those friends and my friends, it was determined that we would settle the score in the parking lot across the street just after school.

School let out and me, Bryan, and Jerry headed across the street to the parking lot that was owned and used by a neighboring business. There must have been fifty kids there by the time we arrived, maybe more. Brad was there and had two of his friends as well. A large circle formed as people gathered around Brad and me. We began to finish what we had started. Shortly after Brad and I resumed, I noticed that one of Brad's friends had started spouting off to Bryan. Bryan stepped up and those two were soon at it as well. I probably punched Brad in the face seven or eight times before he ever hit me. The fight did not last long, and both Brad and his friend went home with their tales tucked between their legs and faces that were now swollen and bloody.

I was proud of Bryan that day. He knew he was on his own, and he knew everyone was there to see it as well. Bryan knew that a different outcome would have had severe negative consequences for the rest of the year in school. But Bryan pressed forward and faced the challenge, and just as happened to me, Bryan's confidence soared after that day. I was egotistical about the way I was shaping the lives of my followers and truly believed that I had done something for him that would make him a better man. Maybe I did. But then maybe I did him more harm than good.

Pam and I continued to heat things up. She had no issues with my drinking, partying, and doing drugs, and even did so herself. She seemed to savor the lifestyle, maybe a little more than I did. Pam and I were at a party one night and ended up having sex, which just took us to a completely different level. We started having sex regularly and not being shy about it either. Not long after, Pam was pregnant, and I was the father.

"Do not envy the wicked, do not desire their company; for their hearts plot violence, and their lips talk about making trouble." Proverbs 24:1-2

Chapter 6

The Child That Saved My Life

I had become a young hellion, seeking only to please my selfish desires, with no thought or regard for the consequences. I lacked any thought or care for others, or how my actions may affect anyone else. I would chase after girls for the short-term satisfying pleasure of the sexual encounter and would use them for their bodies alone as that was what I had learned to desire from the magazines of my younger days. I had become captivated by the soft, luscious beauty on the outside of the girl, but I had never been introduced to the inner beauty and knew nothing of it. There had been many girls over time, and none of them meant anything to me. I did not know how to love. I did not even know what love truly was. I did not know how to respectfully treat another human being, let alone a woman. I only knew how to survive.

I chased after alcohol and drugs as it was something that gave me pleasure as well. It made me feel good. It made me forget who I was and where I had come from. It made me forget what I was unknowingly searching for and so desperately trying to find. It took away those moments when I was left to myself with a clear head, along with all of the sad, depressing thoughts that would haunt me. It also turned me into something that I was not. Something that I was not created to be. It helped me to bury the God given desires of my soul that were trying so intensely to get out and give me the life that God had intended for me........ the life that I knew nothing about.

Growing Up

Pam was pregnant and about to have our child. While I was very reckless and irresponsible with my own life, I still had some basic morals, even as distorted as they may be. I was still a man, to some extent, and knew that it was my obligation and responsibility to take care of and provide for her and our child. More than likely, this was due to the fact that I wanted to be nothing like my father and abandon my children.

Pam and I soon moved into an apartment together just before she had our child. I attempted to be more responsible and carry the new burden which I had placed upon myself. I got a new full-time job that would pay for the apartment and our bills and attempted to change my lifestyle. However, I would still drink, and occasionally do drugs, but not at the level that I had before.

Moving in with Pam and being with her all day, every day, provided an up close and not so glamorous look at the person she really was. She would drink while she was pregnant, even though I strongly discouraged it. She became very possessive and controlling and was jealous of anyone and everything without cause. Her jealousy had caused her not to have any trust in me, or anyone else.

My new job did not always allow me to be off work at an exact set time. I would get to go home when the work was finished, and at times this meant that I would have to stay for an hour or two longer than I had been scheduled. Pam would always call around and check on me to see where I was at, or what I was doing. When I did get home, it was always a fight, because she thought I was out cheating on her with another girl. Pam would also get violent and physical during her outbursts. It was not uncommon for her to hit me and attack me in her fits of rage. However, I would always be the one to walk away, with the wounds, and would never hit her back as that was not who I was as a person.

One afternoon I came home from work and the moment I opened the door; beer bottles came flying at my head. Lucky for me she could not throw very well. Pam had been sitting in the house drinking for the last few hours as her insecurities led her to believe that I was with another girl. Nothing could have been farther from the truth, but there was no reasoning with Pam. She couldn't comprehend rational thinking or reasoning. Pam's instability had brought our relationship to a point that even I knew it was not safe or healthy, for either of us. This is not the life that I wanted to live. I was easy going and laid back. The stress, the fighting, and the never ending accusations were something that I had never had in my life thus far, and were definitely something that I did not want in my life. But I did not know what to do. I had a child on the way, that I was responsible for, but a girlfriend that eventually would either take my life or have me thrown in jail. It was a no-win situation, and once again I was left to myself again to try and figure it out.

After much thought and trying to consider all of the possibilities and outcomes, I decided that it would be best for both of us if we split up. This was not a good environment for either of us, let alone one to bring a child in to. The break-up was ugly, as expected, as Pam was very needy and dependent. Pam again placed the blame on me, and another girl, and even threatened to kill herself if I left. It may have been self-centered at the time, but I figured I would rather have it be her than me. Pam had said on many occasions that if she could not have me, nobody would and always used harmless threats to intimidate me in to not leaving. However, I managed to get through all of the ugliness, and it was done.

Pam had made the choice to be with me against her grandmothers wishes, so she did not have the option to go back and live there. I did not make enough money to afford the apartment on my own, which meant that we were both moving out. My mother chose to side with Pam and agreed to take her in which left me with no other place to stay. Again, I felt worthless and unwanted, by even my own mother.

I spent the next six months living in my car, which just happened to be over the cold Nebraska winter months. I found an empty parking lot where I would park the car at night, and sleep in the back seat. I could not afford the gasoline to keep the car running all night, which meant that I did not have any heat. The temperatures would plummet as the sun went down and I can remember a few nights when I wondered if I would wake up the next morning, or if I would just freeze to death.

I survived the six months, and had found a new friend, Ron. Ron was not living at home either as his parents had kicked him out. Ron was the rebellious type just like me. Ron had an older sister who was dating a guy in a local hardcore rock band. Some, if not all of the band members lived together in an old run-down house. This house had a couple of rooms in the basement that somehow Ron and I managed to find our way in to. Apparently, Ron's sister felt bad for us and managed to convince the band to allow us to sleep there.

While it was a step up from the back seat of my car, it was not by much. The basement had its own door at the back of the house, which would not close all of the way as it was swollen from rot. There were a couple of windows down there, which had been busted out for some time. And to top it off, there was no heat in the basement. The house was a much older home where basements were not finished and were used for storage only. We had one electrical outlet in the entire basement that we could run one space heater off of which barely kept the temps above freezing.

Ironically, some twenty years later, I would come to find out that one of the band members was my future wife's older cousin.

Don't Give Up

Pam eventually moved back in with her grandmother, soon after giving birth to our child – a little girl. Pam and her grandmother decided to keep me out of everything, and I wasn't even made aware of the birth until several days after. Pam's grandmother was just like her, except for the fact that her insecurities and anger had become full blown as she had many more years to perfect them. In their eyes I was the spawn of Satan, and they would do whatever they could to keep me from my own child.

I was overwhelmed at the thought of being a teenage parent but was excited at the same time. I wanted to be the father that I never had, and to give my child everything that I did not have. I would be better than my father was, and I was sure of it. I could see myself doing all of the things with my child that a father does. I could see myself taking her to dance classes, playing Barbie dolls with her, playing dress-up with her as most little girls do. I could see myself comforting her as she cried on my shoulder during times of pain. I could see myself protecting her from the guys like me when she grew up and even walking her down the aisle when she got married. That is the dad that I wanted to be. And that is the dad that I wanted to be for her.

As Satan does in our lives, he is always trying to creep back in with any given chance. Even when we may be wise enough to walk away from a situation that will ultimately lead us down the path of his desires, he is always out there lurking, just waiting for that opportunity to get back in and try again. He never gives up. And he didn't give up with me either. I had walked away from Pam as I knew that the end result would not be good, and I could clearly see where that life of destruction would lead me. However, even though I had walked away, she was not completely out of my life. That meant that Satan still had ways to get back into my head and try to pull me down his road of death and destruction, which is exactly what he did.

After many months of trying to deal with Pam and her grandmother on being able to see my daughter with no success, the thoughts began to come back in to my mind that maybe I should give it another shot with Pam. Maybe she had changed with the birth of our daughter. Maybe it would be different this time. And I finally justified all of this with the reasoning that it would be best for our child. I now find it rather ironic that the same reasoning that I used to end the relationship with Pam the first time, it would be best for our child, is the same reasoning that Satan put into my head which caused me to consider getting back together with her. Satan is the king of liars, and his key method of attack is by deception. He tries to deceive us in to believing that what we are doing, or the choice that we are making, is the best thing, or harmless. He then will help us to justify that choice or decision and will always do so with a cloud of lies.

The Merriam-Webster dictionary defines Deception as *the act of causing someone to accept as true or valid what is false or invalid*[1]. That is the thing about deception – If you knew it was not true or valid, you would never fall for it or believe it to begin with. It is as if Satan has put a veil over our eyes, causing us to see things, or believe things, in a way which they really are not. Once we accept this deception or falsehood as a way of thinking, and as being the truth, Satan has his way in to our lives and now controls our path and direction.

I fell for the deception, and shortly after Pam and I worked things out and moved back in together. It was not long before we were right back where we left off. Nothing had changed. The fighting, the insecurities, the jealousy, the anger and rage, and the violent outbursts. The only thing different now was that we had a small child who would bear witness to it all.

While I still remember all of the miserable times with Pam, I did not let this bring me down or define who I was. I was strong, both mentally and physically, and could overcome her actions towards me. After all, it was a choice that I made, and I had to endure the consequences of that choice. What I could not bear was the effect that it had on my child.

One particular fight remains vividly clear in my recollections today. It was the last fight that we had. While I do not recall what had started the fight, or Pam's rage, I am sure it was more than likely the same root cause. Pam was drinking again and now throwing furniture items and knickknacks at me while screaming, cussing and yelling. Furniture had become tossed about the apartment in her fit of anger. I glanced over across the room and saw our daughter, crouched down, hiding behind the couch with the most dreadful look of fear on her face. At that point I knew this had to end, once and for all, regardless of how Pam and her grandmother would treat me.

In that one specific moment I began to realize that my choices, my decisions, and my actions – affect other people – and right now they were affecting and hurting the one person that I loved more than anything in the world. The one person that I never wanted to hurt or harm. They affected my precious, innocent little girl.

Pam and I split up, for the last time. Again, she moved back in with her grandmother, and our child. Pam and her grandmother filled my daughters head with so many lies about who I was and convinced her that I was an evil monster. I fought for years to be able to see my daughter with no success. I had court orders that allowed me visitation, and even though I paid child support, Pam and her grandmother did whatever they could to keep my daughter away from me.

Pam's life continued on a downward spiral. Different men, different drugs and alcohol, being abused by all of them. Someone once told me that Pam would go to the bar and drink all day and take our daughter with her as she did not have a sitter. Over the years Pam would call me on the phone, out of the blue, begging for money and telling me that she would let me see our daughter if I did give her the money.

My heart was crushed for my daughter, and the life that she would have to live. Knowing that this little girl was destined to become just like her mother and that she did not stand any chance at having a so-called normal life was now my burden to bear, and one that would consume half of my heart over the years.

I had brought a child into this world and had placed her into an environment that would be pure hell for her entire existence. The choices I had made had literally destroyed that child's life before she was even born. I know there are two parts to every equation, and that while I was not the direct source of influence that caused her to go astray, I still should have made better choices, especially when bringing a child into this evil world. I should have thought long term and been more responsible with my choices, knowing who and what Pam was, and that the child would be directly influenced by her, with or without me around. I do not regret having that beautiful little girl, and to this day I still break down in tears when I allow myself to see her little face, and that perfect smile in my mind, which is then quickly wiped away with the guilt and pain that I carry of putting her into a life where she never stood a chance. God...... please forgive me!

Don't Ever Give Up

As my daughter became of legal age, I tried to make contact with her directly in hopes that I may be able to salvage some type of relationship and be there for her as her father. Much to my surprise she agreed to meet. It became obvious in our first few meetings that she was truly afraid of me; however, I kept in mind what she must have been told and what she had been through. I started slow with her and just assured her that I wanted nothing from her, and that I only wanted to give her the love of a father that she so deserved. I am not sure that she knew what that meant, but hopefully I would be able to show her over time. I told her the truth about her mother and I, without placing blame, as well as her grandmother. I told her that I had always wanted her, and wanted to be with her, and had never stopped fighting to try and be with her. I could tell by her look and her reactions that she had been lied to for years, and that this was all new information to her. Unfortunately, her mother and her grandmother were still in the picture and still had full control over her thoughts and beliefs.

I did manage to see my daughter many times over the next few years and even brought her into our family at one point. This did not last long though, as at that point, in my home and with my family, there were responsibilities, obligations, and consequences. It was not a legalistic environment or a dictatorship, but everyone had their responsibilities as a family member, and there were consequences for all of your actions, good or bad. My daughter, however, was not fond of being held accountable or having consequences for her actions. One morning I woke up and realized that she had packed all of her belongings and left in the middle of the night. I was heartbroken as a father and knew that my one and only chance for turning her life around and being a father to her was gone. I then realized that the dichotomy in my story had come full circle – the little boy who so badly wanted and craved the love and attention from his father, was now the father who so badly wanted and craved the attention from his child – and got neither.

My daughter got married several years later and had three boys of her own. She later abandoned all three boys and their father and disappeared, only later to be found living in close proximity to where her mother was. Pam never got better. More men, more drugs, more alcohol. The last I had heard of Pam was that she was serving time in a Federal Prison, for what I do not know. The apple does not fall far from the tree.

While some would look at this chapter and say that it could easily be the low point in my life, which it sure felt like at the time, I would now disagree. For many years of my life that was my perspective, rock bottom. I went through a lot with Pam, and experienced times that I do not wish on anyone. I initially had a lot of hatred and anger while going through this phase of my life. However, I can now say that Pam more than likely saved my life. Yep, saved my life. I was headed down a road of destruction with nothing to stop me. I was so wrapped up in my self-life that I didn't care about anyone or anything else. I have done things to other people which I will never reveal to anyone, and have not revealed in this book, as I am very repulsed and saddened by the way that I lived and the ways in which I used and abused other people. While Pam was a lost soul who caused me much pain and torment, she gave me something that I loved more than myself, and more than life itself. She gave me that little girl. That little girl caused me to stop and look at my life and the direction that I was headed and made me realize this was not the person that I wanted to be or the life that I wanted to live or give to others. For the first time in my life, I saw something that I valued more than myself.

"Children are a heritage from the Lord, offspring a reward for him...... Blessed is the man whose quiver is full of them..."
Psalms 127:3,5

Chapter 7

A Better Man, A Better Person

At some point in my life, I learned to live by a very simple, yet powerful statement. This one statement has become a deeply ingrained part of my belief system, and I still live by it today:

If you don't like what your life is or has become, change it!

Let's break it down a bit, as it can be more complex than just that one simple sentence.

If you don't like what your life is or has become, change it!

First, we must understand that we are where we are today, and we are what we have become, simply as a result of the choices and decisions that we have made up to this point in our life. We all face choices in our lives, every single day. Most of them are smaller and trivial and don't really have much significance or importance in the outcome or direction of our lives. For example – You get up in the morning and have to make a decision on what you will have for breakfast. You get ready for work and have to decide which clothes you will wear today.

You get the point. Insignificant to the overall outcome of our lives, in a sense, but yet they are still choices that we must make every day.

Habits

The average adult makes roughly 35,000 decisions, or choices, every day. Assuming you sleep like a normal person, unlike me, that equates to over 2,000 decisions per hour. Dang, no wonder why we are all so worn out. Children, on the other hand, make roughly 3,000 decisions per day. Most of these, good or bad, happen automatically through information that we have subconsciously stored away in our minds over our years from past experiences.

More than forty percent of the things that we do every day are automatic responses, without any conscious thought or effort from our brain, and we just simply do them as they have become a habit. Habits are the brains way of increasing efficiency and conserving energy. They allow the brain to focus on the more important issues at hand. The brain is always looking for a way to make something routine, so that it can become a habit, and require less thought and effort. Our brain also uses these habits to help minimize risk. Our brain is essentially wired to take the easy way out. So, whether we realize it or not, our brains are always looking for ways to simplify things, make them routine, and take the easy way out by having us do things that require little to no thought at all.

I love to play golf. *'Love'* is probably an understatement. Several years ago, I met another of my good friends while on a golf course. This is actually how I have met most of my friends. His name is Mike. I was playing as a single the day that I met Mike, and he had come up behind me playing with another single. They had caught up with me as I was waiting on the group playing in front of me. Mike would tell me later that he saw my pre-shot routine from afar and wasn't sure that he wanted to join up with me. I guess it didn't look to captivating to him. Later on, after playing many rounds with Mike, he asked me one day why I moved my feet like I did in my pre-shot routine. I gave Mike an inquisitive look, and then said, *"Like what?"* He tried to explain and mimic what I was supposedly doing, but I had no clue what he was attempting to describe. I would make a few more swings, and he would say *"There you go, you did it again!"* I still had no clue.

After several holes, and multiple attempts by Mike to get me to recognize what I was doing, I then began to focus on my footwork prior to hitting my shot in hopes that what he was describing would suddenly make sense. This was hard and took a lot of effort as my brain was trained to focus on the shot that I was trying to hit, and not what my feet were doing. But once I did, I could clearly see what Mike was talking about. I would constantly keep my feet moving, shifting my weight from right to left prior to hitting my shot. This was something that I had learned to do long ago when I started golfing, and now it was just habit. It took no thought. Heck, I didn't even realize that I was doing it until Mike pointed it out. It was the same way, the same tempo, the same cadence, every time – with no thought or effort at all. I had initially started doing this to keep the body loose, and not rigid or static. At some point my brain just made this a habit so that it could use my energies to focus on the actual swing and the shot, which were more important. And now I have been doing it for so long that I don't even realize that I am doing it.

This is exactly the way we are with most of our habits. We don't even realize we are doing them. They just happen – over and over again – without thought. Unfortunately, we have good habits, and we have bad habits. But they are both habits, and our mind handles both in the same manner. And since we have bad habits as well, habits being the things that we aren't even aware we are doing most of the time, wouldn't you find it strange that you could actually be doing things every day that are harmful to yourself and your future – and yet you aren't even aware that you are doing them? Seriously – think about it for a minute. It's kind of an oxymoron. You have to dig deep, really deep, to think about something that you may be doing which doesn't require any thought to do.

The remainder of the decisions that we make every day are the more complex ones that we have to stop and intentionally think about.

Here is how the brain deals with the process – The easy, simple (good and bad) decisions are ones that we make with all of the built-in stuff that we have acquired over the years, and we do almost automatically (habits), without even recognizing it most times. The so called '*Auto Pilot*'.

Now, the tougher, more complex decisions are where it gets a bit hazy. Even as powerful as the human mind is, our working memory can only hold about three or four thoughts at one time. The more you practice with that 'working memory', the stronger it gets, and is then able to hold and deal with more variables at any given time, and in return allows you to make better, more sound decisions, and in a sense shuts the Auto Pilot off. This is done by utilizing both sides of the brain at the same time, which many believe can be achieved through writing. If both sides of the brain are now working together, you are now able to make decisions not only based on the logical, or the creative, but of both. It discontinues one side from totally running the show and allows you to be the best that you can be, in all aspects, making better choices and decisions which lead to better outcomes and results.

Of course, the best that we will ever be will always be limited by the extent of our knowledge, or what we have come to learn and understand through our years, as well as how we perceive that knowledge and information. The brain, or our 'database', can and will only provide information to the extent of that which we have allowed into that database. We are only as smart, informed, or knowledgeable as our own actions allow us to be.

Those tougher choices or decisions, the ones that we have to stop and think about, have long lasting effects that not only shape the direction we are headed, but variably may also have an impact on others around us. Just as we discussed with Satan and his main strategy, deception, we don't always initially realize the long-term effect that many of these tougher choices will have on our lives, and we surely don't see or believe that they will have any negative consequences in our lives – or we would clearly choose the alternative every time. That simple harmless conversation with the new blonde girl at the office because you are just trying to be friendly. Nothing wrong with being polite and friendly, is there? It opens the door for more casual conversation, which opens the door for an unexpected lunch, which opens the door for unhealthy thoughts of you and her, which opens the door for that affair.

Every choice that we make, every day, has consequences to it, one way or the other – Good or Bad.

Our common shortcoming is, as stated, that when we are faced with the tougher choices and decisions that will have a long-term effect on our lives, especially in the case of the negative, we most always don't see it as being harmful at the time that we are making that choice or decision. Again, this is Satan's plan and methodology for getting into our lives and wreaking havoc and destruction. It is not always that one simple little choice or decision that you make that causes you the harm or issue, but that one simple little choice or decision which seems harmless that leads us down a path of more little choices that gradually get more and more harmful to our lives and who we become. That is Satan's methodology – to hide in the background, unnoticed, and cause you to do just enough that you would never even consider that you were being influenced by an outside source.

We have the power to choose every single little detail within our lives. Where we live, who our friends are, where we work, what we like, what we do for fun, what we watch on TV, and so on. This is a God given gift to us called Free Will. It's intended purpose is something different, but we will get to that in a later chapter.

Our free will gives us the freedom of choice, to choose what we want and how we want it. Again, our life today is a result of all of our past choices and decisions. Recall the simple auto pilot choices that we make every day. That forty percent or more of things that we do automatically, out of habit. Well, our habits, or the things that we do almost every day without even thinking, can be just as destructive to us as the tougher more complicated choices as most times they become so routine that we don't even give much if any thought to doing them at all. We just do them, because it is what we have always done, and it is easy.

Now that we have a basic understanding of how our brain deals with the choices that we make, lets break down the one statement that I have come to live by:

If you don't like what your life is or has become, change it!

Simply put, if we don't like the way our life is going, who is in it, or what direction we are headed in – we have the power to change it. We are the ones who put all of those things or people or habits into our lives, by the choices that we have made in the past. If we want a different future, we just need to make some changes with what is in our lives now that we don't like, and then start by making better, more informed choices and decisions, and changing some of our habits.

If you are tired of that dead-end job with the boss who never realizes your potential, then choose to get a better job where you are valued and appreciated.

If you are not liking the way your body looks or feels, choose to start a workout plan or eat more healthy.

If you have a bunch of deadbeat friends who drag you down and don't make you a better person, then choose to replace them with friends who are supportive and encouraging.

If you don't like the person you have become, for whatever reason, change the person that you will become. Get a better job to make more money, go back to school to get a higher education, get involved with a group of people that do something that you would like to do or become. You have the power of choice, to change anything in your life. After all, you are the one who put that thing there to begin with. You can remove it from your life just as easily, and just as quickly.

Reflection

At this point we all need to stop and go take a look in the mirror. What do you see? Do you like what you see? Are you who you truly want to be, or how you want others to see you? Is your life playing out the way that you thought it would? Or do you see more, want more, and desire more? Be honest – I think we all see, want, and desire more. Well, we all have the power to change all of that!

We also need to be honest with ourselves in accepting the fact that it is nobody's fault but our own that our lives are the way that they are. Sure, things happen to us that we cannot control. But we can control how we perceive them and react to them, and we can control if we let those things shape and determine who we become. Every little thing (as well as every big thing) in our lives is there because of us, and us alone. We may not have asked for it to come into our lives or caused it to happen – but we surely have allowed it to stay. Every little thing in our lives is there simply because we have allowed it to stay there.

"So do not fear, for I am with you; do not be dismayed, for I am your God. I will strengthen you and help you; I will uphold you with my righteous right hand." Isaiah 41:10

"For the Spirit God gave us does not make us timid, but gives us power, love and self discipline." 2 Timothy 1:7

"You, dear children, are from God and have overcome them, because the one who is in you is greater than the one who is in the world." 1 John 4:4

There is one exception to this belief and way of thinking. Divorce. I am not a fan or proponent of, nor do I suggest in any way that you get rid of your spouse and go find another if things are not going well or as you would like them too. Marriage is a sacred covenant that you make not only to your spouse, but to God. It is forever. Marriage is not easy, and it does takes work, an entire life full of work, from both parties.

Unfortunately, in the world that we live in today, it has become acceptable in society to so quickly and easily just give up on that commitment. Many people think that it is just much easier to go out and find someone else and start over, instead of putting in the work and effort required to make the marriage that you have work. Marriage and divorce are a book on their own that I am not qualified to dive in to – or maybe I am, as thirty years of hard work and endless effort with my wife has taught me well.

This easy-come-easy-go mentality reminds me of the well-known saying '*The grass is always greener on the other side*', meaning that the things we see from afar always look better and more attractive than the pathetic view that we hold of our own lives. While this statement may hold some validity in certain scenarios, I have always had one response to this utterance – ***You still have to mow it!***

No matter how good it (things) may look from a distance, it (they) still requires care, maintenance, and constant attention.

I love a nice, thick, healthy, green yard. I put a lot of work in to maintaining my yard so that it has that 'perfect' look most all of the time. I water it, I mow it, I fertilize it, I use preemergent. I get comments from the neighbors frequently on how nice my yard looks. If you drove by my house and looked at the yard you may think it was perfect as well and wish that your yard looked just as nice. What you don't see when you drive by and take a quick look is all of the weeds that are still trying to sprout up every single day. You also don't see all of the work and effort that goes in to getting the yard to look this way. It takes a lot of work and effort, and if I slack off for even just a bit, things get out of control, and I have to work twice as hard to get it back to where it was before.

The grass on the other side always looks greener because we are not seeing the full picture. We are seeing but a mere glimpse, a quick snapshot, from far away – and even then, only the good part and most always what someone else wants us to see.

Nonetheless, people that leave their spouses hastily in search of an easier and less troublesome mate all have one thing to remember – ***Wherever you go, there you are!*** What does that mean? It means that a marriage, or any relationship for that matter, takes two to make it work. You are one of the two in that marriage and if it is not working, you are just as much at fault as your partner. I know this may rub some of you the wrong way, and that some marriages may have that unusual circumstance which we won't dive in to now.

My point is that if you run off to go find that 'easier and less troublesome' mate, **YOU** are still part of the equation. **YOU** still have baggage and drama, and problems of your own that you are taking with you into that relationship that will more than likely cause the same problems to arise, eventually finding yourself in the same place that you are in now.

Whether we want to admit it or not, as we will come to understand more deeply in later chapters, we all have issues, baggage, trauma or wounds that stem from our younger years that have defined who we are today. And we continue to carry these wounds around with us our entire lives, most times not even acknowledging them ourselves.

As for your relationship or marriage - Get involved with a good Christian Marriage Counselor and follow their plan. Swallow your pride and your ego and remember why you fell in love with this person to begin with. Make every effort to bring those feelings and emotions back into your marriage, no matter how awkward it may feel, and fight for your spouse just as you would have when you were dating. God will bless you for this and will do wonderful things in your marriage if you allow Him in.

Remember this as well – marriage is a covenant with God. And since it is in a sense a connection that we have with God, Satan is trying to do everything that he can to undo it. Many of the issues and problems that we have in a marriage, or a relationship for that matter, are a direct result of an attack by Satan in an attempt to cause separation and division. Separation between us and God, and division between us and our partner and our family unit. Don't always be so quick to point the finger at and place blame on your partner, as it may not be them at all that is the direct cause of the issue.

We also need to start looking into that mirror on a daily basis, and not in a way that we become so absorbed in our physical appearance. We need to start fixing our inner selves before we can expect to have everything in our lives fall into its place of that perfect story book fantasy that we think we should be living. Every relationship, every encounter, every interaction, requires at least two people. You are one of those two people. If you are not adding value or benefit to the relationship, encounter or interaction – you are only bringing it to its demise. Without added value and benefit, from both parties, it is destined to fail. We all need to work on making ourselves better, while forming better habits and making better choices, which will in turn lead us to better situations, encounters and relationships.

My Choices

As I left Pam, I realized that I had ended up where I was as a result of all the choices and decisions that I had made over the years. I was hit in the face with the actuality that this way of life was not working, and most likely never would. This life did not make me happy, and caused nothing but trouble, pain and problems. I realized that it was very self-centered, and that I had no thought or care for any other human being. I looked to the future and saw a lonely old man with so much bitterness, anger and hatred for the world that I couldn't bear the thought of that being the person who I was destined to become. I had to change. I wanted more out of life, and I wanted to be a better person. I wanted to be loved and appreciated, and so badly yearned to be wanted, loved, and desired by someone else.

I vowed to myself to make changes in my life as well as the direction that I was headed in. I sought out a better job with more stability and income. I started looking at people with a different perspective, and treating them more kindly, as if they mattered to me. I truly wanted to be a 'good guy' and to have people like me for what was on the inside. Unfortunately, I had not been taught where true happiness and success comes from, and I surely did not have anyone in my life as a role model to teach me those things now. I had to keep trying though, no matter how hard it may get and no matter how many times I might fail. I had no other options. Once again, I was on my own.

My life had become more of a trial-and-error exercise. I had to attempt to try and figure out what would be the best way to accomplish something and then abandon that method for another when it failed or did not work out as I had planned. Trial and error is a tough way to live and can be very discouraging and frustrating at times. It requires solidified determination to reach your end goal as there will be more failures than successes. It is always the longest and most difficult road of any search, but at times can be the most rewarding as well.

In the 1897 novel Dracula, written by Bram Stoker, the author is quoted as saying *"We learn from failure, not from success"*.[1]

Albert Einstein also said – *"A person who never made a mistake never tried anything new"*.[2]

We learn so much more from our failures, or the mistakes that we make in life...... If we allow ourselves to. We all make mistakes in life, and those who let the mistakes define who they are never rise up and move on to achieve the greater things that they set out to accomplish, which they are fully capable of. The failure, or mistakes, must be understood as a part of the process to reaching your destination.

So, I kept picking myself up, analyzing where I may have gone wrong, made changes to the process of how to be a better person and kept moving forward. Some parts of my old life were still present though, such as drinking, partying and chasing girls. I was, however, committed to remove the drugs from my life, and to start treating girls like more than just an object for sexual gratification. I came to realize that these girls had to have a perceived value, and that if they did not, I was only cheapening or lessening the value of myself by entering into a relationship with them.

And so went my life for the next couple years. Consistently trying to be a better me and trying to add value to the world I lived in instead of tearing others apart while scratching and clawing to try and get everything and anything that I could.

This was a laborious time in my life, and as previously stated, I had not been taught the commonplace life lessons that most all parents teach their children in preparing them to venture off into the world on their own. My current view of parenthood is that we as parents are blessed by God with the gift of our children, and that we are being entrusted by God to raise, educate, discipline and prepare those children so that one day they may go out on their own and become Godly men and women of their own.

It is not a mindset of ownership, but of stewardship. The children are not ours and were never ours to begin with. They are God's children, and He is asking us to raise them and prepare them for Him and then set them free to be on their own. Once we truly and deeply understand who our creator is, we can clearly see where the true ownership of everything lies. With this legitimate understanding we then do not see our children as an object, a burden, or a hindrance to our lives, and we begin to treat them with the love and care they so much deserve, while educating and preparing them for a life of their own. A life that would be greater than ours, as they come from and belong to a power and creator that is much greater than we are.

My parents did not see their children that way, and even more devastatingly, did not have that perspective of God either. My father had the *'Me'* mentality his entire life. What could he get for himself and what could he get to please himself. All with no thought for the consequences, or how his actions would impact others. My mother was forced into one of the toughest choices in life – having to choose between providing for her kids or raising her kids. She chose the role of a provider and thus neglected the first and foremost responsibility that God had asked of her.

I still struggle today with trying to understand how two grown adults can willingly step in to the act of bringing children into this world and then neglect them and fail to love them and nurture them.

So, in growing up, I was never taught even the most basic principles of life that one would be expected to know as they become an adult. My siblings and I were not educated on personal hygiene, health, dietary intake, finances, savings, how to budget, or more importantly, moral obligations to others and how to be respectful or courteous. We didn't have social skills and did not know how to treat other people, or how to do so with respect. All we knew was what we saw every day – our mother trying to just survive and doing whatever she had to do just so that we could stay above ground.

This was my life, day in and day out. Trying to be a good observer of someone else who appeared to have it all figured out and then trying to do the best that I could to be a likeness of that person and their actions.

There are two main problems with this formula, however. First, an individual's perception or interpretation of what they see, or perceive to see, will never be of any higher quality than their education or understanding of all things. It is not possible for us to see things in a way that we have no knowledge or understanding of. There is much that we do not know, and if we do not know something, we do not have the ability to apply it to our lives. It may be good for some to go back and read this paragraph again, as most all of us hold firm to the belief that what we know is true and correct, and that the knowledge that we possess is more than sufficient to handle all things.

Second, I was a phony, a fake, a counterfeit, a poser. I was not the real me. I was trying to be someone else and was imitating someone else and what they were doing. I was disregarding the true me, and who God had created me to be. And I was doing so with the sole intention of trying to please others in hopes of gaining their admiration and attentions.

But for now, this was the only way in which I knew how to attempt to better myself, and it was working....... to some extent. I did not know any other way – and I did not know that there were other ways.

Getting Better

I worked hard to get a better job, which was in the restaurant business as it was something that I knew and was good at. I was a hard worker and moved my way up into management, making more money and working more hours. I worked on the image that I displayed to others by upgrading my wardrobe and purchasing a newer car. The car was not brand new, but boy was it sharp. It was a two door Chevy Z24 sports car. It was blue in color and had a gray interior, and dark tinted windows. The stereo system had been upgraded and was extremely loud. The car had a back seat, but I surely would not want to be the person who had to sit back there as your knees would be up against your chin because it was so cramped. It had front bucket seats, a center console with the shifter on the floor, and was one of the first cars to have a digital dash display. It was in those days what we called a 'chick magnet'. All the guys wanted a car like that because they knew, or at least believed, that the girls would be drawn to it. I saw that car on a used car lot one day and knew I had to have it. However, I did not have enough money for the down payment. So, I worked and scraped to get the money in about a month and a half, and hoped they still had the car for sale. They did, and it was now mine!

I made a conscious effort to be a positive, upbeat person when dealing with others, and to try to be respectful and polite as well. I even tried reading books like *How to Win Friends and Influence People by Dale Carnegie*[3]. That wasn't helpful as I soon realized that reading was agonizing to me, as if I was being forced to do something against my will.

I then made a much more stable upgrade to my housing situation when an old friend and I decided to rent a house where we could each have our own separate level to live on. It was a small house, in an older neighborhood, in a decent part of town. Most all of the neighbors were elderly and had likely lived there most of their lives. It was quite and secure, and you could get a good night's sleep without the loud chaotic noises of the old neighborhood, and the fear that every little noise that you did hear was someone either stealing your car or trying to break into your house. Life seemed to be getting better, or at least it looked that way on the outside.

On the inside, I was still an insecure child with no confidence who was looking for affirmation from others and just wanting someone to love me and want me for who I truly was. My biggest problem though, was that I still did not know who I was.

"...A man reaps what he sows. Whoever sows to please the flesh, from the flesh will reap destruction; whoever sows to please the Spirit will reap eternal life. Let us not become weary in doing good, for at the proper time we will reap a harvest if we do not give up." Galatians 6:7-9

Chapter 8

The Change That Didn't Happen

The turning point in my life came in 1993. I was still enduring the attempt at bettering myself to just be a 'good person'. Things in life were beginning to get better, or at least they weren't getting worse. Progress was at a snail's pace though and always had its occasional setbacks. While I may have been cleaning up the outside of me, the inside was still a mess, and I had not even become aware of the true issues in my life that had been and were causing all of the carnage.

There is an old saying that goes *"You can dress up a pig, send it to school and teach it manners – but it is still a pig."* That is about how I felt. I was still a pig. I was still broken and damaged and was unknowingly trying to pretend to be someone else to impress others and fit in. I did not know how to be me, let alone someone else.

The Day of Change

The day that changed my life for the better, was the day that Sandi asked me if I would like to go out for drinks and meet her sister. The day that I met Robin.

I remember that day so clearly, and every day after that as well. Robin was in her last year of college; I was twenty-five at the time. Robin was younger than I was, therefore, by simple societal standards I should have been the one who was more educated, more refined, more disciplined, and more well-rounded. In actuality, it was just the opposite.

When I met Robin and got to know her better in the following weeks, I could clearly see that I was playing in a league that I did not have the skill nor the aptitude for. Robin was drop dead gorgeous. She was tall and had long sandy-blonde hair. She had an extremely proportionate body with legs that just went on forever. Her face and complexion were flawless. She could have easily been the cover model on any magazine. And that was just what was on the outside. Guys are much more 'visual' than women are, it is our natural instinct to look at and crave the beauty of the woman's body. That is just the way we are made and created. For me, it was all I ever knew in the past, up until now. For the first time in my life, I wanted to know what was on the inside as well.

On the inside Robin appeared to know who she was. She was confident in who she was and knew what she wanted out of life. She too had been in some bad past relationships, but she did not let that determine her future or harden her heart in any way. She was cautious, but open. Robin was going to school and was in the process of moving her life forward with goals and plans. Robin had an infectious smile and personality, and while she wasn't the most outgoing person, once you became her friend, she was very open and bubbly. Robin was laid back and easy going, just as I was, which made it effortless for us to bond. Robin would drink, but not in excess, and never did drugs. I didn't quite understand what this thing was that had just been dropped in to my life, or what I had done to deserve it – but oh man, did I want it!

This was going to be the biggest challenge that I had ever aspired for in my life, and even though I did not understand how a girl like that could ever see anything good in a guy like me, I was going to fake it for as long as I could in hopes that something may come of us. However, I was sure that she would soon figure out that I had no clue how to live life, and would soon move on to something better, just as everyone else had in my past.

This brings us back to Chapter 1 – The Question, and the last paragraph where Robin and I got married in the spring of 1994. Yep, somehow, someway, I did it. I managed to capture the most beautiful girl that I had ever seen, who also just happened to have the biggest and kindest heart that I had ever known. I finally had someone who loved me and was true and sincere with their love and affection. I say that I captured her, but in reality, I know that this was God's will for my life and the direction of my life, and that I had nothing to do with it (well, very little anyways).

C'mon...... do you really think that a hot Super-model type girl with an even more desiring inner beauty would fall for a stoner loser like me? I had nothing going for me, and nothing to offer her.

As I got to know more about Robin, as well as her sister Sandi, I found out that they had come from a broken family as well. Their parents were divorced too, as the result of an even more shocking and possibly devastating scenario. Their parents had been married for some time and had three children – Sandi who was the oldest, then Robin, and finally a younger brother. Soon after, their father turned his attentions toward men and outwardly admitted that he was gay and then divorced their mother. While I cannot comment on the reasoning for this, or attempt to justify why either course of action may have happened, I can say that this must have been an extremely difficult family dynamic to be raised in. I look back on my upbringing and see the road that it led me down; and then ponder how both Sandi and Robin were able to become so well rounded and confident in who they were and where they were headed. I didn't get it, and it surely made no sense in my limited depth of knowledge.

The Answer to the Question

The answer to the question, is in the question. The question that Robin asked me back in Chapter 1. *Do you believe in God?* Over the following years I came to learn that the answer to the question on how they were able to become who they had become was very confusing, but simplistic in nature. Both Robin and her sister believed in God! More so, they knew God, knew His promises, knew that He was their real Father, and they knew who they were in Christ. They also knew that God was their priority and the main focus in this life that we live, and with that knowledge and confidence, they chased after the right things, for the right reasons.

Both Robin and I had come from broken homes, some might even say that her upbringing had the potential for being more harmful to a child's future than mine, but we ended up going down two completely different roads, in opposite directions. My road was a life of self-preservation and destruction and always chasing after the wrong desires in an attempt to please and satisfy only myself. Her road was a life full of love, promises and riches, surrounded by others and filled with joy and happiness. Robin could have had any guy that she wanted. Someone better looking, someone with money, someone with an education, someone with a future, someone who could offer her safety and security, and even someone with a much nicer sports car. But she chose to stick with me.

So how do two different people who are going in two completely different directions on two completely opposing roads, manage to cross paths at some point in life? This is one of the great mysterious events of life that can only be explained by our Creator Himself. God tells us many great things in the Bible, which can and will guide us through life if we allow them too.

In Jeremiah 29:11 God says: *"For I know the plans I have for you, plans to prosper you and not to harm you, plans to give you hope and a future."*

The Bible also tells us that God knew each and every one of us before he even created us in the womb. God knows every little step in our lives well before we take it and wants more than anything for us to turn to Him, seek Him, and allow Him to guide us. God also likes to keep things mysterious, which is a great point to keep in mind as we progress. In fact – If we knew all of the answers, if we knew how things would play out, we would never turn to God with the realization that we don't know how to live this life on our own. If we did know all of the answers, which many of us seem to think we do, we would believe that we ultimately have control and direction over all that happens in our lives and would therefore have no need for God. And with this newly found wealth of knowledge, we would become just like Satan – thinking that we are equal to or greater than God.

As previously mentioned, God also gave us free will. The freedom to choose, the freedom to make our own decisions. God truly desires us to chase after Him, and choose Him, but He is not going to force us to do it. Although God does have the power and ability to force us, or make us do something, He never will. Doing so would make God a dictator or a tyrant, which He is not – and would essentially make us robots, which we are not and were not created to be.

This can be comparable to that of any other normal, healthy relationship as well – You want the other person to desire you, chase after you, and love you. You want the relationship to be real, and from the heart. Not fake or forced. Just like Robin and I chased after each other when we first met. I wanted nothing but her, and I would like to think that she kind of wanted me too. If it is forced or fake, it is not normal or healthy for either individual.

The choice to choose God is ours. God already knows that He wants us, but now He wants us to step forward and say that we want Him, with our hearts. We all need and desire to be wanted and to be loved. That is the way that God made us. Genesis 1:27 tells us that *"God created mankind in his own image..."*.

God created us to be like Him. We want to be pursued and loved, just as God does. And we want that love to be real, not forced, just as God does. God also tells us in the Bible that He has complete control over everything, which is an important side note for now.

With this free will that God has given us, He has allowed us and actually requires us to make choices at many crucial times in our lives which determine the direction that our lives will then take. Many times throughout our life we make choices that lead us down a road that is not pleasing to God. Such as in my case, with my life and my choices. However, with my life, I did not know the word of God, or that such promises and hope even existed. I had not been exposed to God's calling or His word. I was what people refer to as 'The Lost'. Those that have not heard God's word. This 'not knowing' did not give me a free pass, or exemption, or allow me to be held accountable at a lower standard though.

Although I was unaware of it, I already had made a choice. A choice to follow and live by the ways of the world. The world that is ruled by and run by Satan. I had chosen to make the world and Satan my god, and to live by their beliefs and standards. And as we will discuss in later chapters, the choice that I had made, albeit unintentional and unaware of that choice, was still a choice, and in being so had consequences to the action of the choice itself.

We are all born sinners, and without the blood of Christ, which was given to us through His sacrifice for our sins (our redemption), we have no hope at salvation or knowing God. I believe that God allows certain things and events to happen in our lives as an invitation to us, or a wakeup call. It is in a sense God's way of saying - *"Hey, look at me, here I am. Do you want me?"*

God allows our path to cross the paths of other people and things, that are but just a brief moment in our lives where again we are faced with another choice, this time being presented to us by God. God is saying to us - *"Here I am, do you want me?"*

As is the case with any other normal relationship that we have, God doesn't just come out on the first date and show us everything. After all, He made us in His own image. He doesn't show us all of the good stuff right up front. He gives us a little peak and then hopes that with our free will, we will choose to seek and chase after Him, that we will desire Him and seek to strengthen that relationship.

While many believe that God does not exist, or that He is distant and not actually involved in our lives today, nothing could be further from the truth. This is yet another lie fed to us by Satan to keep us from seeking or knowing God. God is alive and well and very much a part of your life every single day, whether you have come to accept Christ or not, and whether you believe in God or not. We are all God's children, His creation. Our Father, our Creator, has such a desire and love for us that He follows our lives wherever they may go, continually trying to get our attention, and hoping that we will turn to Him and come home. It does not matter how far you have strayed, how dark and desperate the hole may be that you are in, or how despicable the things are that you have done – God is still right there desiring you to turn to Him so that He can shower you with love and forgiveness.

"And God is able to bless you abundantly, so that in all things at all times, having all that you need, you will abound in every good work." 2 Corinthians 9:8

In retrospect I can clearly see many points in my life where God was right there trying to get my attention, seemingly trying to flirt with me. I was so focused on ME and pleasing myself, however, that I did not recognize that He was even there. On that particular day that Sandi had asked me to go have drinks with her sister, I could have easily said no, and came up with some lame excuse in an attempt to justify doing so. I could have easily found something better to do. I wasn't enthusiastic about blind dates, and the potential of having to spend time with someone that I had never seen before. I could have easily kept my eyes focused on the path that I was on and chose to ignore the other paths that were crossing my way. That day, God was allowing my path to cross with a much greater path, one that led to Him.

I did not say no on that day, and I chose to go on that blind date. A simple choice that changed my life forever and took me off of the path that I was on, to lead me in a new direction. As I am writing this book, Robin and I have been married now for thirty years. I would again like to brag about how I have managed to hang on to 'The Beauty' for thirty years, but just as well, I know that it has had very little to do with me.

Over those thirty years, we have never split up, separated, or taken time away from our relationship. She is still, more so than anything, my best friend. I love her, I crave her, I lust for her, and I desire her more now than I ever have. I still have a long way to go as far as hopes of being in the same league as her and I am not sure if I ever will be as she keeps teaching me new things all the time. But, by the grace of God, I wake up every day to keep trying, because she is my love, my beauty, my princess, my best friend and the one that I always will chase after.

Robin and I have been blessed with four children, all of whom have been shown the love, affection, and discipline that should be an unquestionable part of a child's life. Thirty years is a long time, and longer than I would have ever been able to see myself as a part of anything. We just recently had an anniversary party as I wanted to celebrate the accomplishment. Thirty years doesn't just happen by itself. It happens one day at a time, fighting all of the battles of life – together! I know it was a special day for both of us, but for me it was a sense of victory and success.

It was, and is, a milestone and a major accomplishment. I have successfully broken the repeated cycle of divorce in my family which was the role model that my siblings and I grew up knowing. I am the first person from my family since my Grandparents that has not allowed Satan to achieve his goal of separation and division in our family unit. Robin and I both pray that we have been good role models for our children as well, and that this new value system will carry on for many generations with our children.

I must add one other new perspective that Robin taught me recently. She amazes me every day with her depth of thought, and her relationship with The Lord. Robin told me recently that when she prays, she asks God that if at any point in our parenting lives we may have done something against His will or desire with our children, that God would not allow that lesson to sink in with them and become a part of their lives.

What a woman! Father – again – You have given me more than I could ever deserve!

Okay – the guy comes from a rough background, has no role models or direction in his life and therefore heads down a dark desperate path that only leads to destruction, and then stumbles upon the perfect girl of his dreams and they live happily ever after. That must be the end of the story, right?

WRONG! That was just the backstory. This is where the real story begins.

"Therefore, if anyone is in Christ, the new creation has come: The old has gone, the new is here!" 2 Corinthians 5:17

Chapter 9

Out With The Old, In With The New

By this point, you have most likely formed a mental illustration of the world that I grew up in, and an image of me as well, just as most people do when something or someone new is being presented for the first time. People will then attempt to assimilate that view with their own lives, and how they perceive themselves, which I am sure you have also done by now as well.

I made the statement in the *Introduction* of this book that you were probably a lot like me. Some may have become disconnected with that view by now and may feel that they have nothing in common with me, or that they are in no way like the person that I have laid out. Maybe you were fortunate enough to have a good family dynamic and were shown love and support. Maybe you were raised with good morals and values and were taught right from wrong at a very young age. Maybe you were educated, obtained a degree, and even have an outstanding career. Maybe you were raised in good Christian surroundings and know all about God and Jesus Christ. Maybe everything in your life has gone well, and just as you have planned. Maybe you believe that you are nothing like me at all.

The preceding chapters of this book have portrayed what my life looked like growing up, which, in most cases, forms the person which we become and the direction that we take in life. One could say that I did not have a good childhood. One could easily say that I had no clue how to live that life, and I would wholeheartedly agree. Many of you, in one way or another, will likely be able to relate to my past. However, some may struggle to make any connection with me, my past, or my ways of thinking, and might perceive that there is nothing to be learned or gained by reading any further.

I am biased of course, but the best lessons, and the primary deductions from this book are yet to come and will show that we all have inherent fundamental flaws which keep us from living life the way that we were created to live it, and from reaching our fullest potential. They will show that the world which we live in is nothing other than a facade that has been created to keep us from ever realizing our true capacity. These lessons and deductions will further show how all of this has come to happen, and how we have just accepted it as the norm. You still may be reluctant to admit it, but regardless of what your upbringing may have looked like, whether it mirrored mine or not, you more than likely don't have a clue how to live this life either.

Now, if we can put the ego aside for just a bit, and muster up the ambition to read on, we might just end this book with a new perspective and understanding of life and who we really are as a person.

The New

Robin and I married in the spring of 1994. Robin had just graduated from college and wanted to move back home. She was originally from Texas and could not wait to go back. I had nothing spectacular holding me in Omaha, so we moved south to a suburb on the north side of Dallas. Robin began her new career in the medical field working for one of the top cardiologists in the country, as that is what she went to school for. I really didn't have a desire to get back into the restaurant business, so I tried a few different jobs to see what I may like, and where I could fit in.

My first job after our move was at a local Ford dealership as a new car salesman. Car dealerships, and Salesmen, were much different back then than they are now. People dislike car dealerships nowadays because of the way salesmen were back then. It was cut-throat. It was high pressure and very demanding. We had meetings every morning with the sales staff and the Sales Manager where they would teach you how to counter any and every objective that a customer had. They would also offer what were called 'spiffs', which were bonuses or incentives for selling a certain number of cars that day. Then the lot would open, and it was game on.

Each salesperson had his own desk, which were up front in the open showroom area just as they are today. We were not allowed to be sitting at our desk unless we were with a customer and working a deal. At a minimum, we were told that we had to be standing on the 'porch' (the entry doors to the showroom), but were expected to be out roaming the lot just waiting for someone to drive in. And once that customer stepped foot on the lot, they were ours and the games began.

I had learned over time that the Sales Managers understood that no matter what the customer told you, no matter how interested in a vehicle they may be, no matter what personal information they gave you – if that customer left the lot without buying a vehicle, there was a 90% chance that they would never come back and they would end up buying their new vehicle elsewhere. With that mentality, we would actually be scolded for allowing a customer to leave the lot without a vehicle. It was commonplace back then to send them home with the vehicle that they were interested in, even before purchasing it – another psychological sales tactic used by management. Management knew that if a person walked off the lot without a car, the car became 'out of sight, out of mind'. But if we sent you home in the vehicle you were interested in and you could drive it around for a couple days, you would basically talk yourself in to buying it. I was good at sales and liked the job at first, but something just didn't feel right about the deception and forced sales tactics.

I soon found another job working for a Carpet Restoration company. I had done some carpet work in the past, and knew I could fit right in. This company was a small outfit that had the owner running the show, and then four technicians working in the field. We each had our own company van which was fully stocked with everything that we may possibly need. The company offered carpet/upholstery cleaning and repairs. We weren't the common 'bait and switch' type of carpet cleaners though that lure you in with a super low price and then tack on numerous add-ons that you 'must have'. We offered an upscale service to a higher end clientele, usually at an all-inclusive price.

The company was small, but we were very busy and each of the four field technicians were very good at what they did. I really enjoyed this job, and being able to excel in a field while truly being able to give something of value to our customers. The company was located on the far south side of town. Robin and I lived on the north side which made the commute less than desirable, but it was worth it as I made good money and enjoyed what I was doing. Robin and I seemed to be off to a good start with our new marriage and were just beginning to enjoy this new life that we had stepped in to.

Within a short time, Robin was pregnant with our first child. I was once again a bit overwhelmed by the thought but was very excited. The nine months went by, Robin went into labor, and we went to the hospital that night to have our first child. In what seemed like a very short time to me, but probably an eternity to Robin, we had our first boy, Joshua Allen.

Robin was my whole world at that point, and this was our first child, so I was intent on staying at the hospital until she had been released and then taking both of them home. I called my employer and informed them of the birth and that I would not be in for a few days, which they were supportive of. The phone call and the time off came as no surprise to my employer as everyone knew that Robin would be going into labor soon.

The company that I worked for offered 24-hour emergency services, specifically for our commercial clients, for problems such as water damage and flooding from a pipe break or such. Our commitment was that we would respond within one hour, no matter what time of day it was. This meant that each one of the four field technicians carried a pager, and that one of us was always on call, with a weekly rotation. Since the other three techs lived close to the main office, they could just drive to the office and pick up their van within the hour. I lived up north and did not have that option, so the owner reluctantly allowed me to take my van home during the weeks that I was on call, which just happened to be the week our son was born.

My employer knew that we were having a child and was also supportive of me taking the time off when I called him at the birth. However, within one day of my son being born, they repeatedly called me to say that they wanted their van brought back and brought back now. While the owner of the company was a nice man and always appeared very caring, he had many security and trust issues which he let get the better of him. The frequent phone calls with increasing levels of paranoia for his van continued. A couple days later I took both Robin and our new son home and then drove my van back to the shop and left it, never to return again. The owner of the company, with his insecurities and misguided priorities, had turned one of the most memorable days of my life into one of frustration and anger.

I was a go-getter and never had difficulty finding a job, so I wasn't too worried about my situation at that immediate moment. After marrying Robin, and increasingly more so after having our first child, I was determined to be a better man and the best husband and father that I could be. Looking back now I see that this was undoubtedly due to the fact that I was determined to be nothing like my father. I was determined to make sure that I was always there for my wife and kids, and that they knew that I would protect them, provide for them, and love them with all of my heart.

Life was going well, and things appeared to be on the right track. As Robin had a strong belief in God, she wanted us to start attending a church. We searched around and even visited many of the local churches trying to find that perfect one where we fit in. Every week it was a new church, new people, and more pressure as you could just feel the eyes upon you with everyone knowing that you were 'new'. I felt completely out of place as I did not know anything about religion, what I was supposed to do, or how I was supposed to act. I was now the man of my family and was supposed to be the leader of my family, but I felt like that insecure childhood boy once again who would do almost anything to gain the approval of others.

After a couple of months of searching, Robin's sister told her of a church up north that was highly recommended and supposedly had a good pastor. That church was Denton Bible Church, and the pastor was a man named Tommy Nelson. We did some research on the church and found that their core values and beliefs aligned with what we believed, or should I say what Robin believed, so we decided to give it a try the following week. Denton Bible Church was about forty-five minutes north of where we lived, but we figured the drive was worth being involved with a good church. The church was large, as many are in the DFW area. There were over four thousand people who attended every week, so it was easy for us (me) to not stand out as the 'newbies'. Robin and I began to attend that church regularly and eventually became members.

As we were now going to a church that preached the True Word of God, I began to learn more about the scriptures and what they actually meant. The seeds of The Word of God began to make their way in to my mind and my understanding. I was in no way an all-in, Bible thumping believer though, and my religious life was kept only to those few hours on Sunday. And even though the scripture was being preached to me, it was never being taught to me. I would hear it, but the interpretation was limited to what I was able to understand and comprehend. I did not know, and was not taught, that this is a way of life and not just a Sunday thing that we did to be good in God's eyes. The seeds had been planted in my mind, but not in my heart.

"Above all else, guard your heart, for everything you do flows from it." Proverbs 4:23

Back to the Heartland

Robin soon realized that after having our first child, she wanted to be back closer to her mom and her sister, both of whom lived in Nebraska where we had recently come from. So, we made the move back to Nebraska which I was dreading the entire time. I always had a saying about Nebraska - *'The best thing about Nebraska is the sign at the border that says You are now leaving Nebraska'*.

I wanted to do what was best for my wife and kids, and I could understand her reasoning for wanting to be near her family. Even though Nebraska was the last place that I wanted to be, I would soon learn that God had His hand in these plans as well and would soon bring another person into my life that would have an everlasting effect on me.

Once we got back to Nebraska, Robin and I began the process of looking for another church, once again. We attended many churches over the next few years, most of them simply because we knew someone else who was going there.

None of them had any impact on me or my new family, and most were quickly forgotten.

Robin and I quickly had two more kids. Our second child was a boy as well, Kristopher Michael. Our third child was a girl, Katelynn Marie. I feel that God has blessed us with all of our children as they are all beautiful, healthy, and more than we deserve. However, I feel that these two children were a special message to me, from God. They would eventually teach me more about life and about being a caring, loving father than any one or any book ever could.

After several years, we found a church located in a small suburb on the southwest side of Omaha called First Baptist Church. The church was fairly small in attendance when we started going, with roughly one hundred people on any given Sunday. A far cry from the large DFW churches. I feared that I would have to 'fit in' here, and that others would be looking at me and judging me from the get-go. The church had a relatively new pastor who preached The Word straight from the Bible in a practical sense that made it easy to understand. We liked this church, as well as the pastor and his way of communicating God's word and transferred our membership.

At First Baptist, we would not only attend the regular Sunday service but had our kids involved in Sunday School as well as Awana's on Wednesday nights. Robin and I also signed up for a weekly Bible study group which was held once a week at someone's house. With the new pastor, the church began to grow very quickly, and soon after they were adding on a completely new addition which would include a new sanctuary and offices.

The membership in the church grew to a weekly attendance of roughly four hundred people in a short time and the entire congregation was excited about the direction of the church. Robin and I felt that we were at home, and that we were raising our kids in a strong Christian environment. Little did we know at the time that nothing could have been further from the truth.

Over the next several years we were involved in most all of the church activities. I played my role as the good Christian father and supported all of the involvement that my family had with the church. I went to church every Sunday with the wife and kids (when I didn't have something better to do), I went to the Bible study groups that my wife wanted to be involved in, and I pretty much let Robin handle all of the kid's activities that they were involved in. I was still trying to be the best father and husband that I could be and was trying to figure out how to be this 'Best Christian' thing that the church said we should be. The problem was that I had never been taught or shown a good example of what any of these things should be. I was not able to fully comprehend how I was to live this life mostly due to the limited understanding and knowledge that I had obtained up to this point in my life.

I would always listen to the sermons and attempt to figure out how they would apply to my life, and how they would make me a better person. I would pay attention during the Bible studies and again would try to understand the scripture and what it meant to my life as well. But none of these scriptures, sermons, or studies made any sense to me as they were so old and were directed and related to people over two thousand years ago. I had difficulty relating to them, and how I could apply them to my life today.

I had accepted Jesus Christ as my savior, so I knew that I was going to Heaven. This was the one thing that I made sure that I understood clearly. I truly believed that since I had accepted Christ as my savior, all of the other things that I didn't understand were just insignificant details and it really didn't matter whether I had a correct understanding of them as I knew where I would be going when things were all said and done. I had also heard the many sermons explaining how living this Christian life was hard and that we would be tempted by sin every day, and that it is just our nature to screw up and make mistakes. I just couldn't make it make sense. I had even heard many times that God was immeasurably smarter than any of us and therefore we would never be able to comprehend His ideas or plans, which only added confusion to the matter.

I just didn't get it. I had been taught that if we accept Jesus, our sins are forgiven, and we are saved. But then I was taught that we are all still sinners and will struggle with sin every day. I had learned that we would never be able to comprehend God's plans or ways – but yet was told to read the Bible and God will make the scriptures clear in their meaning. Complicated and confusing at best.

So, I thought that this was it as a Christian. I came to believe that being a Christian meant accepting Jesus as your savior, going to church to honor God, and then trying to be a good person all of the other times during the week, even though we know we will sin and fail at doing so. That is what I was learning. That is what they were teaching. That was, and is, the Christian message being preached by most all churches in the Western world today – Accept Christ, go to church, try to be a good person, and then keep trying harder when you are faced with struggles and setbacks. And if you are sinning more, or doing things that you shouldn't be doing – well, you are just not trying hard enough.

That is how my life played out for many, many years. Putting on my good Christian face when I needed to and then going back to my other life and trying to just survive and provide for my family.

I had come to understand and accept that the quality and depth of my Christianity was determined by my efforts, and how those efforts appeared to the world. At the same time, I had been taught that it did not matter what I did, as a Christian I would never 'arrive'. And I had been fed the man-made religious lie that the more of the Christian life that I took on, the more difficult and miserable my life would become.

To say that I was not fascinated with what this new life had to offer would be a huge understatement. Why would one want to give everything they have for this life? My life was painful enough as it was. Why in the world would I want to pile on more difficulty with no offer of reward? If there is nothing to be gained from the work and efforts, then the work and the efforts are futile at best. I saw no reward. I saw nothing to be gained through a complete overhaul of my life. So, I learned to be a Christian, or to at least act like one, when the time or situation that I was in called for me to do so. By my perspective I had become a Christian – albeit a Christian as defined by modern day man and the modern-day church.

An Unexpected Turning Point

One of the things that I enjoy doing most in life is Golf. I could write twenty more chapters on my life in golf, and those experiences, but we will save that for another day, maybe.

Occasionally I would venture out to one of the local municipal golf courses to play and would 'walk on'. This means that I would just show up at the course without having a reserved tee time and they would put me out on the course as a single player with other groups of two or three that had booked tee times. This is a common occurrence in golf for single players as most courses do not allow singles to book a tee time for logistical reasons. I would do this frequently, and when in Omaha it would most always be at Johnny Goodman Golf Course.

Johnny Goodman Golf Course is one of Omaha's 18-hole championship courses. It opened in 1972 and was originally named Applewood, along with the apartment complex that surrounds the course. The City of Omaha decided to change the name of the course in the early 2000's to honor the native Omaha golfer who won the US Open Championship in 1933, as well as many other prestigious events, as an amateur. The course is a par 72 and plays to a length of 6928 yards from the back tees. It is heavily tree lined on most all holes, many of which are doglegs to the left or right and is a great challenge for players at all levels.

You meet many interesting people on a golf course, and over my years of playing at Johnny Goodman I had the privilege of coming to know the Head Pro, Gene 'Spider' Johnson. Gene was an older fellow and had been the Pro at the course since the day it opened. Gene told me a story one time about a charity fundraising event held at the course for The Nebraska Heart Association in 1977. They had invited PGA Tour Pro Jack Nicklaus, Tom Sieckmann who was the top amateur in the state and would soon turn pro and play on the PGA Tour, and another top local amateur to come play, and Gene would join them for an eighteen-hole match.

In the early 1970's Jack Nicklaus was in his prime, as was Tom Sieckmann. Nicklaus had just finished tied for 10th place in The US Open the week prior. Gene Johnson, or Spider, had been playing some of his best golf in recent years as well. Gene had qualified for The PGA Championship in 1962, and then during military service, beat the likes of Orville Moody, the eventual US Open Champion, and Homero Blancas.

Gene went on to describe that match to me hole-by-hole, just as if it were yesterday. The excitement began to flood his aging eyes as he came down the par 5 16th hole, just like we were standing there watching it play in person. While the final scores of all of the players were questioned over time due to it being a charity event, Gene, as well as Sieckmann, went on to beat Nicklaus by 1 stroke, which would be an inexplicable accomplishment for any golfer at any level.

Gene had become rough and hardened on the exterior over the years if you did not know him, likely due to his physical ailments and inability to play the game that he so loved any longer. But as you got to know him, he would let you in a bit more, would soften up a touch, and the stories would eventually seep out over time. Gene came to have issues with his legs as he aged, which kept him from walking or standing for an extended period of time. As I came to know Spider on a more personal level, I realized that it must have been torture for him to have to spend all of his time at that course, gazing out the window at the lush fairways and undulating greens, knowing that he could no longer do what his heart truly desired. I cannot imagine the pain that he must have lived with daily in having his greatest desire laid out openly before him and not being able to quench that desire.

One day I was sitting in the Pro Shop after I had finished a round when three younger men came in boisterously complaining about how bad the greens were, and that no one could make a putt on them. Gene took offense to this, as this was HIS course, and he was not going to let some uneducated novices ramble on meaninglessly while degrading his pride and joy. The three young men went on for about five minutes, at which point Gene was no longer able to hold himself back. Gene slowly pushes himself up out of his chair, grabs the oldest, cheapest, piece of junk putter that he can find out of some scrap golf bag, along with three random old golf balls and then confronts the three guys in his grouchy old voice saying - *"C'mere boys, let me show you how bad the greens are!"* and gestures for them to go out back to the practice putting green.

Gene was never disrespectful to anyone in a direct condescending way. Gene was all about teaching people, and at times these teachings involved the lessons of life. I think I jumped up faster than Gene, as you did not get the chance to see the Spider in action that often. I knew what was about to happen and I kind of had a feeling how it would play out as well.

Gene meanders out the back door and makes his way to the practice putting green. Gene then drops the three balls on to the green at the first spot he comes too. The three young men reluctantly arrive greenside and await Gene's schooling. On that day there were three holes cut in to the green off in the distance, one about fifteen feet away, the second maybe twenty feet, and the last maybe thirty feet away. Each putt would have a substantial amount of break, or bend to it, as well as some elevation change. A PGA Tour Pro would have less than a 10% chance of making one, let alone all three. With no practice strokes and no warmup, Gene takes one stroke of the putter with each ball and sinks one ball in each of the holes. My jaw just dropped. I thought I was a good putter, but this was insane. Gene then glances over to the three guys and says - *"It ain't the greens, it's the player!"* - and then casually walks back into the shop to resume his position in his chair.

Gene Johnson was a man who truly knew what he loved in life – to golf and to fish – and he lived for both. Gene was inducted into the Nebraska Golf Hall of Fame in 2001. Gene served our country in the military for some time, and served many Nebraskans afterwards with his humble position as our Head Pro. Several years later, Gene retired from the job that he loved so much and said that the only place you would find him now would be out on some lake, fishing. Gene touched many people's lives, and hearts, and he is truly missed.

The Hustle

One particular thing that I love about golf is the solitude, and the peace and serenity that it offers. Robin says that I play because it challenges me greater than anything, and that while I may feel like I come close at times, I can never beat the game. I can never win, even though I think I can. It also gives me time to be alone, on occasion, and to just get away from all of what I call 'the noise', all the distractions in life that pull at us every day and eat away at our soul.

On one particular day I headed up to Johnny Goodman with the hope of that solace, and a feeling of escape. I walked into the clubhouse and asked Gene to go out as a single. They were busy that day and Gene said that he would pair me up with a threesome, a group of three guys that had booked a tee time. This was fine as well.

This is also one of the many other benefits of golf – you get the chance to meet people that you normally would not and spend roughly four hours with them. I have met many great people on the golf course, and most all of my current friends have been acquired through a round of golf. However, just as with anything in life, this can be very challenging at times and even ruin your day if you allow it to, when you get paired up with someone that you just can't stand.

On this particular day I was paired up with three guys that each knew one another. They were an eccentric group of guys to say the least. Right away your mind tries to figure out their relationship – father/son, brothers, workmates?? I could not put a finger on these guys though. I made my way up to the first tee and introduced myself.

The first guy was Troy. Troy was my age and seemed to be the most like me. He was a Type A kind of guy and was flamboyant and confident. The second guy was Don. Don appeared to be just a touch older and appeared confident, but in a secure way. Don was more laid back and easy going. Don was the one who would watch the fire and enjoy its comforts, as Troy poured gasoline on it and lit the match. The third guy was much older and just kind of stood off to the side. He introduced himself as Gary. Gary was not shy; he was what we would call reserved. Gary wasn't quick to just spew words out of his mouth just to be noticed but would instead listen and ponder before making a comment. All three seemed to be nice and friendly, and it looked like it was going to be an enjoyable afternoon.

Right away, before we even tee off on the first hole, Troy exclaims boldly that they have a 'game' going and then asks me if I want in on it. A 'game' is any type of wagering, usually dependent on the score of each individual. I said *"Sure, why not!"*, without even asking what the game was, or the amount being wagered.

It was a common practice for many of the regular guys that I played with to 'hustle' other unsuspecting players into a bet. Part of that hustle was being able to correctly assess the abilities of your opponent before they even hit a shot. And most guys nowadays that play golf play the part of the Poser, just trying to look like they are good. They buy the nice clubs, have all the latest gadgets, wear the latest fashions, and waste money on things that will never improve their game. These 'tells' can be easily spotted from the parking lot, and you quickly know who the real 'players' are, and who just wants to look like a player.

This 'spot' was easy – Troy was a loudmouth who tried to intimidate people with his talk and constantly raising the wager amount whenever he was down in hopes to make you uncomfortable. Don was not such an easy one to figure out. He might be able to play, but Don was larger in size and did not appear that athletic, so I figured he was of no major concern. Gary pretty much took himself out of the picture. Gary was a decent player, but knew his abilities were hit and miss at that time.

Troy then asked me what my handicap was. The golf handicap system was designed to make it possible for a player of any skill level to compete with any other player. It levels the playing field so that all players are presumably equal. The one flaw with the handicap system is that one's handicap is based off of scores that the individual enters into the system themselves. Therefore, if a player wanted to 'pad' their handicap, they could enter scores higher than they actually shot which would cause their handicap to go up. And when they show up to a match, such as this, they would be given so many more strokes by the better player based on that inflated handicap and are therefore likely to win due to the false information that they had been inputting.

I answered Troy's question and told him that I was a +2 handicap. He responded by saying - *"OK, I'm a 6 so I'll get 4 strokes from you."* This statement right away confirmed what I had presumed about Troy's ability. He really did not know much about golf or the handicap system.

The handicap system provides you with a number of what your handicap is. This number generally goes from zero (or what would be called a scratch player) up to fifty-four. These numbers cover the scoring abilities of just about 99% of all golfers. What most people do not know is that once you get better than zero, or scratch, you start adding strokes. It's simple positive and negative numbers, just like in math – only reversed. From zero to fifty-four the number is actually a negative, or a subtraction off their gross score for the day. If you get better than scratch, you then have a + (plus) handicap and have to start adding scores to your gross. What Troy didn't realize was that if he actually was a 6 handicap, and I was a plus 2, I would have had to give him 8 strokes instead of four.

What Troy also did not know was that I had just shot the course record at this course a few weeks prior and that I knew this course like the back of my hand.

Nonetheless, we figured out the bet. I asked the guys what tee box they were going to play from, and Troy said the white tees which were one tee box up from the back tees. I looked at him and said that I would be playing the tips (the back tees), at which point I could see a look of concern in his eyes. He responded with the comment - *"What, are you some kinda Pro or something?"* I simply replied to Troy, *"Not anymore."* Troy also did not know that I used to play professionally. I was good enough to play at that level, but not good enough to make a living at that level.

The day went as I had expected as far as the golf, except for the fact that I had underestimated the abilities of Don. Remember – Don had that reserved confidence. That should have been a warning sign. Don did not have the prettiest swing in the game and surely wasn't going out on tour any time soon. But just like my wife, Don knew who he was, he knew what he had, and he could repeat it over and over again. Don ended up being the one who gave me the best run for the money.

The round was very enjoyable with talk and banter going back and forth all day. Each of us exchanged numbers at the end of the round and looked forward to meeting up in the future. I had initially thought that Troy and I would have a better connection and friendship but was wrong in that as well. While Troy, Don and I stayed in touch for many years, and played many more rounds of golf together, we eventually went our separate ways.

The one 'spot' that I had completely missed was Gary. Gary was twenty-five years older than I, therefore, I initially put him in the position of not being able to keep up with me. Gary was the oddball that day. He was the one guy that just didn't fit in to that group, and I never really could figure out why or how he got there. I now know the answers to those questions – and Gary deserves a complete chapter of his own...........

"I will instruct you and teach you in the way you should go; I will counsel you with my loving eye on you." Psalms 32:8

Chapter 10

Mr. G

My first encounter with Mr. G was in 2003, on that golf course in Omaha. I did not know much about Gary Barker at that time, and we didn't exactly commence our relationship expecting to be best friends. As I had stated in the previous chapter, Gary was much older than me and the one that I found myself least comparable to at the time. Gary and I did have a few similarities that paralleled in our lives though, which neither of us realized right away. In hindsight I can now see the incredible power of God once again in the merging of the paths of two dissimilar individuals and bringing them together for His glory and purpose. I can confidently say that, at least to this point in my life, with exception only to my wife, Gary still is, and was, the biggest reason for the changes in my life, and where I am now. This chapter is the story of Gary and I, and how God can and will bring people into your life to help you achieve greater things than you could have ever imagined, when you least expect it, and with the person that you least expected it from.

When Gary and I met on that golf course, there did not seem to be much of a connection. Gary was very friendly and respectful, just as you would want anyone to treat you. However, Gary was reserved, in a knowledgeable way. Gary too, knew who he was and what he believed in. He had core values and beliefs that he would not waver from. Gary was a man of character, and it was clearly evident in that first encounter that Gary's character was different. It was something that I had not seen before, and something that I was unsure how to interact with.

Deception

I had been married now for almost ten years and had three children. My marriage was going well, and I was continually trying to be the best husband and father that I could be, even though I really did not know what that was, or what that should look like. I also knew that God was important, and I was trying to be the best Christian that I could be. But then again, the knowledge and information that I was using to try and achieve this goal was derived from others who had not been adequately informed themselves. Most of the friends that I had in my life were not Christians, but they were comfortable to me as they allowed me to be me. What they really allowed me to be was lazy and unaccountable.

The churches which we had attended, and more so the church that we were members of at that time, had a worldly view of the gospel and of how to teach and govern over its members. The church was very inwardly focused and was more concerned about how the world viewed them, instead of being concerned with how God viewed them. The church, as with my friends, was focused on what was best for themselves, and had very little, if any thought or care for you after you left the building on Sunday.

The church that we were members of at that time, which had started small and then grew quickly, had one Senior Pastor and then one Assistant Pastor. As the church grew, it was decided that positions would be opened up for Deacons to help govern the church. I believe that we had three Deacons at one point in time, who were three men chosen by the Pastor himself. These men were Godly men which was evident in and out of the church. However, the three

Deacons, along with the Assistant Pastor, were all still accountable and under the control of the Senior Pastor. Over time the Assistant Pastor stepped down but continued to attend the church, which should have been our first red flag. Deacons also began to step down and give up their role in the church and were never replaced with other Deacons. All the while the Senior Pastor was hand picking much younger men, who were more like boys, to fill roles and positions of leadership. Younger men that he could control and influence which would aid him in carrying out his agenda.

We had also noticed that several families of the church began to leave for reasons that no one would speak of. Anytime a family would leave, they would be treated as if they had the plague, or shunned in a sense, and no current member of the church was allowed to talk to or associate with them. All ties would be cut off. It became the unwritten rule within the church, and if you were ever found to have associated with these 'shunned' families, you would then be treated as an outcast as well.

Robin and I experienced this firsthand when our eyes were finally opened, and we left the church. Robin suddenly began to be 'unfriended' on Facebook from other church members. At times, when we were out in public and would see someone that we knew who still attended the church, we would be friendly and attempt to say hello, but the other person would turn around and walk away with a glaring sinister look of repulsion. We came to see that church for what it truly was – The Senior Pastor's abuse and confusedness of the calling that had been given to him by God, where he had taken that calling of service to others and turned it into a power grabbing church, run his way, serving him as the ultimate power and authority.

The simple understanding of this is that sin affects all of us, especially pastors and those in leadership positions in the church, and that Satan is at work in all aspects of our lives trying to keep us from knowing the true word of God. Satan can, and will, deceive and attack church leaders to easily mislead an entire group of people, causing separation and eventually leading some to fall away from God.

This was the case with my family. We started attending that church because the pastor was preaching the true word of God, and his sermons were so powerful, true, and to the point. We needed this and truly wanted to be learning the true word of God and how to apply it to our lives. The predicament was that we were not able to see behind the veil until long after we had already been with the church for many years.

By this point we already had our kids involved heavily in the church, now being led by the Senior Pastor's junior soldiers of destruction, and Robin and I had also wholeheartedly committed ourselves to the church and its teachings. You might ask how someone can so easily be persuaded, and if it was that bad it should have been very evident at an early stage. This type of misguidance, and corruption in leadership, has happened in churches all over the world for centuries, and is still happening today. This is the power of Satan, and again the power of his deception. If you knew you were being deceived, or fed information that was harmful, you would quickly turn and run the other way.

Deception happens in very small ways which we accept as being normal and harmless, or insignificant, thus causing us to continue down the path we are going, assuming that everything is fine until we reach a point of giving up, or in this case, being separated from God. I had very little, if any, background knowledge of religion or God, therefore, it was easy to lead me down a delusive road. I knew that the sermons being preached were from the Bible, but what I did not know was that all of the other things going on behind the scenes, as well as how we were being taught to interpret those scriptures were both wrong and sinful. So, I blindly followed along, placing my trust in a pastor who appeared to have good intentions, trying to mold my new life by believing that what I was being taught was the correct way to be a Christian. It is a power play that is commonly played out by Satan and his demons – If Satan can deceive a Pastor, a leader, a Governor, a President, or any person in a leadership role, then that person now becomes one of Satan's tools to deceive and mislead the many that are following that person.

Gary came from a different background than I had. While I do not know Gary's entire history, I do know enough to form an adequate opinion on why he is who he is. Gary was married to a gal named Colleen. Gary and Colleen never had any children. Gary was a former Pastor at a church in another town in Nebraska prior to the time we met. From what I understand, it was a very successful church that was growing quickly. Gary's life was good, filled with the joy and peace of God, as well as many of the luxuries that most folks who are well off enjoy nowadays. For reasons that I do not know and will not assume, that church to some extent fell apart and Gary ended up leaving.

Somewhere around this point, Gary and Colleen split up as well. Again, I do not know the exact reason and will not make any assumptions either. Gary had a background in construction and was very knowledgeable and competent in that field as well. When I met Gary, he was living in that apartment complex which surrounded the golf course where we met and was living by himself.

Gary had recently started doing work as an Independent Insurance Adjuster, on a nationwide level. His job required him to travel all over the country to handle insurance claims from losses that occurred due to large catastrophic events such as hurricanes or wildfires. Gary would get a phone call from his employer and then be deployed to a certain area of the country and would stay in that area and work those claims until that specific event was completed. It was an interesting job to say the least, and one that aroused my curiosity, as Gary would be gone for many months straight, but then would come home and do nothing but play golf until the next call came in.

At this point in my life, I wasn't exactly financially stable. I was closer to financially insolvent. I was still struggling to figure out how life worked, how to be a good husband, and a father to three young kids, all while trying to pay the bills that came along with those obligations.

When times get tough in our lives, when our backs are up against the wall, it is a natural instinct for us to always revert to what we know and believe – our core values. Core values are the fundamental beliefs and principles that we have which guide our behavior and choices. They are deeply ingrained in our sense of self and shape how we view the world, interact with others, and prioritize the issues in our lives. They are, in a sense, our compass which guides us through life.

My core values, or at least my self-taught beliefs, were to do whatever I had to do to survive. Just as long as I was not harming anyone else or breaking any laws. I didn't know any other way of living. My life was about survival and had always been that way since I was young. While I had a job, it wasn't a very good job, or one that would support my family very well. And I never really applied myself or stuck with anything for very long during this time as I could not foresee how it would make things better for myself or my family.

Technology

So, Gary and I met on that particular day, and ended up golfing together a few more times over the next couple months. Nothing that would really create a bond or strong friendship, but enough to keep us in touch with each other. Gary and I both had an addiction to the game of golf. We both wanted to play all the time. This was our initial fondness and connection in each other. And even though he was older, I didn't mind, as Gary seemed like a good guy to be around. He was always polite and respectful, and treated me like a real person, not like the failure that I was seeing myself as. Gary did not know the real me at that point, and I didn't want him too either. I liked our friendship, even though it was only on brief occasions. And maybe in some peculiar way I looked up to Gary as a father figure – one that I still desperately wanted and needed.

A few months later Gary called me up and said that he had just been deployed to the east coast to work a hurricane that had just hit and wanted to know if I could come with him and be his assistant. You see, Gary is what we would call 'old school'. Technology was not Gary's friend. As I think of it, Gary still had a flip-phone, (one of the first ones that they came out with) up until about five years ago, and the only reason that he finally ended up getting rid of it was due to the fact that the carrier had told him they no longer would provide service for it due to the phone being outdated. He eventually ended up buying a new smart phone - and had no clue what to do with it.

While Gary was and still is the smartest guy that I have ever seen around a construction site, he is like a five-year-old when you put him in front of a computer. I take that back – because even five-year-olds know how to navigate their way around a computer nowadays, which Gary did not. And with the dawn of the new century, computers and technology were being implemented into almost every aspect of every business around. Gary now had to learn how to use a computer to write all of his estimates, which meant not only learning the new computer but learning the new programs as well, and the mere thought of this was more than he could bear. Gary told me several years later that he thought he would be long gone from this world by the time the whole computer 'fad' caught on. He was greatly mistaken, and now he needed my help.

I was good with computers and had even just recently built and designed my own website, which was not such a common thing back then. I had also figured out how to program my website so it would be listed in the top spot of searches on Google, as well as several other search engines, for every prominent keyword related to the site. This may sound like no big deal nowadays as there are companies that will do all of this work for you, or you can even buy your way in to the listings and rankings.

Google had just come out in 1998 and was the primary search engine for the internet. People were still trying to figure out the algorithms and what Google bots searched for on your website, and how they prioritized each bit of information. I was able to single-handedly determine what needed to be programmed into the different parts of my web pages, where it needed to be placed, and to what extent, to get my website ranked as number one by Google, and I did it in my own basement, in a short amount of time. I knew my way around computers pretty well.

The New Job

Gary had called me with the offer to go with him and be his assistant. I really did not know much about his job at that time, or what all it entailed, but I knew that I had to support my family, and this would offer good consistent money, even if only for the short term. Gary offered to compensate me by covering my expenses, along with $100 per day, for a six-day work week. That would equate to $600 a week, or roughly $2500 a month. The proposition was very tempting, and while it surely would not drastically change our lives, it would pay our bills and relieve some of the pressures from me, at least for now. I needed to make a quick decision though as Gary had to leave the next morning. Robin and I talked it over and decided that I should go. So, the next morning Gary and I loaded our necessities into his van and made the nineteen-hour trip east to Virginia.

Gary and I spent several months in Virginia while working that storm. Gary managed to obtain a short-term lease on a small two-bedroom apartment, which was now our new home. Gary and I were together twenty-four hours a day, every day. Gary taught me the ins and outs of his job and took the time to teach me the right way, which was the only way Gary knew. Gary was unrelenting in every aspect of what and how he would teach me these things as well, there was no middle ground. There was one way to do everything, and that was the right way. Gary would also insist that I would not learn anything further until I had learned how to do the current task correctly. While I am a quick learner, I am sure this must have been frustrating for Gary at times, having to allot the time to develop my skills, which only meant less time for him to do the work which provided him a paycheck. Gary saw the big picture though and was not concerned with the here and now. Gary understood the benefits that would be realized in having a helper that knew as much as he did and knew that there were no shortcuts.

With all of the time that Gary and I spent together on that storm we got to know each other very well. I became aware that Gary had a religious background, only through casual conversation though. The more time I spent with Gary, the more I could see the principles of this background being applied every day. At no point did Gary ever force his religion or beliefs upon me, and he never made any of our conversations appear to be about religion either. Gary was the first person who was actually teaching me how to live this life, and unbeknownst to me, doing so in a Godly way.

I worked with Gary on several different storms over the next year and a half, and we would spend most of our time with each other, even when we returned back home. I could relate to Gary in a way that was unexplainable. Gary would never lower his standards or beliefs to my level, but would always make it feel, at least to me, that he was right there on the same level with me. I never felt inferior to Gary, and always felt like I could tell him anything without fear of judgment. Gary and I would become more relaxed around each other, just as most do when a relationship goes on. However, no matter the situation or environment, Gary was always quick to point out and address an issue or situation that dared to drag him out of his core beliefs.

In 2004, Gary was deployed to Orlando, Florida. Hurricane Charley had just ripped across the state, and it looked like there was going to be a lot of damage and a lot of claims. Again, we loaded up the van and then headed south to the Sunshine State. By now I was becoming fairly competent with most all aspects of the job that Gary did. We were finally beginning to work well as a team and were becoming more productive.

Gary and I had been in the Orlando area for about three weeks and were just plum worn out from fifteen-hour workdays. The claims that we had been working were large. The hurricane had passed through the Orlando area slowly, and dumped massive amounts of rain on to homes which had already been battered by the wind. The wind damage wasn't that severe in and of itself, but it was enough to tear some shingles off the roofs which then allowed the deluge of rainfall to come pouring in.

Almost every home that we went to revealed the same story – shingles torn off the roof, some other minor exterior damage, and then you would go inside. That is where the job became difficult. All of the insulation that was in the attic spaces became soaked, and very heavy. The drywall ceilings then started to get wet and soggy. It wasn't long before all of the drywall ceilings, as well as the insulation above, came crashing down in almost every single room, in every home, on to all of the furniture and personal belongings. It was it a complete mess.

And then there was the 'M' word. Mold. Nasty Black Mold. Most areas in the city were without power for many days, if not weeks. By the time we made it to many of the houses, the mold was growing halfway up the walls as well. Then, several days later, came the good news – another hurricane was coming in to Florida. We were forced to evacuate the area and head up to Atlanta for a few days. It would be much needed rest.

The Dangling Carrot

Hurricane Frances hit the east coast of Florida near the Ft. Pierce/Vero Beach communities and brought extensive damage to homes and business. Three weeks later Hurricane Jeanne made landfall on the east coast of Florida in nearly the exact same locations. In the time between Frances and Jeanne, Hurricane Ivan made its way up through the Gulf of Mexico and made landfall in the panhandle of Florida. Four hurricanes – back-to-back-to-back-to-back. Florida had not seen this measure of damage since Hurricane Andrew in 1992.

Hurricane Andrew was one of the most powerful storms to hit the US. Andrew made landfall just outside of Miami as a Category 5 hurricane and packed winds up to 165mph[1]. The official wind speed data is said to have been much higher but has been highly debated due to the lack of technology at the time as well as insufficient data due to the cataclysmic destruction that was a result. Andrew completely destroyed over 25,000 homes and inflicted damage upon well over 100,000 others. After the storm had passed, more than 160,000 people were left homeless in Dade County alone. Many lessons were learned in the aftermath of Hurricane Andrew, and many of the building codes that are in force today in Florida, as well as other parts of the country, are a direct result of that storm.

Gary and I returned from Atlanta a few days later after Hurricane Frances had passed, and due to the chaos and complications of doing so, chose not to evacuate for Hurricane Jeanne. While this choice may sound pretty foolish to some, one who has been through a large-scale evacuation, that of a hurricane or similar natural disaster, will know exactly what I mean. It is a task that arises abruptly, requiring expediency and a well thought out plan of intent, with the goal of ensuring safety for yourself and your loved ones. Even those who are fully prepared and have a very logical and sound plan of action find that achieving that goal becomes next to impossible as more than likely a couple hundred thousand other people are attempting the same feat at the exact same time, all utilizing infrastructure and resources that were not designed to handle that volume of traffic or people. You soon find yourself sitting on an interstate highway, at a dead stop, with traffic not moving sometimes for hours – and all of the necessities that may be needed along that journey (food, gas, hotels, etc.) are either completely overwhelmed or have already closed their doors in an attempt to evacuate as well. It becomes a futile effort, at best.

A few days after Hurricane Jean made landfall, Gary and I had stopped into our local office and were speaking with one of Gary's supervisors. I had worked with Gary long enough now that others knew who I was. Gary's supervisor explained that the damage down in the southern part of Florida was extensive, and with all of the storms so far that year, they just didn't have enough adjusters to fill the demand. As the supervisor was saying this his eyes glanced toward me. He then practically begged Gary to let me go out on my own and handle my own claims.

That day was another huge and very impactful day in my life. This could be life changing - in more ways than I could ever have been able to contemplate at the time, and in ways that I wish now I would have been able to understand and foresee. A good, experienced adjuster can fairly easily make over $150,000/yr. That would be three times more money than I had ever made in my life. This was the break that my family had been looking for. Now, if only Gary would agree to the same.

No, Gary did not have control over me or my future, and we certainly did not have a contract between us. I was helping Gary out as a friend, for the benefit of us both. It was a 'gentleman's agreement'. Think back to the earlier chapter and my friend Steve. The night at the 7-11 and the fight with the punk-rockers. Steve was all in without any hesitation. I did not want to fight, and given the option, most likely would have chosen not too. But I had already chosen Steve and committed myself to our friendship. And in the world that I came from, that commitment to Steve meant that he could count on me, no matter what. Gary had given me an opportunity that had paid my bills for the last year plus. And in a way, I had that same commitment to Gary that I did with Steve many years before. I was in this because of Gary, and I wasn't going to go running off to the next big thing that came along just to suit myself, even if it hurt.

Gary and I talked it over as we drove back to our hotel. I could sense that Gary did not want to lose me as his helper, but I could also tell that Gary had something deeper inside giving him direction. Gary knew long ago that I was not his, and his alone. Gary also knew that we had been brought together in some unrecognizable way for a different purpose. And Gary knew that the day would come when he had taught me and prepared me to a point that he would have to release me on for greater things. Gary's self may not have liked it, but deep down in his heart, Gary was jumping with joy. That day was today. As if someone had just lost a loved one, Gary gave me his blessings to move on and become my own adjuster, to become my own man.

No Stopping Me Now

I then became certified and licensed to handle my own claims and quickly moved up in the industry. This was fairly easy for me to do at the time, as unlike most other new adjusters just starting out, I already knew all of the ins and outs of the business, how to handle claims, all of the policy language, and how to take a claim from start to finish, thanks to Gary and his training. I suddenly was being acknowledged and recognized by management as the new guy who gets things done. I soon became the 'go-to' guy and then forged on to become one of the top adjusters in the industry. My income skyrocketed and the $150,000 that I initially thought I would be making; I could now make that in a few months.

I not only easily understood the insurance industry and the claims process, but I was very efficient at it as well.

Every year I would work to simplify the processes of anything that I did, even if it meant saving only a couple of minutes on each claim. I knew that this would allow me more time to handle more claims, which meant more money. I would even deconstruct the process further to understand that if I could save five minutes on each claim process, that would net me another half of an hour each day, which would equate to another three hours per week. That would easily create time for one more claim a week, which would equate to an average of roughly $500 per week, or another $2000 per month, or $24,000 per year. A $24,000 raise just by being more efficient and cutting five minutes on each claim. It was not long before I was making over $300,000 per year, consistently.

Gary and I continued to stay in contact, and many times we would both be out on the same assignment, working the same storm in some other part of the country. We would then have dinners together, play golf on Sundays together, and even share accommodations at times. Gary never stopped being Gary - and never stopped being my mentor or my brother. Gary again knew that our relationship, or this world for that matter, was not about what we did or how much money we made. He knew and understood that there was a bigger picture and that there was a bigger purpose and goal for our lives. He knew what he believed in and never wavered from that belief. Looking back now, I wish I would have had the wisdom that Gary did at that time, but I guess that is why God put Gary into my life.

God puts gifts into our lives all of the time. The question is, are we paying enough attention to recognize those gifts, and what they are truly for. I could have easily dismissed Gary on the golf course that day back in 2003, and on any other day thereafter. But God had greater plans, for both Gary and I, and I would like to think that even if only in some small way, I have made a positive impact on Gary's life as well. Gary is one of those gifts that God sent into my life, and to date he has been the most profound. Gary worked with me, had patience with me, trained me, and helped me develop as a man, just as God asked him to do. And when my time came, Gary supported and encouraged me to move on to bigger things, just as God wanted him to do. But Gary didn't stop there. Gary is still an active and influential part of my life and will be even when we move on to be with The Lord.

Gary and I are still friends today. Friends, however, just isn't enough to describe how I perceive my relationship with Gary. Gary is my mentor, my best friend, my brother, my....... everything! Even those words do not come close to describing the love and respect that I have for Mr. G.

Gary has taught me many valuable lessons over the past twenty plus years. Some about life, some about golf, and some about numerous other things. However, the most valuable and important lesson that Gary has conveyed to me is how to live this life, in the world that we are stuck in. Gary did not teach me how to be religious – Religion is man made and of this world. Gary taught me how to be Godly, and how to live a life that honors our Lord and Savior Jesus Christ. Gary took the time, and still does, to show me the difference and to show me what the role of a true man should look like.

You see – Gary loves God more than anything. And because God loves me more than anything, Gary now loved me more than himself and therefore went out of his way to care for me like no one else ever had, out of that love for God.

I look back now and see that Gary taught me the lessons that he did just as God had taught all of the leaders in the Old Testament – slowly and compassionately. Gary had his eyes fixed on one thing, and one thing only, the entire time - serving and honoring God. He knew what his end goal was, as well as what he was to do along the way. And since he knew what his purpose was, every decision and choice along the way was an easy one for him to make. Everything that Gary did was for God, not for himself. I didn't have any goals or a purpose and therefore was easily distracted by the next greatest thing; to please and satisfy myself, my needs, and my desires.

Gary is now a pastor at a growing church in northern Arkansas. Gary and his wife Colleen are back together and working in everything they do to serve The Lord and serve others. I am sure that Gary and Colleen have touched and affected many others just as they have done with me. My only hope and prayer is that others would recognize the gift that has been placed right in front of them as well – just as I did.

"My command is this: Love each other as I have loved you. Greater love has no one than this: to lay down one's life for one's friends." John 15:12-13

Chapter 11

The Beginning of The End

Life seemed to be falling into place at this point. I now had the promising job that would provide me peace and security, while allowing my family to do things that would have not been possible otherwise. My world was showing signs of stabilization, and with my new income it would certainly be much easier to become the man that I was so wanting to be for my wife and kids. I looked at this new opportunity as a gift, one that I did not want to squander or take for-granted. I saw it as my way out, away from the images and views of myself which I had created in my own head. That little boy struggling to just get by, that teenager with no confidence, that boy who still wanted so badly to be identified as a real man. My new status in life would undeniably elevate the way that others perceived me, as well as the ways in which I viewed myself.

Robin and I had to learn some of life's lessons the hard way as we were commencing our marriage. Neither of us had been prepared or equipped by our parents to successfully make the transition from childhood to that of an adult. There were many aspects of life which we did not comprehend or fully understand, especially when it came to how these matters were relative to our lives and the ways in which they are applied by our society. We racked up some pretty hefty debt starting out simply because we did not fully understand the credit system, and the consequences of abusing it.

We had no clue how the 'credit' system worked, and had no idea that almost everything we would do going forward would then be based off of and judged by some score that in one quick view would be able to tell anyone exactly what type of people we were. We were irresponsible with many aspects of our lives, as well as the choices and decisions that come along with them. At the time I met Gary, Robin and I were still suffering the consequences of those poor choices.

Robin and I are not ignorant people. We are both very intelligent and are capable of learning just about anything if we are taught in a credible manner. Unfortunately, many of our lessons had to be self-taught, while we were suffering the consequences. Such was the case with our finances. But things would change now with my new income. We could pay off the debt that we had racked up and start over. We could now actually save some money and have a safety net. We were also smart enough to realize that there was a whole lot more about this 'money' world that we did not know, so we should probably attempt to learn as much as we could.

One of the first things that we did to better stabilize our financial situation was trying to understand God's view on finances and debt. This showed us a completely different perspective on money, which almost instantly made a huge change in our lives. We began to understand that the money that we do have was never truly ours to begin with. It was God's money, and He was just allowing us to be stewards of it. Our job is to be the best steward that we are able to be with what we have been given. That led us to finding out about a man named Dave Ramsey. If you have not heard of Dave Ramsey by now, you probably have been living under a rock for the last thirty years. Dave is more than likely one of the most knowledgeable people on finances, with a Godly perspective.

At the time we found Dave, his biggest educational tool was a program called 'Financial Peace University'[1]. It is a step-by-step program that teaches you how to become financially independent, no matter what your current budget or debt level may be. Dave's program was incredibly helpful to us, and Robin still uses the 'envelope' system today. I say *'Robin uses'* the system as we have also learned along the way that the finances of our family are best handled by her. I make the money and provide for my family and Robin handles all of the money and pays all of the bills. Basically, she is our accountant. It is not that I am incapable of handling the task, or that I can't be trusted in that area. We have just learned over time that this area is not my strength. I tend to find it rather tedious and painful. I have a propensity to slack off a little bit in that area as it bores me, which only creates problems for us that can be avoided by utilizing the skills and talents of Robin.

Many years ago, before everything became computerized, people would pay for items and services with a check. A piece of paper that you could write out to pay for any item or service, anywhere and at any time. People would have a 'check book', which is just as it sounds – a booklet full of blank paper checks that were linked to their bank account. A person did not have to carry cash all the time, they could just write a check.

This 'check' system created two major problems, however. One, you could write a check for something even if you did not have sufficient funds in your bank account to cover the amount of that check. Two, when writing a check, people like me would often forget to write down the amount of the check in the ledger, and therefore, when you went to balance your check book, the numbers would not balance or align with what you actually had in your checking account. You would essentially think that you had more money in your account than you actually did. This was my biggest flaw, and also how we came to learn that for the success of our family, it was best if Robin handled all of the financial matters.

There is an old saying – *Money won't solve your problems*. Most all people that are financially distraught hold an opposing belief that money actually would make things better; and make all of their problems go away. This regressive way of thinking is also known as the Poverty Mentality, or Scarcity Mindset. I had this same mindset as well, for most all of my life. However, money is not the problem, and money, or a lack of money, does not get us into that difficult position either. Our mentality did, at least in the ways which we view the choices related to money and the use of it!

The choices that we have made are what have put us right where we are. Therefore, we can throw all of the money in the world at our problems if we want too. We may get rid of some of them, at least the ones that we have now. But you are still you, and I am still me. We have done nothing to change who we are, specifically the ways in which we think and the processes which we go through in making those choices. Before you know it, we will be right back in the same position that we are in now, only our problems will be much bigger this time as we now had more money to create even bigger problems with. You have to change YOU first, and the choices that you make, if you want the results or outcome to change.

Dave Ramsey says that after thirty years, his main principle has not changed - *"Have a budget, live on less than you make, and don't owe people money."*[2] Robin and I took this advice seriously when going through his program and realized the power in these principles. Dave also says, *"If you live like no one else, later you can live like no one else."*[3] That simply means that if you scrimp, budget and get things under control now, you can have a much greater life later on.

Dave's course, as well as other books by Dave, greatly increased our knowledge and understanding of the financial world and system, as well as how God views financial matters and debt. I would highly recommend any of Dave Ramsey's books or courses for any one in life, no matter what your financial situation is. You can find all of Dave's information and products at ramseysolutions.com.

Robin and I followed the steps in Financial Peace University exactly as listed. We created a budget that we lived by. We used the debt snowball process. And we did whatever we could to not owe people money. We also took this one step further to honor God by paying back anyone in our past that we owed money too, or that I had at some point taken advantage of financially, with interest. This was painful to some extent at first, but I had to learn to swallow my pride and do the right thing. I have since learned the peace that this one step alone has given me, and how it has released me from the bondage of that sin.

Proverbs 22:7 says - *"the rich rule over the poor, and the borrower is slave to the lender."*

Our financial situation changed greatly over the next few years, and while some may say that it was due to the significant increase in my income, I would strongly disagree. It was due to the change in our mentality on finances and money. Had we not changed that, we would have easily continued to make poor decisions, poor purchases, and been irresponsible with the money that we had, allowing nothing to change at all.

Adversity – The Catalyst for Growth

My new career was skyrocketing, at a pace that even I found hard to believe. The principles that I had adopted at a younger age were finally proving to be worthy and were taking me to the top of my field. *Work harder than anyone else - Be willing to do what others will not do - Do more than others will do - Do what you do better than others would do it - Do whatever you have to do to survive.*

The opportunities kept coming, the money kept increasing. I had fallen into a world that looked for one thing, and one thing only – Production. If you were a producer, and got things done, you were the one on top. You were the one that all others were judged by.

There was a saying in our field back when I started out – *He who closes the claims is King!* That meant that the guy who was the most productive (closed the most claims), got whatever he wanted, and was basically left alone to do his own thing as his production made the bosses look good and that is all that they cared about. The bosses, at each and every level, all reported to other bosses. And the main concern at each and every level was that they stood out to their boss, or that they (or those below them) performed and looked good on those weekly reports. I was the closer. I was the King. I made everyone above me look good, while making those at my level appear inadequate. This was my new position in life, and I relished it. I was finally being recognized, even though in a very small way, for who I was and what I could do. I was appreciated and wanted. Or so I thought.

However sweet it may have been, the recognition and accolades never lasted very long. You were only as good as you were, on that one storm. Once that storm was over and you were released to go home, you might as well have wiped the slate clean. As when the next phone call came around and you were deployed to the next storm, it was like starting all over again as a newbie. Nobody had any status, and everyone was quick to forget what one may have achieved in the past.

This really did not bother me at first as I always knew that I would be the one up at the top again in just a matter of days. But I always had to keep proving myself over and over again, every time working harder and harder to do so with the increased requirements of the job. And then, all of a sudden, as if someone had just flipped a switch – any recognition that I had once received suddenly stopped. I was still the top producer and could do more work than anyone else. I was still the go-to guy whom management always turned to when they had a problem and needed to be bailed out. It was as if no one cared who I was anymore though. Like it did not matter if I was there or not. An oh too familiar feeling of my past coming back to haunt me once again.

In 2006, Robin was pregnant again. Our fourth child. Dylan Matthew was a bit of a surprise during a brief trip home that happened during the busy 2005 season, and a slight break between Hurricane Katrina and Hurricane Wilma which had just hit south Florida. However, we were both excited and could not wait for his arrival. Dylan would be almost eight years younger than his next oldest sibling, which most always causes difficulty in that child's life as they feel separated from their siblings. Dylan would go on to show us a side of life that we did not know before and would actually bring all of his siblings closer together. Dylan was given gifts by God that we had not seen before in other children, which would (and will) impact many others over the years.

Between the years of 2010 and 2020, the workload increased dramatically. As I am sure is the case with most major companies, costs were being cut, and the simplest way to do this was to eliminate jobs. The people in those positions did work that was vital and needed. That work could not just go undone, so it had to be shifted to another person or role that was still around. That new workload most always fell upon us adjusters. The amount of work required for our job increased almost tenfold over the years, with no increase in compensation. The increased workload always came about slowly, bit by bit. In such small increments that while you may not have liked it, in and of itself it was not enough to cause you to look for other employment.

In 2010 I was able to completely handle roughly 8-10 claims per day on any given storm and be finished with that day's work by roughly 6-7pm that evening. By the time 2020 rolled around I was only able to complete four claims a day due to the increased work that had been abounded upon us over the years, but only then if I started my day three hours earlier and everything went smoothly throughout the day. Even then it would take me till roughly 8pm to finish all of the work for just those four claims.

Year after year, storm after storm, the job was beginning to take its toll on me, both mentally and physically. I would find myself increasingly frustrated with the changes that were being made, and the additional work being dumped upon us, and could never rationalize how any of these changes would make one bit of sense in the business world. Many times, over those years, the thought of searching for another job crossed my mind with great consideration. I would always find myself back at the same conclusion though. I made too much money doing what I was doing, and I would be hard pressed to find another job making what I do now. It was the money that kept me there, no matter how hard it got.

There are many deeper issues, and lessons, that can be extracted from the difficulties and the struggles that I experienced over these years. Issues and concerns that have a much more profound effect on one's life than just the money. We all have a weakness, and we all have wounds which have likely led us to that weakness. My weakness was insecurity – both emotionally and financially. I had no security in either of these areas in my younger years which led me to a belief that I had to create it on my own and also led me down the never-ending road in search of that security, even though I had no clue what it was or what it may look like. It led me to having a fear that I will never have this security or safety as well. Satan knows our weaknesses and will use every one of them to get into our lives and begin his dirty work, eventually keeping us from God and from becoming who we were created to be. I realize now that this was exactly what Satan did with me and my life in the promising new career that I had fallen in to.

The quick rise to the top and the massive amount of money that I was now making were the two elements in life that I had always pursued. Elevated status and financial security. I now felt important and secure. And soon after Satan gave me exactly what I had desired the most, he began to pile things on making life more difficult, more stressful, and more busy. The workload then increased more and more to keep me busy – to keep me from my family, from any friends, and from knowing any joy in life at all. But more so to keep me from God – from knowing God, from seeking God, and from hearing or seeing God.

And then when Satan knew he had me locked in right where he wanted me (remember my thought – I would be hard pressed to find another job that would pay me what I was making now), he slowly began to take it all away. No more appreciation. No more respect. I was once again a nobody. The money was the only thing that held me where I was and pushed me to keep going no matter how hard things got.

And when Satan had beat me down and worn me out, he then went after my soul. The accusations and attacks on who I was as a person became never ending. Day after day, hour after hour. Constant bombardment on my mind and thoughts, coupled with the surrounding affirmations from other people and situations that I would at the time only recognize as a sign that I had become a complete and utter failure as a person. I was worthless. I would never amount to anything. It was true. I could never be any good at anything, and nobody liked me or wanted to be around me because I was such a loser. I began to hate life, and to hate everyone and everything in it.

This is usually the point where you stop and look back on your life and ask *How the heck did I get here? Where did I go so terribly wrong?* Again, it is Satan's master plan – Attack your weaknesses by giving you the sinful things that you desire, build you up with false securities and promises, lead you down a road that you are completely unaware you are taking, and then slowly tear it all away piece by piece until you are such a hardened mean person that no amount of reasoning or understanding will help you to realize that life was not meant to be lived this way. You begin to truly believe that life sucks, that you suck, and that your life was just meant to be painful and crappy. You give in and you just accept it.

Throwing in the Towel

Robin and the kids were very supportive and understanding of my job, and me being on the road away from home for months at a time. They would visit me fairly often when I was in another area for an extended period and sometimes would stay for a couple weeks which was a really nice interruption in my chaotic days. During these visits I would still continue to work during the day, and Robin and the kids would go see the sights of that area. This was nice for our kids as they got to see different parts of the country, along with its history, that one would not normally see as they most always were not places that one would usually take a vacation too.

But soon after they would arrive, they were headed back home, leaving me to myself and my stress filled days again with no support or encouragement. I always had a very hard time leaving the kids to go out on a storm. It was difficult for me as a father, especially since I wanted to be the best father that I could be for them. I always justified it with the fact that I was giving them a life where they would now have more choices due to our income, and they would never be left wanting or in need.

I think back to one specific day long ago, before I started this new job, when Robin and I were struggling financially. We had three kids at the time, and I didn't have much for a job. I was finding it hard to provide for my family, and it was taking a toll on all of us, especially Robin. Robin and I sat down at the table and had a talk. She said one thing that day that changed my future and my way of thinking. I will never forget the words that came out of her mouth that day, which crushed me like nothing ever has before. She said, *"I don't even know if I will have money to go to the store and buy food for the kids."*

Providing for my wife and kids was not only my job, but my responsibility as well. And I had just failed - miserably! I swore to myself on that day that from that point forward I would never put my wife into that position again. How terrifying this must have been for her. To put all of her trust and hope in a man, a man who was not coming through for her. That day changed my life and my future, and thereafter I defined my value and worth by my ability to provide financially for my family.

The words that have come out of this woman's mouth at times over the years have had more of an effect on me than anything possibly ever could. Robin was my entire world. I lived to please her and looked for her affirmation in everything that I did. I loved her more than life itself and wanted nothing more than to give her everything and make her life easier. She deserved it, and she was worth it. She was a caring, loving wife, who was more than I could have ever imagined or dreamed of. She was the one I wanted to spend the rest of my life with. She was my best friend, my lover, my so-called soulmate.

I had placed Robin on a pedestal so high that she could do no wrong, and my main goal in life was to gain her approval and love in everything that I did. I must inject that this was in no way by Robin's choosing or doing. This was simply due to the way that I was raised, and the views and beliefs that I had come to accept as being true. I was constantly looking for that love, attention and affirmation that gave me the validation of being a man. Robin had become my idol, my false god, and the one that I worshiped.

No matter where I looked, no matter how hard I worked, no matter who or what I chased after, I would not find the validation that I so desperately sought and needed. I did not know where it came from, or how I would ever get it, or if I would ever get it. All I knew was that I was wearing myself down trying to get it. Continually pushing harder and harder every year, trying more and more to prove myself. Harder at work. Harder in my relationship with my wife. And trying more and more to be perfect in everything that I did, just to maybe get a tiny bit of admiration and recognition.

This process went on for over twenty years. The first half was full of drive and ambition as I saw changes happening in my life, albeit superficial. The second half of those twenty years was the world wearing me down to a point that I just had nothing left to give. I was physically and emotionally drained. I had let the world, and all of the people in it, eat away at my soul bit by bit, and there was now nothing left. I began to see that it did not matter how hard I worked, or how hard I tried, or how perfect I tried to be. Nobody cared. Nobody cared about me and how I felt, nobody cared about me as a person or where I was headed. Nobody liked me and no one wanted to be around me. It did not matter to anyone if I was here or not.

When a man reaches the point in his life where he deeply feels that there is no recognition to be gained in life, from anyone or anything, that man loses any and all hope, dreams, or desire for anything and everything. His soul becomes barren and desolate. He no longer has aspirations of anything and begins to question any existence at all.

About this time, in 2020, work became increasingly difficult. The lack of recognition and admiration had now turned to threats and intimidation to produce work. The workload kept increasing. The job that I once enjoyed, where I was at one time referred to as *'The man-the myth-the legend'*, now just saw me as another liability and offered me no feeling of gratification. The work environment continued on like this for the next couple of years in which I finally started to realize that I did not matter to them either, and they would go on just fine without me. Just as with everyone in my past - They did not care.

All of a sudden life had become a huge struggle. I then began to lose friends, mostly through small and minor differences which just seemed to arise out of nowhere. Robin and I began to struggle in our relationship, which was really the first time in twenty-five years that we had any relational difficulties. The guy who once seemed to have everything figured out and going in the right direction, not so suddenly realized that he didn't have a clue on how to make things work or live this so-called life.

How could this be happening? I was making more money than I ever thought possible. I owned multiple properties, and several different classic cars. My wife and kids pretty much had whatever they wanted. I had arrived! I had made it out of the poverty-stricken neighborhood that the little boy grew up in and now lived in the much more desirable west side of town. I had made something of myself and achieved the goals that were supposed to leave me with a life of peace and happiness.

In the random moments that I did have to reflect back on my memories, I began to realize one thing – that I didn't have any memories! Well, we all have memories. I just didn't have any good memories, any joyful memories. I had run my life in a direction that I believed would give my family and I that peace, happiness and joy.

The truth is that I did not get to enjoy one single minute of it. The never-ending pressures to get to the top, and then stay on top, along with my wounds of insecurity and abandonment always kept me pushing for more and worrying about the future. I never allowed myself to live in or be present in the moment.

I did not know what to do at this point and was ready to give up on life. I was ready to throw in the towel. I was ready to be done with everything. I was done!

When I say I was done, I do not in any way mean to imply that I had suicidal thoughts or wished to end my life. This may sound strange in some sense, but that is quite contrary to the way I was raised, and my skewed beliefs. I believe that the human life is much too valuable to take, and that there are always other ways out of any situation or depression that you may have been or be going through, and that things will always get better. However, due to my past, and the fact that I have always felt that I have 'missed out' on things, one of my greatest fears is missing out on things that others get to enjoy or experience.

That one thought is my primary reasoning for not ever wanting to take my own life. The fear that I would, in a sense, miss out on something in the future. I do not want it to be over. I do not want to not be a part of life. Maybe that is a tiny bit of the optimist in me, that there is more of the 'better' in my future. Or maybe it is just me thinking once again that if I just adapt and change a bit more, everyone will like me and this sad, miserable existence will suddenly be filled with happiness and love.

"Be strong and courageous. Do not be afraid or terrified because of them, for the Lord your God goes with you; He will never leave you nor forsake you." Deuteronomy 31:6

Chapter 12

Yaqats - (yah-kats')

(to awake - original Hebrew)

My life had pretty much come full circle at this point. I had begun as a young boy who was dirt poor, with no morals, values, or religious beliefs, and the only thing I had learned was how to survive. I then grew into my teenage years, focused only upon my self gratification, with no regard or concern for how I was damaging other people. I evolved into a young man who finally began to see that the self-life did not work, and that others did hold value. And then eventually transformed into a so-called adult with the responsibilities and obligations to provide and care for the family that I had created – and to be entrusted to the care and survival of others, and not myself.

I had also adopted some sense of moral virtues and values along the way, and had become religious, so to say. I had advanced in my career to become one of the best in my field with my annual income now exceeding that of 98% of the people in the United States. I now had complete control of my life and everything that happened within it. I could do what I wanted, have what I wanted, and go where I wanted – whenever I wanted. Life was good. I had plodded my way to the top and life was pretty much on cruise control.

When Times Get Tough

Then came the difficulties in 2020. Out of nowhere, everything seemed to become difficult. Extremely difficult. One of the so-called 'qualities' that I had taught myself over the years was perseverance, or determination. In my mind at least, I was mentally stronger and better at anything than everyone else was, as I firmly believed that I could outlast, outwork, or hang in there longer than everyone else. I would always be the one who would come out on top, many times due to the fact that I was the last one standing, or the one who would endure any situation more than everyone else.

I had learned that tough times do come, but if I just got tougher or worked harder, I would always come out on the other side stronger and better, and ahead of everyone else. I also had come to believe that I could make anything work. It was just a matter of how much effort I had to put forth to make it work.

Well, in 2020, everything changed, and not just because of the Covid-19 pandemic. Just as quickly as the Coronavirus spread across our planet, people's lives were changed in ways which they had never conceived before. Many businesses closed for good while others cut staffing levels dramatically and then forced those employees to work from home. The Insurance industry would not find itself exempt from these changes either. However, the need for the position which I held would always be in demand as long as that insurance company was still in business. We handled claims – and an insurance company lives and dies by the way in which it handles or pays out its claims. And since I was now at the top in my field, there would always be work for me, and I would not have to suffer the financial impacts of a worldwide pandemic.

In 2020, everything in life became extremely difficult for other reasons. Nothing seemed to work or be going my way any longer. I would attempt to make these difficulties 'go away' just as I always had, but those efforts soon became pointless. I would fight and hang tough as I always had before, but that was not working either. Before I knew it, everywhere I turned in my life, everything that I did, anything that I touched, became a problem. A problem that was just getting bigger, and much worse as time went on. Nothing in my life was immune to the adversities.

I was a so-called Christian, and we did attend church regularly, so as life became difficult, I figured that I would pray and hoped that would help change things. I then began to occasionally pray and asked God to make things easier and better for me, to just let my life get back to normal, but the prayers were never anything consistent. And in the times that I did pray, it was only to ask God to make my life better, simply for what I wanted and desired.

Life continued on and increasingly became more problematic, and just as before, nothing that I endeavored to do would rectify the situation. Shockingly, for the first time in my life, I could not fix the problems or make them go away. I eventually reached the point one day where I had become so mentally, physically, and emotionally worn out that I uttered two words to my wife that I have never spoken before in my life. Two words that I had never contemplated coming out of my mouth. Two words that were contradictory to everything that I so truly believed.

Robin and I were having an argument. I use the word argument as Robin and I have never had a so-called fight, in my eyes at least. We don't scream and yell at each other. We don't call each other names or say things that we would later regret either. But as two grown adults who live together, we occasionally have disagreements and argue about them. I do not recall what the argument was about on that day, but I can assure you it was more than likely due to my mental and emotional state, and I probably went off for some unjustified reason or another.

I had reached a point in life, as well as in that argument that I said to Robin – *I'm Done!* My meaning was that I give up, I now realize that I cannot win, and I'm tired of fighting. I have nothing left in me to fight with. I said it again – *I'm Done!* And I recall saying it a few more times over the next couple weeks as well. This, however, did not mean that I was done with Robin (think back to a previous chapter – Divorce was not an option).

I'm Done meant that I was throwing in the towel on life. I had fought so hard and so long to make things work, to provide for my family, to have a nice home and nice cars, and to give my kids a good life – and had nothing to show for all of my efforts. Nobody cared. No one valued me. I didn't have any friends left. I didn't have a nice nest egg saved up for my future. My status and image with my career had been reduced to the equivalent of someone who had just been hired off of the street. And I did not feel that my wife was supporting me physically or emotionally as she should have been. I had nothing left.

I had worked so long and hard to get ahead and to reach the point of what I had perceived as being 'successful'. I had literally given everything within me to attain the position in life that we held. And now that I had arrived, the destination that I had thought would be comforting, relaxing, and full of joy and happiness – was anything but. I had no joy in my life. I had no happiness. And any thoughts of getting comfortable and relaxing were quickly driven out by the fact that I had to keep working harder to even maintain the position that I had already given everything I had to achieve.

I had given all of my energies, all of my heart, all of my soul, all of my entire being to reach a standing in life that offered me no comforts or securities and only left me feeling depleted and empty. I hated life and what I had become and was content with the thought of becoming an irritated, hardened, bitter old man.

My life continued on like this for some time after that argument with Robin. Anger, frustration, and hatred filling every minute of every day. I didn't like anyone or anything. I soon began to ponder the reason for my existence and let the thoughts of my failure at life consume me. I could not extrapolate how my life had come to this. I was a pretty smart guy. I had traveled the country to numerous places with my job and had seen all types of people from all walks of life, their different cultures, and how they lived. I knew, or believed anyway, that I was smarter than the average Joe, and I had seen many people who were a lot 'less smart' than I was who were enjoying a successful, happy life. I also knew that I could out work anyone, so that was not the issue. I just could not comprehend how I had arrived at this point of complete failure, when I had worked so hard to be better than everyone else.

Shutting Out the Noise

My morning routine is pretty much the same every day. I am not a morning person, so it usually takes me a bit longer than others to fully wake up. This is most likely due to the fact that I have never slept very well. Every one that knows me knows this. If I am lucky, on a good night, I am able to get about three to four hours of sleep, and I have been this way for as long as I can remember.

After I wake up in the morning (and hit the bathroom), I grab a breakfast bar and a bottle of Mountain Dew and head to my recliner in the Living Room. I flip the TV on and usually watch The Golf Channel for about an hour or so until I become somewhat coherent. The house is most always quiet at this time as I am the only one awake. Then, once I become functional, I go about my day.

The title of this chapter is Yaqats. In Hebrew it's meaning is 'to awake' or 'to awaken'. That word has a special meaning to me now as it is exactly what God chose to do with me one morning during this period of self-ruin to my life. In hindsight, I can now see clearly that God had been intentionally transforming my life, and all of the happenings within it, over the last two years to bring me to this exact point – completely broken with no assurance of anything.

I woke up on this particular morning as usual. Nothing different or note-worthy had happened recently, and I was still wallowing in my pit of despair. Hating life, hating everyone, and even more-so hating myself. I got out of bed around 6am and headed to get my breakfast bar and Mountain Dew, and then to my recliner. It was the middle of December so the sun would not rise until around 7:30am. It was still dark outside and as usual; I was the only one awake in the house.

Just to the right of my recliner is our sectional sofa, with the end closest to me being about five feet away from my chair. I had a small table lamp turned on which cast dim lighting throughout the room. I sat down in my chair, and for some unknown reason, I seemed to interrupt my usual routine for a moment with a significant hesitation. I did not turn the TV on, but instead just sat there staring across the room as if something had just grabbed my attention. I was not sure why at that time, but looking back now, I am confident that it was the Holy Spirit causing me to pause and grabbing my full consideration.

Within moments I could feel a very strong and powerful presence sitting on the end of the couch just out of arms reach, and then heard a soft, soothing voice clearly say - *"Come into My presence"*. I knew right away that this was The Lord. At that exact same moment, I became overwhelmed with emotions running through my entire being that I did not know were even possible to have or experience simultaneously.

I immediately felt an overwhelming guilt from being in His presence with my sin, while at the same time feeling an overpowering joy and happiness that I did not know existed. I felt complete sadness for all of the things that I had done and the ways in which I had chosen to live my life, while at the exact same time feeling loved and wanted in a way that I never had before, like I was the only one that mattered to God. I instantly felt and understood that nothing in this world mattered, as I was made aware of its insignificance, and as I was being shown the reality of our actual existence. I began to cry like a baby out of both sadness and joy, unable to stop, which is very unusual for me as I have cried maybe three times in my entire life. The tears of joy came as I now truly knew that I was loved, wanted and desired, and in a way that I have never comprehended before – and by the only One that mattered. The tears of sadness came with my self disappointment, as I realized how badly I had let me true Father down.

I have come to learn that this lack of crying, or showing any emotion, was a defense that I had taught myself for self-preservation. If I did not get emotionally attached to anyone or anything – I would not get hurt. Now that I think about it, I had also passed this harmful skill on to my children.

Many times, in our lives we make decisions and choices based off of our emotions, and how we are feeling at that time. This can be very harmful as well as we are not using sound judgment and facts to decide our future outcomes. I would always tell my children – Remove the emotion from the equation and you will be much better equipped to address it.

In an effort to train my children to make sound choices and decisions, I had also taught them how to be emotionless, and even heartless to some extent. This is the way that I had taught myself to live, to survive. This detached state also would keep me from experiencing the joy, beauty, happiness, and love in life – which I would not realize until after my morning of Yaqats.

Back to that morning - My whole world stopped, literally, including my way of seeing things and trying to understand things as I normally would. My mind, my spirit, and my heart were overtaken by the love, mercy and understanding of The Lord. I felt the love that the Father was pouring out upon me. I felt the mercy and grace for all of the things that I had done in the past, and that I truly had been forgiven of my sins. I felt and understood that my life did matter to God, and that in God's eyes I was His treasured son whom He would do anything for. I saw the pain and sadness that my life, and my current state had caused Him. Not one of anger, frustration, or disappointment - and that I could have done so much better. But the pain in that He wanted so much more for me and wanted me to have and experience so much more. The pain that He wanted to give me so much more, but I was the one who had been preventing that from happening. The pain and suffering of a parent seeing their child suffer unnecessarily.

And if even for only a brief moment, He gave me a glimpse of life in His world, the world that we were intended to live in. He gave me the perspective and view of another life, another world – that of the one that we are truly from, and that of what reality truly is.

I know at this point some readers will be skeptical about the claims that I have just made. Maybe it was just a voice in your head? Maybe you were just tired and feeling emotional? You were in fact run down and worn out. Maybe you wanted a change so badly that you just created all of these images in your mind, on your own? Maybe you are just not mentally stable?

Valid points – and I as well would have the same skepticism had I not experienced it myself. I will counter each of these concerns as we go forward. And while I may have been tired, run down, and emotionally distraught – I have never had any issues with my mental faculties and have always been very sharp, in-depth with the knowledge that I do possess, and stable in my disposition, outlook, and attitude.

How Do We Know for Sure

Many people often have the question – *How do I know if God is speaking to me?* How do I know if it is God, or just a voice in my head, or an intuition that I have? I will discuss how God speaks to us throughout our daily lives later in this book, but for now, we will touch on the question – How do I know if it was God (talking to me, or His presence)?

If you have ever wondered, or had that same question, the answer is very clear and definitive. You will have no doubt! There will be no question in your mind whether it was God, or not. The power, presence, grace, love, and peace that you will feel in His presence cannot fully be explained in human terms and can only be felt. You will feel and experience things that you did not know were even possible or existed. You will feel multiple things at the same time, many times even having emotions that are conflicting to each other. And the thing that you will feel the most is His love. A love like you have never known, and cannot even come close to imagining in this world that we live in. It is a love that I am unable to thoroughly put into words, a love that is greater than all things that exist.

If you are unsure and have to ask the question, chances are you were not in the presence of The Lord.

I am not claiming that I saw God, or even Jesus Christ. I in fact did not see anything. I felt, and I heard. Those are both inner workings of the mind and the spirit. However, if one were to say that I was 'imagining' that I heard God, and my mind then created a feeling of those warm fuzzy experiences, I would counter that statement with this:

We all know that our brains are like computers. They collect and store information over the entirety of our lives based off of the past experiences and encounters that we go through. The sights, sounds, smells, feelings, emotions, etc. As we encounter new things or experiences in life, our brain quickly searches through its data base trying to find a similar occurrence to help us understand or associate with the new thing that we are encountering. If we do not have any past information in that data base that the mind can relate the new experience to, the mind becomes confused and then attempts to learn whatever it can from that new stimulus.

However, it is also not possible for the brain to create something (an object, an image, or a feeling) that it does not have a basis for. Again, our brains are like computers – you are only able to get out of the computer what has been put into the computer, or what can be calculated through the information put into the computer.

It would not have been possible for me to create those thoughts, feelings, or emotions on my own as my brain, my mind, did not have any comprehension of them, or any variation of their parts, beforehand.

The feelings and the emotions that I experienced on that day were like none that I have ever encountered before and thus could not be just injected into a situation, as I was unaware of what they were or that they actually existed. I also would not have been able to create those feelings or emotions on my own as the human mind does not have the knowledge, comprehension or ability to know or understand the extent of the full power of God.

Furthermore, I firmly believe that the feelings and emotions that I experienced were a direct result of the Holy Spirit within me, allowing me to see, feel, and experience feelings and emotions that are not of our world, but of the Spiritual World, and more so of God. If you have ever been in the presence of God, Jesus, or the Holy Spirit – you will know. There is no mistaking it, and there is no feeling in this world like that of being in His presence.

Back to my awakening. God said to me that day *"Come into My Presence".*

As with most things God directs us on, I had no clue what that meant. I mean, I was in His presence right now, and to say that it felt amazing would be a tremendous understatement, but I also got the feeling that He meant something more. Then, through the Holy Spirit, God showed me the way that I had been living my life, and then how He wanted me too, and intended for me to live it.

God showed me an image of me driving to church, and then just sitting in the parking lot the entire time, never getting out of my truck. God said to me – *"That is what you are doing, you don't get involved! You are not committed. You are not willing to take the first step towards Me. You need to open the doors, come into my presence, and get involved."*

He also showed me that 'getting involved' meant, simply put, relationships. He said that I needed to build relationships with others through the church, that I needed to get involved in serving and helping others both inside and outside of the church, and that church and religion did not stop once I walked out the doors on Sunday.

Most importantly, God showed me that being in His presence meant that I needed to be in a constant relationship with Him. I needed to seek Him. I needed to trust in Him. And I needed to be in constant communication with Him. Just as I would with a best friend.

God woke me up! He showed me and helped me to understand why I was created, and why I was here. God showed me a much bigger picture than I could have ever imagined or drawn up on my own, which was very overwhelming at first. The questions began to flood my mind, some of which He answered that day, some He answered over the next couple weeks, and some I assume He will answer when He feels the time is right. The entire experience that morning seemed to last for an hour but was more likely only a few minutes. The most powerful, eye opening few minutes of my life. My Yaqats – My awakening.

His Presence

If you are ever in the presence of God, your life will never be the same after that moment. This again is difficult to put into words that would accurately convey the fullness of the experience. You see things and feel things that you did not know existed or were even possible. Your heart, your mind, and your soul instantly have not a care in or of this world. You get a glimpse of Gods world, from His perspective, as it was meant to be for us – and all of a sudden, your greatest craving and desire is something that you did not even know existed five minutes ago.

Stop for just a minute and try to think of the one thing in this world that you have desired more than anything. The one thing that you have never been able to attain. The one thing that would give you absolute peace, happiness, and satisfaction. The one thing that seems to be completely out of your reach, but if you could obtain it, it would satisfy all of your desires. It would make your life complete. That perfect spouse, that new job with the lavish pay, that vacation home in the Bahamas, owning your own business, or maybe for some it is just having enough money to get by every month.

Okay, now take that feeling and magnify that by one hundred, one thousand, one million. Hmmm.... You're having a hard time even imaging the expanse of that. But even that would not come close. That feeling that you get from your one thing doesn't even scratch the surface of the feelings and perspective that you get from being in the presence of God. You can't help but be changed. Your inner being, your soul, knows instantly that this is what it has always sought after, and this is what you were made for. Your perspective and view on life and the world changes instantly as you now are able to see people and things from a Godly view. You now truly understand what true love is, and it is nothing like you have ever thought it was or have ever experienced before.

One of the first questions I had for God was - *"Why did You wait so long to wake me up, or call me?? You could have called me twenty-five years ago after I met Robin, and I could have been serving You the entire time."* I think I heard God chuckle before His response. (And yes, God does chuckle. He laughs, He is joyful, and He is playful) God answered that one pretty quick and showed me multiple times over the last twenty-five years when He did try to 'call' me. He wanted me and wanted my attention – I was just too busy and focused on my own life that I chose not to notice Him. I was in that fog.

God showed me the time when He brought Robin into my life, and that I only focused on what was right in front of me. He showed me the time that He brought Gary into my life, and the multiple attempts that Gary made to reveal things to me. He showed me several other occasions as well and then took me back to the time a few years ago when my life became increasingly difficult. God told me that all of that was Him, trying to get my attention, and that is what it had to come to as I was too arrogant and self-centered to recognize Him otherwise. He had to shut out the noise around me, so I could hear Him.

Ohhh the noise, the dreaded noise. In this modern day and age, we like to call it life. The hustle, the job, the distractions, social media, television, the busyness, technology and everything that keeps us chasing after someone or something else. Our modern-day life. And that is exactly what it is – It is the life that Satan has created around us in this world to keep us from hearing and knowing God.

God does not shout. He speaks softly. God does not, and will not, compete with all of the noises and distractions of this world that we let ourselves get caught up in. God doesn't have to compete. He is The Alpha, The Omega, The Almighty!

We as a society have become a 'busy' people. We always have to be doing something, watching something, scrolling through something, and are constantly being distracted by something every single minute of every single day. We as adults have come to have the attention span of a two-year-old. We are unable to sit still in peace and quiet for more than five minutes, and we always have to be occupied by something. And when we do manage to sit still for more than five minutes it is only as we are binge watching the latest reality TV show or scrolling through Facebook or TikTok.

Then we wonder why God is not in our lives. Honestly – Where is there room in your life for God?? We are overworked, overloaded, overstimulated, and just plain burned out. I read somewhere that if we were to put the information into a computer that we put into our brains every day, that computer would be overloaded and basically 'melt down' within about three years. How do we live this way, and more importantly WHY?

Our hearts, our minds, and our souls were not meant for this. They were meant for something greater, much greater. And while much greater – so much simpler. We have longed for it since childhood and have always tried to fill that yearning with a substitute that seems so meaningful and fulfilling at the time but eventually ends up draining our souls and depleting any last bit of hope that we may have had. Our problem is that which our hearts and souls truly desire, and were truly made for, cannot be found in this world – but we endlessly attempt to fill that desire with things that will fade away, and actually deteriorate our lives at a much faster rate.

We fill every moment of our lives with these 'busy' things in search of that one true thing that will satisfy us and make us complete. We never find it, so we keep jumping from one thing to the next, hoping, searching, craving. We never find that one sure thing, but in that search, we have also subconsciously taught ourselves to never be committed to any one thing or process, and to quickly jump to the next sure thing if we do not receive instant gratification.

That one sure thing that we have been in search of our entire lives is the one thing that was stolen from us before we were even born. It is our innocence, our purity, our wholeness. The things that were given to us by God, our creator, and the things that can only be found and restored through Christ. The things that are still available to us today.

When God speaks to us, He does so in a whisper. I then read 1 Kings 19:11-12 which talks about Elijah and his encounter with God. *"The Lord said, "Go out and stand on the mountain in the presence of the Lord, for the Lord is about to pass by." Then a great and powerful wind tore the mountains apart and shattered the rocks before the Lord, but the Lord was not in the wind. After the wind there was an earthquake, but the Lord was not in the earthquake. After the earthquake came a fire, but the Lord was not in the fire. And after the fire came a gentle whisper."*

When God speaks to us, He does so in a whisper. God is not in the noise and distractions that we use to fill our lives every day. God was in the whisper. He whispers because He is so close. He whispers to draw us close.

The things that God showed me on that day opened my eyes to what reality truly is. (Again, just because we believe something to be true, does not make it reality) The feelings and emotions that I experienced were ones that are not possible to be garnered in this world that we live in. And ever since that morning, I have so desperately yearned to be in His presence all of the time as I now realize that is what makes us complete.

I now had the answers and information that made my path seem so clear and evident. I now knew where my life was headed. I now had a clue how to live this life................. so I thought!

"But seek first His Kingdom and His righteousness, and all these things will be given to you as well." Matthew 6:33

Chapter 13

The Lies

"I have told you these things, so that in me you may have peace. In this world you will have trouble. But take heart! I have overcome the world." John 16:33

Over the next couple weeks, I began to make changes to my morning routine. I will now get up (and hit the bathroom), grab my breakfast bar and Mountain Dew, head to my recliner – and then go straight to The Lord in prayer. I follow that up with reading of the Bible and the reading of other books in an effort to increase my knowledge and understanding of God and Jesus Christ, as well as what truth and reality actually are. I wanted to start learning as much as I could about my new best friend. I wanted to get to know Him close and personally, so that I may become the best possible friend that I could be. I truly desired to, first and foremost, seek the Kingdom of God.

Proverbs 1:7 says: *"the fear of the Lord is the beginning of knowledge, but fools despise wisdom and instruction."*

I wanted to increase my knowledge and could now see that my ways of the past were undeniably that of a fool.

I also began to change my routine throughout the day, as well as my priorities, placing God as FIRST in all that I do and think. I took the verse of Matthew

6:33, memorized it, and repeated it to myself over and over again throughout the day until it became deeply inherent in my memory as well as my heart. During this process, I could feel God directing me to put an emphasis on *"Seek First"*, and that He should be first in everything that I do. The first thought in my day, the first thing that I seek and chase after, and even first above my wife and kids.

I remember the day when I came home from work and told Robin that I needed to have a conversation with her. I explained to her that I loved her more than anything in this world and that nothing between us would ever change, but that I did not live for her any longer, and she was no longer the priority in my life. I now lived for God, and He was my first priority. I then told her that I had become aware that I had placed her upon a pedestal, and she had become my idol, which was wrong. Robin cried with excitement and joy as she knew what this meant, that God had finally gotten through to me. Robin was crying for another reason as well, one which I was not aware of at that time but would soon find out.

As I had stated in the last chapter, God exposed me to many other things, and answered many other questions as well, over the next few weeks. One substantial image in particular that He showed me was the life of my wife, Robin, and what faith truly was. God revealed to me that for the last twenty-five years my wife had never stopped praying for me, praying that I would someday become a Godly man.

Robin knew what was important to her from the time that I first met her – God. She knew that God could handle anything. And she knew that when she needed help, all she needed to do was turn to God in prayer. So, for twenty-five years she kept praying....... and praying....... and praying – for ME!

When I look back at my life, I am unable to see how I could ever be worthy of a woman like this. However, I am now able to see the love of both a devoted wife and a grateful, loving God that placed that woman in my life – which I do not know if I will ever be fully capable of comprehending. I had never experienced love like this in my life, and even with Robin and all of her love in my life every day, I was kept blind to that love as I had cemented the lies that Satan had fed me deep into my heart. The lies implying that no one would ever love me. No one desired me. And that no one truly cared for me as a person.

Twenty-five years.... day after day. I still am unable to wrap my mind around that level of faith and belief – although I am trying. I have much to learn from this woman, things that I am sure I am not even aware of yet. Don't ever underestimate the power of a Godly woman who has faith.

The Truths

God then set out to show me the Truths. The Truths are the true word of God, and His promises.

Jeremiah 33:3 says: *"Call to Me and I will answer you, and tell you (and even show you) great and mighty things, (things which have been confined and hidden), which you do not know and understand and cannot distinguish."* AMP version

I was unaware of any of these so-called Truths or Promises, or their true meaning, as I lived in the darkness. The darkness, or the world which we live in and use to occupy all of our time and energies, is Satan's domain. We currently reside in Satan's realm and therefore fall victim to his controls, powers, and the veil that he places over us which keeps us from seeing the light, the truths, and the promises. The veil that keeps us in the darkness, unable to see God, any of His joyous plans for our lives, or the true understanding of what our lives were meant to be.

We then go on to live our everyday lives believing that we are knowledgeable, smart, educated, and are living a good life free from sin and evil, all the while still having no connection with God. We are in the dark, kept there by Satan, and are deceived by Satan in to believing that we are 'good people' because we are not sinners, and we do no wrong.

Satan deceives us with the ways of the world, which are his ways, and then misguides us into believing the lie that we are in fact good people, all while covering us with his veil of darkness that beguiles us to believe that there is nothing further to know – as we already know it all and have it all figured out. We are kept in this darkness, under his veil, and unable to distinguish between good and evil, right or wrong, or that we are being deceived and misled.

All of this is exactly why God said to call out to Him, and He would show us and tell us great and mighty things, things that we did not know and understand, and cannot distinguish. As in our current state of deception, with Satan's veil draped over our eyes, hearts, and minds, we believe that we have a good understanding of all things. The truth is that we only know and understand what Satan wants us to know, which are his lies. That is all we know – and we sadly accept it as being accurate and credible. When we call out to God, and truly seek Him with our hearts, He will show us what truth and reality actually is.

While I may have been briefly introduced to the Bible when growing up, I had never been taught much of the scriptures, or their meanings. This lack of knowledge does not provide me an excuse however, as I knew what the Bible was and who God was, and had the choice to learn more, to seek God, and to call out to Him. I chose other routes and fell victim to the lies and deceptions of Satan. Even in the most simplistic sense of understanding, we are all responsible and accountable for our own actions and the choices which we make, whether they are taken with a spiritual view or a worldly view. This fact of life is undeniable no matter how you may look at it – and whether you choose to accept God or not.

The Darkness

So how does all of this happen, and why? I am aware that our discussion may have reached a point where it has become a bit difficult for some to grasp. I know this because I too was in the exact same spot that you may be in right now, with the same questions, making the same attempts at trying to rationalize this new information so that it might make even the slightest bit of sense with the knowledge and understanding that we do have. As we had discussed earlier with the ways in which our minds obtain information – we are now taking in this new information and attempting to validate any possible truth of that information based off of what we already know, and our past experiences. This validation, or attempt at confirmation, becomes almost impossible through our commonly used methodologies as we are now attempting to rationalize facts about the spiritual realm with the knowledge and understanding that we have of our limited worldly view.

The attempt at making things make sense becomes rather confusing as we are using the ways of the world, which again are the ways of Satan and the ways in which he wants us to think and believe, to put the stamp of approval on something that is completely contrary to the world itself. This confusion is further compounded by the simple fact that we live in the world, and it is essentially all that we have known since our birth. It is what we know, what we have come to base our entire lives off of, and what is right in front of us every day – which only adds to our confirmation bias that what we see, and experience is true reality.

But just as God told us in Jeremiah 33:3: *"Call to Me and I will answer you, and tell you (and even show you) great and mighty things, (things which have been confined and hidden), which you do not know and understand and cannot distinguish."* AMP version

Things which have been confined and hidden, which you do not know and understand and cannot distinguish.

We are unable within our own ability to find, determine, or understand these things of which we may seek to understand or attempt to validate. These things are only revealed to those who call out to God, at which time He will reveal such things to us and begin to show us what truth and reality actually is.

The previous statement only increases the confusion of those in the position of questioning. One is left now to ask *How am I supposed to determine if this whole God thing may have any validity to it or not if the answers to my questions are to remain hidden to me until I fully surrender to a God that I am not even sure exists, is real, or that I may even want to surrender to?*

These are all valid points which are common amongst those who have spent their entire lives in the darkness, and now may be considering the possibility of God, for whatever their reason may be. I too was in this same predicament and was perplexed with the conflicts that arise when one is seeking to better themselves. And as is always the case, Satan is aware that you may be seeking other information than what he has provided you and is always there to bombard your thoughts with more falsities in regard to the truth that you are seeking.

So how does one find the truth, the real meaning of life, the actual understanding of reality, and begin to know and understand who God and Jesus truly are? The answer is simple, yet not one that is always comfortable at first. You take a step! One step. That's it. You take a step of FAITH! Faith that all you can and need to do is open yourself up to God, call out to Him, and then let Him do the rest. If you simply have the faith that God can and will provide all of the answers to your questions, and you are willing to step out into the unknown – God will do the rest!

Resistance

We have free will, right? Can't we just resist or ignore Satan as well, just as we do God? They are both of the spiritual world, right? If we can ignore or deny the one, then we should be able to ignore or deny the other as well. The effortless answer to these questions is once again a foundation that we must come to accept in who we are: *Just because we cannot or will not accept or believe something as being true or real, does not stop that thing from actually being true or real.*

However, for the more detailed answers we must dive into the matter of spiritual warfare.

I can see you cringing now. Touchy subject, I know. Which is also the attitude with most every topic of discussion where we possess a lack of knowledge concerning the subject matter. Hang in there, I will again make it simple and painless. Spiritual warfare is one of the biggest problems affecting our society, and our churches today, which I will explain as well. And it all boils down to our perspective, or how we see things, and what we believe to be true. But keep an open mind though and remember that just because we may not perceive something to be true or real, does not mean that our version of reality is always accurate.

How we see things, or our view on things, is derived from the ways in which we have been shaped into the person that we are today. The ways in which we have been taught or learned things over the course of our life. Over the course of our lives, we then choose what story we believe, and what we believe to be true – whether what we have come to accept and believe as being true is in all reality the truth or not. Each and every one of us holds a view, or perspective, on all matters, which we individually accept and believe as being true and accurate. You can have one matter, one subject, one topic, one object, and so on – but each and every one of us will have a different perspective, or view, of what the reality of that matter actually is.

Here is a simple understanding of that principle.

Let's say you were born in Mongolia and were raised in a family that believed in Buddhism. Your life would be completely different right now, correct? (Unless, of course, you actually were born in Mongolia) You would have come to believe that there are no gods, but there are instead deity's that can help you on your path to enlightenment. You would also have many other inherent beliefs that were taught to you, or learned, through your family or the environment which surrounded you.

That is what the Buddhist believes to be true, and what is their perception of reality, and what they form and shape their entire lives around. Now you may not be a Buddhist, and if you are not, then you will most certainly have a different set of beliefs and perceptions; and you, just as the Buddhist, have formed your life around those beliefs and views from the environment which you were raised in. Two different viewpoints and two different perspectives on what reality truly is.

Reality, and what something truly is, cannot be two different or separate things. Unfortunately, either you or the Buddhist are wrong - or, maybe both of you are wrong. My point is that what we see, and what we believe to be true is not always what it seems to be. Just because we perceive something to be true, does not make it the truth – and does not make it reality.

Now, for a fun little mind teaser – let's expound on that principle and go one large step further. Take a moment and think about your friends, your co-workers, people that you see or meet in passing each day, or better yet, the people at your church. Each and every one of them were raised in a different environment, with different views and different beliefs, even if only at the most basic level. Tens, Hundreds, Thousands, or even Millions of different viewpoints or perspectives on what reality truly is. Can all of them be right on what they perceive to be true? (Remember – reality cannot be two separate things.)

Or - is it just you that is right? As harsh as it may be, each and every one of us like to hold tightly to the belief that what we know, what we believe, what we understand, and the way in which we perceive things – is right!

The Father of Lies

Satan has shrouded our hearts and eyes so that we are unable to see what is true. This too is a fact from the beginning of time in the early chapters of the book of Genesis. Almost ninety percent of what we see and perceive to be happening in our lives every day we do not fully understand, even though we may like to think that we do. The actual truth and reality is that there is a whole lot more going on in our lives and in our world than we care to admit to or can even understand. Try and wrap your mind around that for just a minute......... ninety percent of what goes on in your day-to-day life is not actually what you perceive it to be! On average we are awake for roughly sixteen hours each day. That equates to roughly fourteen and a half hours each day in which we don't have a clue to the actual meaning or purpose of the things that we are experiencing.

This is not a new phenomenon either. Let us take the story from Luke Chapter 24, which happened over two thousand years ago. Jesus had just been crucified and was then buried in the tomb. Three days had passed and on that day two believers and followers of Christ were walking back to their town of Emmaus. They were talking among each other about the happenings of the last few days and were deeply depressed and downcast as they had believed and hoped that Jesus was the Messiah and Redeemer. They did not understand how things could have played out the way that they did. They did not understand how the one whom they believed to be the Messiah could have allowed himself to be murdered, thus ending his life, and all of their hopes.

Then, out of nowhere, Jesus appears on the road to Emmaus and begins walking with the two men. The two men were kept from recognizing Jesus and perceived him to be just another traveler. Jesus asked them *"What are you discussing together as you walk along?"* One of the men looked to Jesus and in a sense said - Are you the only one on the planet who does not have a clue what things have been happening here in these recent days? Jesus then replied - *"What things?"* The man then replied stating – *"The things of Jesus of Nazareth. He was a prophet, powerful in word and deed before God and all the people. He was handed over, sentenced to death, and crucified. We had hoped that He was the one to redeem Israel."* Jesus then tells them - *"How foolish you are, and how slow to believe all that the prophets have spoken. Did not the Messiah have to suffer these things and then enter His glory?"* Jesus then explained to the men all of the things that the prophets had said about Him since the time of Moses. But the men still did not see who Jesus was.

As the two men arrived at their village, Jesus kept walking on as if He was going farther. The two men urged Jesus to stay with them as it was nearly evening, so He did. When they all sat down to eat dinner Jesus took some bread, gave thanks, broke the bread and began to give it to the men. Immediately their eyes were opened, and they recognized Him, and then He disappeared from their sight.

The men then realized that it was truly Jesus, and that their hearts had been burning with desire as He had talked to them during their walk. They also realized that their hearts and eyes had been blinded as they were not able to recognize Jesus, the one whom they were talking about at that moment, even when He was standing right there with them and carrying on a conversation with them.

That story is the perfect example of our lives, and the world that we live in today. We have been so blinded and veiled by Satan that we do not see the things that are right in front of us for what they truly are. Satan does not want us to know the truth and does not want us to see what God actually has planned for our lives, so he keeps us from seeing these things as they truly are.

This is our environment every single day. We are being kept from seeing and understanding what true reality is and are being fed a constant barrage of lies and misinformation all day long which we come to accept as being true and real. Almost every single thing in our lives is a decoy to keep us distracted and away from God as well as keeping us from knowing and reaching our true potential.

Christianity has the one and only True and Living God, which no other religion can claim. With even a basic understanding of God, we come to learn about heaven and the creation of the world. The Bible does a perfect job at explaining to us how all of this came about. The Bible is God's word, His true and living word.

Herein lies the problem however, which is twofold. First, most people have never read the entire Bible, including Christians, and therefore only know bits and pieces. Second, most if not all churches in our society today do not preach or teach ALL of what the Bible has to tell us. While they may teach and preach sermons from the Bible, and do so in the correct understanding of that scripture, they pick and choose the scriptures or topics to be preached on, and it is most always a 'feel good' scripture which is more in line of the redemptive work of Christ, in attempts to make people feel good so that they will keep coming back and that their church will grow. While I wholeheartedly agree with that line of teaching/preaching, there is a lot more in the Bible that we as Christians and believers need to know and become aware of.

You cannot truly and fully understand the God that you serve and worship, or the world that we live in for that matter, while having only half of the picture. These two errors lead us to an incorrect perception of God, and who we see Him to be, as well as the world that we live in and the spiritual world that is frequently mentioned and discussed throughout the Bible – which we will discuss more in-depth in the next chapter.

If one were to read and study the Bible, with intention and focus, they would clearly begin to see that there is a whole lot more going on in and around our world that the modern-day church does not touch upon. This was not the case nearly two thousand years ago when the Apostle Paul was walking around carrying out the mission that Christ had left to him. Paul was spreading the word of salvation, setting up churches, and fighting demons. Yep, mean, nasty, evil demons and spirits.

It was common practice for the churches of that day to cast out the evil spirits from any new convert once being accepted into the church as they knew and understood that the world we live in is a sin fallen world, run by Satan. Hmmm.... I'm getting a little deep here, right? Let's break it down a bit further.

In a simplistic explanation – Before the world was created, there was God, the heavens, the angels, and the spiritual world. Then one day, for some unknown reason which God does not reveal to us, one of the angels decided that he wanted to be equal with God and managed to deceive other angels in to believing that they could be all powerful as well.

Well, God found out (go figure, I mean, He knows everything), and that angel who is now known as Lucifer, along with the other rebellious angels were cast out of heaven and down to earth. Lucifer despised God and wanted to do anything that he could to spoil Gods plans. Then, God created man – Adam and Eve. He placed them on the earth in the Garden of Eden, which was a perfectly peaceful place with no sin or evil. They were to live forever and rule the earth and all that was within it. God had only one rule for Adam and Eve – You are not to eat from the Tree of Knowledge and Power! That one tree in the middle of the garden. They could have the whole world, but not that one tree.

In walks, or slithers, Lucifer. It was actually a serpent, a snake, and most certainly being controlled by Lucifer, or Satan as he and his fallen angels were the only sin in the heavens or on earth.

The serpent could actually talk, and deceived Eve in to believing that she could eat from that one tree and made her question what God had really said and meant. Satan deceived Eve in to believing that if she did eat from that tree, she would know all that God knows (Does that sound familiar with your life).

Although God had already given Adam and Eve everything in the whole world, except for that one tree, they wanted more – just as we do today. Eve fell prey to the deception and the lies of Satan and ate that apple from the tree and then gave some to Adam who was nearby. At this point, the actions of Adam and Eve had allowed an opening for sin to enter mankind and sin entered man and began a never-ending war. Sin was now an inherent part of mankind and would be so for all of eternity. Soon after, God placed punishment upon the man and woman, as well as the serpent. God gave Lucifer, or Satan, reign over all of the earth........ for the time being.

The Earth became populated with mankind, and Satan had his free run at each and every one of them, as allowed by God. God had created man in His own image, to honor, obey and serve God. Satan's main purpose was to keep all of mankind from knowing God, or knowing the word of God, and the battle between good and evil had begun. That battle, or war, has played out every single day since then and continues to play out and affect our lives as well.

Satan's tactics are the same in our lives today, just as they were in the lives of Adam and Eve.

First, Satan filled Eve's mind with lies and questions, just as he does with us every single day. Then he tempted her to question and disobey God, and to eat from the Tree of Knowledge – the tree that would make her knowledgeable about all things, just as God is.

This familiar scene replays itself over and over again in our current day – as we continually seek out knowledge and information which we perceive will ultimately give us power. And with this knowledge and power, we no longer believe there is a need for God. Exactly what Satan wants.

Evil, sin, and Satan existed before mankind did. They were cast down from Heaven as Satan desired to be greater than God and still believes that he can be. This ongoing war between good and evil, God and Satan, has been transpiring since the times prior to the creation of Adam and Eve. You, me, and everyone else on this planet are in the middle of that war, which plays out every day, whether we choose to accept the fact or not. God wants us to choose Him, and an everlasting life filled with riches, Satan does not want us to make that choice. Therefore, Satan will do everything and anything that he can to keep us from God, from knowing about God, and from ever getting close to God, including keeping us in his darkness so that we are incapable of seeing the light, or what is actually true.

Two of Satan's most powerful tactics and frequently used weapons are deception and lies. Just as he did with Eve in the garden, Satan will attempt to deceive us at first and will then fill our head with lies – to keep us from knowing the Truth of God, or what reality truly is.

Deception is a very powerful thing, we do not even realize that we are being deceived, leading us to believe that there is nothing wrong with what we are doing or the choice that we have made. If we did realize the attempt to mislead us, we would surely not be naive enough to succumb to it and therefore would not be deceived. Satan will deceive us in to believing that something is harmless, or that it will not lead to any ill intent, so as to get us to sin, and go against the will of God. He will lie to us and provide us the reasons that we then use to justify those choices as being acceptable. And once we fall victim to that deception, it always leads us to sin. Satan will then inundate us with the lies about how worthless we have become because of our sin, and that God would want nothing to do with us as we are hopeless.

This is where the shame is piled on. Satan has already deceived us, lied to us, and caused us to turn away from God, and toward sin – or the darkness. Now he needs to keep us in that darkness. Shame is the strategy that Satan utilizes to keep us in that damaged, darkened state. He drowns us in that shame to makes us feel as though we were deserving of it, and that there is nothing good in us at all.

Shame comes at us from many different angles and can be self-inflicted or brought on through the acts of others. This shame most always manifests itself in the early years of our childhood as we are beginning to form our decision-making abilities. Satan has to hit us there, at that point, before we can come to know God and form a true belief and understanding of who God is and who God truly created us to be. As we are young, we learn from the environment around us, trying to fit in and adapt, and then are quickly led to that shame by the rejection of others or the fear of being seen as inadequate in just being ourselves. We never believe that our true self is ever enough.

It is a never-ending battle. Day after day, Satan is continually manipulating us and the world around us, trying to get into our heads and our lives, intent on keeping us from God, keeping us from realizing the truth, and keeping us in his darkness.

The Apostle Paul knew firsthand that these battles begin in our mind. That is where Satan initiates his attacks on us. Paul warns us in Romans 12:2 - *"Do not conform to the pattern of this world but be transformed by the renewing of your mind."*

This sin and deception can play out in a multitude of ways, and over the course of many years as well. It can range from the smallest of sins such as telling a lie to your friends, or evils much more devastating such as murder, rape, incest, adultery, and many, many others.

Dr. Ed Murphy states in *The Handbook for Spiritual Warfare* – *"The danger of any deception is directly proportionate to the seriousness of the matter about which one was deceived and how thorough is the deception."*[1]

This deception does not always have to cause a direct sinful action either, which was the case with me, and my childhood. Satan fed me lies as I was young which I then came to accept and believe as being my true identity, and which I then let define my character and actions through the shame.

The lie that I was worthless, and no one wanted me. The lie that I had no future as I had no value. The lie that I would never amount to anything because I had nothing of value to offer. The lie that everyone else was better than I was. The lie that since I had come from a broken family without a father, I would never be whole, and I would never be a man myself. The lie that women were just an object for my self pleasure. And then the continual lies and deception that I might as well keep on doing the bad things that I had done as I was already no-good anyway, and no one would want me now. These were ALL LIES from Satan, striving to keep me going down the road that I was on, and to keep me away from any chance of learning and knowing God and His word........ and the TRUTH.

The Attacks

Satan can, will, and does come into the lives of believers as well (those who are Christians), trying to deceive them just the same, and pull them away from God. As long as we live in this world, we are at risk of Satan's attacks.

Satan does not have the capacity or sovereignties equivalent to God though. He is one being, and is not omnipotent (having unlimited power), omnipresent (present everywhere, at all times), or omniscience (knowing everything), as God is. Satan cannot be in more than one place at a time; however, he does have many demons and evil spirits that help him in his attacks. Satan is limited in his powers to only that of which God will allow. Satan does not know everything that God does, does not know God's plans, and cannot read your mind either. However, Satan is very intelligent and most always will determine how to deceive you by judging your past actions and then determining what you are likely to do in the future.

Another great misconception that many of us have comes about when we finally accept the fact that God does control all things. We then deduce that because God does control all things, He must also then cause and allow people to sin. And He must cause and allow all of the evil and bad happenings in our world.

Nothing could be further from the truth. Sin is completely antithetical to God, who He is, and anything which He has created. God created man without any awareness of sin. It was man, and the abuse of the free will that God gave him, that choose to entertain sin.

God also does not cause people to sin or to be sinful. However, God does allow sinful people, as well as Satan, to do evil to further His will. Likewise, God does allow Satan to act upon mankind, in modern-day times, just as the apostle Paul warned us about almost two thousand years ago. Do not interpret that to mean that God is evil Himself, to any extent. God controls all things, both good and evil. God does not create evil, or sin, and He surely does not direct it to happen. Satan causes it and directs it – God just allows it to happen at times, all for His glory and purpose, which again we are not able to fully comprehend.

Again, we must consider and conceive that there is a much greater story playing out in what we call our lives, and that the things which we see and perceive may not be what the true reality of our world is. Let me say that again...... the things that we see and perceive are not what the true reality of our world is.

The story that we must begin to comprehend, which is the true story that we are a part of, is one of love and war. A constant war between Satan and God that has been ongoing since the time prior to the creation of man. And the never-ending love of our Father, our Creator, who is fighting for us and our souls, every single day, so that we will not spend eternity in bondage to Satan.

But as is the case with any war, there will be casualties, and people will get wounded every day as well. Just because we are Christians, and are therefore under the protective hand of God, does not mean that we are now exempt from being attacked, or being wounded. We specifically are the ones that Satan is coming after, to attack and plunder. Satan knows that he cannot defeat God, therefore, he comes after God's people in an effort to indirectly attack God.

We will be attacked, and almost assuredly every single day. And there will be casualties. Misfortunes will happen in your life, as well as evils that are so dreadful that one cannot make any sense of them. Events that will leave you questioning God, questioning His love, His mercy, His grace, and His power. And that is exactly what Satan wants – for you to question God.

We will spend our entire lives in the middle of this ongoing war. Traumatic misery happens during wars. People get wounded and lives are lost. If you are a

Christian, you can rest assured that we will be on the winning side. However, it is still a war, and you can also be assured that you ~~will have to fight~~ must fight every single day and that many of these battles will not go as you thought they should have.

On an opposing note – some may find the idea of such a war difficult to swallow and may even be saying that life is not so bad. That they don't see or feel this ongoing battle, or any of these evils playing out in their life every day. That everything is just fine, and they love their life just the way that it is. They find the notion of such a war ridiculous, as their life has gone well so far, without any of the struggles or challenges previously mentioned.

You, my friend, are the one who should be the most troubled then. You perceive everything to be just fine, and you do not feel or see these so-called evil attacks every day because you are of no concern to Satan. You are living your life just the way that Satan wants you to. You are not a threat to Satan, his plans, or his purpose. You are of no concern, and therefore do not see these attacks, because Satan knows that you have already been defeated. Satan's lies and deceptions have misled you so deeply into your current state of beliefs that without a miraculous intervention from God himself, you will continue to follow the ways of this world and of Satan, and remain on the side of evil, even though you may not feel evil at all.

Satan is alive, Satan is real, and the fall of many Christians around the world is ongoing proof that spiritual warfare still exists in our current day and age, just as it did two thousand years ago. Most people nowadays, including the modern church, view spiritual warfare in one of three ways: *we know little about it*; *we don't know what to do about it*; or *we chose to ignore it*. All three of these views are extremely harmful not only to our lives here in the world that we live in, but to our lives in Christ as well.

• If we know little about it – we chose to be ignorant to one of the most powerful influences on our lives and our world. Ignorance as a defense mechanism will only result in harm to the one choosing not to become informed or educated on the matter at hand.

• If we don't know what to do about it – we then are aware, but choose not to prepare or equip ourselves to have a fighting chance at surviving the environment which we live in. There are many resources, as well as many good, in-depth books which discuss the topic while making us aware of the gifts and powers that we have in Christ which allow us to combat the issue – mainly the Bible.

• If we choose to ignore it – This again is ignorance, albeit on a much larger scale, as we now have at least some limited knowledge and awareness of the matter but choose to believe that it does not affect us directly, and therefore we just ignore it completely. This was my view for the longest time. I did not know anything about spiritual warfare and simply chose to believe that if I did not acknowledge evil spirits, they would leave me alone. Ha! Nothing could be further from the truth. Ignorance does not provide us protection, or the weapons needed to fight the daily battle. All the while I was being attacked, to keep me in the darkness, and my ignorance kept me from seeing the reality of what was actually happening.

All three of these views keep us from knowing who we truly are in Christ and knowing the powers which God has given us through Christ, who has already defeated Satan through His resurrection. Satan has been defeated, we cannot lose, but the battles still rage on in our lives every day.

What are we fighting for then if Satan has already been defeated? We are fighting for the unredeemed. Those who do not know Christ, and those who have not accepted Jesus Christ as their Lord and Savior. We are fighting for every last soul in this world to come to know Christ. And as we fight that fight, we will be attacked as well, having battles of our own, as Satan fights to keep us from doing God's will, and to keep everyone else in complete darkness.

We are also fighting for The Kingdom of God. For His glory and honor, and as warriors in the army of The Great King Himself. There is no middle ground, my friends. It is purely and simply Good or Evil. God or Satan. Everything else is just background noise. So, who are you fighting for? Which side are you on?

That is the choice that all of us must make, and God has given us the free will to make that choice. As with all choices in life – there are consequences, good and bad. Choose God – and the road may be rocky and difficult while here in this world, but we are promised eternal life, everlasting riches, sonship, and that we will inherit the Kingdom of our Father.

Choose Satan – and while you may have a happy, joyful life on earth, you are promised eternal damnation and separation from God. I find it rather ironic though that if you choose sin and evil, the God which you chose to deny and resist, is still gracious and generous enough to give you what your heart truly desires – albeit an eternity with sin and evil. You have to make a choice.

And by making no choice you are simply falling victim to Satan's schemes and are living in the darkness as well.

David said in 2 Samuel 23:6 - *"But evil men are all to be cast aside like thorns, which are not gathered with the hand."*

The Powers Within Us

So, what are these powers and weapons that we have been given to fight this war? First and foremost – we must have accepted Jesus Christ as our Lord and Savior. Once we do this truly from our heart, our salvation is guaranteed. This cannot be taken away from us – no matter what (see the book of 1 Samuel 28:19 and the story of King Saul). You are now a son or daughter of God and rightfully owned by God Himself.

While Satan can still attack us, torment us, and may even pull us away because we still live in this world, which control of was given to him for a limited time – Satan can no longer possess us or own us. We belong to God. Possession implies ownership. While Satan and his demons cannot actually possess or own believers, they can still attack our lives and even inhabit our souls and control us and the things that we do.

Jesus tells us in the Synoptic Gospels (Matthew, Mark, Luke) that once we have accepted Him, He will send the Holy Spirit to dwell within us until His return. The Holy Spirit is the Spirit of God and our direct link to God. The Holy Spirit is something like our interpreter for God. It is the Spirit of God living within us. God is so much greater than we are, as are His ways and His words. Left to our own abilities we would not be able to comprehend or understand His will or desires. That is where the Holy Spirit comes in. When we pray, the Holy Spirit sends our prays to God and then, in a sense, relays what God is telling us. The Holy Spirit also leads us through life, with a good moral compass, convicting us of things that are against Gods will, in a very simplistic explanation. The Holy Spirit is part of The Deity, or The Divine Godhead – The Father (God), The Son (Jesus), and The Holy Spirit.

Jesus gives us the Holy Spirit, and the Apostle Paul tells us in Ephesians 6:10-12 - *"Finally, be strong in the Lord and in His mighty power. Put on the*

full armor of God, so that you can take your stand against the devil's schemes.
For our struggle is not against flesh and blood, but against the rulers, against the
authorities, against the powers of this dark world and against the spiritual forces
of evil in the heavenly realms."

Paul tells us clearly that our battle is against the evil forces, not against one
another. And Paul also tells us to *Be Strong – in the Lord and in His mighty*
power. These powers are the powers that we have, through Christ, as Christians.
We are called to stand up, fully confident, with a loud and vigorous spirit and
fight for the Kingdom of God with the powers that have been given to us
through Jesus Christ.

The armor of God that Paul mentions consists of the belt of truth, the
breastplate of righteousness, the shoes of the gospel of peace, the shield of faith,
the helmet of salvation, and the sword of the spirit (the word of God). Paul also
adds prayer to the list.

In my opinion, prayer is the most important, and primary tool that we have
in our Christian life and the foundation for the relationship that we have with
God and Christ. The powers that we have in Christ have been given to us, but
they are not to be looked at as some object that we possess. These powers come
through Christ and God alone, who have all power. We can only access these
powers through constant, continual prayer, and the Holy Spirit.

So, we have the Holy Spirit, and we have put on the full armor of God. What
other powers might we have which we may be completely oblivious to? Well,
Jesus also told us several other things before He left. Jesus told us upon His
resurrection that *"all authority in heaven and earth has been given to me"*. We
have come to learn that once we accepted Christ as our Savior, we (our old sinful
self) have died with Christ at the cross, have been resurrected with Christ as well,
and have been born again and made new. Jesus tells us that we are in Him, as
He is in us, and that all authority which has now been given to Him has been
given to us as well, through Him. And since we are already in Christ, who is now

seated at the right hand of The Father, we are already there with Him as well, in a sense. This is where it may begin to get a bit fuzzy for some and takes a bit of further reading to fully understand the positioning that we have in Christ. But we can be confident that through Christ, our salvation, and the powers Christ has given to us, that we have the power and ability to defeat Satan and all of his evil forces in any battle.

So why then does Satan and his evil forces still continue to attack us? As I mentioned earlier, Satan is not like God, he does not know everything. He does not know or at least will not admit that he has been defeated yet, so the battle rages on until the last days when Christ will come again and defeat Satan and evil one final time.

Satan, and death, were defeated through Christ's crucifixion and His resurrection so that we may have a way out of that bondage and death which Satan inflicted upon us, at which time Satan was bound in chains (limited in his powers and abilities) until the return of Christ and Satan's final defeat.

We could go on with the topic of spiritual warfare for many more chapters. The information provided above is rudimentary at best, but should allow for a basic understanding of a realistic overview of the world that we live in. I am by no means an expert on the matter, nor do I claim to have an in-depth knowledge of the subject either. As with everything in my life now, I am just beginning to learn what is true and right. I would highly suggest that you continue to do the same. Find some good books and decide for yourself. Remember, you have free will and can choose whom to follow. I am confident however, that when you do know the Truth, the choice will become very easy. Two great books on spiritual warfare are:

The Bondage Breaker by Neil Anderson[2]
The Handbook for Spiritual Warfare by Dr. Ed Murphy[3]

The Bondage Breaker[2] is an excellent book to start with for dealing with sin, past sins, and understanding how to get out of the bondage that sin and Satan creates. It is very easy to read, follow, and comprehend.

The Handbook for Spiritual Warfare[3] is probably the most in depth, comprehensive book on spiritual warfare available to us today. I ordered this book solely based on a recommendation in another book which I was reading, and did not know much about it at the time. When it arrived, I was a bit intimidated by its size alone. The book is over six hundred pages long – and is in small print. (Keep in mind, I had not read any books until six months ago)

I managed to muster up the courage to dive into it one day and am so glad that I did. *The Handbook for Spiritual Warfare*[3] gives you a complete understanding of sin and spiritual warfare, from not only the authors perspective, but from other leading experts as well, and does not simply 'tell' you the information, it makes you aware of the information and then breaks that information down even further by explaining the reasoning, background, facts and basis for all of the information. It covers sin from the time Lucifer was cast down from heaven, all the way through the book of Revelations. I would say that ninety percent of the book is fairly easy to read. There are a few chapters that dive a little deep on the breakdown of information, and depending on your knowledge of the Bible, they may seem a bit confusing. Even with those tough chapters, the book is a must, and what I feel should be read by any new Christian.

As with any knowledge that we acquire, or anything that we allow in to our minds, we must seek to find the truth, and what is right. And we must do so through our own efforts and endeavors, attempting to validate any and all information that we encounter. The Apostle Paul again gives us more great advice in 1 Thessalonians 5:21 *"Test all things; hold fast what is good."* NKJV

We live in an instant gratification society, which we have unknowingly created on our own, where it has become the norm to just accept everything at 'face value'. The news outlets, social media, magazines, gossip. If we hear something, see something, or become aware of something – we immediately accept it as truth and believe it to our core, without ever checking the validity of that information and whether it may hold any truth to it at all.

One of the benefits of our modern technology is that we now have the ability and the resources to obtain information about almost anything that we want to know, in an instant. With all of the cable channels and outlets, all of the internet sites, cell phones, and so on – anything that we may want to know, and many times things that we did not want to know, are just a few clicks away.

This can be just as harmful as it is helpful. All of these platforms are so readily available to those seeking information, and they are just as easily available to those who provide false or incorrect information, wishing to mislead others or guide them in a direction that benefits the deceivers own personal agenda.

Our predicament is that we perceive knowledge as power. We have come to believe that the more knowledge we can attain, the more powerful we will be. This feeling of power offers us a sense of control over matters in our lives, as well as a false sense of security and safety. And in our continual search for knowledge and power, we blindly listen to, read, or view the latest, greatest advice on anything and everything, and then believe that we are all knowing on the truth of the matter.

In reality, we are simply packed full of useless, inadequate falsehoods – which we then build our lives around.

A great insight given recently at one of our church services by my pastor and bestselling author, Craig Groeschel, which would be very beneficial to jot down on a note card or save to your phone, is the Bottom Line Test.

Bottom Line Test:
• If it does not bring freedom and it does not bring life – it is not Christianity.
• If it does not restore the image of God and rejoice in the heart, it is not Christianity.[4]

We all must do our own homework! We have to take what we are reading or seeing and then run it down further to determine if any truth lies within it. Don't just take everything as being 'the gospel truth'. That saying, 'the gospel truth', came about because The Bible is nothing but truth. The true and living word of God.

So go find some good books, but don't just take every word as being correct just because someone wrote it in a book. Satan is filling our heads every day with lies – in the TV that we watch, in our social media platforms, on the internet, and yes, in books as well. Seek out the truth and then seek to validate that truth as being correct. Does the information that you are reading or seeing align with what the Bible says? If not, then discard it quickly as all false information and lies come from only one source – Satan, the father of lies.

I cannot stress it enough, friends – we are in the midst of a battle every day. A life-or-death battle which will determine our fate. We can either choose to acknowledge that fact, and prepare ourselves for the fight, or we can do nothing and become a casualty and lose everything, for eternity. It all begins in our mind. Our thoughts, our desires, our motives. Every little thing that we let in to our mind has an influence on our life, one way or the other, and determines which side we will be fighting for.

The world which we live in has a set of laws and rules in which it operates, which we may never fully comprehend, which are all controlled by powers much greater than us. There is God, and there is Satan. This is fact. This is true. This is reality. And if we choose to run from or ignore God – Satan will always be right there ready and willing to help us do so. You ARE on one side or the other, even if you choose to deny the fact that either may exist.

"Fight the good fight of the faith. Take hold of the eternal life to which you were called when you made your good confession in the presence of many witnesses." 1 Timothy 6:12

"I have told you these things, so that in me you may have peace. In this world you will have trouble....... But take heart! I have overcome the world." John 16:33

Chapter 14

Perception

The Merriam-Webster dictionary defines *Perception* as: *(an) awareness of the elements of environment through physical sensation, or (a) physical sensation interpreted in the light of experience.*[1]

For this discussion the definition conveyed through Wikipedia seems to be more fitting, and the one that we will use. Wikipedia states that *Perception*: *is the organization, identification, and interpretation of sensory information in order to represent and understand the presented information or environment, and goes on to state that: Perception is not only the passive receipt of these signals, but it is also shaped by the recipient's learning, memory, expectation, and attention. Sensory input is a process that transforms this low-level information to higher-level information. The process that follows connects a person's concepts and expectations (or knowledge), restorative and selective mechanisms (such as attention) that influence perception.... Perception depends on complex functions of the nervous system but subjectively seems mostly effortless because this processing happens outside conscious awareness.*[2]

Social psychology is the study of individual or group behavior and how that behavior is influenced by the presence and behavior of others. As it applies to social psychology, we use our different mental processes in perception to form our impressions of other people, which also includes the different conclusions that we make about others based on those impressions. Perception, or how we view something, will also influence our personality, as well as our behavior, depending upon the extent of the relationship between these aspects of our psychology.

In unsophisticated terms – our brain analyzes and attempts to determine a rationale for everything that we encounter, based off of past data and experiences, and then categorizes and assigns a value and/or belief of how we should understand and view that new data in relation and importance/significance to our lives.

Basically – we place some form of judgment on anything and everything that we do and encounter.

We subconsciously place this 'judgment' upon anything and everything in our lives, from the time we are a young child. And even though this 'judgment' is placed upon everyone and everything within the subconscious level of our minds – each and every one of us are consciously aware that judgment is being placed upon us during any interaction with others.

We are all too familiar with the expression '*you will never get a second chance to make a first impression*'. So much emphasis throughout society has been placed on that 'first impression' as we have all come to learn that the beliefs, as well as the judgment, that others have about us are all formed within that small window of our first encounter. Yes, it is possible to learn more about someone or something as time goes on, and we can also learn more from those subsequent encounters or situations as well. However, any additional information that we may derive at a later time is almost always used only to validate our initial impression, and perception of that encounter, and rarely do we ever change our first impression.

It is also understood that most people make that judgment, or determination of what they perceive, within the first seven seconds, and will
then, almost instantly, make up to eleven decisions (judgments) on how
they perceive that person or thing. New research and studies actually show
that with most people, that 'first impression' or judgment which we make,
comes within the first tenth of a second. Almost instantaneously! Then, we
stick to our guns, and rarely ever change that view or perception, regardless
of what new information may be received.

This is a sad and disappointing fact of the way that we so quickly place
someone or something into a nice, tidy box within our minds, most likely
never to be moved, or reconsidered. And with many things in our adult lives,
we have placed this 'judgment' based on experiences and information which
we acquired many years ago, even dating back to our early childhood years.

We, as grown adults, are making choices and determinations that not
only affect our lives at the moment, but our future lives as well, based on old,
outdated, past information, that we have refused to go back and reassess.
This perceptual form of thinking is childish at best, irresponsible at any
adult level, and to some extent could be considered what psychologists refer
to as a cognitive distortion – an irrational thought pattern which causes
one to perceive reality inaccurately. It keeps us confined and protected in
our own little 'bubble', a world of our own which we have created through
our skewed perceptions, never to experience the countless diversions of
other people or experiences which God had originally planned for our lives,
and that God still desires for us. We therefore intrinsically bring harm to
ourselves.

Furthermore, when we put someone or something into that 'box' based on
our own perceptions, views and beliefs – doing so has little to no effect on the
person or thing that we have placed in that box. The only thing that it does
affect is us, and our potential. The person or object that we have placed in that

particular box is still the same as it always was, unaffected by our limited views and understandings, and our refusal to expand and grow.

More than likely you have heard the saying *'Think outside of the box'*. That saying refers exactly to these perceptions which we have. We perceive something as one way, then place it in that box, and refuse to ever adjust that perception which then limits the full extent of our potential to the outer boundaries of that box, and our own outdated knowledge and understanding. When in reality, something greater, something far better than what we have come to believe, may be lying just outside the boundaries of that box. All we have to do is be willing to open that box and consider the possibility that the information inside may need to be reevaluated or updated.

Ne plus ultra

The words inscribed on The Pillars of Hercules on either side of The Strait of Gibraltar. The Strait of Gibraltar is the gateway that connects the enclosed Mediterranean Sea to the wide-open Atlantic Ocean, on the south side of Spain.

In the 15th century, exploration of the world had not widely begun and sailors from Spain feared the unknown that was on the other side of The Strait. Few sailors had ever attempted to venture out into the great unknown, only to never return again. This led the people, as well as the Spanish Government, to believe that there was nothing else beyond the Pillars of Hercules, at the opening of the Strait.

As a warning to all sailors considering any type of venture outward, the Latin words Ne plus ultra were inscribed on to The Pillars of Hercules at the point where the Strait opened to the Atlantic Ocean. At the time, the meaning of Ne plus ultra was – *Nothing more beyond*, or *No more beyond*. It was to be a warning to all sailors that nothing existed beyond the pillars and cautioned them to go no further. From that moment on, no sailor dared to challenge the warning heeded by the Spanish Government.

Then, in the late 1400's, along came a man by the name of Christopher Columbus. Columbus had sailed many seas before and managed to persuade the Spanish Government to fund several voyages beyond The Strait, allowing Columbus to search for the new world and venture out into the Atlantic. Columbus had a new way of thinking. A way of thinking that was contrary to the beliefs of the Spaniards. However, Columbus knew things that neither Spain nor its sailors knew.

To the amazement of Spain, Columbus was successful in his voyages and later returned with maps, charts, treasures and stories. Shortly after Columbus' voyages, Spain changed the inscriptions on those Pillars to read *Plus Ultra*, and removed the Ne. They also declared Plus Ultra to be the national motto of Spain which now implies *'Further beyond'* and encourages all to take risks and become the ultimate that one can be.

Spain had originally perceived the Atlantic Ocean as 'a place that no man returned from' and insisted that nothing existed beyond the pillars, and did so based upon inaccurate assumptions and information, and a tendency to be dogmatic in their views and beliefs out of fear. They were making assumptions without having the facts to validate those beliefs and held firmly to those incorrect assumptions as being reality.

We utilize this same tendency today, more than five hundred years later, in the 21st century. We perceive something or someone to be a certain way based on false or incorrect information, outdated views or beliefs, and past experiences or encounters – Just as the Spaniards did in the 1400s. We, however, take this dogmatism one step further.

We hold firm to that belief, or perception, as if it were the only truth, regardless of any new information that may be presented to us, and regardless of the source or the credibility of that source. Again, self-destructive, harmful, and sad behavior that only leads to our own shallowness. We use this process with most everything in our lives – and we do this with God as well. And the perception which we hold of God greatly influences not only our day to day lives, but how we view and perceive the world and others as well.

Once again, this perception that we have is often derived from false, incorrect, or inaccurate information that is inferred from the experiences which we have gone through, therefore, we end up possessing an incorrect view, or perception, of God and the world that we live in. This incorrect perception leads us to having beliefs and views that are so contrary to the way that we were meant to live, what reality truly is, and who God truly is and the love that He has for us – not to mention giving us a flawed view and understanding of our world and how things actually operate.

Psych 101

Psychologists believe that by the time we have reached seven years of age, most of our beliefs and habits are formed. They also believe that by that age we have formed one core false belief – one which defines who we become and which we will carry with us for most if not all of our lives. More often than not this core false belief is that we are unlovable. (Recall the previous chapter and the point made that Satan begins his attacks on us when we are young, before we can come to know who God truly is.)

Furthermore, psychologists believe that our major values of life are 'picked up' between the ages of eight and thirteen and are based on where you were and what your surroundings were during that time in your life. In other words – your environment. Again – we are all products of our environment, no matter how much we may deny it or wish that it were not true.

Sociologists refer to this as the Cognitive Bias, which is defined as *a systematic error in our thinking caused by the tendency of the human brain to simplify information processing through a filter of personal experiences and preferences.* There are over 180 different types of Cognitive Bias, and every one of us has at least one. The Biases help us to make decisions very quickly, and to make sense of the world around us.

The most common and well-known type of Cognitive Bias is Confirmation Bias. Confirmation Bias is when we look for and interpret information that would support an assumption of theory that we already have. We look for ways to confirm a belief or view which we already hold. We basically seek out ways to validate a belief or assumption that we already have, whether that assumption be correct or not. And if we look long enough, and hard enough, eventually we will find something that our minds will rationalize as supporting evidence to confirm that our belief is true – even though that belief, in reality, may be completely false. This too is a harmful way of solidifying our foundations and is a backwards process to say the least. We grab hold of a belief or assumption, and then we seek out ways to confirm it as being true.

By now we have hopefully established that we are a product of our environment. We also know that many of our core beliefs and habits become ingrained at a very young age. We also know that our perception, or how we see and view all matters, is shaped by how we learn, what we chose to remember, and what our expectations are. Therefore, as we grow older and supposedly mature - We simply evolve into grown-up juveniles living our lives with a foundation of perceptions and beliefs that we came to accept as a child and refuse to change or correct.

I am sure at this point that some may say – *"That is not me! I am educated. I am sophisticated. I am refined. I have a diverse set of skills. I am very intellectual and well rounded."*

While it may be true that all of these attributes can be noted in the person that you have become, they are just that – attributes. They are 'add-ons' which we often tend to utilize to portray an image that we have determined as being necessary to either 'fit in', or to simply survive.

The biases, tendencies, perceptions, values, and beliefs which we are discussing are who we are at our core level, and not who or what we have become, or portray ourselves to be – although, who and what we have become is always a direct result of these core level beliefs and values.

These perceptions, or beliefs, are applied no differently when it comes to God, and the modern-day church as well. For many different reasons, which we have come to accept as justifiable, we find a way to make a viewpoint reasonable and then tell ourselves that "God just doesn't fit into my life". We may not like a certain thing about a religion, we may not like a certain church, we were treated poorly at a church or by some Christian at one point – and that single action or behavior then becomes our view and perspective of God, and therefore we just write God out of our lives – again, without even an attempt to dig deeper or obtain any further facts or information.

I am hoping and praying that by the end of this book, if not the end of this chapter, that through the power of the Holy Spirit I may be able to change your view and understanding of who God truly is, help you to understand what role the modern day church plays in our relationship with God, as well as dispel many false perceptions and beliefs of both that most of us have come to accept as being true over the course of our lives.

Misconceptions

Listed below are just a few of the most common faults with our perception of God and the church, and are by no means in any order of significance or importance:

The Comfort Bubble

This has to be one of the most commonly assumed positions or beliefs held by those who may attend church and is just as common with the so-called Christian in our society today. I am sure that anyone who has ever stepped foot into a church, including myself, has fallen victim to this at one time or another, in one way or another.

One day we either decide to start going to church, or maybe we have been attending a church for some time. The pastor, or maybe someone else on staff, rubs us the wrong way. He doesn't preach the way we like. He's too young. He's too old. Maybe there is no one standing at the door to greet you when you arrive. Or maybe the people greeting you are just too pushy and all up in your space. The message just is not what you want to hear on Sundays either. It is not convicting enough for you. Or maybe it is too convicting, leaving you with something less than that warm fuzzy feeling you expect to receive from church. Or my personal favorite...... they don't serve doughnuts at that church. Whatever excuse we manage to come up with – we decide that it is not the place for us, and we don't go back. Furthermore, we then speculate that all churches are this way, so we don't bother to look for another church either.

All of us like to have things our own little way. This is also known as our comfort zone. It is the way and order in which we have arranged and organized everything within our lives so that we feel in control of all that is around us. The comfort zone keeps us safe and protects us from getting hurt, like we had been in the past (which is why we created a comfort zone to begin with). We only allow things that we can control to exist within our comfort zones. The feeling of not having control is fearful to us, and most likely the same feeling that we experienced when we were hurt by something in our past – which then led us to create this comfort zone in an attempt at self-preservation.

While comfort zones may make us feel safe and protected, the actual ramifications are quite the opposite, they harm us more than protect us. They create an introverted person living in a false reality who is now afraid to experience anything new. And if we don't ever step out of that comfort zone, we will never be able to experience the joy, love, passion and the beauty of the other people and provisions that God intended for us to experience.

You've heard the old saying - '*you can't teach an old dog new tricks*'. Well, if you are like I was, you are 'the old dog'. You want the church to be your way, you want it to be comfortable, and you are not willing to budge on anything that might make you uncomfortable. You want the church, and its people, to change or conform so that it/they will fit into what you think it/they should be. This mentality of the modern church consumer has been the prime mover of our modern-day church, prompting the church to evolve more and more into a worldly business that is more concerned with filling seats and paying the bills, than saving souls and helping people.

One fundamental belief that we must all comprehend is that the church IS NOT GOD. Don't get me wrong. I am by no means implying that we should do away with the church. There are many good churches out there, with many good pastors, that are firmly grounded in The Lord's word. However, the church has become exactly what we as people have become in this modern day and age – an adaptation to those around us in an attempt to fit in and be found worthy. The church as we know it today was started by man, run by man, and is controlled by man.

The Bible clearly tells us in Romans 3:23 that ALL have sinned and fall short of the glory of God. There is not one person on this earth that is perfect in any sense, which includes pastors and leaders of the church as well. Our great misconception in the 'comfort bubble' is that we base our perception of God on what we see and feel in the man-made, man-run church. It does not matter what church you go to in this country, or any country for that matter, the church is not God and will never be completely representative of who and what God is.

The church is but one of our places to worship God, while fellowshipping with other believers. The church is where we gather with other believers to 1) worship and glorify God; 2) have fellowship and build relationships with other believers; 3) learn to become disciples or followers of Christ; 4) teach others about God's word and the Scriptures; and 5) serve others within our church, and within our community.

While there is much more to the church, what the church does, and its purpose as directed by God, these are the basics that every church should have and should be doing. But again, the church, which is led by, run by, and attended by man (or woman) is just as much at risk of Satan's attacks as anyone else in this world. Satan's main goal is to keep us from knowing and growing close to God, and to thwart God's plans, therefore, the church is a main target for his attacks. This includes pastors, elders, leaders, and their families as well.

If you must be judgmental about a church, which I highly discourage, make it about that church and that church only. Not about God. That is not who or what God is. And that is also not what every other church is. The only person that you are hurting by walking away is yourself.

Jesus tells us in Matthew 7:1 *"Do not judge, or you too will be judged"* and goes on to say in verse 3 *"Why do you look at the spec of sawdust in your brother's eye and pay no attention to the plank in your own eye?"*

The Father Figure

Another common misconception that we have is one which we have formed ourselves, in our view or understanding of God and who He truly is. It is one where our perspective and expectations of God have been formed based upon our relationship with our worldly, or biological father. This goes back to our discussion on how we perceive things, how our beliefs are formed, and being a product of the environment from which we come. Our cognitive bias comes in to play here as well.

As we go through life and learn new things or meet new people, we again place judgment on and categorize these things or people into certain 'boxes' in our mind, which is then stored along with other data and information about that person or the experience as we have perceived it. This 'other data' includes sights, sounds, smells, and other extrapolations that we derive from that moment, as well as the related emotions or feelings that we may be experiencing at that time. When we encounter people or situations that we are unfamiliar with, our mind quickly scans through our database of prior experiences and attempts to find something similar to which it can relate the current scenario too. This is called associative learning – the way in which we learn something new, which the mind always seeks to do in the quickest way possible, is done by associating it with something that we are already familiar with.

Our propensity is to apply this method of learning to God as well. However, we are unable to see God, we are unable touch God, and we surely cannot smell God. These three senses (sight, touch, smell) are bodily functions which we utilize in learning as well, to gather that 'other data', which then aids our mind in making that perception, or judgment. We are therefore unable to apply these bodily senses to the learning and understanding of God, which causes our mind to lean more heavily on the association of things that we do know from our past experiences. And almost always, the mind most closely associates God, our Heavenly Father, with that of our worldly or biological father.

We are also told that we must simply have faith that He exists, that He is real, and that everything in the Bible is His true word. All while living in a world with a 'I have to see it to believe it' mentality. So, for many of us that do become Christians, and even more who do not, we place a worldly view on God, one that aligns Him with the views and perceptions which we hold of our biological father.

Our tendency is to base our perception of God, including His power, love, grace, abilities, sovereignty, and much more on the ways in which we view each of these aspects within our worldly fathers. Again – associative learning – but wrong. In our effort to learn about and understand the true character of God and all that encompasses that character - we are attempting to understand an all-powerful and mighty creator, who is full of more love than we will ever be able to comprehend - and we are doing so by comparing God with the likes and abilities of a common man.

If our worldly father was firm and harsh, that is more than likely the how we will perceive God as well. If our worldly father abused or neglected us, we see God as one who is never there for us either, and has abandoned us. Or maybe your father was kind and loving, and what you perceive to be the perfect father. Even then we incorrectly assume that God is only love and peace and that He cannot have an aggressive side. It does not matter what type of relationship we had with our biological fathers, or what view or perception we may have of our earthly fathers – all of these associations are inadequate, and once again we are seeking to make God fit into something which we can understand and are able to relate too. We instinctively 'dumb down' God to a level that we can understand and feel comfortable with.

God does not and never will FIT into any perception that we may have of Him, and we should stop trying to make Him. We should instead be trying to make ourselves fit into God's world, God's views, and God's perception. While we should continually strive to learn more about God, and Jesus Christ, as well as strengthen our relationship with them, we must be content with the fact that there are many things which may never be revealed to us, thus limiting our understanding of God, as long as we live in this world. And this limited understanding, or lack of knowledge, is perfectly pleasing to God. In fact, it is the way in which He planned it to be. If we actually did know all things, and we actually did understand everything about God – we then would want to take the lead and have control over our lives.

God knows all things for a reason – because He is our Creator and our Guide. We do not know all things for a reason – because it is ours to seek out the one who does, our Creator and our Guide.

Good God – Bad God

The next common misconception that we often see is one of conflicting views, with a resolute belief of one side or the other. People will either have a steadfast belief that God is either fully loving (good), or fully malicious and does not care (bad).

The 'Loving God' view sees God as all loving, all caring, and unable to cause harm to anyone or anything. They see God as soft and gentle, and see a God that would never hurt, or allow harm to anyone or anything. This view sees God as peace, love, hope, promises, salvation, healing, comforting, and providing for our every need and desire.

The 'Bad God', or malicious God view sees God as one who does not care about the world, or any of us in it, and for the most part He just sits back, and watches things play out. They may also see God as being pretty much non-existent. At times they may also hold a view that while God may have been involved and very active in the lives of those in the Old Testament, He has not been around for a couple thousand years and just really doesn't care anymore.

These people, along with others who believe that God still does exist, see God as a dictator, a tyrant, an authoritarian. They see Him as an unfair ruler watching our every move and just waiting to dole out the punishment, which is the only end result. They see God as having no thought or concern for what we may desire, or how our lies may turn out.

So, which view is correct? Neither. They are both wrong, or both right, to some extent at least, which Scripture clearly shows if one would take the time to learn God's word with focus and attention. Here are just a few scriptures which contradict, or affirm, both of these views.

The Loving God view:

We don't have to look very deep into the Bible to find out how angry, jealous, and aggressive God can be. We could start in the first book of the Bible, which is Genesis, chapters 3-9.

In Chapter 3: verse 16, God tells the woman (Eve) *"I will make your pains in childbearing very severe; with painful labor you will give birth to children."* God punished Eve, and every woman after her, with pain during their birthing.

In verses 17-19, God tells Adam that because he listened to his wife and ate from the tree that God had commanded them not to eat from - *"Cursed is the ground because of you; through painful toil you will eat food from it all the days of your life. It will produce thorns and thistles for you, and you will eat the plants of the field. By the sweat of your brow you will eat your food until you return to the ground......"*

God punished both Adam and Eve (as well as mankind), along with Satan, for disobeying His commands, and then kicked them out of the Garden of Eden to go work the ground from which Adam had been created. The Garden of Eden had provided everything for man until that deceitful moment.

Chapter 4 – Adam and Eve had two boys at first – Cain and Abel. Cain would eventually kill his brother Abel out of jealousy. God punished Cain and told him – 12 *"When you work the ground, it will no longer yield its crop for you. You will be a restless wanderer on the earth."* The verses leading up to Cain's punishment show that Cain's heart was hardened against God, and that God had directly given Cain several chances to repent and be forgiven, Cain chose to live in sin and therefore was punished by God. These verses show both a merciful and loving God who gave Cain many opportunities to repent of his sins, but then chose to punish Cain after his heart became full of evil.

Our lives are exactly the same as Cain's life was. We continually sin over and over again, and God is always right there giving us many chances to repent from those sinful ways and to receive His full blessings and mercy, and He is always hoping that with the free will that He gave us we will make the right choice.

Genesis 6 verse 6-7 - *"the LORD regretted that he had made human beings on the earth, and his heart was deeply troubled. So, the LORD said, "I will wipe from the face of the earth the human race that I have created – and with them the animals, the birds and the creatures that move along the ground- for I regret that I have made them "".* Then in verse 13 God said to Noah *"I am going to put an end to all people, for the earth is filled with violence because of them. I am surely going to destroy both them and the earth."*

I think we all know the rest of the story – The Great Flood. God flooded the entire earth to kill all mankind, and every living creature that inhabited it. Yes, our Great and Mighty loving God killed everyone and everything. Well, except for Noah and his family. But why did God spare them? Because Noah was the only man on earth who had kept his family obedient to God.

I am mindful that there are some of you reading now who are saying - "well ya, but that was in the Old Testament. God has changed, or things have changed."

The Bible also tells us that God does not change.

Malachi 3:6 says, *"I am the Lord, and I do not change."* NLT

And in the New Testament Hebrews 13:8 says, *"Jesus Christ is the same yesterday, today, and forever."* NLT

And if we recall, Jesus and God are one in the same. The triune God. Jesus was there with God before all creation and has never changed since that time.

God is forever the same, forever faithful, and forever consistent. We know we can always count on Him to be there and always keep His word and His promises. But, for those that are not so easy to convince, here are some verses from the New Testament:

Romans 1:18 - *"The wrath of God is being revealed from heaven against all the godlessness and wickedness of people, who suppress the truth by their wickedness"*

1 Thessalonians 1:10 – *"and to wait for his Son from heaven, whom he raised from the dead – Jesus, who rescues us from the coming wrath."*

And you could close it all off by reading the last book in the Bible, Revelation, which cites hatred, anger, wrath, and the hour of trial that is going to come upon the whole world.

Again, those who feel that God is only a peaceful, loving God have not read the entire Bible and are only picking and choosing select verses in an attempt to validate a belief which they already hold. Once again – our confirmation bias, we look for ways to validate a belief or assumption that we already have.

God is surely a loving, kind, patient, peaceful God. But He is also, at the same time, a jealous, angry, vengeful God who hates evil, sin, and those who disobey his will and commands.

The Bad God view:

This is the view where one thinks that God just doesn't care anymore. That He has given up on mankind, hence the reason that no one hears from Him anymore, or that we don't have miraculous signs like there were in the Old Testament. Or they just don't believe that God is all that powerful, and that He is really nothing to be feared. They will then attempt to justify this view by saying - *"If God cared, why does He let so many bad things happen to good people?"*

Signs and miracles did happen more frequently in the Old Testament than they did in the New Testament, or even now. There are a quite a few reasons for this. The biggest reason is that in the Old Testament, people did not have direct access to God as we do now through Jesus Christ and the Holy Spirit. God had to, in a sense, talk to people directly, and did so many times through signs and miracles.

I believe that signs and miracles still happen today, maybe just not in the way that some people are looking for. Jesus tells us directly in John Chapter 8. Starting in verse 43 Jesus says - *"Why is my language not clear to you? Because you are unable to hear what I say. You belong to your father, the devil, and you want to carry out your fathers' desires."* Jesus then goes on in verse 47 to say - *"Whoever belongs to God hears what God says. The reason you do not hear is that you do not belong to God."*

I do know that when we become a Christian, and grow closer to God, He begins to reveal much more, and much greater things to us. Things which may have been present in our life all along, but we had never noticed. We also start to see the things that God wants to show us, such as signs and miracles. They happen every day – for those that can see.

Others say that God has given up on us, or that He just no longer cares about mankind. The truth of the matter is just the opposite. Mankind has given up on God, and has chosen to walk away from Him, believing that they can figure everything out on their own. The feeling that God is abandoning us only comes as we get further and further away from God. It is the 'self-life'.

We have become so absorbed in ourselves that we rarely ever stop to think, even for a brief moment, that maybe WE are the ones who are at fault, but instead always point the finger at someone else. We not only do this with everyone in our worldly lives, but we do this with God as well. The further away that we find ourselves from God, the harder it becomes to see anything good, and the more Satan covers us with that veil of darkness. Satan then continues to fill our head with the lies that we can handle everything on our own, that we can be smarter than God, and that we do not need God (remember how that worked out in the Garden? - Not so good!).

The fullness of God's love for us is something that we truly cannot even come close to imagining. The simple truth is that our hearts and our minds just don't have the ability to do so. But yet we still try to compare His love to a love that we know or understand. There are two problems with this comparison – One, again, we are humans and are imperfect in every way. No being in this world could ever show you what perfect love is, or what it feels like. Two, again, we are trying to bring God down to our level so that He will make sense to us.

We also fill our lives with so much other junk as well. We have become so consumed with chasing the latest thing, and keeping up with the Jones', that there is no room in our hearts or souls for God. We make ourselves so busy with everything else that we are completely unable to recognize any of that love which God does put into our lives.

God has shown His love and desire for us so many times that it is mind boggling. His continual pursuit and desire for our lives, and our souls, clearly shows how much He loves us. I know that I do not have that kind of patience, let alone love. I would have given up a long time ago, as I am sure most all of us would have as well (not that we can or should be comparing ourselves to God).

But God did not. He wants us so badly that He will never walk away. He wants us so badly that He sent His only Son down from a perfect heaven, to live in our sinful, crappy world, and then be mocked, abused, ridiculed, and beaten till the skin on His body was coming off, only then to have nails driven through His hands and feet as He was hung on a wooden cross with the sun scorching down on his exposed wounds. And while He was grasping for any breathe of air that He could get, He was further mocked and then impaled in His lungs by a spear. God loved us so much that He sent His only Son to go through pure hell just so that Satan could not have us, that we could be with Him.

I have three boys of my own and would like to think that I am a good, loving, protective father. I would do anything to protect my boys, and my girl, from anything that endangered them. I have asked myself many times if I could do that same thing with one of my sons. Maybe I am weak. Maybe I just don't have a close enough relationship with God. Maybe it is just because I am human. Whatever the reasoning may be – There is no way that I could ever sacrifice any one of my children, for anything or anyone! That is a love that I will never be able to fully grasp. A love that we as humans cannot fully comprehend.

So, loving God or mean God – either way you were right. God is both and always has been. I must also touch on the one other comment, but only briefly as that explanation could go on for chapters.

Why does God let bad things happen to good people? The simple answer is – Because He is God! He gets to do whatever He wants and pleases.

As God tells us in the Bible, we do not know His plans. Many times, something bad happens to someone we love or care about, whom we think is a good person, and we immediately question God for the pain and suffering. God is not always the cause of the pain and suffering. You must remember that we live in a world with the prince of darkness, Satan, who is always trying to cause us pain and suffering. I know, I know. The next questions that pop into your head are – *"Well, if God is in control of everything, why didn't He stop Satan or stop the bad thing from happening. Why does God allow evil to happen to good people?"* Again, I will not pretend to know what God's plans are, nor should anyone.

We do know this though – God promises us protection if we are within Him. Psalms 121:7-8 says, *"The Lord will keep you from all harm – He will watch over your life; the Lord will watch over your coming and going both now and forever more."* Unfortunately, just being a 'GOOD' person is not what God asks of us. Being good does not put us under His protection either. And since Satan is out there just waiting to attack, just being good is actually what Satan wants.

And lastly, there is the comment - *"But Aunt Phoebe was a devout Christian and knew God closely. So why did God let her die of cancer?"* The simple answer to this would be that we live in a sin fallen world which is filled with all kinds of evil and diseases, that will affect us all, because we live in this world. They affect our bodies anyway. If Aunt Phoebe was close to God, they will not affect her spirit, her soul. And now Aunt Phoebe is living a life with Jesus and God which is better than we could ever imagine. She is the lucky one. We don't always know why certain things happen, especially when they happen to Godly people. We do know that God is the Creator, and all things, good or bad, work for His glory.

Perspective

The modern-day church's illustration of God, and heaven as well, has misled us and the world in to seeing, or perceiving, both God and heaven as a soft, gentle, kind, innocuous person and place. The redacted portions of the true image of God and heaven, as are clearly seen in the Bible, also show battles, wars, wrath, anger, envy, jealousy, and a stern, fierce God who is uncompromising in His fight for our souls and our love. As we have been led to accept this modern image of both God and heaven, we are simply unmoved and unmotivated as our perception of who God really is has been lessened, all in an effort to grow the modern-day church and fill seats. We perceive God as something less than He actually is, and therefore, perceive a dumbed down, over simplified, cheaper version of both God and Jesus.

As all of us do in life, we want to have the nicer, better, higher quality option of whatever it is that fills our lives. We want the nicer car with the fancier upgrades, not just the base model. We want the 80-inch big screen TV with the highest resolution and refresh rate. And almost every one of us can't wait to get the new cell phone with the enhanced features that no one else has. We all want the best, the biggest, the brightest, the loudest, and the most expensive.

We apply this same view to God and Jesus as well. After we have let the world downgrade the qualities and personality of both God and Christ for us, they no longer seem appealing to us, and we no longer desire Him as we now want something bigger and better.

It is a proven fact that if you are repeatedly exposed to misinformation, you are likely to believe and accept that misinformation as being true. This is called the Illusory Truth Effect, and it is playing out in our lives more so in our technologically advanced world than it ever has before. We are bombarded by falsehoods over and over again, so we come to accept them as true and correct. And since our perception, understanding, and image of God has been lessened, so has our faith, and our desire to pursue Him for who and what He truly is. We perceive God as something far less than He actually is and see Him as much less authoritative and omnipotent than He actually is.

It is our view and our perception which has been flawed, not God. It is our tendency to attempt to make everything understandable in our minds so that we can rationalize our life and our way of living and justify bringing God down to our level. To us, and our minds, it is much easier to bring God down to a level that we can understand and relate too, than it is to attempt to appreciate and perceive God for who and what He truly is. We will never fully and truly understand or know who and what God truly is while on this earth.......... and that is okay!

Our perspective (perception) is nothing more, and never greater, than the cumulation of our past experiences.

So maybe we have been perceiving God the wrong way. Maybe we just did not know how we actually perceived things in general, or about the many outside forces that influence our perceptions. Maybe it is our perception of ourselves (and the world that we live in for that matter) that is flawed – I know mine was. We all have cognitive biases that cause us to see things that are not reflective of what the reality of a given situation truly is. While we cannot control what happens to us, we can control how we perceive those happenings.

Whatever your perception was, or is, it can change, if you will allow it too. It is time to erase the lies and misinformation that we have been fed, and have allowed ourselves to believe, and start learning who our true loving Father is, and what He is like.

The truth is that our Father is The King of all kings. He is all powerful and loves us more than we could ever imagine. He wants us to come home to Him so that He can show us that love. His grace and mercy will wash away anything in our past just so He can be close to us. He wants you; He loves you, and He is willing to fight for you....... till the end of all times.

"For from Him, and through Him, and for Him are all things. To Him be the glory forever! Amen" Romans 11:36

Chapter 15

The Christian Life

We hear people say it all the time – *I am a Christian!* They claim to be a Christian while living a life that approximates very little of the true meaning of the word itself, if any at all. The Christian label has become so cliche in our vocabulary, more notably in the modern Western culture, that most people are clueless to its actual meaning.

So, what exactly is a Christian? What does it mean to be a true Christian? And more importantly – Why do so many self-proclaimed Christians actually discredit the true meaning of the word, all the while turning others away from any possible appeal of wanting or learning to know more about Christ?

By definition, Christianity is a religion that is based upon the life and teachings of Jesus Christ. Therefore, a Christian is one who is a follower of Christianity, or a believer and follower of Jesus Christ.

Believer, by definition in the Merriam-Webster dictionary, is *one who has a firm conviction as to the goodness, efficacy, or ability of something.*[1]

So, by uniting these two definitions, if we say we are a Christian, we should be followers of Jesus Christ and firmly believe in His words and teachings.

The Bible

Christianity, or any religion for that matter, is a very complex subject and can present many challenges and difficulties when attempting to break down and accurately comprehend all of its subject matter. The primary hurdle within this challenge being that the perception and interpretation of God's word, by man himself, leads to many different theories or interpretations of God's word, which are often times opposing and conflicting views of that interpretation, and contrary to the original meaning and intention of that word.

One may wonder how a word, or combination of words, can be misinterpreted or perceived to mean something other than its original intention. Again, we go back to our last chapter and our discussion on how our perceptions are formed. Each and every one of us will encounter different experiences over the course of our lives. And even if two or more people were to go through the same experience, each will almost assuredly grasp a different perspective of that experience. Each one of those experiences has had some effect, even if minor, in the shaping and molding of our views, beliefs, and understandings of what we see and encounter going forward.

I was shocked to discover that there are roughly 45,000 different types of Christianity across our world today. There are roughly two hundred different types in the United States alone. All claiming to be Christians, and followers of Christ. That lead me to the question – *Why are there so many different denominations, or variations, of Christianity if they are all supposedly followers of Christ?* After all, Jesus did not teach us in 45,000 different ways.

While I do not have the background or knowledge to attempt to dissect each of the different denominations and their convictions or differences, I do possess the knowledge and experience to tell you this - The simple answer, once again, is man!

God gave us His perfect and always true Word in the Bible. Over the years, the Bible has been translated into many other languages in an effort to spread the Word and the Gospel of Christ. There are currently over 3100 different versions of the Bible, which have been translated into more than two thousand different languages. As these translations occur, the original words of the Bible are interpreted from one language to another. As with many of the original Hebrew, Aramaic and Greek words, the words used have multiple meanings, which are all dependent upon the structure of the sentence which they are being used in, and the context of the time, place, and people that those words were being used for. As man attempts to translate these words, he does so by using the knowledge and information which he has acquired, based on his own past experiences – or the depth of his own knowledge.

To a great extent, man is biased and will always lean toward the under-standing or perception of life which he holds, through his own eyes, based upon his past experiences. What we get is a slightly different translation of the Bible with slightly different verses or meanings that do not align word for word with the original scriptures. The followers of these new versions are now in fact Christians as well, even though the true word of God has been skewed or altered to some extent. These followers of the newly 'skewed' translation are then taught, and firmly believe, that their translation is the true and accurate word of God.

Many versions of the Bible have also been created to accommodate our modern lifestyles, or to aid in spreading our social and political views and beliefs. Once more, we don't even bother with an attempt at transforming our lives into the word of God – we take the easy way out and attempt to transform God to fit into our lives.

In 2004, a team of translators created the INT version of the Bible, otherwise known as The Inclusive New Testament[2]. The goal of the INT was to system-atically introduce the principles of feminism into the Holy Scriptures by way of removing gender specific titles. The mere act of doing so is contradictory to God, and being a Christian, at even the most basic levels. Doing so would be implying that they believe in God, as the Creator and Ruler of all things, while simultaneously implying that God's Word and direction are not sufficient and therefore must be modified by mankind as we know better than He does.

The simplified truth of this matter is that the proponents and followers of this line of thinking do not truly believe in God at all, they are simply using God, and His Word in an attempt to glorify themselves and further their own personal beliefs and agendas.

The final verses in the book of Revelations unquestionably tell us that the Word of God is complete, and nothing shall be added to it or taken away from it without severe punishment. 2nd Peter 1:21 cites that *"..prophecy never had its origin in the human will, but prophets, though human, spoke from God as they were carried along by the Holy Spirit."*

Reading the Bible

One of the biggest stumbling blocks that Christians face today is in how we read and interpret God's word in the Bible. We give our lives to Christ, become a Christian, and are then taught that to learn more about God and grow closer to God we must be in His Word every day. Meaning that we must read the Bible every day. Again, we are brought right back to our initial predicament – man and his perception.

When we read the Bible, just as with any other book, our mind will always attempt to paint a picture or visualize the story which we are reading, as we perceive it to be. As we are unable to assimilate any of our modern-day experiences with the times or happenings in the Bible, that picture or image which we create is most always inadequate and lacking. We therefore paint that picture based on our own limited knowledge, experience, and understanding – ones which we can equate to in modern times. Once again, we attempt to rationalize the words, or that image, into an understanding that we can relate too. Then we place this newly formed understanding, perspective, or belief, in to our minds and label that new perception as being fact, and our truth. But hold on, our minds are not finished yet. You guessed it – Our confirmation bias then kicks in and we seek out ways to validate our newly formed belief, while rejecting any other possible view or understanding of what that scripture may actually mean.

This is how we have come to have over 45,000 different variations of Christianity today. As man begins to interpret the Bible, he comes to a belief or understanding of what he perceives the words to mean, or even more unacceptable, what he wants the words to mean. Many of these beliefs or perceptions are minor in difference, and do not change the view of Jesus Christ as our Lord and Savior, which is the focal point and foundation of Christianity. However, these differences cause one, or a group of people, to part from their original denomination or religious group and to form a new denomination, or variant thereof, holding firm to these new beliefs.

The second, but likely the most harmful way in which we as Christians read the Bible is referred to as 'pick-and-choose'. Again, we have given our lives to Christ, become a Christian, and are then taught that to learn more about God and grow closer to Him we must be in His Word. However, we fall significantly short in the first step and stating that we would give our lives to Christ.

We like our lives, the way they are, and the ways in which we have arranged them. They are comfortable, and there are many things in our lives that we enjoy. We really don't want to let go of those things, and we see no harm in hanging on to them, while at the same time being a Christian. So, we then seek ways to justify their existence in our lives by searching for any justification in God's Word that would endorse these practices or beliefs. (Our confirmation bias again – We believe (or want) something to be true, and then we seek out ways to validate that belief).

We seek out words or scriptures within the Bible that would allow us to justify keeping these sinful habits in our lives. And, as no part of God's Word, or Scripture, at any point, gives any inclination that keeping this sin in our life is acceptable, we 'pick-and-choose' little bits of a verse, or smaller sections of a paragraph and use them completely out of the context or the meaning that they were intended to have. We then go around citing this part of scripture to others as justification for our sin, allowing us to remain unchanged, and even more appalling, showing others that being a Christian has no real meaning to it at all. In a sense – We want to call ourselves Christians, but we want Christianity to be on our terms. We tweak and distort the Bible to make it conform to our lives, instead of transforming our lives to fit into what the Bible actually says and means.

One of the most common examples of this 'pick-and-choose' fault uses the verse from Philippians 4:13. The book of Philippians was written by the Apostle Paul and was written as a letter to the believers of Philippi, which was a prosperous Roman colony. Paul's letter to the Philippi is short, biblically speaking, and is only four chapters in length. Paul's overall intention with the letter was to thank the Philippi for supporting his mission work, as well as to encourage all Christians to live joyfully in Christ – regardless of their circumstances.

Paul states in Philippians 4:13 – *"I can do all this through him who gives me strength."* (New International Version)

In the New King James Version, it reads: – *"I can do all things through Christ who strengthens me."*

The NASB 2020 version reads as: – *"I can do all things through Him who strengthens me."*

The two major differences which we see in the three versions above are:

1) the descriptor word used to identify Jesus Christ as being the one who Paul is strengthened through. Three different variations are used: *Christ, Him, and him.* While each version offers a different interpretation of the original translation – these differences are of no significance as it is a common inference that all three are referring to and describe the same being.

2) The specificity of what it is that Paul can now do through Him – *all this, all things.* Here we see what could be considered a significant difference in the use or interpretation of a simple phrase. One version, the one which is most commonly grabbed for our own personal advantage, is the NKJV or the NASB version using *all things.* The NIV version uses the phrase *all this.*

Things is described as meaning an object or entity not precisely designated or capable of being designated.[3]

This has the meaning of a person, thing, or idea that is present or near in place, time, or thought, or has just been mentioned.[4]

Therefore, by definition of these words, one is likely referring to things of the moment or that have been recently noted or experienced (this) – and the other refers to a more generalization of the word itself and has no designation or may be all encompassing (things).

So how are we to know which verse is correct, and what the actual intention or application of that verse is? The answer is very simple and is most always one which the 'pick-and-chooser' will never do.

We have to read more! We have to read more than just the one or two verses. We need to read the paragraph, and possibly the entire chapter – to be able to determine the context and environment that the words were said in and used for. Doing so will help to give us a more precise picture of the meaning and intent of the verse

And in the case of our example verse, if we would open our Bible, we can clearly see that verse 13 comes at the end of a paragraph which begins with verse 10. Throughout this entire paragraph Paul is explaining that he has learned to be content, whatever the circumstances may be. The end of the paragraph concludes with verses 12 & 13 where Paul states: [12]*"I know what it is to be in need, and I know what it is to have plenty. I have learned the secret of being content in any and every situation, whether well fed or hungry, whether living in plenty or in want.* [13]*I can do all this through him who gives me strength."*

While I personally believe that I can do all things through Christ who strengthens me, I do not believe that Paul was referring to any and all known or unknown things, in the past, present, or future. Based on the entire letter that Paul wrote, the specific paragraph and its subject matter, and the fact that Paul states in the verse immediately preceding our questionable verse – I believe that Paul was advocating a fact that he knew very well, and which he considered a well-guarded secret. Paul was implying that Christ was the one who gave him strength to be content, at all times, in any situation, whether good or bad.

'Pick-and-choose' simply does not work. We must know the full context of the Scripture itself, as well as submit ourselves to an intimate and personal relationship with Christ. That is when we truly become strengthened in all things!

Many of us also have a tendency to read the Bible using a systematic approach, a process based on the application of clearly predefined and repeatable steps, using it as a self-help guide to life. We read through the Scriptures in an attempt to garner tips and shortcuts on how to attain and live a better life. Or, as we like to call it today, 'a life hack'. We are looking for the easy way out, or the little 'cheat' that will all of a sudden make our lives painless and uncomplicated.

At the time I was in High School in the 1980's, we had little pamphlets called CliffsNotes. For those not familiar with CliffsNotes, they were basically a study guide that gave you all of the important information, the highlights, that you needed without having to actually read or learn the entire book of the subject matter that had been assigned to you. It allowed you to take a short cut or essentially take the easy way out. I have come to learn that kids now-a-days use what is called TLDR, which is the modern-day version of CliffsNotes. TLDR stands for Too Long Didn't Read.

This methodology is very much how we approach the Bible as well. We just want the important tips, the highlights, which will help us in passing this class called life, so that we can get back to living and the ways of this world. Most all of us view the Bible in the same ways which we did Advanced Literature class, Trigonometry, or Advanced Calculus. We care very little about actually learning anything or retaining the information– we just want to know enough to get by.

The How to of the Bible

The Bible, God's true and living Word, is anything but a shortcut. It is a love story, a drama packed action movie, a romance novel, a bloody battle, and a self-help guide all wrapped up into one book. It is God showing us how we were meant to live, how we were created to live, and how so many others have failed at doing so by choosing to pursue other paths. It is God showing us that He has always and will always love us, desire us, and fight for us. And it is God showing us that He will go to any length to find us, help us, and save us from ourselves and this world.

We would benefit ourselves if we approached the Bible just as we do with any other book or movie that we may read or watch. When we read those books, or see those movies, we find ourselves intertwined with the story and perceive an emotional connection with the characters and the story that is being told. There is always at least one character that we grow fond of, can relate too, and in a sense bond with.

We then allow ourselves to become a part of that movie or book, and that character. Many of us will then go one step further and make this character a part of our daily lives by placing posters on our walls, bumper stickers on our cars, and buying clothing items that flaunt an image of that character. We become so intertwined with that story or character that we begin to revolve our lives around it.

This is how we need to approach the Bible as well. Becoming so intertwined with the story, and the main character Jesus Christ, that we revolve our entire lives around it. We fail to do so as our perception of Jesus, thanks to modern day religion and the views of the world, is that of some stuffy hippie who was just freewheeling it through life. He then becomes someone that we cannot relate to, and we therefore choose not to be associated with Him. We need to learn who the real Jesus is, not the CliffsNotes version.

Jesus - The laid back, easy going, fun loving, party guy who would drop anything that He was doing to give anyone the love, attention and care that they so desperately needed. The guy who knew exactly what it was that you truly needed, and not just what you desired. The guy that made you feel like you were the only person in the world when He was interacting with you. He went to parties, He went to BBQs, and He even created alcohol out of water. He went camping and fishing with his buddies and even took road trips with them. And then, no matter where He was or what He was doing, He would drop everything and walk to another town just to be there for one person who was in need. We would do ourselves well to learn who the true Jesus was and is.

My favorite character in the Bible, aside from Jesus and God obviously, is Saul/Paul. I can relate myself and my life experiences to his in many ways, at least up to the point of his conversion. I too was headed down the wrong road, with a brutal and ugly past. I too thought that my way was the best way. And in that one moment, God put my entire world on hold to show me how much He loved me and what my life was truly created to be, just as He did with Paul, which caused both of us to change instantly. I can now only hope and pray that it is God's will that the rest of my life would be as Paul's was as well.

More Golf

My friend Mike and I went to play golf the other day. Mike had booked a tee time for us that had us teeing off mid-afternoon. It was a Friday, and the beginning of summer, so the course was packed. As we had expected, we were paired up with another twosome which turned out to be two younger men in their early twenties.

As I commonly do, I refer to people of this age group as 'kids'. Robin always gives me a hard time when I do so, reminding me that they are no longer 'kids', but young adults. I still see them as kids, being uneducated and very impressionable.

One of the kids that we played with that day was extremely cocky and arrogant. This became evident on the first tee box. Mike fancied this attribute in the young man and in a sense befriended him quickly. Mike is a leader and a mentor and cherishes the opportunity to make a positive impact on a younger man. I am more of a 'be quiet and let your skills do the talking' kind of guy. Either way, the day was full of good conversation with the younger twosome, and it was an enjoyable round.

When we had reached the fourteenth tee box, I noticed that the bois-terous kid had some numbers written on the side of his golf shoes with a black permanent marker. The numbers were 4 13. I asked him what the significance of those numbers were, to which he replied, *"It's a bible verse - Philippians 4:13".* I of course knew what Philippians 4:13 said, but asked him anyways - *"What does that verse say?"* He responded in a way that was rather shocking, as if he was embarrassed. In a muted and sarcastic tone, he stated, *"For I can do all things through Christ who strengthens me."*

By now we had spent roughly three hours with these two younger men. And in the course of that three hours, I had witnessed both of them being full of pride, cussing profusely, and at one point almost initiating a fight with another group – just because they felt up to it.

This is the so-called Christian life in our world today. We call ourselves Christians, grab a verse from the bible because we think it empowers us (even though we have no clue of the context behind that verse), and then feel like we are in the good graces of God by doing so. We do not know God. We simply try to use God to give ourselves a better life or existence.

As you can see, Christianity and the Bible can become very confusing and difficult to completely understand. The effort to do so becomes even more complicated when you factor in the external forces of spiritual warfare, false prophets, and those who simply confound the meaning of Scripture with false and inaccurate information. Man, left to himself, will never fully understand the true Word of God. This can only be achieved through the Holy Spirit, who dwells within us once we become Christians. By the power of the Holy Spirit, and constant prayer and reading of God's Word, God reveals to us the true meaning of the Scriptures.

What Kind of Christian are You?

I am hopeful that by this point in the book you are starting to see some of the possible flaws in the ways which we view things, and how that view, or perception, has a significant impact on our lives and who we become. Your life does not have to be falling apart or at rock bottom to have these flaws either. My early years reveal a story of bad choices, wrong directions, lies and deceptions, which fully consumed me and formed my perspective on life and the world that we live in. They were wrong, they were skewed, they were flawed. I really did not have a clue how to live life at that point as I was being guided by the ways of the world, and not by The Spirit.

Then, by the grace of God, over time, many people were placed into my life who made an impact on my future and my direction. Of course, I had a choice in choosing whether or not to accept these people into my life. I could have taken the easy way out and continued down the path that I was on. But deep down inside, I knew that something was missing, something was not right with the way of life that I had been living. I knew that there had to be more, or at least that is what I so desperately wanted to believe. I was not sure what it was – but I knew that there had to be a better reasoning and purpose for our lives.

Then, good things began to happen in my life, and before you know it, I was on top of the world. I had made it! I had the girl, I had a job making a ton of money, I had the cars, I owned multiple houses, I had all the toys that I wanted. My confidence and self-esteem grew incredibly, and it was evident that I was not the same person that I was before. I now had morals and values as well. I went to church, and I was a Christian. I had changed my views and perceptions on life, and I now acted like and believed that I was in the top 2% of people in our country – financially speaking. I had gone from being a lost wandering soul who did not have two nickels to rub together, to becoming a man who had complete control over every aspect of his life and who had more than enough money to do whatever he wanted too. But even though I had 'made it' in my own eyes, deep down inside I could still tell that something was missing. I could sense and feel that a piece of the puzzle was still missing. I would never have admitted it back then, but the real me felt shallow, superficial, and incomplete. Even with all of my success and the rise to the top, I still felt like that abandoned little boy who was always trying to be someone else, and who could never do enough to have someone truly love me.

And then, on that one December morning in my living room, God showed me how my views and perceptions were wrong, skewed, and flawed. I had 'made it' by worldly standards. But not by God's standards. God showed me that this is not what we were created for, or how we were meant to live this life, in this world. God also showed me what it meant to be a TRUE Christian, and what that life should look like. And God showed me what true love is, and that I have always been loved by my true Father.

I must, although, make it clear that while God has made a major transformation in my life and has revealed many things to me since then, I am in no way insinuating that I have been shown or told what the secrets to The Kingdom of Heaven are. I am not claiming to be all knowledgeable or greater than anyone else. It is actually the opposite. The only thing that I can truly claim is that just as before, I still have no clue how to live my life, albeit for different reasons now. I am still learning, I am still growing, and through His grace and love, God is still showing me and teaching me new things every day. But as I have now come to understand that everything that I thought I knew, everything that I believed to be true, and every way that I understood how to live this life were all wrong, I once again find myself in that oh so familiar place of not having a clue how to live this new life either. I must wipe away all of the thoughts and beliefs that I have and relearn how to do everything all over again – the right way, just as God had intended.

I know the question that may be popping into some of your heads right now - *"Whoa! Wait a minute. Now you're telling me that I have to live up to some standards to get into heaven?"* No, that is not the case. Paul tells us clearly in Romans 10:9 that *"if you declare with your mouth, "Jesus is Lord", and believe in your heart that God raised Him from the dead, you will be saved."*

If you have professed Jesus as your Lord and Savior and believe in your heart that God raised Him from the dead, your salvation can never be taken away from you. You will go to heaven.

So why then do we have to live life a certain way? Why do we have to 'act' or 'perform' in a certain way? If our salvation cannot be achieved by any 'works' of our own, why does it matter what we do? If we are going to heaven anyway, what does it matter? Well, it matters a lot. This as well is a very deep topic which we could devote an entire book too, in fact, several authors already have. For now, however, we will just touch on the aspects related to the meaning of a Christian, and Christianity.

As we learned in previous chapters, a Christian is a follower and believer of Jesus Christ. A believer, as we outlined earlier by definition, is one who has a firm conviction as to the goodness, efficacy, or ability of something. Therefore, if we are believers or followers of Jesus Christ, we firmly believe in His goodness, effectiveness and ability. We follow Jesus to learn from Him, in His teachings and examples on how to live life, and how to be obedient and glorifying to The Father.

In Matthew 16:24-25, Jesus tells us *"Whoever wants to be my disciple must deny themselves and take up their cross and follow me. For whoever wants to save their life will lose it, but whoever loses their life for me will find it."*

These two verses were an enormous stumbling block for me at first, simply because I did not understand their true meaning. Again, we go back to the images and perception of things which we have formed in the past, that shape our views of our world today. To me these verses meant that I had to give up everything that I had, literally – all of my cars, all of my toys, all of my houses, all of my possessions, everything that I had worked so hard to obtain – and take all of my money and give it to some 'good cause', and then live a life of poverty just to follow Jesus. I had painted a picture in my mind of the twelve disciples, wearing nothing but their robes and sandals, who had literally given up everything they owned to follow Jesus. It would be very plausible to see how one could say - *"Umm, No Thanks, I'll pass!"*

However, what God has shown me and what I have learned since that day, is that my perception, or how I viewed reality was wrong. My mental image of those two verses were that of poverty and a life of nothing. But through God's grace, in studying His word, He has shown me that my perception of those two verses was completely inaccurate. God has shown me that in the first part of verse 24 when Jesus says we must deny ourselves and take up our cross, that I do not have to give up all of my possessions to follow Him. The meaning of that verse is that I need to stop placing myself first and to stop trying to please myself before God and before others. That self-life that we mentioned before. We need to place God and Jesus first in our lives, and they need to be our priority and our focus all day, every day, in everything we do.

To take up my cross can have multiple meanings. The cross, in relation to Jesus, is where He was crucified, sacrificing His life for ours. Our cross is to be where we sacrifice everything as well. All of the trials, struggles, fears, anxieties, pressures and weaknesses that we have in this world. All of the burdens that weigh so heavily upon us. We take up our cross by taking all of these to that altar and letting Jesus handle all of it. We live in Him, fully dependent upon Him, for everything comes from Him.

In verse 25 Jesus tells us that whoever wants to save their life will lose it, and whoever loses their life for me will find it. Hmmm, this was still a challenge for me as I always had that poverty mentality. I did not want to lose anything. My life had always been about what I could get. But then again, God showed me the true meaning of these words. God showed me that we don't actually LOSE anything, we GAIN everything. He showed me that as we give up the worldly way of life and give in to the way of Jesus, we will not only be guaranteed much more numerous and greater things, but we will also be shown the way to true life – the way our lives were meant to be lived. Jesus is saying that to save our lives we must lose our worldly lives, we must stop living in and according to this world and start living in Jesus Christ.

As generations have passed, times have changed, and things have evolved – so has the church and the meaning or definition of a Christian. In this fast paced, technology driven world that we live in today, I could not even begin to list all of the different stereotypes of Christians in our society. There is a growing difference between the self-titled Christians of the Eastern world and the Western world, with the Western world Christian continuing to grow further and further away from God as we continually allow ourselves and our lives to be filled with modern technology and its misinformation and self-reliance. A.K.A. – the lies and the deception. We have come to a point where we do not feel like we need God, as we already know everything that there is to know, or we have the ability to obtain answers to anything within a few clicks of a computer mouse. Does any of this sound familiar?

Let us once again go back to the book of Genesis and the Garden of Eden. Just as Satan tempted Eve in to believing that they could be as smart and powerful as God, and that they really did not need God, Satan continues with the same ubiquitous temptations and deceptions on us today. Nothing has changed – Satan is still luring us further and further away from God with the lies and deceptions – just more so in a modern technological way which we find rather appealing and acceptable.

John Eldredge pushes us to question our modern-day religious culture in his book *Beautiful Outlaw*[5] where he states:

"You must understand an important distinction – there is Christianity, and then there is church culture. They are not the same...... The personality conveyed through much of Christian culture is not the personality of Jesus but of the people in charge of that particular franchise."[6]

Eldredge goes on to say *"So the Deceiver deceives by means of distortion, and his favorite tool is to present a distorted Christ....... through the respectable channels of religion. Consider this one piece of evidence: millions of people who have spent years attending church, and yet they do not know God. Their heads are filled wit h stuffing about Jesus, but they do not experience him."*[7]

Eldredge calls this the religious fog and goes on to state - *"...it would be just a little arrogant for us to assume we could not fall under the same religious haze...... religion gives the impression of having Christ, while it inoculates you from experiencing the real thing."*[8]

The Scottish prophet George MacDonald adds *"It ought to be a startling thought, that we may have learned him (Jesus) wrong."*[9]

The Church

As this world has accustomed us to do, when we do think of God, Christ, or church, we get that awkward, discomforting feeling which we have learned to associate with religion. I cannot stress the importance of understanding that religion is man made and is not of God or Christ. Christ was opposed to the religious views and acts of the Pharisee's, which was merely a human effort to be righteous.

The modern-day church has become much of the same in that their main objective is to grow their membership which most always comes through means of preaching a false doctrine of the gospels, contorting their political views into their theology, or by creating an environment that is dictated by modern culture in an effort to please the world that they exist in.

Man has allowed, and been the causation of, religion and the church to sway so far from God, Christ, and Christianity that what we have today is a religious environment that is actually counter-intuitive to what the Bible and the gospels actually teach – and what and who God and Jesus actually are.

These artificial environments which we commonly refer to as the church are partially liable for shaping and forming the tainted views of Christianity that we hold today, as well as the ways in which we consider God and Jesus to be, and the ways in which we perceive what it means to be a Christian.

The church's goal of leading others to Christ and their salvation has in a sense become a hypocrisy as it is not the lives of the new believers that are being changed, but the church itself that is changing to adapt to the ways of the world.

Recently, shortly after my awakening, I had a brief encounter with a man who pastored a fairly large church. I was on the hunt for a better understanding of the new information which was being revealed to me almost daily. We had a lengthy conversation on that day, as I endeavored to pull answers from someone whom I believed would surely have them. This pastor made a comment about halfway through our talk which, at the time, left me puzzled and even more perplexed. He stated that God has never spoken to him.

This man is a devout Christian, a devoted husband and father, and is unquestionably a 'good person'. He is the sort of pastor that I think most people would want to lead their church. He is very friendly, very open, very approachable, and always has a comforting answer for one's troubles. He had spent the better part of the last two decades devoting his life to God and serving others. So how could it be possible that this man has never heard from God?

Unfortunately, this is what our modern-day church has become. We are being led, we are being taught, we are being educated and trained by those who don't have a clue what it means to be a true Christian themselves. This is no fault of their own either. They too have been misinformed, misguided, and outright lied too – just as we have. They too had been indoctrinated to an image of God and Christ, as well as Christianity, which had been devastatingly altered by the time it reached them.

I must clarify that in no way am I opposing the church, or pastors; or attempting to thwart the primary intention and purpose of the church. God had a plan for the church, just as He did with mankind. And just as mankind has done, the church has strayed immensely from that plan and has chosen to take matters into its own hands.

Christian Stereotypes

You need only to look at a few of the most notable stereotypes of a Christian in our society today to comprise more than 90% of those who call themselves a Christian. We all know them. We have all seen them. They attend our churches, they are our neighbors, they are our work colleagues. And more than likely – You are one as well – Just as I was.

The Legalistic Christian

Our first stereotype is not as common nowadays as it was back in the prior century. This is the legalistic, or what I would call 'hardcore' Christian. It is likely that you have seen them portrayed in older movies. The Mom and Pop, or Grandparents, that lived and died by every single word in the Bible. They more than likely had a Bible within ten feet of them at all times and knew every single word in the Scriptures by heart. Their response to everything was a Bible verse, and most always in a condescending way – which would almost certainly be in a harsh, punishing tone that came with the evil stare of Satan himself. To them, the Bible was black and white. There was no gray area, and there was no room for the love and grace of Jesus either. In their eyes, if you did not follow or live by every Scripture in the Bible, you would be damned to hell for eternity.

This type of Christian is much like the Pharisee's back when Jesus walked our earth. Jesus compared them to Satan and called them hypocrites as they had a greater interest in appearing righteous on the outside than being righteous on the inside.

The Legalistic Christian was more common fifty plus years ago. This extreme legalism of many Christians as well as many Christian churches in the mid twentieth century may also be part of the reasoning for the direction of most churches today. Having realized that this approach to Christianity is not received well among the common public, most churches today have swung the pendulum 180 degrees in the opposite direction and now base their foundation and message on the love and the salvation received through Jesus Christ instead of forcefully imparting the laws and commandments upon their congregation.

The Know-it-All Christian

Another common type of Christian that we often see is the know-it-all. Every church has one, at least one. However, most know-it-alls don't even go to church. More than likely, they were raised in a strict religious environment and were required to attend a private school or endured some type of seminary schooling. They were required, or forced, to learn the Bible and all of its Scriptures. They too, just like the legalistic Christian, know the scriptures front to back, and have memorized most if not all of the Bible.

In other cases, with the know-it-all, they have acquired a fascination with the Bible through an interest in history or a search for prophetic knowledge and wisdom. They have studied the Bible over and over in an attempt to find the secret answers to life, and the revelation of how our world would end.

Most know-it-alls will often cite or use Scripture as a response during ordinary conversations in an attempt to 'appear' Christian. However, these same know-it-alls have read the Word, but do not know the Word. The know-it-all has taken the Scriptures and allowed them in to their mind – but have never allowed any of God's Word into their heart.

The Word of God is a true and living thing. It's true meaning only comes out to us as God is willing to reveal its meaning to us, through the Holy Spirit. If we do not have that true, intimate relationship with God, and we do not truly believe in our hearts, then the Word of God is only being read and interpreted by man with his limited knowledge and understanding alone.

The Cultural Christian

The Cultural Christian has to be the most common type found in our society today. They are also what we have come to accept or refer to as being a 'normal' Christian. They are everywhere. Every church is full of them. Most everyone that you encounter who claims to be a Christian will fall into this stereotype. This was me, as well, after I sought to turn my life around, and more than likely, this is you too if you call yourself a Christian.

The Normal Christian conceivably leads a good life or at least tries too. They attend church on Sundays. Well, they attend church when nothing better is going on, or if they can get out of bed on time, or if they did not stay up too late last night. Whatever the excuse is, they can typically find something better to do to occupy their time. But when they do manage to make it to church, they show up late, don't pay attention, spend half the time scrolling through social media on their phones, and then rush out the door to get back to their good life which had just been inconvenienced by this thing called church.

Another variation of the Normal Christian is one who actually does try to be a Christian, albeit for the wrong reasons. Something, or someone, has led them to believe that if they just go to church, pray, and attempt to be religious, that life will play out more in their favor. Church, and God for that matter, become a safety net for them. It is their back up plan. If all else fails, if they are unable make things work out on their own – well, they are a Christian and they have God so He will suddenly swoop in and save the day for them.

They show up to church, they pay attention to the sermon, they take notes, and they may even hang out for a bit after the service is over. But then it is out the doors and right back to their real life – right back to doing everything else they have been doing, and nothing that the church or God is asking them to do. Much like our society today, they fervently believe they can get an award for just showing up.

Then the Normal Christian (of any variation – and there are many) goes about their worldly life playing the part of a Christian, with the look at me attitude. They put a church sticker on the back of their SUV, they post on Facebook that they attended church today, they tell all of their friends that they are Christians – but only when asked, and they look down upon anyone else with judgment anytime others do something wrong as if they are better just because they are a Christian. They rarely ever pray, and if they do, it is usually only in times of desperate need and most always to fulfill a personal desire or need. They have become so wrapped up in themselves, and their self-image, that they only claim to be a Christian in an effort to make themselves look better and have the appearance of being 'good'.

The Normal Christian forms their view and understanding of Christianity through the ways of the modern-day culture around them. They too become a product of their environment, allowing that environment to shape and form who and what God and Jesus are, and how each should be viewed and understood.

There is a not-so-common variation of the Normal Christian, which looks so much like the previously mentioned one, while having different intentions. This is the Agnostic Christian. The meaning of the word agnostic is - *not having or showing conviction about the existence of God*. The Agnostic Christian truly desires to follow God and be a good Christian but cannot allow themselves to fully have the faith that God exists, and that God is actually involved in and cares about their lives. The Agnostic Christian is focused on the self-life, but more so in a preservation mode instead of one trying to build up their own image as with the more common generic Normal Christian. Like so many of us in our relationships with others, the Agnostic Christian builds up a wall to protect themselves from being let down or disappointed by a God that may or may not really even care or exist.

As John Eldredge put it so well in his book The Sacred Romance, *"Perhaps God will come through, perhaps He won't.......I'll hedge my bets and if He does show up, so much the better. The simple word for this is Godlessness. Like a lover who's been wronged, we guard our heart against future disappointment."*[10]

The Christian Atheist

Those two words do not go together, do they? They are contradictory and divergent in both meaning and nature. However, many people today play the part of the Christian Atheist. How can this be? How can a person be two completely different, opposing things at the same time?

We have already learned what the definition of a Christian is – *one who is a believer and follower of Jesus Christ.* An Atheist is a one who does not believe in God, or gods. But, if Jesus Christ is the Son of God – and a Christian believes in and follows Christ, how can that same person not believe in God, or Jesus's Father?

A Christian Atheist is one who believes in and follows the ideology of Jesus Christ – but yet does not believe in God. They have not bought into the crucifixion, the resurrection, or the Trinity – let alone salvation or restoration - but more so believe in the philosophy and teachings of Jesus as a person, as a guide on how to live a better life.

They are in many ways like the Normal Christian in the sense that they aspire to live a so called 'good life', doing the right things, being kind, generous, loving, caring, and helpful, while desiring to look good for the world to see, and doing so only in an effort to glorify themselves. Many Christian Atheists believe that God has never existed, while some believe that God has ceased to exist, or is dead.

The reasoning for the thoughts and beliefs of the Christian Atheist, along with their justification for this way of thinking, is not as apparent as with the Normal Christian, but can most always be traced back to their childhood. But again, to be simplistic, the Christian Atheist lives the self-life believing that they have full control over everything and every outcome, and lives only to satisfy their own desires.

While these are just a few of the most common stereotypes of Christians today, there are many others, and many variations of the ones listed above as well.

I am fully aware that this next statement may rub some of you the wrong way and may even offend some others. However, I have always been a straight-forward and direct type of person. Rarely do I sugar coat the words that I say only to ensure someone's feelings do not get hurt. I am always honest, sincere, and to-the-point. I am also not a big talker and usually do not say a whole lot. Throughout my years I have learned that my words will have more value and meaning and will also be much better received if they are not diluted with meaningless fluff. Therefore, seldom do I say much unless there is something to be gained from the message.

With that said, I am going to make many of your lives so much easier and free up a lot of your time.

You can stop going to church - and stop doing the things that you do to be a Christian!

Not what you were expecting, huh? It is true though. You can stop, and you can stop right now. I am not using the word CAN as in your ability to go to church. I am using the word CAN in a permissive sense. As in it is okay.

Maybe this will help – You are wasting your time, and everyone else's as well. You are putting on a show in an effort to make it appear that you are righteous and holy. You show up, put in your time, and then go right back to living your worldly life until the following week. You even have yourself convinced that you are a Christian, and doing the right things. However, it is not truly in your heart.

You are playing the part of the poser, just as I once did, in an effort to appear as someone or something that you truly are not. And the worst part is that you are doing it so well that you even have yourself convinced that this is who you truly are.

Shame

Most all of us are fake, to some extent at least. Imposters, phonies, frauds......... and, well, even deceivers. Don't get bent out of shape with the accusation. Heck, I was one too, and probably one of the best (or worst) at doing so.

We do not allow ourselves to be real, to be authentic, to be our true selves. It is the way we were raised. It is what we have come to accept and believe that we must do to survive. We adapt and change to whatever environment or situation we may find ourselves in. And we even go to the extent of doing so multiple times a day.

But why? Why would so many people go to great lengths, most times requiring great effort, to be something that they are not when it would just be so much easier to be who they truly are?

Genesis 3:9-11 is where it all started. Adam and Eve had just eaten the apple. God was going through the garden looking for Adam. Adam and Eve hid among the trees. God then calls out to Adam, who replies *"I heard you in the garden, so I hid. I was afraid because I was naked."* Then God asks, *"Who told you that you were naked?"*

We could dive in to so many different conversations on what these verses unfold, but for now we will just stick with being afraid. Adam had eaten the apple from the forbidden tree and had suddenly become aware that he was naked. And now he was afraid, or even ashamed of his nakedness. However,

Adam had been naked his entire life, and it had never been a concern to him before. So why now?

When Adam ate the apple, sin and Satan entered man. Adam did not know what sin was before this time. And as Satan always does, first comes the lies and deceptions to get us to sin, and then he pours on the guilt and the shame to make us feel bad about what we have done, and unworthy of being close to God. Adam now felt that shame and for the first time in his life he felt that he had to hide from God out of that shame.

We do this same thing when we are always trying to be something other than our true selves. We are ashamed of our true selves, and therefore we always attempt to blend into whatever situation we find ourselves in, portraying an image of something that we are not. We are afraid of being exposed for who we truly are. We are fakes, we are phonies, we are all frauds. And we do so because we are ashamed of who we truly are, and what others may think of us if we show our true selves. We allow the world and mankind to shape and mold the person that we should be all in an effort to fit in and be accepted. All to receive that affirmation and validation that we desperately seek and crave.

We have been misled to believe that we will get this acceptance from other people as well as the world, and in that acceptance we now will be complete.

Union

All of these 'things' that we do, do not make us a Christian. There is one way, and only one way to be able to call ourselves Christians. There is one way, and only one way to knowing and understanding God as well – and that way is by being in complete union with God and Jesus Christ. As Christians, this should be our first and foremost priority, focus, and intention.

Being in union with God and Christ comes from the heart. If it is not our hearts true desire, we will not seek it, chase it, or desire it. God wants our heart, not our efforts.

Probably the simplest, yet most impactful quote that I have ever heard, which defines us to our core as human beings, comes from Dallas Willard.

"Actions reveal beliefs 100% of the time."[11]

So concise, so powerful, and so true. Our actions, what we think, do, and say – reveal what our true core beliefs are 100% of the time. Spending an hour or two on Sundays in an attempt to be a Christian and then running back to spend the other 166 hours of the week seeking our own pleasures clearly reveals the core desires of our hearts.

We spend those few hours on Sunday, or maybe even a few hours each day, doing things that make us feel like we are Christians. We dabble in Christianity here and there, just enough to make ourselves feel better about who we are and where our lives are headed. We read Godly books, we listen to Christian radio, we get involved with a church group, and we even make the ever so rare attempt to go out of our way to help others. But before long we begin to question why we are not growing closer to God. We begin to question Christianity. We begin to question God. We then come to believe that this Christian life is not attainable. That it does not apply to us in this day and age. That living a life as Jesus did is just not possible for us as we are sinners.

Dallas Willard describes it best in his book *The Spirit of the Disciplines.* Willard says: *"Our mistake is to think that following Jesus consists in loving our enemies, going the 'second mile', turning the other cheek, suffering patiently and hopefully – while living the rest of our lives just as everyone around us does."*[12]

Willard goes on to explain that it is not that living a life just as Jesus did is unattainable, or impossible – it is that we are not disciplined in our training and preparations to live our lives as Jesus did, and as He lived His life all day, every day.

We go about our lives sprinkling a little 'God stuff' on it here and there and then wonder why we do not feel close to God, or that we are actually one with God.

The Cross

If you have truly accepted Jesus as your Savior and believe that God raised Him from the dead – your salvation is guaranteed. We have discussed in a previous chapter the specific scripture that validates this statement.

Our salvation through Jesus Christ does not offer us a free pass though, to just go live our lives however we may choose to. As Jesus told us in Matthew 16:24-25 - *"Whoever wants to be my disciple must deny themselves and take up their cross and follow me. For whoever wants to save their life will lose it, but whoever loses their life for me will find it."*

Therefore, when we choose to become a Christian, we are making the choice to follow Jesus and to stop following ourselves. We are also choosing to stop following others, and the ways of this world that we live in. This means that we are to look to Jesus, and God, for guidance, direction, advice, counseling, support, and help on how we should live, what we should do, and how our lives should play out. We ultimately give up control of our lives (don't worry, you never really had control of it anyway) and turn it all over to God and Jesus. We let God decide our direction, and we constantly seek out His advice and then follow it. We transform every aspect of our lives to live more like Jesus did.

Our admission into heaven is based solely upon one thing, and one thing only – Accepting Jesus Christ as our Savior! Once we accept Christ as our Lord and Savior and truly believe in our hearts that God raised Him from the dead, our salvation, and our inheritance of ALL of God's promises are guaranteed. This cannot ever be taken away from us either. At that point, God now has ownership of our lives and our souls. Satan can no longer own or possess us. We have then become the children of God and are entitled to and promised all of His riches and powers as his sons and daughters.

The meaning of the word *salvation* as defined in the Merriam-Webster dictionary is - *the deliverance from the power and effects of sin.*[13] Jesus Christ is our salvation and is who and what delivers us from the power and effects of sin. Christ was crucified and died on the cross to conquer sin and death and the separation from God that being in that sin delivers. Once we have accepted Christ, that sin and that separation no longer has a hold on us or our lives.

Since the beginning of time as we know it, starting with Adam and Eve, God has always known that man (and woman) would be separated from Him by this sin, and that our true nature and existence would be sinful to the core. As you learn more about God, you will come to understand that this sin cannot be in the presence of God. God is too pure, too holy, and too righteous. This too has been the case since the beginning of time.

In the Old Testament days of the Bible people could not come to God as we do now. People did not have a direct relationship with God, as it was not possible due to their sin. The groups of people in the Old Testament, or tribes, had what was called a High Priest. This High Priest was their connection to God. The High Priest was the only one who could directly connect with God, and even then, it was under certain specific conditions that the High Priest could come in to contact with God. The High Priest was a person just like you and I, but was chosen by God to be the one to hold that position. They were sinful by nature just as you and I are, but were hand picked by God for that time of intercession.

At the times when the High Priests would come to God, certain rituals and sacrifices had to be followed prior to that High Priest then going behind a curtained off area where only he would be in connection with God. When the High Priest would go into the temple and pass beyond the curtained area, a rope would be tied to his ankle so that he could be pulled out if he were ever to be struck dead from being in the presence of God. Just being in the presence of God with our sin is enough to have us struck down and put to death immediately. But as God knew that we were full of sin, and left to ourselves we would choose sin all of the time, there had to be an intercessor for us that would give us a bridge or allow us to connect with God Himself. In the Old Testament, those high Priests were our intercessors, or our connection to God.

In the Old Testament, people also lived by what was called The Law. The Ten Commandments, The Law of the Prophets, the words and directions given directly by God on how we were to live. These laws told us what we were to eat, how we were to handle certain matters, how we were to work, how and who we were to marry, and so on. The Law was our only path to righteousness, or being holy, and was our only pathway to God. The Law was based on our works, or our performance and how we did things. We had to perform a certain way to be righteous. Over time it became evident that no man could live up to the law completely, and that man himself could never become righteous, or therefore have a relationship with God.

It is very apparent throughout the Bible that God knew this all along, from the beginning of time, as He had already planned for an intercessor to be our only hope and our only salvation. This intercessor is first mentioned in the early chapters of Genesis, once Satan and sin entered our world. The intercessor would not come in the Old Testament, however, and man would attempt to live by The Law for many hundreds of years.

That intercessor would be Jesus Christ, the one and only son of God. The birth of Jesus Christ by the virgin Mary was the beginning to the end of death and separation which sin had placed upon us. His birth from a virgin holds significance as well. Jesus Christ was and is perfect in every way and could not have been so if created by the imperfect seed of man.

Jesus would live a human life just as we do, facing all of the struggles, challenges, temptations, and deceptions that we do every day. Jesus would go on living this life for thirty-three years, just as we do. While not utilizing his omnipotent powers, which He had the full ability to use, Jesus lived a perfect life never sinning or giving in to the temptations of sin. Jesus knew His purpose was to live a sinless life, and then be beaten, tortured, and crucified on the cross, so that death and sin would be conquered, and we would therefore be able to come to God directly through His crucifixion and resurrection. Jesus became our bridge, our intercessor, the one who connects us with God and allows us to be able to come to God directly. We no longer needed the High Priests, because Jesus was and is the Ultimate High Priest.

If you are not familiar with the crucifixion and its reasoning or all that it offers us, this may seem a bit confusing at first. Jesus lived a perfect sinless life to show that sin has no control over us through Him. Jesus died on the cross so that His perfection would conquer that sin. The blood from his crucifixion would be what is washed over us once we accept him. The perfect sinless blood of Christ then covers us, and that is what God sees when we come to Him. He sees us as perfect and pure – sinless. The blood of Christ is what now allows us to now be able to go directly to God and have a relationship with Him. We are now clean, pure and righteous in God's eyes.

Jesus lived a perfect life to conquer sin, was crucified on the cross so that His blood would be the atonement, or the proceeds that were paid for the purchase of our souls from Satan and sin. It did not end there though. Jesus was then wrapped in cloth and buried in a tomb where He lay for three days. On the third day Jesus was raised from the dead and conquered death itself showing that he was more powerful than Satan, sin and death. That is the resurrection.

As Jesus hung on the cross, badly beaten, bleeding and grasping for air, His final words were tetelestai. Tetelestai is a Greek word and means *It is finished*. As Jesus said these words, he let out His final breath and His spirit left His body.

It was finished! Jesus had finished the work He had been sent to do, and had conquered Satan, sin and death. Our lives have been forever changed since then, but only by the perfect and pure love and grace of God, our true Father.

Many people call themselves Christians – Many people have faith in Him – But very few actually **follow** Him!

The Works

The question popped up at the beginning of this chapter that we may feel like we have to live a certain way to be able to get into heaven. That we must perform certain tasks or do certain works. As stated previously, this is not the case. While I know some may disagree with this statement, that does not make it untrue – Once saved, always saved!

In the antithetical world that we live in we have been taught that our value comes from performance, or what and how much we can do. We learn that if we work harder, work faster, and work more efficiently than others, we will be seen as better, or more valued. We are rewarded for these works through a promotion, a raise in salary, or some type of recognition that gives us a sense of validation and self-worth, only pushing us to keep working and trying harder to do even more. We crave that affirmation and validation, just as we crave to be loved and wanted.

We spend our entire lives wearing ourselves down in an attempt to receive any type of affirmation that we are desired, that we are valued and appreciated. We eventually find that all of this wasted exertion is meaningless as no matter how hard we work, or attempt to produce results, we are never able to quench that craving that lies deep inside of us. No person on this earth is able to provide us with the validation that we so desperately seek. We eventually find ourselves old and worn out, with souls that are empty and desolate as we have been unable to fill them with what they truly crave.

Pretty bleak, huh? This was my life over the past forty years and is the case with the modern-day Christian as well. Even in an attempt to be a Christian, and grow closer to God, we confuse the gospel and the message of Christ with the worldly views and ideologies that we have been led to believe all of our lives. Again, our perception of who God and Jesus truly are, and what they offer us, is faulty and something that we have attempted to assimilate with what we know and understand. We as Christians see the power and saving grace of God, and the love and salvation offered through Christ, but we still feel that it is something that we have to work for. Something that we have to earn or work to deserve. Nothing could be farther from the truth.

If you have ever read through the Bible, or listened to it on audio, you can surely understand that since the beginning of life on earth man has never been able to do or accomplish anything that would make him righteous in the eyes of God. Man could not live up to The Law in the Old Testament and would always fall short. God knew this but wanted us to be with Him regardless, so He provided a way for us to be with Him, united forever. That way was the life and crucifixion of His son – or the works of Jesus Christ.

Jesus has already done all of the work for us that we need to spend eternity with God. There is nothing more that we can ever do or need to do to accomplish this.

Tetelestai – It Is Finished! The perfect work of Christ is finished, and therefore, there is nothing more needed or required by us. Jesus paid the price for our sins, released us from the bondage of Satan, and completed all of the work required for our salvation that ensures us of a never-ending relationship with God. Any attempt or effort of works in any way to try and work our way in to heaven, or into the good graces of our heavenly Father only cheapens the work of Christ, and our faith and belief in His works and whom God is.

Ephesians 2:8-10 makes it clear and evident in telling us *"For it is by grace you have been saved, through faith – and this is not from yourselves, it is the gift of God – not by works, so that no one can boast. For we are God's handiwork, created in Christ Jesus to do good works, which God prepared in advance for us to do."*

There is nothing that we can do or ever need to do for our salvation – other than turning to Christ and having faith. And even this faith is not something that we produce ourselves. This faith comes from God, through the Holy Spirit. But why then does our wonderful teacher, the Apostle Paul, tell us in the second half of that message that we were created in Christ to do good works? First, there is no work that we can do to earn our salvation. Then, we must do works.? Sounds a bit contradictory, doesn't it?

The works that Paul refers to in the second half of that passage is what we should be doing, and how we should be acting or living once we have become Christians, through faith. These works are the disciplines that we as followers of Christ must begin to impart on our lives, our mind, and our spirit. They are the works in preparing our body, our mind, our heart, and our souls for the Kingdom of Heaven and true righteousness. As Paul instructs us in Ephesians 4:22-24 - *"You were taught, with regard to your former way of life, to put off your old self, which is being corrupted by its deceitful desires; to be made new in the attitude of your minds, and to put on the new self, created to be like God in true righteousness and holiness."*

The *"putting off of our old self and putting on the new self"* is a work, or an action that we must perform, or work at, to obtain true righteousness and holiness. It is the work and constant process of renewing our minds and bodies with the ways of Christ, and removing the old sinful habits that were all that we once knew.

I understand that this may be a bit confusing to some as it was previously stated that through the crucifixion and resurrection of Christ, all of the work has been done for us – there is nothing more that we can or need to do. This is a completely true and accurate statement in regard to our salvation. Our salvation is a gift given to us by God, and God alone, and is something that we cannot earn or work to achieve on our own.

However, as was also mentioned, after we receive our salvation, the process of sanctification begins. The process of becoming holy and righteous in the eyes of God. This is where our works come in. As with our salvation, the process of sanctification cannot happen through our own doing and does require the grace and blessing of God. But in this process, we must actively choose how our body and mind will be used going forward, and we do so in the choices that we make and the works that we do, which allow us to either 'put off the old self' or remain unchanged and continue to live a life corrupted by its deceitful desires.

Some may say that this is incorrect, and that man is sinful in nature and cannot become holy or righteous. They may also say that there is nothing that we can do to achieve any level of holiness or righteousness, and that these are things that can only be given to us by God. This way of thinking is incorrect and has evolved over time as well through the distortion of Satan in our view of Christ and God.

We do have a part to play in the big picture of things. We do have work that is required of us. God never said *"Hey, don't worry about it. Just sit back, do nothing, and continue living life as you always have. I will save you and give you a free pass to my Eternal Kingdom."*

He did not do it for Moses. He did not do it for Abraham. And He didn't even do it for His only son Jesus Christ. They all had to partake in the transformation process through their own actions and works. And so do we.

Sanctification

As Christians we should now be devoted followers of Christ. And since we are followers and believers, we should strive to live more like, and act more like Christ every day. And not just every day, but every minute of every day. We do this, or these works, out of obedience, love, and faith in an attempt to honor and glorify God, our Father. We do these works because we love Him and want to please Him. We do these works because we know deep down inside that it is only through God and Jesus Christ that we will ever truly receive that affirmation and validation that we have forever longed for.

I am walking a fine line here, but these works are also the difference in the process of our sanctification, or our restoration. Once we receive our salvation through Jesus Christ, the process of sanctification begins in which we are set aside specifically for God, for His use, and for His purpose. Through this sanctification, we are being restored, or renewed, to the holy beings that we were created to be. Sanctification, or restoration, does not and will not happen if we have accepted Jesus Christ as our Savior but continue to live in and of this world and its ways.

Wow! Powerful. Say that again - Sanctification, or restoration, does not and will not happen if we have accepted Jesus Christ as our Savior but continue to live in and of this world and its ways.

Let that sink in for a moment.

The restoration of our souls, and our lives, will never happen if we continue to keep running back to our old life and the ways of this world. This restoration is the whole reason that Jesus suffered, was crucified, and died on the cross. For our salvation, and that we may be restored to the perfect image of God.

This restoration, or the works, is one of the main areas where the modern-day church has so greatly failed its followers. Most, if not all, modern day churches preach the gospel of salvation and put forth all of their efforts in to bringing others to accept Christ as their savior. And then it stops! *Congratulations –*

You are a new Christian, alive in Christ........... Next! And they move on to save others.

The church, or the body of the church for that matter, puts little to no focus, effort, or attention on the training or teaching of that new Christian in how to live a life like Jesus did. We simply lead them to Christ and tell them that their lives will be changed forever in doing so but then fail them greatly as they are left to themselves to figure it all out on their own.

This, and this alone, is the main reason why we now have a world filled with so many proclaimed Christians who don't have a clue what it truly means to be a Christian or what the life of a Christian should actually look like.

So, with all of the different stereotypes of Christians out there, and all of the people claiming to be Christians, how are we supposed to know who truly is a Christian?

Jesus tells us in Matthew 7:16 - *"By their fruits you will recognize them."*

Jesus goes on to tell us in Luke 6:43,45 - *"No good tree bears bad fruit, nor does a bad tree bear good fruit...... A good man brings good things out of the good stored up in his heart, and an evil man brings evil things out of the evil stored up in his heart. For the mouth speaks what the heart is full of."*

What is your heart stored up with? What things come from your mouth? How do you act once you leave the church on Sunday? For most of us so called Christians, we go right back to the ways of this world. We claim to be a 'good tree' while at the same time bearing bad fruit. We gossip, we slander others, we fight and do everything that we can to get one step up on everyone else – or as my way of thinking was, to just survive. We have little or no thought for others and their needs and only think of ourselves and what we want. We even do this with the people that we value the most in our lives – our spouses and our children.

The truth is that you do not have to tell anyone if you are a Christian or not, it will be clearly evident in how you act and talk. Your works, or how you act and behave, will show the fruit that you bear, and if that fruit is worth harvesting.

Do you recall my good friend Gary? The older man that I met on the golf course. Gary did not come out screaming and yelling *"Hey, I'm a Christian"*. In fact, I did not learn that Gary was a Christian until much later in our relationship. Gary did not need to boast that he was a Christian though, because he knew the words of our brother Paul and that the faith that he had was not of his own making, but that of the Holy Spirit. Gary knew that if he just honored and obeyed God, his fruit would be evident and would be worthy of harvesting. So that is what Gary did.

Gary remained faithful to Christ and ensured that his works everyday were honoring and glorifying to God. The approach and moments of teaching that Gary took with me have altered my life forever and have brought me closer to God. Had Gary come out screaming that he was a Christian, or trying to shove his Christianity down my throat, I likely would have run the other way. This type of show not only would have pushed me away but would have also been one where Gary would have been boasting in his own efforts in a vain attempt at glorifying himself.

So, what specifically are these works and how do we do them? Again, there is no straightforward answer. This is different for each and every one of us. God has a different plan for each of our lives, and therefore, the route that we take and many of the tasks or works that we do along the way will be different in all of us.

There are many things that each and every one of us should be doing though.

First and foremost, we must come to God in humble submission acknowledging that He is our Creator and has full control over our lives and everything else in this world. We must also understand and accept that not everything in this world, or that we are asked to do, is going to make sense to us at that time. We must again submit to the Father and obey – with faith. We must turn to God every day for guidance and direction, and a true desire to grow and strengthen our relationship with Him. Once we begin to do that, God will reveal to us what direction it is that He wants us to head in, and what things, or works, we are to do.

These works, however, will resemble the works and life of Jesus Christ. We should begin to live and act more like Christ did with our main focus on God. We should be loving and serving others, setting aside time to be alone with God, and practicing the disciplines that Jesus did in his everyday life. We should be giving up our old selves and putting on the new self. We should be discarding the ways of this world and living in the ways of our Father. We should be different than everyone else, distinctively different. And we should be doing everything that we do for one reason and one reason only – to honor and glorify God.

In his daily radio sermon, Dr. Charles Stanley explains perfectly what the Christian life should look like:

"When someone meets us, it should be as if they are meeting Jesus Christ."[14]

Dallas Willard so simply states - *"The overarching biblical command is to love, and the first act of love is always the giving of attention."*[15]

"The Lord says: "These people come near to me with their mouth and honor me with their lips, but their hearts are far from me. Their worship of me is based on merely human rules they have been taught..."" *Isaiah 29:13*

Chapter 16

The Battles That We Face

S ince the first days of Adam and Eve, in the Garden of Eden, we have been at war. A war which threatens our very lives and existence. A war that continues on every single day, and that every one of us is deeply entrenched in whether we may realize it or not.

This war is unlike the type of war that we, in modern times with our technologically advanced world, see play out on TV, whereas one country attacks or invades another halfway around the globe as we sit comfortably in our sofa and watch as a detached spectator. Although this modern-day war is a derivation of the one that I refer too, the war which we face every day has much greater consequences and is much more encompassing. It is the war of the spirit worlds, and the battle for our souls.

Since the days when God created man, Satan has been determined to undermine God's plans and to keep man from knowing God and growing close to God. Satan's goal is to keep every human being from knowing God, and to have ultimate control and rule over all creation.

While we have touched a bit on this subject in previous chapters, let us now dig in a little deeper, discussing the different levels of spiritual warfare and how they affect each of us and our lives. Again, I will concede that I am by no means an expert on the subject, however, the information provided shall hopefully provide a fundamental understanding of what we are up against, as well as what we can do to best defend ourselves in this war. For a more proficient understanding, I had noted a few books in previous chapters which were written by experts in this field, which give a very in-depth background and understanding of the topic. However, my goal in this chapter is to help the reader understand, in a simplistic way, and acknowledge that a war is constantly going on in our lives, and it is a war which we are deeply involved in whether we choose to believe it or not.

This war is one that is rarely mentioned or discussed in our modern-day church as it has since long been pushed aside for the more acceptable 'feel good' gospel, thus leaving Christians unaware of 'the full story', and therefore ill equipped to live the life that we are called to. It is because of this alteration in the church's mentality that nearly everyone in our society today is consequently unprepared for the battles which we face, with most being completely unaware of the root cause of life's problems and difficulties. Regardless of what our religious views or beliefs may be, we have been brought into bondage by Satan from the time we are infants, and all of us are affected by this war. And with the inadequacies of the church, even the Christian world has been led astray from God. The foundations and principles of the early church and Christianity have been devastatingly altered into methods that are more acceptable and favorable to the world.

And us, the everyday average Joes and Janes – we just don't know any better because it is what we have been taught, so we just come to accept it as reality and the way which life is supposed to be.

Accordingly, I do not find it at all surprising that some may struggle to grasp the possibility of a reality that is different than the one which we know and live in – one that is neither dealt with in our churches, nor addressed in our daily lives.

In an effort to explain and help others understand this actuality, I will use the 5 W's (plus H) principle. If you are not familiar with the 5 W's, it is a method which we all should have learned in school. The Who, What, Where, When, Why – and the How.

The 5 W's principle is a set of questions that helps one gather information on a topic and is commonly used by writers when telling a story and/or gathering information. It helps the writer to tell a complete story or convey a message that gives a more clear understanding of what is being laid out.

However, before we can begin to allow ourselves to accept the following realities, we must first have a paradigm shift in what we believe we really are. Much of our problem lies within the belief and perspective that we are human beings, or bodies, with a soul, or spirit. The actuality of our existence is antithetical to this belief, or a complete polar opposite.

We were created as spirits, who just happen to occupy an earthly body. Our spirit will live on, in one place or another, while our earthly body will eventually fail and succumb to death. We were created in the spirit world, by the spirit world, and for the spirit world. It is our spirit which has all of the desires and cravings of love, peace, joy, and happiness that our heavenly Father created us with. It is our earthly body that gives us the desires and cravings of this world that eventually lead to death.

Recent studies show that 60% of Americans believe that Satan is just a symbol of evil, and not a real living being. A cartoon character. An object that we have created to signify the evil things in life. Even more astonishing, 52% of born-again Christians do not believe that Satan is real.

The Who

Just typing in 'The Who' takes me back to the 1970's and '80's and one of the top bands of that time. Coincidentally, the drummer for *The Who* at that time was a man named Kenney Jones (If you have not noticed yet, that is my name as well). However, the band is not the WHO that we are looking for. We are referring to WHO we battle against. WHO is our enemy?

Paul answers this question perfectly in Ephesians 6:12 when he tells us that our struggle is not against mankind, but against the rulers, against the authorities, against the powers of this dark world and against the spiritual forces of evil in the heavenly realms. Let me break it down even further to make sure we completely understand – Our struggles are not against each other – they are against the spiritual forces of evil and the powers of this dark world.

We cannot defeat what we cannot define. If we do not know who our enemy is, and do not acknowledge that they are the enemy, we can never be truly prepared for the battle that lies ahead. When we do not know what to prepare for, or how to fight that battle, we will come out on the losing side every single time.

I am sure that many of you, if not all, have had the same or a similar experience in life that I have. You feel like you are making no progress at all in what you do, no matter how hard you may try. You go through your day and everything is a struggle. You just want to bang your head against a brick wall as it feels like everything, and everyone is set against you.

The predicament that we find ourselves in, once again, comes from our faulty perception of reality and who our enemy truly is. We see other people as our enemy and therefore attempt to adequately prepare ourselves for the battle with them. It is as if we are being sent to storm the beaches of Normandy in World War II, with sticks and stones as our weapons. We don't stand a chance of surviving. We don't know who our true enemy is, and therefore we are not adequately prepared for the battles that we face every single day.

We are told many times throughout the Bible by Jesus, Paul, and many others that our enemy is Satan. Satan is the father of lies and has been out to corrupt our lives since long before we were born. Satan is the fallen one, the angel cast out by God Himself.

Satan is believed to have been an Archangel, or among the highest of angels, prior to his fall. His original name was Samael, and he was the brother to Archangel Michael who is the most powerful angel in heaven, and the leader of all of the heavenly armies.

Samael was created in perfection and was full of wisdom and beauty, just as all of the other angels are. However, just as is the case with us human beings, Samael had been given free will. His pride got the better of him and he wanted to be God. He wanted to be the most high and sit on the throne. The Bible notes Samael as saying over and over again – I will, I will, as in his power being separate from God. (Sounds like all of us today as well – I will, I will)

Samael, along with one third of the other angels, which he had deceived in to believing his scheme, rebelled against God and a great war broke out. Samael was defeated by none other than his brother Michael and was then cast down from heaven along with all of the other rebellious angels.

Samael's name was then changed to Lucifer, and is also known as the father of lies, the deceiver, the accuser, the adversary, the destroyer, the devil, the evil one, the god of this world, the prince of darkness, the tempter, the thief, and the wicked one. Satan is a real being and has all the traits of one, such as a personality, feelings, emotions and intelligence. Satan appeared to Jesus in the wilderness and had lengthy conversations with Jesus at that time. Jesus was not talking to himself or some imaginary figure, He was talking to a real being.

When God placed Adam and Eve in The Garden, He gave them dominion over all of the earth, and everything within it. It was theirs to rule and control. When they sinned against God by falling to Satan's temptations, that dominion had been lost, and stolen by Satan. Satan now had the dominion, or control, over the entire world.

Satan, along with the other fallen angels he had deceived in to rebelling against God, now prowl the earth looking for souls to devour. These other fallen angels are what we now know as demons, or evil spirits. They will stop short of nothing to keep us from knowing God, and to keep us from serving God.

The war that broke out in heaven when Satan thought he could be God, had spilled over into our world. You and I were born in to and placed right in the middle of a war that has been playing out since a time prior to the creation of mankind. And since every one of us is God's creation, Satan desires to destroy and punish each and every one of us and seeks to do so every single day of our lives.

While Satan does have supernatural powers, he is still subject to the powers of God. These supernatural powers allow Satan to do many things, in many ways that we as humans cannot even imagine. However, since Satan is not God, he is not like God. Satan is not omnipotent as God is, which means having all power. He is still under the control and authority of God. Satan is not omniscient as God is, meaning that he would have full knowledge of everything, and even foreknowledge of things to come. Satan is also not omnipresent as God is, meaning that he cannot be in all places at one time. Satan can only be in one place at any given time.

However, Satan does have his army of demons who scatter about and attack us just as if it were Satan himself. Satan does still have contact with God, as is evidenced in the book of Job. While Satan does have controlling power over our world, he does not have controlling power over those who are Christians. We are able to defeat Satan and his evil forces by the power and authority given to us through Jesus Christ, and by putting on the Armor of God. This takes us back to the beginning of this chapter – the vast majority of Christians today are completely uneducated, uninformed, and unaware of the powers that they have as Christians, and how to access and utilize those powers – thanks to the modern-day church.

So, what power does Satan have? And how much power can he use against us? Satan's biggest attacks come against our minds and our thoughts. For this main reason – we are told many times throughout the Bible to guard and protect our hearts and our minds. Satan does have the power to get us to believe something or think certain thoughts as we are misled or deceived. These deceptions then lead us to doing sinful actions against ourselves, or others, which can change our lives forever, and even at times cause us to take our own lives or the lives of others. Satan does not, however, kill us or other people – he causes and creates the thoughts and deceptions that cause us to sin and do such things on our own.

Satan is limited in his powers though, as he is still under the control of God. Since we live in this world, a world under the control of Satan, we are subject to his ways and his attacks every single day. The Bible tells us that we either live by the spirit, meaning the Holy Spirit, or we live by the flesh, meaning the world and the ways of the world and flesh. If we live by the Spirit, then we are under the protection of Jesus Christ and God. If we live by the flesh, then we are under the control of Satan and his demons.

However, even if we live by the Spirit and are under the protection of Christ and God, our bodies still live in this world, a world controlled by Satan. We are therefore still subject to his attacks every single day that we are on this planet. We must remember, it is a war that is being fought – just because one may be on the 'good' side does not make them exempt from these attacks.

God does allow these attacks to happen, to some extent, which I am well aware is a major question and misunderstanding for many believers and non-believers. However, God assures us that since we are in Christ, Satan can no longer own us or have full control over us. As Christians, we belong to God.

The What

It has become a common phrase in our society today – *The battle between Good and Evil*. That is exactly what our battle is, or the struggles that we will face every day. We have also heard the saying that *while we may lose the battle, we can still win the war.*

The definition of the word *War* according to The Cambridge Dictionary is: *Any situation in which there is strong competition between opposing sides or a great fight against something harmful.*[1]

A great fight against something harmful – that is the war which we are involved in. The war between God and Satan – Good and evil – the war that has been going on since the beginning of time. It is this war which we have been positioned in to from the time we were created. It is this war which is the central theme and environment of our existence. It is this war which encompasses everything that we know, and everything that exists. It is the primary basis for all that occurs in the world that we live in. Everything else is just happenstance.

God created man in His own perfect image. Adam and Eve were perfect in every way, as was the world that they lived in. No sin, no hate, no anger, no lies or deception. Everything was beautiful and perfect. Even the animals all co-existed peacefully with each other, and with man. This was God's plan for our lives – to live a perfect, peaceful, joyful life – just as the image of God is.

Then the war began. The war, which began in the heavenly realms between God and the Archangel Samael, overflowed into the world that we know and live in when Samael was cast down from heaven in his attempt to overthrow The Kingdom, and become God himself. Samael became Lucifer, also known as Satan, and was free to roam the earth as he pleased.

The war did not end there, however. Satan believed then, and still does now, that he can defeat God and have all control over everything in existence. And since man was created by God, in God's own image, Satan began to attack man as our original purpose for existence was to serve, honor, and glorify God.

Simplistically put, we are created by God, of God, and into the army of God, as His soldiers.

The war itself is the overall, bigger picture, that has been ongoing for thousands of years. More than likely, the war will go on long after we are gone as well. However, as with any war, there are numerous battles that play out in an attempt for one side to gain a stronghold or further advance their cause in an effort to win the overall war. The war does not stop, it never has, and it never will until the return of Jesus Christ and the final defeat of Satan. Until that day comes, Satan will always be fighting this war against God and His people, in an attempt to win control over everything that exists – in an attempt to defeat God and be god himself.

These battles go on every single day, just as they have since Eve plucked the apple from the Tree of Knowledge. Satan and his demons are constantly fighting against God, and against us, for his own cause and benefit. To truly understand this and vigorously believe that it is truth, we must first acknowledge that Satan is real, and that the war itself is of much higher significance and meaning than our petty little lives are. The world does not revolve around you, me, or anyone that resides in it.

The world was not made for you, me or anyone in it. The world, as well as everything we know of it, would have and still will exist with or without us. We do not make the world go 'round, no matter how big or powerful we may think we are. We are but a speck of dust in a very tiny spot somewhere in the middle of an existence that our feeble minds will never be able to fully understand or comprehend. And although many of us think more highly of ourselves than we ought – We are not God either.

Hopefully, to some degree, we have come to grasp that this war is prelusive to our own individual existence and is for a superior reasoning than our existence. We must also know and believe that since this war is related too and directly involves the Creator of all things, the war, and each of its battles, involves everyone and everything made by the Creator, or God Himself. Therefore –

there are no innocent bystanders. We are either on one side or the other of all battles that will be fought, and of the war itself. Let me say that again as to make it perfectly clear – We are either on one side or the other of all the battles that will be fought!

Let me now explain it in a way that brings it home, into your world, in a way which we can grasp on an individual, daily level –
Every single thought, choice, action, and reaction that you make or have during every single day is one that is supportive of one side or the other.

While many others believe that there is such a war, and that God and Satan do exist, they refuse to acknowledge that they are a part of that war, or any battle in that war. They choose to believe that they can just go on living their lives, not accepting it as actuality, and that they do not need to be involved in the war or the battles. They believe that one can exist without the other and therefore choose to be a bystander believing that the war can and will go on without them, without any harm to themselves.

Nothing could be further from the truth. And those who choose this view and mentality are actually choosing to be casualties of this war and are choosing to be on the side of Satan and evil. This is exactly what Satan wants us to do – NOTHING! Satan does not want us to fight for God. He wants us to believe that we do not matter, and that if we just ignore the war and its battles, everything will work out just fine.

Well – spoiler alert – if your choice is ignorance, your fate has already been sealed. The Bible tells us clearly that we will spend an eternity in the fiery pit with Satan and his demons.

There is no middle ground people! You do not get to be a conscientious objector. It is one side or the other. Good or evil. God or Satan. The choice is ours to make, but we still must make a choice.

The Where

So where are these battles, and the war fought? The simple answer is everywhere. As God is omnipresent, has created all things, and has control over all things, the war and the battles are multidimensional. This discussion of *The Where* may become a bit profound for some, therefore, I encourage you to do some research on the topic and obtain a more in-depth knowledge to help provide a better understanding and comprehension of the matter.

The where is multidimensional - the war is fought in and on three different levels – the spiritual level, the worldly level, and the self (or individual) level.

The spiritual level, or realm, includes all of the heavens and the spirit world. It is the realm that is outside of our world as we know it. It is inhabited by the angels, demons, spirits, and God. The war is constantly ongoing in that realm just as it is in our world.

The worldly realm is one which we can relate to slightly easier. It is the world in which we live, but on a much larger scale than just our own personal lives. Think of a country, a nation, government officials and their leaders. Think of the church and all of its leaders. If Satan can attack and deceive a high-ranking leader or official, the power of Satan's attack is then multiplied as that leader is now being led to deceive the multitudes of their followers.

The self-realm, or individual realm, is our own individual lives and the battles and struggles which we face every day. Now we are hitting home. This is the level that we can relate to much more easily as it is what we face every day. The biggest problem that we have as Christians, or even non-Christians for that matter, is that for many of the reasons which we have discussed in previous chapters, we refuse to truly accept or believe that Satan exists, or that he is causing havoc in our lives every single day. Therefore, we fail recognize or acknowledge the battles and struggles that we face every day for what they truly are, or where they truly come from.

Many bad or evil things happen to us and to others around us all the time. Divorce, assaults, fights, arguments, thefts, car accidents, incest, rape, torture, the loss of a job or a loved one, a financial crisis, or even just the simple mean words that someone said to you in passing today. The list goes on and on. Our lives are crap, and it makes us feel like crap. We soon start to believe that we were not meant to have a good, meaningful life filled with joy and happiness and then begin to question God or question if God even exists.

This madness goes on in our lives day after day, and we continue to let ourselves believe that God must not care – *How could He let all of this happen if He truly were a loving God? How can He really care about me and my life when He is letting it go so badly?*

I am hoping that by now some of the pieces of the puzzle in your mind are starting to magically fit together, and just maybe that light bulb is going off in your head. Satan is real, the attacks are real, and the attacks come at us every single day – with one intention and one main purpose – To make us question the existence of and the love of God. Just as with Adam and Eve in The Garden, we too are being attacked by Satan and his demons on a daily basis with the intention of drawing us away from God.

And as we learned earlier, these attacks are not always so straight forward and evident. They seem just like a normal part of life, so we come to accept them just as that and hence fail to recognize that we are being attacked by the Father of Lies himself. Our lack of knowledge and belief in Satan and his evil forces keeps us from accepting any possibility that the happenings in and around our lives could be that of Lucifer himself.

Furthermore, we have refused to accept this reality, or even the possibility of it, due to the pressures of the world and society that we live in today. We don't want to be seen as a whacko, somebody who has lost their mind and believes in supernatural beings. We have been taught that we have to see it to believe it, and it would be pure foolish to place the blame on something or someone that we cannot directly see.

This is where the worldly battle comes in to play in our daily lives, and our personal battle. Satan has so corrupted the worldly systems, that the accepted views and beliefs on a local, regional, national, and even worldly level have become so skewed that the normal or acceptable virtues and beliefs of the past are now just ridiculous and outdated to our modern society. Little by little, bit by bit, Satan chews away at what we deem to be acceptable and good, and then gradually keeps stretching that boundary as we willingly tolerate more and more. These attacks happen every single day, in very small ways so that in and of themselves they seem insignificant and harmless.

Then one day we wake up and find that it is commonplace and increasingly acceptable in the world that we live in for a biological adult male to share the same public restroom as a six-year-old girl, at the same time. We have become apathetic to doing the things, seeing the things, and participating in the things which would have made our grandparents walk away with shame and disgust. We have just given in, bit by bit, and here we are.

All we need to do is look back twenty, thirty, forty years ago. Take television commercials for example. Thirty years ago, you would have had to buy a pornographic magazine to see a half-naked woman other than your spouse. Now we see these women every day in TV commercials on all channels, at all times of the day. And even more damaging, we let our children become exposed to it as well, as it has become acceptable and is now the new norm.

We also give our children access to the whole world, and everything in it when we give them a cell phone, many times before they are even fifteen years old. We open up a whole new world to them, making anything and everything viewable and available within seconds, not to mention allowing the entire world to become an active participant in their lives. We give them a gift out of what we see as love and kindness, failing to recognize that we have just allowed our children, at such a young age, to be corrupted and influenced with information and images that their minds and lives are not ready to handle, comprehend, or interpret.

Thirty or forty years ago, we had consequences for actions that were wrong or hurtful to others. Punishment was normal and acceptable for children, just as it was for criminals. Nowadays a person can basically do whatever they want, wherever they want, without the fear of consequences or punishment. It is accepted and we are forced into the view that this person cannot be punished as if we do so, we are then being unfair to them. The person or group that has been attacked or offended cannot seek punishment against the attacker as it would be hurtful to the one who was causing all of the hurt to others. Does that even make any sense? Crazy – but this is the world view that we have come to accept.

And how about moral standards? The Bible shows us over and over again that as Christians we are to be held to a higher standard. This should be the case as we have a higher calling, a higher purpose. Some may think this is unfair, and our new worldly view has taught us that all people should be equal and should be able to live and act out their lives and personal beliefs the way that they want to, regardless of how it may offend or affect others.

We as Christians have allowed our standards and morals to be eaten at bit by bit, giving in to the ways and thinking of the worldly in increments so small that they are unworthy of a fight. We lower ourselves and give in, each time giving up a bit more of who we are and what we once believed as these things have become the new acceptable. The modern-day church has been excellent at leading us down this path in an effort to remain relevant.

We as Christians quickly forget the calling of our brother Paul. Paul wrote the books of 1 and 2 Timothy. Paul was writing to his brother Timothy, who at that time was a young church leader. Paul wrote 1 Timothy to help Timothy better understand his duties as a new church leader.

Paul tells us in 1 Timothy 6:12 - *"Fight the good fight of faith. Take hold of the eternal life to which you were called when you made your good confession in the presence of many witnesses."*

This verse is a very popular and well used verse from Scripture. One that is not well used is the verse which precedes 6:12. In 1 Timothy 6:11 Paul says: *"But you, man of God, flee from all this, and pursue righteousness, godliness, faith, love, endurance and gentleness."* (Another great example of the 'pick-and-choose' Christian from Chapter 15)

We as Christians succumb to the worldly views and standards, and forget who we are, what we stand for, and the fight that we were called too. Paul also told us in other books of the Bible that we would be at war, and that a battle would rage on in our lives every day. Paul warned us of this and prepared us with the knowledge and weapons that we would need for this war and the battles – The Armor of God, and it's seven pieces.

We as Christians need to learn to recognize the enemy that is attacking us and then stand up and fight the battles and confront the enemy with the powers and weapons given to us through Jesus Christ.

We are at war, every single day that we are alive. Plain and simple, Satan is attacking you whether you choose to recognize it or not. From the negative thoughts and self-inflicted torture and pain that we have in our lives, to the worldwide wars and genocide happening throughout our world – Satan is more than likely behind the scenes causing the havoc and chaos.

The When

Again, the simplistic answer to *The When* is – every single minute of every single day. Satan and his demons are constantly prowling around looking for any possible way into our lives and our minds to set the trap. But again, just as with *The Who*, we fail to recognize what is actually happening, who is actually the root cause of the problem, and just chalk it all up to being a part of the depressing life that we have.

Let us consider a quick, simple scenario to start with, where the attacker, or the attack is not so obvious:

You have had a long, hard day at work and finally make it home utterly exhausted, two hours later than you normally do. The boss had been yelling at you all day demanding one thing or another. Or maybe it was that co-worker that succeeded in reaching their goal of getting on your last nerve. The know-it-all who gets everything right. The boss's favorite. Others have been pulling at you all day long as well with the demands, expectations, deadlines, and pressures. Every single outlet that you have turned to today – the news, social media posts, the gossip, the rumor mill – they are all negative and dark and leave you feeling hopeless and run down. It seems as though you have a target on your back, and the entire world had one shared objective today - to ruin your day.

You've had enough. Completely fried, frazzled, and fatigued. You just want some alone time, some peace and quiet. Just one unadulterated minute without all of the noise and chaos. You walk in the front door and your kids come charging at you like a freight train wanting this and wanting that. They demand your attention, and they need your help to fix this, or play that. They will not stop. Like hamsters on a little wheel just running and running and running, a hundred miles an hour. It's loud, it's chaotic, it is anything but peaceful. And then it happens. You can no longer take it and at the top of your lungs you shout *Just shut up and leave me alone for a minute!*

Yep, you guessed it. That is the enemy! Or at least the intended results of what the enemy has been doing all day. Not the kids, and not you. But Satan's evil workers. They have been prowling around in your life all day long pushing your buttons, getting you agitated, making things bother and irritate you. These evil spirits have been wearing you down all day just so that you would get to this point, where you are completely worn out and want nothing to do with anyone.

And when you could no longer hold back the urge to rip someone's head off, it just so happened to be in front of your children. The one's who love you more than anything.

The enemy has intentionally caused things to happen throughout your day knowing that it would wear you down, and that you would eventually break. The enemy knows you very well as they watch you and your habits all of the time. They know how hard they have to push, where they have to push, and exactly what they have to do to get you to cross that line. And they know precisely when they want you to break as well. And it just so happened that on this day, the enemy wanted you to break right in front of your kids. The enemy wanted you to take all of that anger and frustration out on the ones that you love the most. They wanted to cause separation and division among your family. They wanted to hit you where it would hurt the most.

The worst part of this whole scenario is that those same demons are still there. They don't just go away once their goal is achieved. They are right there, lurking once again, waiting for the next opening which most always comes in the aftermath of your explosion – either from you or your children. And if a door opens, which it likely will, they are ready to put the thoughts into your children's minds that you are a monster and that you never loved them to begin with. The enemy will keep attacking us, our lives, and those that are around us – as long as we keep giving them a way in.

Let us try another scenario:

Maybe the attack comes through our spouse. You notice that he or she has started to dress differently, maybe a little nicer and more appealing than usual. You begin to ponder why. Almost immediately, the thoughts pour into your head. Maybe they are having an affair. Maybe they have found someone better than me and want something new. Someone with more money, someone that is more outgoing and fun, someone who is more attractive. Maybe I am just not good enough anymore. You feed on the thoughts for some time and eventually tell yourself that you do not have to take this, you are better than this.

So, you head down to the bar for some drinks or call up the girlfriends for a gal's night out. The thoughts continue to grow, and continue to make you feel less wanted, and more worthless. You have a few drinks and then the next thought hits you...... *Why not? If they can do it, I can do it too.* You suddenly find yourself flirting with the guy or gal sitting nearby while having numerous lascivious thoughts of what it would be like to be with them instead of your spouse. Maybe you get up the nerve to act on it, maybe you don't. Either way, those thoughts have now been planted in to your mind and they will only grow deeper and stronger as you begin to question every little action that your spouse now makes.

Those thoughts were put there by the enemy because you allowed them an open door. You had the choice when first confronted with the thought to either accept it and run with it, or to take it captive and submit it to Christ. Well, you ran with it, which only opened the door more for the enemy to add on to it ever so easily.

And pouring more salt on the wound, when you get home, your spouse is all gussied up again and those thoughts start working away at you even more than before. Fortunately, you did not act on those initial thoughts at the bar and ruin your marriage, as your spouse then informs you that they did all of this for you, as they were hoping to spend some quality alone time with you.

That is exactly what we do every single day. We allow the enemy to fill our minds with evil thoughts, lies, and deceptions. With the falsehoods and self-doubt that consume us all day. It is no great surprise that we not only hate ourselves, but that we hate most everyone else as well. After all, that is the person that Satan wants us to be.

God's plan is union – Satan's plan is division, and he is at work every minute of every single day trying not only to separate us from God but to make us question God as well as everything in our lives that is true and good and is of God.

The Why

The why should be pretty evident by now. Satan wants to rule and have control over all things. Satan wants to be God, and he will fight the war, along with all of the battles, until the return of our Lord and Savior Jesus Christ when Satan will be once and for all defeated and cast out of our lives.

I know there are many other WHY questions out there as well. Why does God allow sin? Why did God even create Satan? Why does God allow Satan to do the evil things that he does? If God is all powerful and in control, why doesn't He just stop Satan from doing these things?

While I cannot answer all of these questions, I can hopefully provide a bit of perspective to some of them. The first thing that we must comprehend is that we are the creation – not the Creator. It is not ours to ask and wonder why. When God, or anyone for that matter, creates something – it is the creator's choice as to what purpose the creation will serve. The thing that was created does not get to decide what it will be or how it will live out its life. We are God's creation, and were created to serve, honor and glorify Him according to His will and His plans. Not our will, and not our plans. HIS!

God also tells us in the Bible that we will never have the ability to fully comprehend or understand all of His power, wisdom, knowledge, and plans. But He assures us that if we follow Him through Jesus Christ, that we will always be taken care of and provided for. We must have the faith and trust that our Father, our Creator, truly wants the best for His creation and that He will lead us to a life that is better than we could ever achieve or imagine on our own.

Second, we must recognize that God was not the one who brought sin into our world. We can only blame ourselves for that. Man is the one responsible for that affliction – not God. God gave us free will, the freedom to choose, and man chose to sin and turn against God. This was not what God wanted or desired, for God has always wanted us to be pure and righteous and in close union with Him. From the early days in the garden when man used that free will to make an erroneous choice, Satan and sin now had an open door to every man and woman on earth.

God was not oblivious to these possibilities though. He knew what could happen with our free will. He had just hoped that we would choose Him, just as he still does now. And even though generation after generation chose the life of self-pleasure in place of God, He still loved and desired us so much that He gave us a way out of the bondage that the self-life and sin trapped us in to. God had his very own son, Jesus Christ, sacrificed on the cross so that His perfect blood could wash away our sins and make us pure.

God also did not create sin. Yes, God created Samael (Lucifer). But God created him to be holy and righteous, just as He did with us. It was Samael in using his own free will that chose to turn against God and create sin – just as is the case with us and our lives.

And the question that stumps most all of us – If God truly is all powerful and has control over everything, why doesn't He just put an end Satan? Why does God allow Satan and evil to continue? These questions are very complex and have been answered in multiple different ways by man through his own perception and views over the years.

Simply put – It is God's story, not ours. God is the author and had written the story which we are such a small part of long before we ever came into existence. Just as is the case with the book that you are reading now. It is my book, my story. I get to decide the layout, the subject matter, the order, and what does and does not get to be included in the book. You, with your free will, get to decide whether you will follow along and buy in to the story, or if you will take alternative routes. In regard to my book, a much less complicated choice, but again just one of the innumerable choices that we must make every single day which will undeniably have an effect on the outcome of our lives.

We may never know all of the *WHY's* until that day when we are in heaven with our true Father. Until that time we just need to trust in who He is and have faith that He always wants the best for us.

The How

We have discussed in previous chapters how Satan, and sin, came into this world. Now we will consider HOW he gets into our lives.

The How is a very deep topic as well, much deeper than I have the knowledge or the space to allow for. Sticking with my simplistic approach, we will only touch on the basics of how Satan and his demons get into our lives and minds throughout our day-to-day activities and routines.

This should at a minimum give you a better understanding and perspective of the happenings going on around you, and will also hopefully encourage you to seek out more knowledge and a deeper awareness of the battles and the war that we are in.

As was explained earlier, Satan's first and primary weapons are lies and deceptions. Satan and his evil demons will make every attempt to gain an entrance in to our minds. This is where the battles are fought. Paul tells is in Romans 12:2: *"Do not conform to patterns of this world but be transformed by the renewing of your mind. Then you will be able to test and approve what God's will is – His good, pleasing and perfect will."*

The world that we live in is subject to and manipulated by the powers of Satan. Paul tells us not to conform to the patterns of this world, and in doing so would equate to us being in union with Satan. This is where matters become difficult for most of us – as we still live in this world and are confronted by its challenges and trials every single day. We are a part of this world, we associate with this world, and therefore by mere association we allow ourselves to evolve into what the world has become.

Paul knew this as he faced it as well. So, Paul then tells us to be transformed by the renewing of our minds. Paul knows that our minds are constantly bombarded with the sin, lies, and deceptions of this world every day. However, Paul is also aware that we have a choice as to what we allow in to our minds, so therefore he tells us to be transformed, or to change from our worldly ways, by renewing our minds to the ways of the Spirit.

Well, how does one renew their mind, especially those of us who have been beaten down for so long that we are unable to determine what actually is true or real. We renew our minds through the Scriptures, the Word of God, and the Holy Spirit. We allow only God's truths and promises in to our mind, so as Paul tells us, we will be able to test and approve what God's perfect will is.

A faulty perception which I had believed in my past is one that many others latch on to nowadays as well. We come to accept that the Bible and the Scriptures are no longer suitable in this day and age. The Bible, the Scriptures, the teachings which the disciples provided – just do not fit into or apply to the world that we live in today. Things have changed so much since their time, and our world has become so different now that those practices just do not and cannot be applied in modern times. We look at verses such as the one in the previous paragraph and tell ourselves that Paul would have no clue how to live in our day and age, and that the instruction which he provides us no longer has any relevance or application to our lives, or the world that we live in.

But there again, it is our perception that is flawed, and not the message. We place our main focus on this world, and how to live in it and adapt everything else to it. We make the world our primary focal point and then try to pick and choose what may or may not fit into it. The way we see reality, and the priorities that we focus on are simply backwards. The Bible, the Scriptures, and all of the disciples' teachings are never wrong. They apply just as much nowadays as they did two thousand years ago. We need to shift our focus to the Bible and Scriptures and then endeavor to make everything else fit into that understanding. We need to wholeheartedly believe that we live in the Kingdom of God, and not in this world.

There are a multitude of verses in the Bible that discuss the importance of our mind and our thoughts, as well as how we must guard them, protect them, and allow only pure and righteous thoughts in. Once we learn to control what we allow in to our minds, we quickly begin to see all of the attacks that are being made against us and those around us. Therefore, we begin with ourselves, our own minds, and learn to regulate what we allow in. And we then take every thought captive and make it obedient to Christ.

Well, that sounds silly. How does one take their thoughts and make them obedient to Christ? This is a lot simpler than it may sound, however, it does take some discipline and practice. Any thought that comes in to our mind that is not a truth of God or honoring to God – we squash it right away. We learn to immediately 'fact check' all of the information that we are taking in, or the thoughts which we are having. And if any of those thoughts, or information, are not from God and honoring to God, we send them to Jesus to let Him deal with them, and we then replace them with the truth of our Father.

We send them to Jesus to have Him deal with them for Jesus is the Ultimate Authority. Satan is the father of lies, and all lies, falsehoods, and deceptions come only through Satan and his evil spirits. While we may be able to remove these lies and deceptions from our lives, Jesus Christ is the only one who can administer judgment upon them, and the evil spirits involved in bringing those lies upon us.

Here is an example of this process, using a thought from my past which I had allowed to be planted into my mind.

When I was growing up without a father, or any parental figure for that matter, I really did not feel loved or wanted. I had come to accept and believe, through the help of Satan and his lies, that I was worthless, and that no one would ever want me or love me. I let this thought continue to grow in my mind, so much that it became my identity. That is how I saw myself, and every time something would transpire in my life, it would be viewed with that perspective, and the evil spirits would then pile on more and more confirmation, convincing me that this had to be true.

Then one day I met this amazing girl. You know her – Robin, my wife. Robin loved me for who I was. Robin saw things in me that even I did not see. But no matter how much Robin would tell me or show me that she truly loved me, I would never fully accept it or believe it. I would always reply to her that one day she would wake up and see the real me, who I really was, and would leave me just like everyone else had. I always did so in a sarcastic, jokingly way – as not to be demeaning to her – but deep down inside this had become my core belief, which I had accepted as reality, and what I perceived as the fate of all of my encounters.

Pretty stupid, huh? Why would I do this? Because I had been fed the lies and deceptions for so long that they had become my reality. That is what I truly believed, no matter what anyone else would say or do. No matter what truth was right in front of me, I would only accept the lies that I had allowed myself to believe as being the real truth.

Fortunately for me, Robin knew what the real truth was, and took no part in the thoughts, comments, or beliefs that I had. Robin could have easily jumped on board with my negative comments, and I am sure that at many times Satan was trying to get her too as well. Robin did not allow that to happen though. She would not let those thoughts and beliefs enter her mind, and she took them captive and made them obedient to Christ. She knew that God loved me, and she knew that she loved me and that my thoughts were not coming from God.

So, what did Robin do? She prayed and gave the thoughts to Christ and let Him deal with them, and she kept on loving me just as God had asked her to do.

Then one day, by the grace of God, my eyes were opened enough to be able to see that this was not really who I was. That I had been lied to all along, and that I had accepted and believed the lie as being the truth. I then went on a search to find out more about these so called 'Truths' that I had heard everyone talking about. What I found changed not only my perspective but changed my life forever. I then replaced the lies that I had been told my entire life with the Truths from God. The Truth that I used to replace this specific lie was:

"I am a child of God, who loves me unconditionally. His love for me is never-ending, and greater than I could ever imagine. And since He is my Father, I have been promised the inheritance of all His riches. My Father is the King of all kings."

The process is rather simple but does take some effort and determination as we are so conditioned to believe that those lies which we have been told are truths and are our reality. Start right now – What is one of those lies in your life that you have accepted as being true? Write it out in the spaces provided on the next page. Squash it out, send it to Jesus, and then go find a truth from our Father to replace it with.

<u>**The lie that I have always accepted as my reality is:**</u>

<u>**The truth of God that I will replace that lie with is:**</u>

"Hear us, our God, for we are despised. Turn their insults back on their own heads. Give them over as plunder in a land of captivity." Nehemiah 4:4

Chapter 17

The Warrior In You

Growing up, one of my favorite bands in the '70's and '80's was a trio from Canada. Ahhh, if you are like me, Rush comes to mind right away. While Rush is my favorite band of all time, it is not the band that I am referring to. The other trio from Canada is Triumph. Darn near as good as Rush, but not quite on the same level.

Triumph released a song in 1981 titled *Fight the Good Fight*[1]. The lyrics basically entailed our daily struggles and how we try so hard to fit in, but so often find ourselves giving up, and giving in. As with many songs that we hear over time, this song was a huge motivator for me as I am sure it was for others as well. It gave you the urge to keep fighting and to not give up. It gave you motivation to fight for what you believed. And c'mon, it had the word 'Good' in the title and verses, so it gave you the sense that doing so would be meritorious and honorable.

I still listen to Triumph today, as well as many other bands from that era. I love to listen to, and now watch, someone who has excelled greatly with a talent which they have been given. Someone who is above average at what they do. Someone who takes their skill and makes it a lifelong journey to perfect it – and not just make a bunch of noise.

Music was different back then. Just think about it for a minute. The two bands that I have just mentioned consisted of only three members. Each band member played multiple instruments. There was no lip syncing, no pausing, and nothing counterfeit about what you saw or heard. It was truly a show of excellence when you were privileged enough to see one of these bands perform live.

My all-time favorite musician is Neil Peart, the drummer for Rush. To call Neil a drummer is an insult to his talents and abilities. Neil did not just play the drums; he made them come alive in a way that no one ever had before. It was not uncommon for Neil to play in front of a live audience with more than forty different drums in his set – and to use every single one of them when doing so. Die-hard Rush fans like me referred to Neil as 'the Professor' as he was an absolute genius at his craft. If you have not had the chance to hear or see Neil play, I strongly recommend that you put this book down for a minute, get on the internet and do a search for *Neil Peart solo.*

Neil was one of the best drummers ever, even in the early days of playing with Rush. Neil could do things that others just could not. Over time, Neil came to believe that what he was doing, the way in which he was playing the drums, wasn't true and was not allowing the full, rich, vibrant sound of each drum to come out as it should. So, at the peak of his career, when he was already clearly better than anyone else, Neil decided to learn how to play the drums all over again, from scratch.

Neil spent years relearning his craft and how to play with finesse instead of just banging the sticks around. Neil could have easily gone down this rabbit hole never to play at a high level again, losing all of his talent in the search for perfection. Fortunately for us this did not happen. Neil resurfaced from this endeavor several years later and created some of his best work, and went on to give many of us live shows which we will never forget.

Neil was very much an introvert and did not like being in the public eye. Neil just wanted to be the best drummer that he could be, and he wanted to do it in a way that no one else had done it before. Neil spent his entire life fine tuning and perfecting the gift and talent that he had been given, and had no concern for what you, I, or anyone else thought about the process in which he did it. He had a goal, a purpose, and a cause that he believed in, and he was willing to risk everything he had to achieve that goal. In Neil's mind there was only one way to do things – the right way, no matter what the cost and no matter what effort was required.

Neil realized that even though he had reached a superior level as a drummer, which most all of us would have considered as being on top, the information and processes which he had learned and used to get to this level were not correct. They were faulty with numerous flaws. Neil realized that the way in which he learned to play was not allowing him to reach his true potential, and that it was actually holding him back, causing him to be something other than what he was truly created to be. Neil then set out to find the truth, and to realize the full extent of the gift that he had been given, regardless of the views and opinions of others or the world.

I let Rush drift in to my mind and I go off on a rant. I could go on for pages about the band and their history, however, Rush is better heard than read. Go listen!

Back to our other three-man band – Triumph. In 1981 they came out with the song *Fight the Good Fight*[1]. I had listened to this song hundreds of times, each one motivating me to push on and keep going. But as I aged, I began to recognize what the lyrics actually said, and how the lies that we are fed by Satan can and do come at us from any direction, many times so innocently and unassumingly. We sing these songs, even if only in our minds, over and over again repeating the words that they contain. We are basically declaring to ourselves that the words are truth, and we then come to believe them as such due to the repetitiveness. This is called the Illusory-truth effect. If we hear something over and over again, we begin to believe it is truth, even if it is not.

One part of the song in *Fight the Good Fight* says:
All your life you've been waiting for your chance
Where you'll fit into the plan
But you're the master of your own destiny
So give and take the best that you can[1]

Then it hit me – *You're the master of your own destiny* – I had essentially programmed myself to accept that my life was in my own hands. That if I wanted anything, I had to go get it or take it. That if I was a success, it was to my credit, and if I failed, there was only myself to blame. A simple little line in a catchy song that in and of itself seems harmless, and in the overview of the song seems uplifting. However, it is the little things like this that Satan and his evil spirits cause to be put into our lives and minds every single day in an effort to deceive us in to believing a false reality. I believed it too, for the longest time. That lie has now been squashed and replaced as well.

Every single day of our lives, and for many of us, every moment that fills our days, we are constantly being attacked by the evil one in an attempt to pull us away from God, from our true reason for being created, and from the undefinable joy and glory that our Father wants to give us. Over time, we come to accept this struggle as the norm, as our reality, as the cards that we have been dealt. It happens so often that for many of us we aren't even aware that another way of life exists. We don't realize that there are other choices, and that each one of us has the full power and ability to make those choices, and those changes, no matter how dismal or bleak our circumstances may be.

For others, while they may realize that there is more out there, it is the simple thought of change that scares the hell out of them. Our minds do not like change. We like consistency and routines. We like comfortable. A change would require strenuous thought, extensive effort and way too much work – and we are all just too tired and worn down already from the life that we live now. We don't want to have to put forth any effort, which would only exhaust us even more. So, we stay right where we are at, even though it may be that miserable existence that we despise so much. It's easy, it's convenient, and we know how to make it work – at least to some extent.

This is right where Satan wants us – tired, worn out, beaten down, and to weary to stand up and fight. Too fatigued to make our life better, or to realize our true potential. Satan has already won the battle and the war in this case, and you my friend have already been defeated.

Why do you think that each and every day of our existence is a complete struggle? Why do you think that every day when you come home from work, and being in the world, you are completely worn out? This is not God – This is not the life that God had planned for us, or that He desires for us to live. God is joy, happiness, peace, comfort, and assurance. God is love, union with your neighbors and fellow mankind, and all things that are good. God is adventure and fun. God is abundant and overflowing with all of his riches and promises – when we abide within Him.

It is Satan that fills our lives with struggles, challenges, confrontations, arguments, and hassles; and who then overloads us with work and problems which leave us with not an ounce of energy, to the point where we just want to go home and veg out in front of the TV all night as we have nothing left in the tank. Our souls are drained of every ounce of energy and joy that we may have possibly had at the start of the day. All with the goal of keeping us completely run down and overloaded, just so that we do not have anything left to give to God, or anyone else.

The Cause

Most all of us meander through life in this beaten down stage with nothing left within ourselves to give. And those of us that are Christians have been reduced to a state where we have become purely spiritual consumers. We have nothing left to give either. We merely take - or at least try too. Our souls have been so depleted of any joy and contentment that we may have once had, and that we were created to be filled with, that all we can muster up the strength for is to take. We are aware of that complete emptiness which we possess and know deep down inside that there is something missing, something that we desperately crave and desire, but yet we have no clue what it is or how to fill that emptiness.

We routinely go about our days trying to grab any slice of happiness that we may find, and even involuntarily begin to sacrifice our beliefs for just a few moments of blissfulness. This bliss and momentary happiness of course do not satisfy what we truly hunger for, so we keep searching, and keep sacrificing ourselves and what is left of our souls.

There are several causes to this modern-day plague which most all of us call our existence. The first being our perspective and how we truly view or perceive our reality and our existence. Going back a couple chapters, we have an ill-conceived view of God, who He truly is, and how we perceive our relationship with God. Many of us, while we may believe in God, do not live our lives to serve God or to be in a direct relationship with Him.

We may believe that God is there and does have control over all things, however, we just want to reap the rewards of His control and powers, so we simply try to be good and do the right things. Much of this is a result of the on-demand, performance-based society which we have been indoctrinated in to. We have been taught that if we perform a certain outward action, a certain reward or result will follow. We are very much result oriented and have been trained to place a certain value on everything in our lives based upon the outcome or result.

We Are Dogs

Have you ever had a dog? And if so, have you ever tried to train that dog to be obedient, and follow commands or hand signs? If you have, you know that when training dogs it is common to use treats as a reward for the dog when they have successfully done what it is that you are attempting to teach them. This is known as reward based training, or operant conditioning. The dog is conditioned, or trained, to understand that if he wants the treat, all that he has to do is repeat what he just did that got him the treat the first time. The dogs brain quickly associates the treat, or the reward, with the command and activity that he just performed. And from that point on when the dog hears or sees the command, his brain quickly links it to the treat and the process which he must go through to obtain the treat. The dog wants the treat, and the dog will do what is required to get the treat.

We are all so much just like the dog! We think the same way, and our brains are wired the same way as well. We want the treat. We want joy and happiness. We want the fun things in life. The quandary that we face is that in our effort and search for those moments of satisfaction we most always put too much focus on the treat, or the reward, out of simple self-gratification in an attempt to grab any little part of happiness that we can find. We become more focused on pleasing ourselves instead of pleasing God, and we find it very easy to do so as we live in a world that promotes and encourages self-pleasure and satisfaction. We put very little focus or concern on the actual task that we are called to do, focusing solely on the reward or the treat, so much to the point where we have become willing to do almost anything to get the treat, as the task no longer carries any weight or value.

Our souls have become so drained that when we are able to experience that one little thing that gives us joy, or the treat, we desperately crave more. So, we keep doing that which gives us the treat, increasing our focus and efforts on the output which offers us the treat in hopes that we may get an even bigger treat, or reward, but with very little concern for any consequences that may come with the activity that leads us to the treat. We as human beings have taught ourselves to seek out the treat first, and then do whatever we must to obtain it, eventually leaving us willing to do anything.

The dog, however, is smart. Even the dog knows that the treat does not come first. The dog knows that unless a certain action is performed, there is no treat. The dog, who is inferior to mankind, also has one other indelible belief without question and never wavers from that knowledge. The dog knows whom his master is. The dog will always follow his master and will always trust that his master will lead him and guide him in the right direction. The dog knows that the true comfort and love that he desires comes only from his master. The dog knows that his master is his protector and provider as well, and the dog remains loyal and obedient throughout his entire life.

Maybe we are not like the dog after all.

So where are we going with all of this dog talk? Well, unlike the dog, we let every little thing in our day bother us, beat us down, and just plain wear us out. We get distracted by all of the things in this world, allowing them to pull us away from our Master. When that happens, our souls begin to get depleted, and we begin to look elsewhere for what we are truly craving. Then, before you know it, we have strayed so far away from our Master that we no longer have someone to replenish our souls with what we truly need. We are left to ourselves, trying to grab any little piece of joy and happiness that we can, wherever we can, from whomever we can.

This was not God's plan for our lives, and He surely did not want us living a life of emptiness. God tells us directly in the Bible that:

Jeremiah 29:11 - *"For I know the plans I have for you," declares the Lord, "Plans to prosper you and not to harm you, plans to give you hope and a future."*

Psalm 32:8 - *"I will instruct you and teach you in the way you should go; I will counsel you with my eye upon you."*

Psalm 23:1-3 - *"The Lord is my shepherd, I lack nothing. He makes me lie down in green pastures, he leads me beside quiet waters, he refreshes my soul. He guides me along the right paths for his name's sake."*

When we have the constant contact and union with God our souls are recharged. We are at peace, not only with ourselves, but the chaotic world around us as well. We also learn to become more aware of the direction which God is leading us in, and we can trust that He will lead us beside quiet waters, refresh our souls, and guide us along the right path. We know whom our Master is, and we do not want to stray from Him as we are aware that He is the one who provides for all of our needs.

We also begin to learn the purpose which God created us for. Each and every one of us has a God given purpose in life, and each are different, to some extent at least. God has a plan and a purpose for every one of us in advancing His kingdom and glorifying His namesake.

While the plan and the purpose for each of us may be different, there are many things that God has given all of us the calling and the command to do. One of those expectations is to fight. Yes – to fight! God has made each and every one of us a warrior. A great and mighty warrior in the army of God.

2 Timothy 1:7 - *"For the spirit God gave us does not make us timid, but gives us power, love and self discipline."*

Nehemiah 4:14 - *".......Don't be afraid of them. Remember the Lord, who is great and awesome, and fight for your families, your sons and your daughters, your wives and your homes."*

Joshua 1:9 - *"Have I not commanded you? Be strong and courageous. Do not be afraid; do not be discouraged, for the Lord your God will be with you wherever you go."*

And there are countless other verses in Scripture that tell us we are warriors, soldiers, and that we must put on the armor and fight. Now, here is the key takeaway:

A warrior without a noble cause to fight for, will find the wrong things to fight against.

The Warrior's Call

What exactly is a warrior? The *You Version Bible plan The Heart of a Warrior*[2] defines a warrior as:

"A Warrior is a Beloved Son with a settled heart who is then trained and equipped to engage in the life-and-death battles that are continually going on in him and all around him.

Being a Warrior involves more than force. It goes deeper: there is a deftness to it, an intuitiveness, and a gracefulness."[2]

A warrior confidently knows who he is, what he stands for, who and what he fights for, and is willing to defend all of these beliefs at all costs.

We must fight, and we must have a noble cause to fight for. Paul teaches us many times throughout Scripture what we must fight for, and whom we are fighting against. Me – I first and foremost fight for my mind, my heart and my soul, to keep them pure with the words and direction of God. Secondly, I fight for my wife and my children. To protect them and guard them from the evils and sins of this world. This comes naturally to most fathers to some extent, more so in a worldly way. As parents, it is intrinsic for us to protect our kids from something which may cause them harm. However, when we do not have a cause that we are fighting for, or against, we have fundamentally reduced ourselves to just being bodyguards for our children. We try to keep them from getting injured, or at times protect them from the bully down the street. But then we let them spend hours alone on the computer in another room with no supervision and let them watch endless hours of cable television just so we don't have to babysit them.

Again – we have our focus in the wrong place. The enemy is already inside your house, and he is running rampant having been given complete access to your kids. We have become more concerned with the bully down the street that may or may not give your kid a black eye (which will heal in a week, by the way), when we should be focused on the corruption, the images, the agendas, the lies, and the predators that are allowed access to our children in the safety of our own homes (which will cause lifelong, immeasurable damage).

We must stand up and fight. Fight for what you love.

Stop fighting for the things that you want and start fighting for the things that you don't want to lose!

When we are in close union with God and Jesus, we will know what we are to fight for. All of us must fight for our families and the family unit as a whole. But what else should we fight for? God will let you know which fights are yours, and which ones to simply walk away from. Not all of the battles that we encounter every day are ours to get involved in. Those battles which are not ours to fight are how we come to lose all of our energy and our souls. Save your energy for the battles that matter most, and the battles that God tells you are yours to fight.

We must understand that individually we cannot solve all of the world's problems, and we also cannot win all of the world's battles. Stay in your own lane and focus on the battles that God has given you to fight. God will give you certain battles to fight as you have certain skills and abilities that others do not have which will enable you to win that battle, through God. You were not given those other battles because you do not possess the certain skills or abilities that someone else has which are needed in that battle. We each have our own purpose and plan.

Another important factor that we must always take into account is that as we become more in union with God and Christ our confidence and the assurance of who we are will soar. Our worries and struggles, at least from a worldly perspective, begin to fade away. We may find it very easy at times to feel and believe that whatever challenges we may face, we can handle on our own with our newly obtained powers and strengths.

The more that we attempt to remove sin and the ways of the world from our lives, the stronger the pulls will be from Satan as he does not want us choosing God. There will be many times when the attack comes at us, and with our new understanding we are now able to recognize that attack for what it truly is and also feel more prepared and equipped to face that attack – on our own. This is commonplace for many of us as we still hold tightly to our self-life and our inherent belief that we can and must handle everything on our own.

We must be overly cautious in not allowing our new knowledge and confidence to turn into arrogance or cockiness. The powers, the strength, the position that we now hold in Christ and the Kingdom of God are not something that are of us, from us, or within us. We are but a speck of dust without Christ, and do not stand a chance in any such fight unless Jesus is in that fight with us.

I will get into the whole 'conversations with God' bit in the next chapter, and how we know when God is telling us to do, or not to do something. But as explained in earlier chapters, when God is speaking to you, you will know. This becomes more evident and apparent as you become more in union with God and Jesus. And as you do, God will let you know which battles are yours to fight – and which battles to walk away from.

Take my wife Robin, for example. God has placed it upon her to stand up and fight for unborn babies, as well as the elderly. She has an undefinable passion when it comes to these two areas. Robin is not the kind of person you would picture when you say the word warrior. She is a girly-girl. She likes to get her hair done up every month or so. She gets her nails done every couple weeks. And just the mention of yard work causes her to break out in a rash. However, it does not matter who you are, where you are at, or if she knows you or not – if the word abortion comes up, you had better stand back as this woman becomes the angry fire of God which is about to be poured out upon everything around her within seconds. I love her passion, I love her desire, and I love her unwavering commitment to obey the Lords calling.

Entitlement

Another paradigm shift that we must coerce ourselves in to accepting to become true warriors is that of gratitude versus entitlement. The world that we live in has again taught us a detrimental lesson that opposes the meaning of our very existence. We are led to believe that we are owed something – from everyone and every situation. We are led to believe that our mere existence and presence is something that others should have to pay a cost for. This belief causes us to elevate our opinion and view of ourselves, while diminishing the view and value of others.

The legitimate view that we should possess is that we are owed nothing – nothing at all. Without Christ, we are nothing and we are dead. We are no better, or more valued, than anyone else and left to ourselves we are dead in our sins. However, in Christ and as followers of Christ, we are made anew and are washed clean by His blood.

Jesus teaches us how to follow Him, as well as what our lives should look like once we do so.

James 4:10 tells us *"Humble yourselves before the Lord, and He will lift you up."*

James 4:7 says *"Submit yourselves, then, to God. Resist the devil, and he will flee from you."*

And Job 22:21 tells us *"Submit to God and be at peace with Him; in this way prosperity will come to you."*

Our entitlement attitude comes from the belief that we are higher and greater than others and therefore should be owed something. Again, our perspective and focus is causing us to view our reality inversely. Instead of looking downward upon others and expecting some type of praise from them – we should be looking upwards to God with never ending gratitude and thanks for what we have been given. We should be quick to remember that you, I, and everyone else were made by the Creator, for the Creator. We should be focused on and grateful for everything that we do have, and which God has been pleased to provide us with. We need to modify our viewpoint from one of entitlement, to one of gratitude and begin to give honor and praise to our Creator instead of trying to continually prove that we are better than everyone else.

In many ways we have become much like the Pharisees of the Old Testament. A Pharisee was one who was a member of a Jewish sect that followed certain rites and ceremonies according to the written law and the traditions of their forefathers. The Pharisees believed that through knowledge and their own works in following these laws, they could be righteous. A Pharisee would be what we today call 'book smart'. They knew the Bible inside and out and lived their lives with this knowledge as the supporting foundation for all of their beliefs. The Pharisees believed that they were better than everyone else, as they knew more than everyone else, and followed God's Law to the letter. The Pharisee's knew what to do and how to act – outwardly. They did not however allow God's word into their hearts, and did not have a personal relationship with God.

I was reading the Bible the other day and came across John 6:39-40. I most always read the NIV version of the Bible, but for some reason on this day I was taken to the MSG (Message) version. I had read this verse before but seeing it in this new context really opened my eyes. Right away I said to myself *That is us (the modern-day Christian) in a nutshell!*

Jesus is speaking to us in John 6:39-40. The MSG version says – *"You have your heads in your Bibles constantly because you think you'll find eternal life there. But you miss the forest for the trees. These Scriptures are all about me! And I am, standing right before you, and you aren't willing to receive from me the life you say you want."*

This is precisely what so many of us Christians do, who claim to truly desire to follow Christ. We want to be good and look good in God's eyes, and we want to please Him so we try to learn as much as we can about His word and how we should live our lives. We become book smart – and we hold that knowledge as a power and a belief that we have grown closer to God. However, we do not know God – we simply know about God.

We do not have that personal relationship with God, or Jesus. That personal relationship that cannot be found in the Bible, or any book for that matter. That personal relationship that can only be found in Christ, through constant communication, union, and prayer.

And Jesus tells us – *I'm standing right here in front of you, let's talk.* The secret, the answer, the solution that we keep searching everywhere else for is standing right in front of us every day, everywhere we go. All we have to do is stop and turn to Him.

A true warrior knows who he/she is – nothing more, nothing less. He/She is honest with their self-perception, is unpretentious in their qualities and attributes, all the while being confident in their abilities that have been taught and given to them from a higher power.

David tells us in Psalms 8 that we were made slightly lower than God, and that God has crowned us with glory and honor, made to have dominion over the works of His hands. Does that sound like your life? Do you live a life that is one step below God? Can you feel that glory and honor? Have you taken dominion over all things created, or have they taken dominion over you?

Regardless of our own individual call to battle, we all must stop being passive Christians. You are either a Christian – or you are not. If you say that you are, then stop being so timid and afraid – and stand up and fight. Fight for your family. Fight for your friends. Fight for your co-workers. Fight for your neighbors. Fight for the Kingdom of God. Every one of us needs help in the fight against the enemy, and you are just the help that someone needs. They are waiting -why are you?

"Fight the good fight of the faith. Take hold of the eternal life to which you were called when you made your good confession in the presence of many witnesses." 1 Timothy 6:12

Chapter 18

Prayers

It is May of 2024 as I begin this chapter. In the Midwest of the United States that means springtime is upon us. Most parts of the country are beginning to make their escape from the winter months, and the long, cold, dreary days and nights. The sun begins to hang in the sky just a bit longer each day. The temperatures continue to gradually rise. And life begins to reemerge from hibernation. This is my favorite time of the year, for several reasons. Mostly due to the fact that everything around us seems to come alive and manifest a complete change of attitude with the warmer temperatures.

The birds are now chirping incessantly (even though I cannot say that I am crazy about that), the landscape for as far as one can see is being restored to life again with bright vibrant colors, and even people seem to be a bit nicer, if only for a brief period of time.

The Job

With my job, springtime means one thing. You had better be rested and ready, as it is time to go to work. Spring in the United States brings many severe storms as old man winter fights with his last bit of energy against the incoming season that wants to take his place. And with these severe storms come torrential rains, large hail and many tornadoes. This year has been no exception, and this year spring has not only arrived earlier than usual but has decided to reveal itself with aggression.

During the month of May alone, the United States had over 6100 severe storm reports, with 475 of those being tornadoes. Twenty-Five of the contiguous Forty-Eight states have had at least one tornado so far this year which is extremely unusual in itself. There have also been multiple storms which have produced hail stones in excess of five inches in diameter, which is a rare occurrence as well. There is a very good chance that if you live in the Midwest, you have either been directly affected by one of these storms or know someone who has. For me and my family, several of these storms hit close to home, almost too close. And for me, this year's storm season began on the afternoon of Friday April 26th.

With my job I always pay close attention to the weather, especially during the spring and summer months. I have a bit more knowledge about meteorology than the average Joe as it was one of the courses that I studied during Flight School. I am by no means an expert meteorologist, but I do possess an understanding greater than just being able to look at a radar and say that it is going to rain. My daughter has taught herself to use my ability as a crutch, or an excuse that allows her to be oblivious when it comes to watching the weather. She is well aware that if bad weather is coming way, dad will call her ahead of time and let her know.

Katelynn, my daughter, lives in Oklahoma and works in the town of Norman, which is a suburb on the south side of Oklahoma City. If the Midwest were a target for tornadoes, Norman would be the bullseye. The Oklahoma City metropolitan area is well known for its large, strong tornadoes and holds claim to the largest tornado on record in the El Reno area at two and a half miles wide, as well as the strongest tornado on record in the Moore-Norman area with a wind speed of 324mph.[1]

Katelynn tells me of days when she has been at work and everyone else is panicking about potential storms forecast for later that day, all while she remains calm and collective. She says that her co-workers ask her how she can be so unconcerned. She looks them in the eyes, and with a convicting voice she replies *It's not going to storm today. If it was going to, my dad would have called me by now!* And then she goes about her day as usual.

On April 26th, that is exactly what I had to do, albeit with my two oldest boys and not my daughter. Robin and I had moved south to the warmer climates and currently reside in Texas, but our two oldest boys still live in the Omaha area. I knew a very strong front was blowing through the upper Midwest on that day, and there would be severe storms somewhere along the central plains. The only question was where these storms would begin to fire up. By mid-afternoon the line of storms began to explode over central Nebraska and then progressed eastward. By the time they neared the Lincoln, Nebraska area multiple spotters and Storm Chasers were following these cells as they had a very strong potential to produce tornadoes. I had been periodically following the coverage of these storms on The Weather Channel as well as I knew it would likely impact my boys in one way or another.

As the line moved through Lincoln and came out on the east side, tornado warnings began to go off. The radar signature showed the clear signature of a tornadic supercell, but nothing had been spotted on the ground....... yet. Then out of nowhere, one of the Storm Chasers following the line who just happened to be sending his live camera feed directly to The Weather Channel got the first glimpse of the monster as it crossed over a set of train tracks and flipped several box cars on the northeast corner of town.

Lincoln is roughly forty-five miles from Omaha, and with the exception of some very small rural towns, it is mostly farmland. Most tornadoes do not last that long or travel that distance either. On this day, and with this storm, things would be different though. The tornado coming out of the Lincoln area only intensified as it drew closer to Omaha. And as it did I began to pay real close attention and instinctively went into 'DAD' mode.

'Dad' mode is a superpower which only dads have, and only dads can and will understand. It is not a power that we have the ability to summon on demand though, it just happens. As Dads, it is our natural instinct to preserve and protect our family (not to incline that mothers don't). When we feel one of them is in danger, Dad mode kicks in. We then become hyper focused on the one needing protection and tend to block out everything else around us. The adrenaline that our body creates can increase tenfold, and in many cases, we have strength, power, and focus like never before. Our brains seem to operate at a much higher level as well giving us the ability to process information, analyze situations, and make rational decisions at speeds much faster than normal. In a sense, we are transformed into something much greater than we were, with powers that are not evident during our normal existence.

By now, The Weather Channel is covering this one storm exclusively as it has become a major tornado and is heading into a major city. The tornado was tracking towards the very western suburbs of Omaha, which due to the population growth of the city over the past ten years, was now sprawling with homes and apartments. And one of those newer homes belonged to our oldest son, Josh, and his family.

I was at home, six hundred miles away, watching everything unfold live on TV. I could tell by the radar image, and the path that the tornado had traveled, that it was now time to take action. Our second son, Kris, lives a little more to the east, towards the middle of Omaha, and it did not appear that he would be in any immediate danger, or in the direct path of the tornado. So, I gave him over to Robin and told her to call him to make sure that he was aware of what was unfolding and to stay out of West Omaha.

I then picked up my cell phone and called Josh. Josh works from home as most people do in these post COVID days – however, Josh actually does work. My first question to Josh was *Where are the girls?* Josh is married to his Highschool sweetheart, Ryan, and they have two little girls. Josh informed me that Ryan was at work. I knew Ryan worked on the far east side of town, so she was safe. He then said that the girls were at school. I had no idea what school they went to, so I asked where the school was. He told me, and I figured they would be okay as well, and not likely to be in the path either.

Josh, as well as my other children, have never been through or close to an actual tornado at any point in their lives. They did grow up in the Midwest though, so making the occasional trip to the basement when the sirens went off was not unusual and had become a normal part of their life. However, they had never seen the death and destruction that one can cause. And just as most of us do with many aspects of our life, they had never considered the full outcome or the extent of the consequences of the road which they were heading down. They had not contemplated the potential possibilities of what life may be like when they come up out of that basement. To them, and many others as well, it is just a safety precaution that you take when the sirens go off. They know what to do when one is coming - but they have no clue what to do, or how to prepare themselves for what happens afterwards.

Such is the case with most of us in this day and age. We have become reactive in character, and most always we only take action when something or someone forces us to do so. Rarely do we ever put much forethought into all of the encompassing factors of an event or action, which only leaves us unprepared for the aftermath and the wreckage that ensues.

Over the course of my life, I have seen the devastating results and the pure shock of many people who have taken a direct hit from a tornado, and survived, but were in no way prepared for what to do after that event. I have seen people buried alive by the debris and rubble as they took shelter underground. And I have seen the death of many from these vicious storms as well. I have also had several up close and personal experiences with tornadoes and actually lived within six blocks of the last major tornado that went through Omaha in 1975, which was an EF4 that ripped through the middle of town. In all of my years I would guess that I have seen over thirty tornadoes up close and in person.

I have also seen the unexplainable power that these things have, possessing the ability to turn massive buildings into a pile of sticks, while at the same time leaving much smaller and lighter objects completely untouched. In the spring of 2011, the Midwest was experiencing another massive tornado outbreak as well, with what seemed to be a large devastating tornado almost every other day. I have many stories from that year but there is one specific event which I do not believe I will ever forget.

A large EF4 tornado had just tore through the western side of Oklahoma City and hit the town of El Reno, Oklahoma. I had been to El Reno before as it is frequently in the path of tornadoes. This particular storm was different though. It was huge, and it would take several lives including two small children that lived in the neighborhood where I was working claims. The memory that I have of that event is not one of destruction and devastation though. It is one of the sovereign hand of God, in all things, and the reminder that He works in all things for the good of His will. It was also a startling awareness to me of the fact that the things that we most always see in a situation, or how we perceive them to be, are most always not the true reality of what is actually playing out in the bigger picture of life.

One of the claims that I had received on that deployment was for an insured whose house had taken a direct hit and had been completely destroyed. In fact, the entire subdivision had been leveled and not one home was left standing. When I arrived at the home, I noticed that the only thing left standing upright was the stone chimney which had been erected in the middle portion of the home. There were a couple interior walls that were partially standing, but only because they were in some form or another attached to the chimney wall. The roof and all of the other exterior and interior walls were gone. The cars had been lifted out of the garage as well and had been thrown hundreds of yards away. Most all of the personal items in the home were scattered about the neighborhood too. This was normal, this was my job, and this was what I dealt with on a daily basis. My job was to try and figure out what the house had looked like prior to the storm, down to every single outlet and piece of trim, and then attempt to rebuild it on paper so that I could determine how much it would cost to rebuild it in real life.

As I began my walk around the debris piles and sifted through the items that I was able make sense of, I made my way toward the rear of the home. I began to make out what appeared to be the Master Bedroom. The bed in that room had been mostly destroyed and only portions of it were left. All of the clothing from the closets had been ripped out and scattered. Three of the four walls were almost completely gone, and what did remain in the room had been left in a huge pile now covered by insulation and tree debris. The room was almost unrecognizable – with the exception of one thing.

There was a small nightstand next to where the bed was which had been left untouched and unmoved. On that nightstand laid a Bible which was open. The Bible had not been damaged, it was not covered in dirt or debris as everything else was, and it appeared as though it had been placed there after the storm went through, which I knew was not the case. The distinguishable difference in the appearance of the Bible made it stand out and create confusion in one's mind being unable to integrate that small, untouched table and Bible into the destruction and chaos of the rest of the home and the surrounding neighborhood.

I made my way over to the Bible for a closer look, and what I saw I will never forget.

The Bible was opened to the New Testament, and the book of John. John 3:16 - *"For God so loved the world that He gave His only begotten Son that whosoever believes in Him shall not perish but have everlasting life".*

Back to Omaha

I then brought Josh up to speed on what was happening and where the tornado was as it was heading into Omaha, and what its likely path was. Josh and his wife are Millennials, so they do not have cable television. Why? I don't know. It's a Millennial thing. Heck, I'm not sure if they have a TV at all.

I then told Josh in a slow, calm manner...... *Here is what you need you to do. First, you have time, so don't panic. I want you to go get your wallet, get your car keys, put on a pair of jeans and some rubber soled boots or shoes. Then come back to the phone and I will tell you what to do next.*

Josh put the phone down and was gone for a couple minutes before he returned. I told him again...... *Relax, you are going to be fine, and we don't need to hurry. Now, go grab a jacket, a flashlight, a pocketknife and some band-aids.* He went off and did that and came back quickly. *Okay, last thing... if you have all of your social security cards and birth certificates in one convenient place, go grab them really quick – if not, don't worry about it. Then grab a blanket and come right back.*

Josh went and grabbed the blanket and was back before you know it. Fortunately for us we had plenty of advance notice with this tornado, which is not usually the case for most people. Then I told Josh.... *I want you to go downstairs into the basement, get underneath the area where the stairs are, cover up with the blanket and do not come out until you hear from me again. And don't worry, you are going to be fine, and you will survive no matter what happens.*

Another good thing for Robin and I is that Josh has always been our nonchalant child. Nothing ever bothers Josh, and he never gets too riled up about anything. He always has the ability to take everything in stride – just as he did on this day.

About half an hour later, Josh and I were back on the phone as he was coming up out of the basement. The tornado had passed close by his home, but not close enough to cause any damage or harm. Hundreds of homes were completely destroyed that day in Omaha and the surrounding areas and miraculously no one was killed. I was grateful that I could be there for my son to not only help keep him safe, but to comfort him as well knowing that he was not alone. We would later come to learn that some friends of ours were in the path and had lost everything that they owned. Little did we know that this was only the beginning of the monsters which we would face over the next month.

You have probably already ascertained what happens next. Yep – the following day I received a phone call from my employer and was deployed to Omaha for work. I jumped at the chance. I am not real fond of Omaha, but my two boys and grandkids are there. If I have to work, it might as well be in a place where I can be around my family. So, I packed up my equipment and supplies and headed off to Omaha.

A few weeks later Robin had come to Omaha to visit me. While I say visit *ME*, I know that her true motivator for coming was to see the grandkids. This, however, left our youngest son, Dylan, home alone, in Texas. Dylan was about to turn eighteen and is quite capable of taking care of himself. However, he is still our 'baby', our youngest.

Robin had been in Omaha for a couple nights at this point. The weather in the Midwest was going crazy again and between tornado warnings in Omaha, severe weather in Oklahoma (where our daughter lives), and severe weather back at home, I believe Robin and I went a full week with being woken up in the middle of the night for one storm warning or another. And the final night would turn out to be our biggest challenge.

That evening, Texas had a chance for severe storms, but they were supposed to be clear of any risk by 8pm. I had been watching the radar all day just to see if anything was headed towards Dylan and our home. Nope, nothing at all. Robin and I had been over at Josh's house grilling out with the family. I had to work the next morning and needed a shower before we went to bed so I left Josh's place before Robin did and headed back to the place where we were staying.

Before I got into the shower I decided to take one last look at the radar. There was one little thunderstorm located just west of Gainesville, Texas, or about thirty miles west of our house. The storm had been moving from southwest to northeast and did not appear to be a threat as it would be well north of our place by the time it made its way east. So, I jumped in the shower and shortly after Robin made it back and we went to bed.

Our home in Texas is in a rural area that has little to no tornado siren coverage. However, the county that we live in offers a service called 'Code Red'. If you register for this service, at no cost, and enter your cell phone number, anytime there is any type of severe weather alert the system will automatically send you a text message, as well as call you with an automated message of what the warning is for. This is very handy for me as it keeps me informed of what is going on at home even when I am out of town working.

Before Robin and I managed to fall asleep, we were startled by the Code Red alert going off on both of our cell phones. The warning was a Tornado Warning, and our youngest son was home alone. My first response was to gather information – I pulled the radar up, and to my surprise, there was nothing near our house. How can there be a tornado warning when there is not even a thunderstorm anywhere in the vicinity? Then I moved the radar image a bit further west. My jaw dropped immediately, and I believe what I said was *Holy Crap! That is a tornado!* The radar signature was unmistakable. I immediately got up and flipped on The Weather Channel to see if they had any information. Sure enough, they were covering it.

Robin immediately called Dylan on the phone to let him know what was going on. Dylan told her that he had just left the house and was taking his girlfriend home. Right away I asked him exactly where he was at and began to calculate if he would be able to make it back home in time before the storm hit. I had an underground shelter installed at our new property when we moved, which most people in North Texas do not have. I knew it would be the safest place for him, no matter what. I quickly realized that he would not be able to make it, or at least it would be risky and reckless to even try. Dylan's girlfriend lived down in the DFW metro area, and at the time he was driving south, away from the storm.

Robin and I ran through all of the possibilities of where he could go to hang out as it would likely be at least an hour or so before he would be able to head back north again and get home. There were no options. The only choice was for him to stay at his girlfriend's house until it had passed.

Robin and I sat and watched the TV coverage and became frustrated with Dylan because he had allowed his girlfriend to stay over so late, and he should not have been out driving her home at this time of night regardless.

As we watched the TV coverage the tornado tore through a small town called Valley View. We would later learn that seven people died there that night. The tornado proceeded to head directly towards our home while destroying many others on its way. Shortly before the tornado made it to our home it turned southward and died out. A short time later we called Dylan and told him that it was okay to head home now.

You are probably looking back at the title of this chapter and might be a bit confused right now. You may be wondering how tornadoes have anything to do with prayers. These are but a few of my experiences in which God has shown me a several key factors about prayer. Let me explain.

I have been doing my job for twenty-one years now. Over those years I have been called in to one area or another immediately after a major tornado has passed through, devastating lives, homes and businesses. That is what I do – I come in and assess your insured losses, write you a check for those losses, and help you get on the road to recovery.

The job was challenging at first, and very shocking to say the least. But just like every other profession that deals with trauma, you become numb to it over time and create a defense mechanism. You put up a wall to protect yourself and your own sanity. I began to see this happening to myself as well over the years. I was becoming insensitive to the situation and began to block out the people involved in the traumatic event in an effort to guard myself. This, however, was not who I wanted to be, and this was not how I wanted to do my job. I had to find another way to deal with the catastrophic events, while being helpful to the people as well. After all, the people are what really mattered, not their stuff.

I began to focus on the WHO, and not the WHAT – from two different aspects. *Who* I was, and not *What* I was. And *Who* the people were, and not *What* they had lost. My original viewpoint was that I was there because of what I did – I was a Catastrophe Adjuster, I settled claims. With that mentality I forgot *WHO* I was, specifically in those most demanding situations.

So, WHO was I? I was one of the most experienced adjusters around. I was also one of the most efficient and productive. I was a Christian that understood the value of people as well. I quickly began to see that by building a wall to protect myself from the emotional aspects of those claims I was only hurting the people who had already been through a major loss even more. I needed to embrace the fact that I had been put there for a reason, and that reason was not just to write a check. I had compassion, I had true understanding and invaluable experience in large losses. I could be a huge blessing to these people and help them through the recovery process much quicker, with much better direction and guidance, and much less confusion. I could make the whole process much easier and much more comfortable for them. But doing so also meant that I had to tear down my wall, get personal with them and open myself up to a lot of heartbreaking memories that would likely stay with me forever. I eventually embraced the opportunity and even believed that it was a gift that God had given me. I would later learn that a small aspect of this whole process actually was the purpose that God gave me for my life.

Throughout all of these traumatic events, and all of the conversations that I had with people who had just gone through these events, almost every story had one thing in common that these people had explained to me when describing how the event unfolded. *They prayed.* Every other detail in their story was different, but almost every one of them had prayed at some point just prior to the catastrophe changing their lives forever.

You may not find that strange, or unusual, but I did. These people were all from different walks of life, different social backgrounds, and at different financial levels, they were in different parts of the country, were of different ethnic backgrounds, and had different religious views and beliefs. I would later come to find out through more in-depth conversations with many of these people that most of them did not even go to church.

However, they must have believed that there was a God or at least hoped at that time that there was. They must have finally come to realize, mostly due to the situation, that they did not and could not control everything. They all came to the realization that there only hope, their last hope, was to look to a higher power and cry out for help.

This condensed view of many people who find themselves in a desperate situation, and how they respond during those moments is who we are as a society today, and how we view God in our society today. We have our nice house with the white picket fence, we have the 2.5 kids, the dog, and all the toys that we desire. We have a good job and a good life. We have everything under control. We even go as far as cherishing the feeling that securities like insurance will keep us whole, even in times of loss. We think that we have a good handle on life and that we have learned how to make everything work. Until it doesn't work.

Therefore, we don't think that we need God as we have a good handle on everything. So, we don't go to church, we don't pray, and we surely do not have a close relationship with God. Then that dreadful day hits us, and we cry out to God like we never have before. We beg for His grace and mercy, and plead with Him, at times even trying to make deals with Him, if He would only allow this bad thing not to happen. We then become so dejected and place blame on God when He doesn't answer our prayers.

Paul tells us in Ephesians 6:18 *"And pray in the Spirit on all occasions, with all kinds of prayers and requests."*

Romans 8:26 goes on to tell us *"In the same way, the Spirit helps us in or weakness. We do not know what we ought to pray for, but the Spirit himself intercedes for us through wordless groans."*

We run through our lives trying to manage and control everything in our sight, with little or no thought to caring or finding out what God's will or direction for our lives may be. Then, when all hell breaks loose in our lives, we run to God pleading for Him to give us our own selfish desires – what we want, not what God wants.

Those prayers never get answered, for several reasons, but mostly due to the fact that we are praying out of greed and self-satisfaction. We put ourselves first, before God, and only pull God out of the closet when we are in need of a lifeline.

My Personal Experience

On that evening when Robin and I were watching the tornado on TV as it headed straight for our home, and our son who was there alone, all we could do was watch, wait, and pray. Our thoughts became focused on the fact that our son had allowed his girlfriend to stay at the house longer than he should have, which frustrated us. I was disappointed and angry with Dylan as he had chosen to make his own rules once Mom and Dad were away. He should not have been out driving at this time of night. He should have been home where he could have quickly gone to the safety of the storm shelter.

That night played out and neither our son nor our home was touched by the storm. We eventually went to bed and got some sleep. The next morning as I began my day, God gently reminded me of my prayers during that prior morning. I immediately felt so foolish, selfish, and absorbed in my own thoughts and desires, once again. And then I stopped what I was doing and cried out a grateful thanks to our Almighty Father for the gift He had given me and for answering my prayers.

Lately I have been trying to be more like Daniel and consistently pray three times a day. Morning, noon, and night. That prior morning, I was feeling somewhat alone and distant from God. During my prayer time I had asked God that on that day He would show me His love, mercy and grace in any way that

He would choose. During that next morning God made it clear to me that He had answered my prayers, and through the Holy Spirit, He told me:

I love you so much that while your home as well as your son, whom you value more than anything, were in danger and it appeared that a devastating result would be inevitable – it was My will and plan to remove your son from that danger under My protective hand.

The mercy that I have for you is endless, and even though the storms may rage on and be headed straight for you, I have complete control over all things and will see you through every trial and storm.

While many people's lives and homes were affected by the storms that night, yours was untouched by my never-ending grace.

The more I reflected on that night, how everything had played out, and the ways in which they unfolded – I was sure that God had answered my prayer of that morning. And how He had answered my prayer on that day was done in a way that only He could do and was done in such a manner that He knew I would be able to recognize as such.

God took what I valued the most – my children – and allowed them to be in harms way to grab my attention. He then allowed many events to happen that would alter the normal routines of others so that His hand of protection would have my son removed from the path of that danger. And even after my son was out of harms way, my life still could have been turned upside down with the destruction of my home. God's mercy and grace did not allow that to happen as His divine power caused the storm to shift and weaken just prior to nearing my home.

One other point which really caught my attention and fascinated me was God's timing. God's timing is always perfect, and always exactly as it should be. In my prayer of that morning before, I had prayed that God would show me these things *in that day*. In reflection, I realized that every one of these events had transpired just as that day was ending, and the time on the clock just as the storm died out was a few minutes before midnight. God had answered my prayer for that day, in that day, with perfection.

I am not at all trying to suggest that I have found the 'secret' to praying, or that my way of praying is better than others. In fact, it is quite the opposite. I do not feel that I am very good at praying and I often feel embarrassed or ashamed when I go to God with my requests as they are many times about me and my own desires. I feel selfish, foolish, and often find myself carrying on about the same simple things.

However, I carry on and continue to pray multiple times throughout the day as I know it is not about me. It is not about my efforts, but God's efforts. I know I am weak in my prayers, and I know that God can and will strengthen me in all areas of my life. I have come to learn that my part is to remain faithful and obedient, to keep trusting in Him and His strength, and to consistently remain in that communication with God and Jesus. I am aware that my prayers are childlike to some extent, and therefore, one thing that I pray for is that God would teach me and show me how to pray in a way that honors and glorifies Him. I trust that as with everything else, this will happen in God's perfect timing.

We must accept and believe that God knows each and every one of us better than we know ourselves. He knows my weaknesses, and they are of no surprise to Him. He knows all of my thoughts as well, before they even come to my mind. More importantly, God knows what parts of me need to be strengthened first, and they are most always parts that I do not expect or that I see as needing improvement. For right now, in my life, I feel that God is working in me to become more consistent in relying upon Him for everything. To learn and understand that He has to be my focal point and the one that I turn to at all times throughout my day.

God has also shown me that one of my weaknesses is in my priorities, and how I have them arranged, and that they must be changed to make Him the one and only priority in my life. And for where I am at right now, He is doing this through teaching me how to be consistent in seeking Him, desiring Him and turning to Him multiple times per day.

All of these changes in my life are the result of a process that we had touched on briefly in a previous chapter. This process is known as sanctification. When we accept Jesus Christ as our Lord and Savior, we receive our salvation. Once we receive that salvation, the process of sanctification begins. This is the lifelong process where we are renewed, trained, educated and set apart for God's special use and purpose. We are transformed in to holy beings, and this transformation does not happen over night. As Christians we are a continual work in progress – but there should always be progress.

How Do We Pray?

What is prayer, and how should we pray? If God knows all of our thoughts, then why do we need to pray? And whom should we be praying too?

There are many tough questions when it comes to prayers and praying, along with many different and opposing views and answers. Again, I am by no means an expert at praying, nor am I all-knowing in the theological understandings of prayer. The depth of my prayer knowledge is limited to what our good Lord has revealed to me through the experiences in my life. However, as I continue to turn to God for growth in this area, He is continually strengthening me and exposing me to a better and deeper understanding each and every day.

In raising my children, I taught each of them an explicit understanding of one core belief which would help them to be successful in life, no matter where life may lead them. That belief was that one did not need to be an expert, or all knowing, at everything in life to be successful. One only needed to find the area which interested and motivated them the most, then learn as much as they could about that area or field to be the best that they could possibly be in that area. And as life progressed, one would certainly run into areas where they had little to no knowledge or understanding of how that part of life worked. At these times one would seek out someone who is an expert in that area and ask for help. The smartest, most knowledgeable and successful people in our world today have all sought help from others when encountering a matter in which they were not experienced or skilled. And all of these experts know, understand, and believe that there is nothing wrong or to be embarrassed about in asking for help. They are fully aware that they cannot and will not reach their full potential without the help of others.

With that understanding and belief, I feel that I am an expert at prayer and that I can answer many of the questions which we have about prayer. What?? Initially, I said I was not an expert at praying, and now I am claiming that I am an expert. You as the reader have to be questioning my sanity at this point. Hang in there with me. It will make sense.

First, I do not believe that any of us as human beings can ever truly be an expert at prayer or praying. God tells us in the Bible that His ways are higher than ours, and His understanding is much greater than ours. While we may think that we have a good grasp on prayer, I do not believe that any of us will ever come to a point that we have 'made it' in our prayer lives.

Secondly, with the insight that God has shown me and revealed to me about prayer and praying, I believe that I do have the knowledge to answer many of the questions about prayer – and then most importantly, help steer you in the right direction of the one who is an expert in the field of prayer – Jesus Christ.

So, let's get started. Just as we did in the last chapter, I will use the 5 Ws to answer our questions on prayer and praying.

The Who

Who do we pray to? God? Jesus? The Holy Spirit? And why should we direct our prayers toward them? Do we ever pray to anyone else? Should we pray to anyone or anything else?

The answers to these questions can become a bit perplexing as well, and to grasp them we must first have an understanding of the Trinity. The Trinity is the concept of God, in three different entities. God the Father, God the Son, and God the Holy Spirit. Each are individual entities, but each are intertwined into the one triune God. They are all God, but they are also separate at the same time.

God The Father is the creator of all things that exist. He is the supreme being and has sovereignty over all things. The Bible tells us that God has always existed and will always exist.

Jesus Christ is the son of God, created by God through His perfect seed into the pure and perfect womb of the virgin Mary, which had not been defiled by man. That, however, is the Jesus Christ that we know through the New Testament - The Son of Man. Jesus did not begin His existence through that birth in a manger though, some two thousand years ago. The Bible tells us that Jesus was with God when the world was created.

John 1:1-5 tells us *"In the beginning was the Word, and the Word was with God, and the Word was God. He was with God in the beginning. Through Him all things were made; without Him nothing was made that has been made. In Him was life, and that life was the light of all mankind. The light shines in the darkness, and the darkness has not overcome it."*

Jesus is The Word, The Life, and through Him all things were created. Jesus is God, is part of God, and has been in existence prior to the creation of all things.

The Holy Spirit is the spirit of God, sent to dwell in and among all of us. The Holy Spirit is our guide, our comforter, our teacher, and our connection with God. And being of God, the Holy Spirit has been in existence forever as well.

All three – The Father, The Son, and The Holy Spirit – are omnipotent, omniscient, and omnipresent. They are all separate beings but yet are one in the same. They are each individual in their existence yet are all one in the same.

To help one comprehend the Trinity, or the concept of a triune God, in a very simplistic way – The Father creates and plans – The Son carries out and accomplishes the plans – The Holy Spirit applies it to all who believe. The Trinity, as well as the role of each member, is considerably more complex and encompassing than just described. However, this perspective should enable one to have a basic foundation of who and what God is.

When we pray, we are praying to God the Father, as He is the Creator and controller of all things. However, with our limited abilities and our sin nature we can only access God the Father through Jesus Christ, whose blood has washed us clean. Jesus has also been given authority over all things by God (Matthew 28:18).

We also do not know how to pray, or what to pray for at many times, so we pray through the Holy Spirit who takes our prayers to God for us, as well as revealing to us God's answers and His Word.

Because God is all three – The Father, The Son, The Holy Spirit – we can and should pray to any of them and all of them. He/They are all sovereign and are all God.

This again is a simplistic view and there is much more to it than that. However, it should allow for a basic understanding of who we pray to, and why we pray to them.

We should also not be praying to anyone or anything else. Prayer is a form of submission – We are submitting ourselves to a higher power, our Creator, and acknowledging that He is the higher power. God clearly tells us in the Bible that there shall be no other gods before Him. When we pray to anything or anyone else, we are placing other gods before the one true living God.

The What

What are we to pray for? There is no formulated answer to this question, as what we pray for will vary from person to person and will also change a multitude of times throughout the different seasons of one's life. As we begin to grow closer to God, becoming more in union with Him and Christ, our hearts will become more in tune with the desires of God. We then begin to understand and become more aware of what God's will is, and as we do so, His will becomes our will.

Just as with any relationship that grows stronger over time, as we grow closer to God we will begin to desire and love the same things that He does. And as that bond and union strengthens with God, He will put those desires into our hearts. His will becomes more evident and clearer to us, as does what we should be praying for.

While much of what we pray for will change, almost daily, there are several things that we should always be praying for.

- We should always be praying that His will be done, and not ours.

- We should always be praying for others.

- We should always be praying that God would lead us, teach us, strengthen us, and show us His will and His ways.

- And most importantly, we should always be praising God for everything that He has done as well as everything that is to come.

Many times, when we do pray, it becomes mostly about us and what we want or what we need. Our tendency is to make praying about ourselves and not about God. We find ourselves asking God to 'give me this, give me that, help me do this and help me do that'. Again, our viewpoint and perspective are askew, focusing more on our will and desires and not His.

The Bible tells us in many books and chapters what we should pray for. The Apostle Paul tells us in Philippians 4:6 - *"Do not be anxious about anything, but in every situation, by prayer and petition, with thanksgiving, present your requests to God."* Paul wrote this in his letter to the Philippi, while he was in prison. Paul was locked up in prison, in a very desperate situation – and yet he tells us not to worry about it, take it to God in Prayer, with thanksgiving.

C'mon. Seriously? I mean – I myself have been in jail, and the last thing that I was at that moment was thankful. I was more worried if I would .make it out of that cell alive or not.

Paul tells us that no matter what our situation, no matter what our worries or concerns – do not let them overcome you, take them to God in prayer. And he tells us to do so in a thankful way. In other words – we don't whine and complain about what it is that we are going through, we give thanks to God for all that He has given us and for being with us and seeing us through the trials that we are in.

This advice comes from the man who was shipwrecked three times, walked over two thousand miles on his missionary trips (through the deserts and the mountains), and was imprisoned multiple times. And he tells us – *Relax, give it to God and let Him handle it!* I am thinking that Paul had a pretty good idea of what stressful situations were like, and he had also learned that there is only one way to deal with them.

Most all of us view these trials and struggles, which we face every day, in a negative way. We whine, we complain, and we become angry about the situations that we are going through and being inconvenienced with. Many times, we blame God for allowing these bad things to happen to us or assume that God must not truly care for us as He is making our lives miserable and frustrating.

A dive into the book of Jonah may provide us with a more reasonable contemplation of our circumstances at times. Many of the trials and struggles which are going on in our lives, or around us, are for a much greater purpose and reasoning than we are capable of understanding.

God had commanded Jonah to go to the city of Nineveh and preach against their wickedness, which Jonah did not want to do. Jonah despised the people of Nineveh and did not care if God destroyed all of them. So, Jonah ran in the opposite direction, to hide from God and His will. Jonah boarded a ship headed for Tarshish, a town five times farther than the distance to Nineveh, and in the complete opposite direction.

The ship was then beaten and battered by storms and waves. The crew of the ship feared for their lives and believed that they would not survive. They all prayed to their gods for the storm to stop, with no avail. Jonah, however, was not praying. Jonah then told the crew that he worshiped the Lord, the God of Heaven, who made the sea and the dry land. The crew then became terrified and asked Jonah *"What did you do?"*, as they knew he must have done something to offend God. And then they asked Jonah what they should do to make the sea calm down.

Jonah knew he was the cause of the problems and told the crew to throw him overboard in to the sea. The crew, however, did not want to cause another man to die, so they tried to row to shore. As they did, the sea grew even more wild than before. The crew then realized that the only way they would survive was if they threw Jonah into the sea, which they did.

God then made a fish large enough to swallow Jonah whole, where Jonah spent the next three days praising and returning to God. The fish eventually spat Jonah out, and he returned to obey God's command. Shortly after, Jonah made that trip to Nineveh just as God commanded. Jonah spread Gods message throughout the entire town, and everyone repented of their evil ways. God then spared the Ninevites from destruction.

I don't know about you – but if I am thrown overboard in to the wide-open sea, and then swallowed by a monstrous fish, I am not thinking that these are good things coming from God, that will benefit me going forward. But they were. They were provisions from God allowing Jonah to get back on track, and to keep him from running down a road that would only take him further away from God.

We should also mention the hundreds of other men who were on that same ship with Jonah. Men that believed their lives were about to end. Men that were frantically doing everything they could to save the ship, and themselves. Men that had absolutely no understanding of the reality to the situation that was playing out around them, indirectly affecting each and every one of them.

The truth of the matter is that while God is allowing these things to happen in our lives, it is most always for our own benefit, and He is trying to teach us something that we need to learn or become stronger in. He is growing us, and it is through these trials and struggles that we grow and learn the most.

Even though the situation that we may find ourselves in may not seem like a gift from God at the time, God sees the bigger picture and is always working in our lives allowing things to happen that will lead us back to Him, and much greater things.

Pray is powerful, and it does work when we do it with our hearts in the right place. Pray for your family, pray for your friends. Pray for that guy that just cut you off in traffic. Pray for your boss, for your co-workers. Pray for your pastor, your church, and for the entire congregation. But most importantly – just pray!

The Where

Where do we pray? Is there a specific place, or time that we pray? The simple answer is that there is no specific time or place – we pray anywhere and everywhere, all the time.

Paul instructed the Philippi not to be anxious about anything, but in every situation present your requests to God. Therefore, Paul is telling us to stop worrying about everything that we are worrying about and take it to God. Well, again, our tendency is to worry about every little thing, all day long. Paul says that we should turn to God with those worries – all day long.

So, wherever we may be when those worries, struggles, fears or challenges confront us – pray. Take them to God in prayer no matter where you are at. It does not have to be at home in a quiet room. It does not have to be in the church. God is alive, God is real, and God is everywhere. God is right there with us in all of those trials and struggles, and He desperately wants us to turn to Him in prayer in those times of need.

Jesus chimes in on the matter as well in Matthew 6:5-15. In vs. 6-8 Jesus tells us *"But when you pray, go into your room, close the door and pray to your Father, who is unseen. Then your Father, who sees what is done in secret, will reward you. And when you do pray, do not keep on babbling like the pagans, for they think they will be heard because of their many words. Do not be like them, for your Father knows what you need before you ask Him."*

Jesus, however, was not stating that we should only pray in our room, alone and by ourselves. While it is very beneficial at times to have that quiet place, free from all distractions, with only you and God present, Jesus was conveying a different message. Jesus was instructing us to not be boastful in our praying. Not to act as though the act of praying itself makes us better than others, and therefore not to stand up and do it in front of a crowd so that we merely draw attention to ourselves.

Prayer is not about us – It is about God. The attention, focus and praise should all be towards God – and God alone.

The When

When do we pray, or when should we pray? Back to Paul's instructions to the Philippi - *"in every situation, present your requests to God."*

The word *every*, also means any. So, in every and any situation we should pray. Prayer takes practice, dedication and commitment. No matter what my own intentions are, I find myself always struggling to be consistent in making time to pray. I write myself little sticky notes and paste them everywhere. I have them on the dashboard of my truck as well as I spend most of my day driving around from place to place for work. Well guess what – I still don't see them. Life gets in my way, Satan tries to keep us distracted with other things, and the next thing you know is that the entire day has passed without you praying.

Praying takes a conscious effort which will wear you out at first as Satan is trying to do everything that he can to keep us from doing it. We must fight the enemy with all vigilance, especially when it comes to our prayer lives. Satan knows how strong prayer is, and he knows that it will also bring us closer to and more in union with God. Satan will do anything and everything to keep us from praying or having the time to do it.

Praying does not come easy, and we have to force ourselves in to doing it at first as it is not our normal routine (remember our sin nature). And just as we begin to remember to pray, or make any effort to do so, in walks Satan with some small distraction that takes us in a completely different direction.

Back when I vowed to be more consistent with praying, I would see my little sticky notes which would remind me that I needed to do so. I would tell myself that I needed to pray, but then would say *Oh, just let me finish up this one thing first*, and then I would end up going in a completely different direction and my little reminder had all but vanished. By the grace of God and the help of the Holy Spirit, I have come to a point that when I now see that reminder, I force myself to stop whatever it is that I am doing – and pray. I have come to realize that if I do not do it right then, I never will. There will always be something in the way and always be something trying to keep me from God.

I had mentioned earlier that I am also trying to be more like Daniel as well. Most of us have heard the story of Daniel and the lion's den. But very few people know anything more about the story of Daniel.

Daniel was a prophet in the Old Testament who had a sincere heart and desire to please God. There is much that can be learned from Daniel and the way that he lived his life in being faithful to God. The book of Daniel also shows us how God is right there with us the entire time, is faithful to us, and provides for our every need when we make Him our priority.

Daniel made it a habit to pray three times a day. Morning, noon, and night. No matter what was going on in his life, he would stop and pray. The ruler at that time was King Darius. King Darius had been coerced in to making a decree, or law, that no one could pray to anyone or anything other than King Darius for the next thirty days. The punishment for doing so was to be thrown in to the lion's den, where death was certain. King Darius had been pressured in to making this decree by a few other men who did not like Daniel. These men knew that Daniel prayed to God three times a day, and their sole intention of getting King Darius to make the decree was to get rid of Daniel.

Daniel knew in his heart who his true King was, and he would not change his beliefs or his faithfulness no matter what the worldly consequences may be. Daniel continued to go home three times a day and go up to his room, which had an open window that allowed everyone to see in. He would get on his knees and pray to the one and only true God. Daniel would do so out loud as well, with praise and worship, and he did not care if anyone else saw him.

If you recall, Jesus told us to go into our room, close the door and to pray in secret. Daniel did exactly the opposite. But again, this was not the point that Jesus was making. Daniel was praying just as he always had, and he was doing so with a pure heart for God. Daniel was not praying openly to draw attention to himself.

The end of Daniel's story is what most people are familiar with. Daniel was caught praying to God, and not King Darius. Daniel was thrown in to the lion's den, which he was well aware could happen, and would likely result in his death. But after being thrown in to the lion's den, an angel appeared to Daniel and told him that the lions would not harm him. God was faithful to Daniel, just as Daniel had been faithful to God.

The next morning, King Darius found that Daniel had survived the night in the lion's den. King Darius was relieved as he was fond of Daniel. King Darius then went on to decree that from that point forward all people in his kingdom were to fear and tremble before the God of Daniel.

I personally do not believe that Daniel prayed three times a day. I believe that Daniel actually prayed more often than that. How can this be? What evidence is there? The Bible does not tell us directly, however, from my own experiences I can assure you that when you do commit to praying consistently, and remain faithful in that effort, you draw much closer to God. The closer to God that you get, the more God reveals to you. And the more that you see of God, the more you desire to be with God which prompts you to go to Him in prayer even more and more. I believe that Daniel experienced the same thing that I had, the presence of God. And just like Daniel and I, once you experience that presence, everything else suddenly pales in comparison and that presence becomes the one thing that your heart truly craves and desires.

The Why

Why do we pray? I think the better question would be why do we not pray? Both are intriguing questions, and both could be answered in numerous ways.

Once again, the simple answer as to why we pray is that this is our way of communicating with God and Jesus. God and Jesus, the Creators and Controllers of all that exist, have a plan and a purpose for everything in this world. We become an active part of that plan only when we are in constant communication with them. Therefore, we can either align with that plan, or we can ignore it and be resistant to what will eventually happen either way.

Our lives, and everything that is encompassed within them, are much more in tune with true reality when we are in communication with God and Jesus. They let us in on the plan and guide us and direct us through this chaotic, sin filled world that we live in. We then have a road map of what the real plan is, what our true destination is, and what roads we need to take to reach that destination. Without that communication we do not ever know what that plan for our life is, what the destination is, or what roads to travel to reach that destination. We are basically wandering around aimlessly just hoping that we chose the right road to get us to where we don't even know we are going.

Praying, or that communication with God, also helps us to keep our lives in check. It keeps us grounded in who we are, and who we were created to be. Our perspective and value of ourselves, our self-image, is more in line with that of God as well. We become confident and strong in who we are through Jesus Christ, while at the same time being humbled by the fact that we must submit to a higher power. It is through this prayer and communication that God begins to refine us, convict us, and strengthen us to become everything that we can be, and were made to be. We become true warriors.

Just as with any trip, journey, or plan there will always be speed bumps or potholes that we hit along the way. This is true when we follow God's plan as well. If I told you that all aspects of your life would be simple and easy just by praying and being in communication with God, you would be greatly misled. It is in fact just the opposite.

As we discussed in earlier chapters, the enemy is still out there. And as we grow closer to God, especially in prayer, the evil one is going to put in overtime trying to lay down as many speed bumps and potholes as he can to try and keep us from God, or to make us think that being close to God really does not help. These times are when prayer is most important and should be leaned on more than anything. This is when we must have that unshakable faith that God will see us through everything, and when we must turn to Him for that guidance and support as we humbly acknowledge that we do not have control over everything and require His support to see us through the adversity.

It is also important to understand and know that as we become more committed to God and prayer, we must not have the expectation or view of that relationship as being like one that is commonly known in the world which we live in. It will not be like the relationships that we have with others such as our family or friends.

And as our relationship with God grows, God will continue to grow us and strengthen us. This is all part of that sanctification process that we touched on earlier. God is always teaching us, training us, and refining us.

There will also come a time when it may seem that God is not there, no matter how much we turn to Him and pray. This too is God at work, strengthening us to remain committed and faithful, even when it feels like we are all alone. God is still there, and He is still working in in us to make a strong warrior that will not run from the fight at the first sign of adversity. God wants to know that we are committed, and that we will show up for the fight every day because it is what is truly in our heart, and now who we truly are.

My life has changed greatly since I have placed God at the top of all things, and since I have begun to pray consistently. I pray for His advice, His direction, His guidance, His counsel, His wisdom, His peace, His comfort, His passion, His love, His mercy, His grace, His teachings, His presence, His forgiveness, His perspective, His will, His understanding, His patience, and many other things as well.

No, my life does not always go perfect, and I still have plenty of challenges and stressful situations that confront me every day. But my perspective and understanding has changed, and I now see reality for what it truly is, which allows me to face all of these situations without the stress and fears. I now understand the bigger picture, and what truly matters and is important. When we learn to have this perspective, we quickly realize how insignificant all of the little things are that bombard us every day, and how inconsequential they are to our existence.

So, if our lives are still going to be crappy and full of pain and misery, what is the point in praying? Well – crappy, pain and misery are all perspectives – or how we perceive the things that we are experiencing. When we are focused on God and in constant communication with God, our perspective changes. The trials and challenges that we face and go through every day may not change, but we are now able to see things with a fresh new perspective, the perspective that God has. All of a sudden, these things do not seem so crappy, painful, or miserable anymore. We now have a higher view and understanding of all things, and our perception of all things changes for the better. We begin to see the bigger picture and begin to not view everything that we face as being about ourselves. We don't take everything personal anymore.

When we pray, and are in constant communication with God, we learn to understand as well as truly believe the fact that we are not in this alone any longer. These battles that we face every day are not ours to worry about or struggle with. We call on our Lord and Savior Jesus Christ and let Him fight the battles for us. We give all of the struggles and battles over to Him which sets us free from the anger, frustration, envy, hostility and resentment that we so unneedingly carry around. We are freed from the burdens of the negative emotions and hostility that keep us in bondage to sin. We are freed up to do more of what we then desire to do the most – Praise God.

The How

So how do we pray? Is there a right way? Is there a wrong way?

There is no right way or wrong way to pray. Any attempt at prayer is better than no attempt at all. And while there may be some who feel inadequate in their ability to pray, even the simplest of prayers, with an open and committed heart, is better than not praying at all. I guess there is one wrong way to pray, and that would be choosing not to pray.

Our Christian lives are very much comparable to our earthly life cycles. Once we receive our salvation through Jesus Christ, we are basically infants in Christianity. We are full of energy, running around, wanting to learn as much as we can. We have some knowledge and beliefs, but they usually do not have very much depth to them. As we mature and grow in our faith, our knowledge and beliefs grow as well, or they should. And as our knowledge and faith increases, we become more like adults, and at this point should be mentoring and teaching other young Christians.

Our prayer life, or the ways in which we pray will also change and grow as we draw closer to God. God and prayer are interdependent. You cannot have one without the other. You cannot have God without prayer, and while one could say that you could pray without having God, that prayer would be artificial and to a false god. The more we pray, the closer we become to God, and the closer we become to God, the more we pray.

As we begin our Christian lives we may feel at times that our prayers, or the style and manner in which we pray is insufficient and not pleasing to God. There are but a few problems with this belief. First, we are basing God's view of us by our works, or how we perform, which is never the way God views us. Second, this thought is being put in to our minds by Satan in an attempt to make us feel that we will never be good enough for God. Take every thought captive and make it obedient to Christ. Third, no two people will ever, or should ever pray in the same manner.

Hmmmmm, that third one is a profound statement, right? How do we come up with the basis for that? The underlying belief that no two people will pray the same way is versed throughout the Bible. It is in God's creation, and the way in which He created us. As stated earlier, however, much of the *What* we pray for should be the same in each and every person.

Nonetheless, each and every one of us are different, in many different ways. And while it is possible to find two people who look very much like each other; the thoughts, emotions, spirit and heart of each of the two are completely different. You could even take two identical twins, raised in the same environment and taught the same views – and each will have a completely different style and personality.

The most important part of any one of us to God is our heart. The true function, design, and intent for our hearts, as created by God, would require its own book to accurately explain. But simply put, your heart is different than my heart and was created differently for a different purpose.

This is important, so get out your highlighter, mark it, remember it, and don't ever forget it:

God made each and every one of us exactly the way that we are for His glory and honor. Even with all of our imperfections and inadequacies that we tend to place our focus on, as well as all of our quirks and idiosyncrasies, we are perfect in God's eyes. God made each and every one of us exactly how He wanted us to be.

While we may be seen as flawed in the view of others, as well as this world, which we have come to believe and accept as being the truth of who we are – It is a complete lie which we have been taught to adopt as our reality.

We are perfect in God's eyes. We were made perfectly, in His image. God made you and me, with every little funky and weird habit or characteristic that we have, for a specific reason. And He wants us to use those weird quirks and habits to connect with others to spread the Word of the Gospel. There are many, many people who have never heard the Gospel, or read the Bible. Many of these people never will unless someone brings it into their lives. This happens as we build relationships and bonds with others, which happens when others find something about us interesting or relatable. To someone, somewhere, our unique quirks and habits are something that they can relate too. Something that they will be attracted too. Something that opens the door to sharing the Gospel and bringing others to know Christ.

For most of us though, we live in the image of how we perceive ourselves and how others in this world perceive us. We do not live in or believe in the image that God has of us. And we therefore suppress the image of who we truly are and were created to be and therefore attempt to hide or fix our quirks and so-called flaws. Whether we want to accept the fact or not, we have become the poser, trying to be something other than who we truly are and who we were truly created to be.

Whoa! Whoa! Whoa! Hit the brakes. I can see many of you already taking the last couple paragraphs and doing what we habitually do with the Bible. Taking it out of context. Using it as a means to justify our sinful ways, our comforts, and our personal desires. This is not at all a validation allowing us to continue in our sinful desires.

God did not create us to sin. He made us perfect, in every way. We, as mankind, brought that sin into our lives, on our own choosing. God did not create us to be homosexuals, murderers, rapists, drunkards, liars, adulterers, cheaters, thief's ...... and the list goes on and on. These are all choices which we have made on our own, in an effort to please our own selfish desires and pleasures.

Let us take a trip back to the Old Testament and visit a couple little towns called Sodom and Gomorrah. I am sure that most everyone is familiar with the names of these two towns. But are you aware of what actually happened, and why?

Sodom and Gomorrah were the first towns in creation to venture in to acts of sin that were so evil and opposing to God's heart that those acts alone caused their own destruction. The primary act that they had resorted to was believed to be homosexuality. The men lusted after men instead of women.

God then sent two angels, appearing as men, in an attempt to save the towns. The angels were met by a wicked mob who had become so evil that they wanted to rape the angels as well. God then destroyed Sodom and Gomorrah, and all of the people that lived there, with rains of sulfur and fire.

God did spare four people on that day though. Lot, his wife, and their two daughters were allowed to escape. Lot's wife would be turned to a pillar of salt as she looked back during the escape though – which is much like us when we are given the opportunity to repent and save our souls, but we just cannot seem to let go of our past and keep looking back.

Our lives, our towns, our countries have become much like Sodom and Gomorrah. We have allowed ourselves to become so blinded by our sin that we are unable to see the destruction that we are creating and causing, and the destruction of our own lives as well.

With that said – How do we pray? You pray like you, and I will pray like me. Just be yourself! God knows who you are, what you are, and every little thing about you. He made you this way for a reason.

As you know by now, I have four children. They are all mine and were all created and raised by Robin and me. Yet each and every one of them is vastly different. When they come to talk to me, they each have their own style and mannerisms in which they do so. They do not try to pretend to be their brother or sister. They are simply being themselves, and that is but one of the things that I love so much about each of them.

Josh is our oldest. Josh is confident, full of wisdom, assured and secure in who he is. When Josh comes to talk to me, he is usually straight to the point, in a casual manner, yet always clear and concise.

Kris is our second son. Kris is the risky, living on the edge kind of kid. Kris also thinks at times that he can reinvent the wheel and has a better way of doing things. When Kris comes to talk to me the conversations can go on for hours jumping from one thing to another with a perspective that is all his own.

Katelynn, our only girl, is our third child. Katelynn looks like her mom (thank you Lord) but acts and thinks like me. When Katelynn comes to talk to me, Robin makes it a point to be around as she finds it rather humorous. Katelynn knows exactly how I think, how I will respond, and what I will likely say – so she is always ready with an appropriate response. Her and I can go on, literally for hours, countering each other's reply. It is very much like having a conversation with myself, and I think this is where Robin finds the humor. It is Robins way of seeing me get a dose of my own medicine.

Dylan is our fourth child. Dylan is easy going and laid back, but at the same time has an emotional side to him as well. Dylan is very studious, especially when it comes to the miscalculations which his older brothers and sister have endured. Dylan is always very respectful to others and is cautious with his words as not to elicit a response that would endanger himself.

Four kids, raised by the same parents, in the same house, and educated with the same values and beliefs. But each are incredibly different. I love each and every one of them for who they are, as if they were my only child, and always encourage them to be themselves, and to be the best themselves that they can be. I love it when any of them comes to me to talk, and I cherish each and every moment of it.

This is the way that our Father sees us as well. He knows we are all different – He made us to be different and made us exactly the way that we are for a specific reason. So, embrace who you really are. Stop trying to hide it or be ashamed of it. And when you pray – Be you! Talk to God like you normally talk. Cry out to God like you normally cry. God knows your requests and your pains long before you ever decide to come to Him with them. He just wants you to come to Him - for help and advice, and to talk.

In being our true selves, when we come to God, we must also allow ourselves to erase any preconceptions of God and prayer which we have been programmed to believe through society and the modern-day church. Many of us do not know where to start, how to start, or how we should perform the action of prayer. We are often led to believe that we should follow a certain 'preformatted' prayer, or that it must be done in a certain manner and sequence.

This line of thinking, and prayer, is nonsense. We do not need to be perfect to come to God, and we certainly do not need to be perfect in our prayers either. All we need to do is bow our heads, or get on our knees, with an open and humble heart.......... and start talking to God. He will do the rest, and He will also teach us how to better our prayer lives so that we may be glorifying Him in what we do.

The topic of how long one should pray is controversial as well. Again, I believe everyone is different. Be you. But get to the point and don't ramble on for hours just so you may feel more Godly. Jesus tells us in Matthew 6 not to ramble on like the Pharisees.

The MSG version of the Bible states in vs. 5 - *"And when you come before God, don't turn it into a theatrical production either."*

We are all different. Some people talk slowly, some talk fast. Some people have the gift of conversation, some don't care to talk much at all. When you go to God in prayer, just be you, who you truly are, and come to God from your heart.

My prayers usually are not incredibly lengthy, though at times they can be. When I find myself trying to force the issue, and rambling on, I most always turn my prayer toward Jesus and the Holy Spirit, asking for help in clearing my mind and helping me to stay focused. And if the struggle continues, I will then spend the rest of my prayer time just praising Jesus over and over again. My wife on the other hand could probably go on with good meaning and intention for hours. That is just who she is.

Do not be mistaken though, praying, and making time to pray is never easy. It is most assuredly at the top of Satan's list of things that he wants to keep us from doing. And therefore, the more committed we are to praying, the more resistance we can expect to encounter when doing so or even planning to do so.

As Satan and the ways of this world have distorted the views which we have of ourselves, we most always turn to prayer and God with the wrong attitude. Satan and the world have made us believe that we are worthless, inadequate, and not worthy of anything that a perfect God would have to offer. We therefore often turn to God with a beggar's mentality, pleading for any scraps or handouts that He may find the grace to give us.

This is the one way in which I believe we should not pray. We should not be turning to God with a servant mentality or a beggar's mentality. This concept requires a deeper appreciation of our relationship with God and Christ, but as we grow closer to God it will become clearer and more understandable.

We are promised many things once we become Christians and begin to walk in union with God. We are brought in to the family of God, as His sons and daughters. We are promised to inherit His Kingdom and all of the riches that come with it. We are one with Christ, in Christ, and are as well seated at the right hand of the Father with Christ even though our earthly bodies still reside in the world.

Again, it is all about our perspective, and how we view ourselves. We need to possess the view and understanding of the reality that our Father is the King of all kings, the Creator of all things, and the Ruler over all things that exist. This is our Father, and we are His children. And as our Father, He wants only the best, and the very best, for each and every one of us. We do not need to plead and beg for things from our Father. He wants more than anything to provide these things to us and wants us to have a completely joyous and enriched life. He wants to give us more than we could ever imagine.

We need to realign our perspective of our Father, and our view of ourselves as His children. We need to accept and believe the fact that God wants us to have the greatest life possible, and that He wants to bless us with more than we could ever imagine or ask for. We need to turn to God with the confidence of a son/daughter of a King, who is loved more than anything. We need to approach God as His children, not as some distant beggar or servant hoping for a handout.

Praise

Prayer is not just about asking for something from God. A good portion of our prayer life should be spent praising God for all things. An attitude of gratitude. Being grateful for what we have and what we have been undeservedly given.

Praise is defined as *the expression of approval or admiration for something or someone.* It is when we exalt God for who He truly is. Through this exaltation, we are placing ourselves into a posture of submissiveness and acknowledging that God is greater than we are. We are lifting God up and recognizing Him as the highest power and authority over all things, including ourselves and our lives.

Praise often becomes intertwined with worship. Although the two are similar in a sense, they are vastly different. Worship is about expressing the love and gratitude that we have for God. While we are still expressing a gratefulness in praise, the act of praise itself is more of a surrendering of all things to a power and authority that is higher and greater than we are.

The act of praising God brings us into His presence which then fills us with His joy, love, and peace.

I recently learned something really awesome, and I want you to try it as well - When things in your life get crazy and hectic, when you are overwhelmed and feel like the whole world is coming down upon you, when that next bad thing happens in your life and you just don't see a way out – Instead of complaining, or even praying and asking God to take it away, stop for a moment and just praise God.

I'm going to let you in on a little secret:

It is emotionally and mentally impossible to feel sad, depressed, or negative in any way when you are truly praising God.

While I have learned so much about prayer, praying, and our prayer lives lately, I will admit that I still feel like a child in my knowledge and understanding of how God desires us to pray and how we should pray. I would highly recommend reading John Eldredge's book *Moving Mountains – Praying with Passion, Confidence and Authority*.[2]

"The god of this age [Satan] has blinded the minds of the unbelievers, so that they cannot see the light of the gospel that displays the glory of Christ, who is the image of God." 2 Corinthians 4:4

Chapter 19

Answers

How does God answer our prayers, and what can we, or should we expect? This may be one of the toughest questions and biggest controversies of them all. And just as with our prayer life, the way that God does and does not answer our prayers will vary greatly for each and every one of us. As I have discussed in previous chapters, God made things happen in my life which would grab my attention. He knew exactly what would make me stop and look to Him. While this worked for me, it most likely would not have for someone else. It is what I needed, not what you would have needed.

We are all different, in countless ways that most of us do not even understand, down to a microscopic level. Each and every one of us was created differently, for a different purpose, and then embarked on a different path through life encountering different experiences which have all left an impression on us, shaping who and what we have become. And since we are all different in so many ways, we cannot expect that one simple set of rules, actions, responses, or methodology would be sufficient in handling the concerns of the masses. We were created individually, and God relates to each and every one of us individually as well, as our needs require. This is God's plan, and by His design.

I have heard it said that God answers prayers in one of three ways – Yes, No and maybe later or not right now. While this may be true to some extent, it is a very naive and inexperienced perspective, which again brings God down to our level in our effort to rationalize His actions and thinking. For simplicity's sake, we will touch on each of these responses and will then dive in a bit deeper as to hopefully achieve a better grasp on how and why God does or does not answer our prayers.

Yes

The YES answer is the easy one to interpret. This is when we pray for someone or something and are blessed to see it come to fruition. It is such an amazing and powerful experience when we are able to see our loving Father in action, especially when it is in response to something we have been praying for.

However, even with the positive outcome of the *YES* answer we face challenges. Our shortcoming with the *YES* answer is two-fold. The first being that we are impatient. We live in an 'on-demand' society and have been taught that we can and should expect to have whatever we want in mere minutes. We do not like to wait. We want it now. As a matter of fact, unbeknownst to most all of us, the technologically advanced world that we live in has actually reprogrammed us and our minds to live this way, and to accept that as the new norm.

Almost everything that we have placed into our lives in this modern day and age serves one main purpose – to provide us with results and information as quickly as possible. Therefore, we have become conditioned to expect an immediate response or result in everything that we do. And when we encounter a situation in which the response or result is not immediate, we quickly abandon that effort and seek out other options. So, when we turn to God for an action or outcome, and it takes more than five minutes to see Him respond, we take matters in to or own hands and attempt to take control and handle matters on our own. We then allow ourselves to contemplate the idea that God does not exist, or that He does not care for us and our lives.

God desires to see many things from us as Christians. What God is ultimately trying to do is change our character and our hearts – back to the way of their original creation. God's true desire is that we would have the heart and character of Jesus. He wants to see that our desire for Him is truly in our hearts and that it is our greatest desire. He wants to see that we have fully submitted our lives to Him, and that we realize and accept that we do not have control over everything. He wants to see that we are faithful and obedient to Him and His word as well, and that we will patiently await His will and His response.

Through this desire, submission, and obedience, our faith grows and becomes stronger. And as these attributes grow within us, so does our character. When we continually turn to God for answers and resolutions, we become more in tune with what God desires and what His will is. God will answer our prayers if they are His will, and not our will. God will also answer these prayers in His timing, not in our timing, and not when we stomp our feet like a two-year-old and demand that we have it now.

God knows better than we do as to what our needs are, how our needs are best met, and when it is best to meet those needs. We need to have trust and faith that our gracious Father who has provided everything for us in the past, will once again provide for our every need in the future as well. And this trust and faith must be accompanied with patience. When we truly have trust and faith that God will provide for our every need and request, we can rest easy knowing that we have already received the answer even though we may not immediately see the result.

Our second greatest deficiency in the *YES* answer, once again, lies within our perspective of our lives, as well as that of the world we live in. We need to acknowledge the fact that there are events playing out on a scale much bigger and greater than we can relate to which we most always do not have a clue about. We need to truly believe, accept, and understand that this world does not revolve around us.

In Daniel Chapter 10 – Daniel was praying for the people of Jerusalem. He began to pray and fast for twenty-one days, with no answer or sign from God. This was a man who had his heart fully committed to God, dare I say that Daniel was much more righteous than you or I. Twenty-one days with no answer, but Daniel kept on praying regardless. On the twenty first day Daniel was struck by the vision of an angel speaking to him. Daniel was told by the angel that God had heard his prayers on day one, and that God had sent this angel to Daniel to answer his prayers at that time on the very first day. Daniel was then told that for the last twenty days the angel had been in a fierce battle with the prince of the Persian Kingdom (a territorial demon) who had been keeping him from delivering God's message, and that the angel had to summon the powerful Archangel Michael to assist him and break free from the battle, allowing him to finally reach Daniel on the twenty first day.

There are many other issues unfolding in our world and around us, which we have no comprehension of, that fight against the will of God. The only significant part about us in the equation is that we remain faithful, obedient and consistent in our relationship with God, and that we obey His command of resisting the enemy.

The third issue we have with the yes answer is in the way we perceive it or respond to it when it does come. We again are blessed by seeing that prayer answered, and certain things come to fruition. We then begin to feel a sense of involvement, or that we had some part in making certain things happen or not happen. Our confidence rises as does our pride and we begin to feel that we must be important or special to God as He heard and answered our prayer.

The truth is that all of us are important and special to God, whether our prayers get answered or not. However, the emotions and feelings that we are having in this scenario do not honor God and are simply an attempt at elevating ourselves to achieve some sense of gratification. The requests of our prayers did come to happen; however, this was by no means through any ability or power that we may possess. They came to happen solely because of God and His ultimate power. Any and all praise, glory, or recognition should be directed and intended for God and Jesus alone.

No

This is the answer that no one likes to hear. Again, in the world that we live in we are taught that we can have anything that we desire. And if someone tells us that we can't, we just need to look elsewhere until we find someone or someplace where we can. We are just like the dead fallen leaves from a tree – we blow anywhere the next wind takes us. We are not attached or anchored to anything, so when one thing no longer suits us, pleases us, or offers us satisfaction – we quickly jump to the next latest and greatest thing in an effort to satisfy our own selfish desires and pleasures. We simply do whatever we have too in hopes of keeping ourselves happy.

Jesus tells us in John 15:5: *"I am the vine; you are the branches. If you remain in me and I in you, you will bear much fruit; apart from me you can do nothing."*

The No's are always hard to take. When we pray for something, we most always feel that what we are asking for is the best-case scenario, or for the best outcome. Again, it is most always our own desire, our will, and our own needs which we ask God to fulfill.

Unless of course we are praying for harm to come to another person out of spite and anger, which will never come from God through our prayers. Again, this is not God's will, this is sin that has filled our hearts which is seeking to keep us from honoring and being in union with God.

And when we pray for someone or something, and we perceive that prayer as being the best possible outcome or result in what we are asking for, we become dejected, and many times offended, when we see these things play out in a way that is contrary to our request. We begin to feel that God does not listen to us, or that God does not care about us, what we want, or what we desire. We then begin to question God, and our relationship with God, and at times will even question if He truly exists.

The true answer to the NO's can be found in Isaiah 55:8-9. God tells us: *"For my thoughts are not your thoughts, neither are your ways my ways," declares the Lord. "As the heavens are higher than the earth, so are my ways higher than your ways and my thoughts than your thoughts."*

We will not always understand why God does or does not answer our prayers in the ways which He does. God has a knowledge and understanding much greater than we will ever be able to comprehend. And when we do reach a point where we surmise that we may have gained enough intelligence and wisdom to assume what God is thinking or planning, we have then only become just like Samael/Lucifer/Satan in thinking that we can become God too.

The best reflection of attitude that we can have, regardless of the answer to our prayers, is one of submission and obedience. Acknowledging that God is all powerful, all knowledgeable, and understanding of things that we are not even capable of comprehending. It all boils down to the faith that we must have and must learn to live in – we must have the true faith which wholeheartedly believes that our Father knows what is best for us, our Father wants the best for us, and our Father will provide the best for us – no matter what we may think or feel in any given moment.

Maybe later – Not right now
The third option to the answer of our prayers is never an easy one to recognize. Most always the answer does not come, and again we are left believing that God is ignoring us or does not care. Many a time we think and feel that when

our prayers go unanswered, or when we do not see immediate results, that God does not care about our lives or what we want, and again, we question whether God even exists.

These thoughts and questions which we create are harmful to our relationship with God and are exactly what Satan is aiming for. Satan is right there whispering into your ear - *"See, I told you He doesn't care about you, He is not even paying attention to you."* Satan wants us to question God and wants to induce the separation from God that these questions create.

The reality of the *Maybe later* answer is that God is still answering our prayers – just not in a way or with the timing that we want. Just as we do with everything else in life, if we do not get the answer that we want, when we want it, we stomp off and throw a fit determined to find someone or something that will give us what we want. We walk away from God, the one who wants nothing but the best for us, in search of what we think is best for us. We then begin to sacrifice our beliefs and values as a Christian in an attempt to satisfy our own personal desires.

Just because God does not give in to our 'on-demand' lifestyle and provide us with instant results to all of our prayers does not mean that He will not answer that prayer in the way that we want or expect. God answers all prayers in His own good timing, no, in His perfect timing. As God's thoughts are higher than our thoughts, He knows the perfect time to answer each and every prayer, and when it will have the greatest effect in glorifying His name.

Therefore, the answer that we receive many times is *not right now*, or *you are not quite ready for that yet*. That does not mean no, it just means that now is not the right time for that. It means that other things have to happen first before that prayer can come to fruition. And those other things may be through other people, or they may be through us.

There are also times when our prayers do not get answered right away as other things have to occur in other people or situations first. God is working in other people as well, developing their hearts and character. And these other people and situations have to develop to a certain level before God will answer your prayer. Without the development of these other factors, answering your prayer now would be like planting the seed on the arid desert soil. It would not prosper or come to flourish.

Just as well, there are times when God is wanting us to develop and mature more in our relationship with Him, and in our faith. God cares about our hearts, what is best for our hearts, and what is truly in our hearts. So, for many prayers, God is saying *Keep coming back to me every day with that prayer and we will see if it is truly what you desire in your heart.* God wants us to strengthen our relationship with Him through prayer, and with that strengthening our hearts begin to desire and crave the things that God does as well.

The Other Answers

Albeit, the truth of the matter, one that many of us may find hard to accept, is that God does not answer all of our prayers, at least in a way which we would hope or expect them to be answered. God is much greater than we are, has a much greater understanding of all things than we ever will, and has much greater plans for us, for others, and for this world that we live in. What we may think or believe to be the best outcome, result, or course of action, for ourselves or others, is never anywhere close to the greatness of the plans that God has for us. We need to stop acting like the spoiled child that throws a fit every time they do not get what they want when our prayers do not get answered and start understanding that the reason for our existence is to be in complete union with God, and not for God to serve our every need and desire.

There are also many times when we turn to God in prayer and ask for something to happen, or for God to change the outcome of a situation. My kids are sick. My aunt has cancer. My boss is making my life impossible. My spouse isn't supportive of me. Just a few examples, but you get the point.

We then turn to God and pray for that person or that situation, asking God to heal them, or change the situation to our liking. The first issue with this type of prayer is that we are seeking our will, and not God's. It is our desires that we wish to come to fruition and not His, and for our glory and satisfaction.

The second, and much more difficult issue to understand, again deals with our perspective. We often do not see what is truly going on in a particular situation. We don't see the big picture and are therefore praying for the wrong thing to happen. Take the scenario with your boss. He is a jerk and makes your job, and life, very difficult. We turn to God and ask that He would make our job easier and less stressful. We pray that our boss would be changed, or maybe even that we would get a new boss. We pray that we would get a transfer or even find another job. What we fail to recognize is what the problem may actually be, and what our prayer should actually be for. Again, there are many outside forces attacking our lives, and the lives of others each and every day.

We pray for the wrong things, at the wrong times, and therefore those prayers don't ever get answered. We have our simple minds focused directly upon ourselves and our own small little world. There may be a reason why God has you stuck working for that miserable boss, or in that relationship with an unsupportive spouse. If we are truly Christians, God will use us in many different ways for His glory and many times this will require us to be in uncomfortable situations that we do not like. We are to be the light in this dark world. We are to be different, and to make a difference.

We should be praying for that boss, for his salvation, and that the Holy Spirit would come into his life and provide him the protection that is needed for him to be able to see the love and mercy of Jesus Christ. We should be praying for his heart, for his life, and for peace and relief in his world. Just as Paul told us in Philippians 2, we need to put others before ourselves – especially in our prayers. And if we find the need to pray for ourselves, we should be praying that through the Holy Spirit, God will strengthen us and enable us to do His will in the situation that we are in.

When we hold it as a core belief that our purpose is to honor and glorify God in everything that we do, we then begin to openly accept whatever answer may be given to our prayers, and we will then honor and glorify God for however He so chooses to answer our prayers.

Our Perspective

As we have learned with so many other things in life, and this world, we may now have also learned that our perspective on prayers and how they are answered could be faulty as well. We go to God with our selfish desires, expect an immediate response, and then think that it is perfectly normal and acceptable to just go right back to living our lives as we do. We view God as a genie in a bottle who is there to grant our every wish, make our lives easier, and then be put back up on the shelf until we need Him again.

Prayer, or life for that matter, is not about us. It is about God and His will and desires. This may seem a bit harsh and unfair to some people, but there is an absolute understanding which we must have about the life that we live – Our lives, our worlds, and everything about our being is not about us! It is about God. Life is not fair, and it was never intended to be that way. However, God is fair and just, and if we remain in God, serving and honoring God, He will ensure that we are rewarded for doing so. Maybe not today – Maybe not tomorrow – But in God we will be the ones to reap His glorious blessings.

We must come to grips with the fact that this world, God's world, would go on just as God has planned it too with or without our presence. We do not make the world go 'round, God does. We do not have the power to control anything,

God does. We do not exist without God, but God does and will exist without us.

We must rewrite our perspective and how we view God; and then carry that new view over into our prayer life with an all-out admiration, love, respect and fear for our Almighty Father. We must stop questioning God when our prayers are not answered in the ways that we want or the time that we want and begin to start questioning ourselves.

Our Pastor, Craig Groeschel, has brought up some self-reflective questions that we can ponder during these times. Over the past couple of years Craig has used these questions in several sermons, and I believe they are also listed in a few of his books as well.

Here are just a few of the questions which we can ask ourselves instead of questioning God:

What is God trying to tell me through this?
What do I need to learn from this?
What is God trying to teach me here?
What issues in my heart is God trying to raise through this?
What is it that God wants me to see through this?
What is it that God is asking me to let go of?[1]

I have tried to make it a part of my prayer life now that when I do not think that God is answering my prayers, or even when I am going through a challenging time in my life, I stop and ask myself these questions. Many times, I am unsure of the answers, so I turn to God in prayer and ask Him for the answers.

How Does God Speak to Us

We have learned in past chapters that God whispers. He does not shout or yell and will not do so to gain our attentions. He is not going to try to compete with the ways and noises of this world in an attempt to get us to recognize Him either.

God speaks to us softly. To hear a soft voice, you have to turn off all of the other surrounding noise. Things have to be quiet and peaceful. Just as God did in my life when I refused to recognize Him time and time again for over forty years – God shut out all of the surrounding noise in my life, or the things that were keeping me distracted from Him. I felt like I was losing everything and everyone in my life at that time, and that I had nothing left to turn too. The truth is that God removed these distractions from my life, one by one, to bring me to that quiet, isolated place in my living room on that one specific morning. That quiet place - physically, mentally, and emotionally – is right where I needed to be to hear God speak to me.

I have never been a so-called morning person until lately. My favorite time of the day now is early in the morning. I find myself waking up between 4am and 5am, and I love it. No one else is awake. The whole world is asleep, so I do not feel the pressures of my work life pulling me in yet. The birds aren't even up yet.

Everything is quiet. Everything is peaceful. I am able to start my day in a quiet surrounding with just myself and God. No interruptions, no distractions, and my heart and mind focused solely on God. Completely open, available, and free to hear what my loving Father is wanting to share with his son.

I also mentioned that I have been trying to be like Daniel and consistently pray three times a day. It becomes more challenging throughout the day though as I am stuck right in the middle of my chaotic life with things pulling at me from every direction. Some days are easier than others, but even then, it takes determination and commitment to remain faithful in prayer throughout the day. It is most often during the morning times, in the calmness and quiet, that I hear God speaking to me as I turn to Him for guidance and direction.

God does speak to us in many other ways as well though. Most prominently through His Word, the Bible. God's word is a living, breathing thing, and brings life and meaning to all of our questions and misunderstandings. It does not matter how many times you may have read the Bible; you can read a certain verse that you may have read ten times already and God will allow that verse to provide meaning, direction and clarity for what you are going through today, in a way that you did not see it before.

God also gives us signs and gifts throughout our day as well. Little treasures meant just for us. Little things that we encounter as we go through life that God put there just for us to show His love and affection for us. Things that other people will not see. Things that will make you pause, smile, and feel a warm comforting emotion as you know God did that just for you. It is only one of the ways in which He is saying: *I love you and you are the most important to me.* The closer we grow to God through prayer, the more evident these little treasures become to us as we go about our day.

These little things: the signs, gifts, and treasures – God has been placing them into your day forever. We are either just too busy with all of the distractions that we have placed into our lives to recognize them, or we have allowed Satan to keep the veil over our eyes keeping them hidden from us.

We need to allow ourselves the time and space to be with God. We need to eliminate the noise and distractions that are vying for our attentions, and that keep God out of our everyday life. This again is part of Satan's scheme – to keep us so busy and absorbed in other things that we have no room in our lives for God. It will not be easy, and the more that we try to do so, the more we will be confronted with other diversions.

But we must make a conscious effort to start, even if we start small. In John Eldredge's book *Get Your Life Back*[2], he introduces us to an excellent practice which he calls *The One Minute Pause*[3]. Eldredge has also created an app for *The One Minute Pause*[3] that you can install on your phone which will give you reminders to stop and pause, taking time to be with God, even if only for one minute.

The app is a great place to start, and while it may only be for a minute or so here and there, it helps us to create a new habit which brings us closer to God. The app has prerecorded prayers that are one minute, three minutes, five minutes, and ten minutes in length. Eldredge also includes five- and ten-minute pauses for Guidance, Healing, Mental Strength, and Praise/Worship.

In his book, *The Power to Change*[4], Craig Groeschel validates the principal intention of *The One Minute Pause*[3] in telling us that to change our habits we must first change our underlying beliefs. Many of us have aspirations, certain goals, lofty ambitions, or attempt new resolutions in an effort to make our lives better. And while all of these are good things, we most always see them fail or end quickly. The main reasoning behind that failure is that we are focused on a certain process or set of actions that we believe will get us to an end result, without making any attempt to change the disciplines or underlying beliefs of who we truly are. To make that new habit a consistent part of our lives, we must first accept and believe that this is who we truly are as a person.

Just as the Apostle Paul told us so clearly, we find that the war, or the battle, is in our minds. It is the thoughts, the perceptions, and the beliefs that we have ingrained so deeply into our understandings that keep us from reaching our true potential, or seeing our aspirations and resolutions become a normal part of our lives. If we truly want to see that change happen, we must first change the underlying belief, the lies which we have come to accept as our reality, which we have that are holding us back.

We all wander through life searching for 'the secret'. No matter what we do, no matter what we put our efforts and attentions towards, we are always trying to find the easier way to do it. Just as we found out in a previous chapter – the human mind is always trying to find the easiest way to do things in an effort to conserve energy and survive.

I can confidently say that I have finally found the secret to living this life that we do – **Prayer!** Life simply does not work without it, no matter how hard we may try to make it.

"Do not be anxious about anything, but in every situation, by prayer and petition, with thanksgiving, present your requests to God. And the peace of God, which transcends all understanding, will guard your hearts and your minds in Christ Jesus."

Philippians 4:6-7

Chapter 20

What Are You Waiting For?

Hopefully by now you have garnered a new perspective of who God is, how much He wants us and cares for us, and the effect that Satan and sin have on our lives every single day. Most discussions thus far have been with regard to Christians, or those who have already accepted Jesus Christ as their Lord and Savior. However, my primary objective with this book is to help others acknowledge and realize that the world which we live in has been successful in its attempts to alter our views and understandings of what reality truly is. We have been adversely duped by falsehoods our entire lives, and we have come to accept them as being authentic and accurate. We have been fed so many falsities that the ways in which we see and understand most of life has now become the polar opposite of its true meaning and intentions.

But what if you do not know Jesus? What if you have not accepted Him as your Lord and Savior? What if you are not sure about the whole God thing? Well, this book was written for you too. You too can remove the constant influx of disinformation from your life and come to know whom God and Jesus Christ truly are, just as is the case with the modern-day Christian.

Much like the Apostle Paul, I came from a dark and desperate path of destruction. My life was filled with the constant barrage of propaganda from Satan with the sole intent of keeping me in the darkness. You too can now begin to know and believe the promises and truths that God has for us through His son Jesus Christ, no matter what your past may have been like.

All that it takes is one little step – a step of faith.

John 3:16 goes on to tell us: *"For God so loved the world that He gave his one and only Son, that whoever believes in Him shall not perish but have eternal life."*

Jesus tells us in John 3:5: *"Very truly I tell you, no one can enter the kingdom of God unless they are born of water and the Spirit."*

Romans 9:9 says: *"If you declare with your mouth, "Jesus is Lord", and believe in your heart that God raised Him from the dead, you will be saved."*

The water and the Spirit that Jesus refers too in John 3:5 is signifying baptism, first by water, and then by the Holy Spirit. The baptism by water is the washing away of our old selves and sinful desires, and the birth of our new life in Christ. And as we are now believers in Christ, we receive the baptism of the Holy Spirit, which is the Holy Spirit dwelling within us.

In Romans 9:9 Paul is telling us that by verbally accepting Jesus Christ as our Lord and Savior and truly believing in our hearts that God raised Him from the dead, our salvation is guaranteed and cannot be taken away from us. We are then one, in Christ, and have now become sons and daughters of God, and inherit the rightful claim to all of His promises.

The Decision

From my perspective, the decision to accept Christ as your Lord and Savior, or become a Christian, is a rather easy one. Obviously, I say this as I am now a Christian. Many years passed, however, where I likely would not have agreed with that statement as I was being misled as well. Now that I have seen both sides (good and evil), with all sincerity and forthrightness, I can truly say that the choice is, or should be, very easy.

However, this choice should not be taken lightly. It goes against everything that we have been taught and led to believe in the world that we know. And since we can actually see, hear, feel and experience (and sometimes taste) the world that we live in – it is something that we are much more likely to fall in line with. I am sure you have heard the old saying *'You have to see it to believe it'*. Well, that is the mentality that we have come to accept in our world and our lives.

Countless others have been led to Christ, have accepted Him as their Lord and Savior, and have been baptized – only to fall away and return to their former life of this world. One should be well aware that in making the decision to become a Christian, the act alone of accepting Christ as your Lord and Savior is not all that is involved nor required to truly become a Christian. This is just the beginning of our new life, a life in which we should change, be renewed, and live to follow Jesus Christ in each and every moment of our days.

We also live in a world full of con-artists, liars, thief's, cheaters and people who are out for nothing but their own personal gain, regardless of the cost to others. We have learned, or taught ourselves, to become very guarded and skeptical of anyone or anything which we do not know and that has not proven itself to be trustworthy. We have also been taught to 'question everything'. We do these things for our own protection and to keep ourselves from getting hurt. Just as it was in ancient times when cities and towns would build extremely high, impenetrable stone walls surrounding the town to keep enemy forces out, and to protect those within – we build walls around our own lives as well to guard and protect ourselves from the evil and sin in this world.

When these cities and towns built these walls, the people living inside the walls felt safe and secure. They knew the other people inside, and this allowed them to let down their guard and relax. They could get comfortable. They did not have to worry about the possibility of an outside danger, or even what that outside danger may be. They did not have to question everything that they encountered on a daily basis. It did not matter what dangers or threats existed outside of the walls, as they knew they were safe living inside the walls.

Once again, just as is our most common issue today, the perception that they had was flawed, and their focus was in the wrong direction. The people in these towns and cities were focused on and concerned with possible attacks coming from outside of the walls, from unknown forces, with no regard for attacks that may come from within, or the repercussions from being imprisoned within those walls.

I know what you must be thinking – It makes perfect sense to build a mountainous wall of defense to keep invading armies out. I agree – It makes perfect sense to protect ourselves and preserve the life that we know and love. But that is just looking at the issue from one side, with only one perspective. And as is most always our case – rarely do we ever believe that the perspective which we hold, personally, is ever flawed or skewed. Almost never are we willing to admit that we may be wrong.

What the people in those cities and towns did not realize was the harm that they were creating in building those walls.

First – while the walls may have kept enemy forces out, they kept the people inside imprisoned within. This meant that their whole existence and under-standing of the world, and its views, only came from within the walls, and what had already existed within the walls, and therefore would never increase or change as the influences would always remain the same. Nothing new would ever be experienced, or learned, as the depth of knowledge was only as great as what had already been learned. They would never have a Christopher Colum-bus to come along and help them to realize that they actually could sail out past the Strait of Gibraltar. (Chapter 14).

Second – As the walls kept people inside, they would never be able to experience anyone new. They would never be able to acquire new friendships. They would never be able to experience the love and joy of others that God had intended for us, even if it meant opening ourselves up to the possibility of getting hurt every now and then.

Third – The intentions in erecting those walls were to keep the enemy armies out. However, no matter how high of a wall you build, you cannot keep our true enemy out. Satan and his demons can still get in, will get in, and will attack. Satan will even tell you that the wall is for your best interest, and that you need it to protect yourself. Satan will tell you that you already know everything that you need to know, and that there is nothing good out there for you anyways.

Just as the people did in ancient times, we build walls around our lives as well. We try to protect ourselves from ever being hurt. We learn what we can from our limited environment, and then believe that we are all knowledgeable and that there is not a better way of understanding things, or a better way to do things. We believe that our way and understanding of all things is the only way, and we refuse to accept any other version or the possibility that our understandings may be incorrect or flawed.

And when someone approaches us with something different than what we know and believe, we immediately write them off as being a lunatic. Our wall keeps us confined in a prison, a prison that Satan has led us to believe is safe and comfortable (remember Satan's #1 tactic – *Deception*. If we knew it was a prison we would not want to stay there, so he deceives us in to believing that it is something else, something enjoyable, something comfortable – and that nothing outside of that prison would give us any more enjoyment or comfort).

I am sure you have also heard the saying *'There are two sides to every coin'*. What does it mean exactly? Any coin that you look at has two sides, and each side has a different image, logo, or inscription. They are always opposing and different. No coin has two sides that are identical, or that share the same view.

In U.S currency, we call the two sides of a coin Heads or Tails. We call the one side Heads as it has an image of one's head on it, which is most always that of a former President. We call the other side Tails as the tail is the opposing side of a head. On U.S. currency the Tails side usually has an image of a building, or the American Eagle.

Nonetheless, there are always two sides to every coin. Same coin – but a different view on each side. Two different ways to look at the same thing. Two different perspectives. In our case, in the world that we live in, there are two different views on how we should live our lives – The way that God wants us and intended us to live, or the way that Satan wants us to live. And from the minute we are born, Satan has been constantly trying to do everything that he can to keep us away from God and to live life the way that he wants us to live it.

The sad thing about this fact is that most people in our world today live this way, and don't even realize it. They don't even acknowledge, or understand, the fact that Satan is an everyday part of their lives.

So when I come to you and explain that your life would be much better off, that you will have life forever and you will be promised riches beyond your wildest imagination by accepting Jesus Christ as your Lord and Savior – I completely understand why you would be so reluctant to grasp on to something or someone that you cannot see, feel or touch. It sounds too radical to believe, and again our mind cannot assimilate any of those statements with anything that we may have already learned in life – so we quickly write it off as being absurd.

The First Step

Taking a step into the unknown is scary – but taking any new first step always is.

It requires us to step outside of those walls which we have built. To venture out into a world that we know nothing about, which I know completely scares the hell out of most people nowadays. It requires us to let down that guard, and to remove any of the preconceived thoughts or expectations that we may have had, and to just be open to experiencing something new, as it is. It requires us to open up and let others in, and experience life as it was meant to be lived. It requires us to take that first step of faith, into something that we know nothing about and to give up control of everything that we do know. It requires us to acknowledge that we do not know it all, and that there is more out there for us, much more that our Creator is waiting to give to us.

We all like our comfort zones. The ways in which we have made our lives comfortable and easy, predictable and safe. We do not like change in our lives, and most always, it takes something profound to initiate a change. My profound moment was being in the presence of God, even if ever so briefly. That is a moment which I will never forget, one that has changed me forever. And that one moment has left me craving and yearning to experience those feelings and emotions, His presence, more than anything else.

I went through life for years in search of the so-called perfect life, and what I believed was the way to live the perfect life. I would always attempt to fine tune or tweak my methods to obtain better results as I went along. I spent decades chasing my own desires and passions, my own thrills and fantasies, and always trying to get the most out of this world. All while building my own walls and comfort zones that would protect me from other things or people that I perceived as a hindrance to my betterment, or that I just simply did not want to deal with. And after decades of hard work, success and gain – I came to the realization that I was still left feeling empty. I was still that same desolate man with no true character and no justifiable reason for my life itself. I was shallow, I was fake, I was a poser. I was living my life based upon a foundation of lies and deceptions which promised me everything but gave me nothing.

All of those years in search of that perfect life has led me to one absolute and certain conclusion – **It Does Not Exist!**

While that may be hard for some to swallow, it is the cold, hard truth. It does not exist in the world that we live in, with the worldly views and beliefs which we have come to accept and chase after. That perfect life only exists in Jesus Christ. And it is a life more exceptional and promising than anything we may ever dream up or imagine on our own.

Denial

The refusal to accept or even consider this as a possibility only further validates the fact that Satan has a very strong grasp on one's life at this time and has dimmed their view on all things good. I do not take these words lightly and use them only with the best of intentions. I deliver them out of love, in hopes that through these words the Holy Spirit may open your eyes, if even just for a moment, to acknowledge that just maybe there is something else out there to be considered. Maybe we have been lied to our entire lives. Maybe we have been deceived. And maybe, just maybe, we don't have a clue how to live this life that we are in.

I am also mindful of the thoughts which many of you may be having right now, and what may be running through your head –

C'mon, this is a bunch of rubbish. Jesus, God, and Christianity are just a story that a bunch of old guys made up a long time ago. It is not real. And it is certainly not going to change my life.

Some may also believe that Christianity is just another form of social control, or that it is harmful to society and the progress of science or humanity. Others may see a Christian as someone who is weird, unintelligent, or weak, as again this is the worldly view that we have learned to accept and associate with Christianity.

However, our biggest doubts when considering to follow Jesus Christ come from fear. A fear of the unknown. A fear of not having control. A fear of having to give something up. And a fear of the 'what-if's'. And when we are unable resolve the 'what-if's', we begin to question the existence of God, Jesus and Christianity as we have also made it an inherent belief of ours that we must have a justifiable explanation for everything in our lives to be able to rationalize its existence.

If any part of this book has made even the slightest bit of sense to you – You will hopefully see and understand that all of the negative and detracting thoughts that you are encountering are coming directly from Satan, in his attempt to keep you from God. As we discussed before, the attacks begin in our mind, with the lies and the deceptions. The more that you ponder the possible factuality of this book, and any of the statements within, the more Satan will flood your mind with lies to counter your attempt at considering any such possibilities.

Here is a great exercise for those who may not believe that God, Jesus, or Christianity are real, or that they truly exist:

Think of something else that you have heard of over the course of your life which you do not believe is real or actually exists. Anything you want – your choice. Whatever it may be, apply the following process to that thing:

For this example, we will use aliens and U.F.O's as our subject matter.

The first U.F.O sighting in the United States happened in June of 1947. However, U.F.O stories go back as far as the 1600's. And just as with Christianity, many who claim to have seen a U.F.O rarely ever talk about it for fear of being seen as a lunatic.

So, are they real or not? I think it would be safe to say that darn near every one of us has never seen a U.F.O, or an alien. We haven't seen one, haven't touched one, and haven't smelled one – yet many still believe they exist.

Here is your exercise – (I will use U.F.O's and aliens in the example below, but you can insert your 'thing' if you wish)

Think long and hard in an attempt to validate why they may exist. Attempt to rationalize their existence and find a justification for their being. How did they become so advanced and create technology far greater than we can even comprehend in our day and age? Where do they come from? And why are they coming to our planet? Are they going to take over our world, or are they here to help us?

A very controversial topic which has been much debated over the years. And a topic that could have many valid points of debate for either side, just as you could say with Christianity as well.

I can assure you that one thing did **NOT** happen in that exercise though, and your internal search for the truth – You were not overcome with opposing, negative thoughts every time that you thought of a reason that would support or validate their reality.

Sure, you may not believe in U.F.O's or aliens – but you simply leave it at that and shrug it off. Again, your mind searches through its vast data base of information which you have assembled over the years in an attempt to rationalize an experience or thought, and then quickly makes a conclusion as to your beliefs based off of that information. And you leave it at that. And if you ever go back to consider the possibility of aliens and U.F.O's again, your mind quickly jumps back to that same conclusion that you had already once predetermined.

Now – try that same exercise with God, Jesus, and Christianity. You do not get one simple contradictory thought, and then it's done. You get bombarded with multiple objections. And if you walk away from that mental discussion, and at some point, come back to hash it out again – the overwhelming contradictions are now more than likely totally different than they were last time. How can this be? If the thoughts you were hearing were truly yours and coming from your mind and your database, your mind would go right back to the predetermined answer that you had stored last time from the previous attempt at finding answers.

The simple fact in this scenario is that the thoughts which are overtaking your mind are not yours. They are the thoughts of an outside source, an influence with greater powers than we can understand. An influence who is the master at getting us to believe and accept that the thoughts which we are having are those of our own. The overpowering resistance that one encounters when pursuing God, Christ or Christianity should alone be more than enough of an indicator that He/They do exist, and they are very real.

Why else would someone or something make such endless efforts to steer you from something that does not actually exist? If something truly does not exist, what is the point in any attempt to persuade others that it does not exist?

My Reservations

As for me – I had those same thoughts as well. I was just like you. I truly believed that if I gave my life to Christ, I would lose everything that I had. I would lose my freedom, my choices, my independence. I would be seen as a weak, wimpy, boring man. Life would no longer be fun, and in a sense, I would become castrated and emotionless. I would be very dull and boring. What point is there to life if that is how life was meant to be lived?

Yet again, these were all lies that Satan had been feeding me to keep me from turning to Christ and knowing the truth. I fell victim to the trap and accepted and believed the lies for so many years. Little did I know that those lies actually kept me in bondage, living a life that wasn't even half as good as it is now that the truth has been revealed to me.

Now, I am truly free, and I feel that freedom every single moment of every day. I see things in a way that our loving Father meant for us to see them in – the beauty, the joy, the happiness, the love. I am no longer bogged down by the fears, worries, stresses and pain which controlled my life in the past. I am free to be me, as I was created to be, and to fully enjoy this life as we were created to do.

Contrary to my initial fears, I did not lose anything either. Actually, I gained more than I ever could have imagined. I am still the same man that I was before, in a sense, only now in a way that seeks to honor and glorify God in everything that I do, and which allows me to freely be myself. Obedient to and serving a God that wants me to be happy and live my life to the fullest.

I still ride my Harley, probably more so now than before, as I have realized that it gives me joy and happiness. I still desire and lust for my wife and take every chance that I can get to be intimate and playful with her – and I am very thankful to say that these times are not boring, they have actually become more fun and enjoyable. And I am still that rough around the edges tough guy who is not afraid of a fight. The difference now though is that I know what I am fighting for, and what battles are mine to fight.

I am now able to truly see and understand that the world is not out to get me. And when someone else does do something offensive, or that may be hurtful, I no longer take it personally. I now realize and see that almost always, the offense and the ensuing attack is not intended for or directed at me. I see the offense and the attack for what it is – sin within the life of another. I realize now that the individual is not the root of the problem, it is the sin within them. Therefore, I no longer instinctively assume a defensive posture and attack them back. It is not the person. Absent the sins and lies they have been deceived into believing, just as I once had been, that person would not be doing what they are doing.

That other person is just like me, and you; filled and deceived by the sins and lies of Satan. The only difference is that I am now aware of the bigger picture and now have the ability to see things for what they truly are. And when one is able to view life with that perspective, they suddenly become aware that all of the little trivial things do not matter – or hurt.

There is much more, my friends. A whole world more. One that is bright, joyful, exciting, playful, and stress-free. One which we were created to have and live in, through Jesus Christ, and that God our Father wants to lavish upon us.

I know how difficult change can be. I know that stepping in to the unknown, and out of our comfort zone is scary, no matter how false that perceived security may be. I know you will feel as though you are all on your own in doing so, as you are leaving everything that you know behind. We are all afraid to fall, we are all afraid of getting hurt. I can promise you this though - Jesus Christ and God will NEVER hurt you. – and they will both be there with you every step of the way.

God created you, in His own image. You are His child. Does not every parent want more than the best for their child? Well, God desires even more than that for each of us, unimaginably more. And more than we could ever conceive from the concept of any worldly parents.

The fear that God, or Jesus, will come into your life and make radical changes through discipline and punishment are absurd and totally inaccurate as well. Our Father is a God of love and kindness, even in times of discipline. Yes, He will take you to some places in your life that require change. But He will always do so in a kind, loving, and gentle way – and He will always be right there with you, hand in hand, guiding you through every last bit of it.

The Places God Took Me

For many years now I have been aware that I cannot recall many memories of my younger days, and I have feared this was due to the fact that they were so traumatic, and I had suppressed them so deeply as to avoid the pain of facing them once again. Rarely do I ever talk about my past, and even now as I try to, I have difficulty recalling what may or may not have happened.

I mentioned in a previous chapter that I had been deployed back to my hometown of Omaha for the recent spring/summer storms which rolled through there this year. Shortly after I arrived in Omaha, I felt Jesus urging me to go to the house that I initially grew up in. I was not sure why, but I felt that Jesus wanted to show me something there, or that something needed to be healed.

I felt Jesus telling me that to move on with my life, I needed to address and heal the wounds of the past. I had now reached a point in my life where I was not only hearing God and the Holy Spirit but listening to and obeying any direction that they gave me. So, I committed to making the trip over to the old house.

I put the trip off for weeks, however, always finding something else to do in an effort to avoid having to face my past. In the meantime, I would constantly attempt to recall what may or may not have happened there that would need to be healed or addressed in hopes of preparing myself for what may be forthcoming. For the life of me, I could not come up with anything. However, I knew that it was not somewhere that I wanted to go or be.

Three months came to pass as I procrastinated, hoping to avoid facing the pain, which I knew was inevitable. Then, the Holy Spirit overwhelms me in saying: *"You need to go, and you need to go today!"* So that night I hopped on my Harley and rode over to the house that I grew up in, the one where I was just a little boy, the one where my whole world and my family fell apart.

I parked my bike along the curb, a couple houses down, and then just sat there taking in the images of the house and the neighborhood, clearing my mind and allowing Jesus to come in and show me what it was that I needed to address. I had to dig deep to picture my past, the inside of that house, and any moments that I could recall.

Nothing! No emotion, no feelings, no pain. I could not see what it was that Jesus was trying to show me. I sat there for probably half an hour asking Jesus to take me where He wanted me to go. Nothing!

Then, out of nowhere, Jesus tells me: - *"Get off the bike and take a walk down the street."* So, I did. I walked down to the end of the block, recalling the people who had lived in each one of the houses as I walked by, and some of the memories that I had of each. I reached the end of the block and still felt nothing. I began to feel as though I was missing the point, and that for some reason I was keeping Jesus from showing me what it was that He had wanted me to see. (This too, is another tactic of Satan. At times, when we may not feel close to God, Satan will try to convince us that we are at fault, that we are doing something wrong.)

I then crossed the street and began to head back up to my bike. I passed the first house, and as I come to the second, a devastating feeling of fear and terror overcame me, which caused me to stop dead in my tracks. Suddenly my mind was flooded with images of the past. That house looked nothing like I remembered it to be, and I had not given this house any thought since I was probably eight years old. The house was evil and dark as I was seeing it, even though it had been completely updated and looked modern and new. All of a sudden, I did not want to be there, but I did not know why. I couldn't move though. It was as if I was frozen in time, and no matter how badly I wanted to be somewhere else, Jesus wanted me to be right here, as that little eight-year-old boy again.

Then Jesus speaks to me softly and says: - *"This is where you lost your innocence. This is where it all started."* Jesus showed me what happened in that house. What had been buried so deeply that even I was no longer aware of its existence.

There were two neighbor girls, sisters, who lived in that house. One day I had gone down to their house to play. We ended up down in their basement, and the older sister decided that we were going to play Doctor. I do not recall all of the details, however, after being in that basement for some time I do recall bolting up the stairs and flying out the front door in response to what had just happened.

I had not remembered that day since it happened, and had completely buried it so deep inside of me that it would have never come out. And I had never shared the events of that day with anyone, not even my wife.

Jesus then prompted me to head over to the other old neighborhood that I had lived in where I spent much of my teenage years where He revealed a few other things to me as well.

As I left the first house and rode down the street, about a block away, I passed the McCarthy's house. The McCarthy's were friends of our family. They had kids the same ages as my siblings and I, and our parents would get together on occasions. As I rode by their house it became evident that they no longer lived there. I also began to notice a small boy who was standing outside of that house in the front yard all by himself. This struck me as odd at first, as it was beginning to get dark and there was not a parent in sight.

As I got closer to the boy, I could see that his eyes were affixed on me the entire time. His position never changed, other than following my movement with his head and eyes. I then passed right in front of the house and the boy, and what I saw still bewilders me to this day. The boy was probably about six or seven years old. He had brown hair and a small skinny body. I could see his face clearly by now. He looked just like me. Exactly like I did when I was that age. The boy then lifted up his hand and waved at me, still looking me directly in the eyes as if we were connected in some way. The happiness and the smile on his face were one that I had not seen in a very long time. One that I have long since forgotten how to bring about.

Then Jesus speaks to me again as to help me understand the million thoughts that were now running through my head: - *"That is you. Pure, innocent, and happy!"* I guess it was me, I mean he looked just like me, but I had long since forgotten what innocence and happiness were.

In short time I arrived in the neighborhood that we had moved to after my parents divorced. Remember – the less than desirable neighborhood. I headed down the block taking in all the houses and recalling who lived there and looking for any sign of anyone that I once knew. Everything had changed. Nothing looked the same. I didn't recognize anything.

Our house was located in the middle of the block, so I rode down to that point and pulled my bike over to the side, shut it off, and just sat there and stared at the structure that held so many memories of my past. It too, looked nothing like I had remembered it.

I then heard the sound of a door opening and closing not too far behind me, and off to my left. I turn to look out of curiosity and am shocked by the person that I now see. An older man, much older, walking out of his home. A man that I recognize, and one whom I had always looked up to and admired. A man that knew me, as well as my whole family, since we had moved into that house forty some years ago.

The man was Curt. Curt was a Captain with the Fire Department when I was younger. He was a single man and lived alone. I guess it was in his nature, or maybe due to his job, but Curt was always there, willing to help everyone in that neighborhood, at any time. He knew everyone, and everyone knew him as well.

I got off of my bike and walked over to Curt, hoping to soak up a good memory of my past. Curt did not recognize me at first, and I had to remind him who I was. And the moment I did, it was like a switch was flipped. This now eighty-year-old man instantaneously went back in time to the loving, caring, father figure that we all once knew. He was excited to see me, and you could see his eyes fill with joy.

Curt and I revisited the old neighborhood and all the people who used to live there. Not one left he says. Most all of them have died. Even the kids who were my age and would be in their fifties now – all gone. Curt and I are casually walking the block as we talk, and we find ourselves standing in front of my old house at some point. He tells me stories of the people that have lived there since we left, and all that has changed. He then goes on to tell me about the gal who is living there now, a lovely lady named Mary. I comment to Curt that everything looked so different than what I remembered as a child.

At that moment, Curt seemed to change as well. Curt was eighty years old now and had been on the Fire Department for most of his life. The Fire Department of old, not the modern-day Fire Department run by bureaucrats who are more concerned with minimizing their liability than protecting the people they serve. And yes, there is a difference. The old school fire fighters would kick down doors, run in to burning buildings, and do anything at almost any cost to save whatever and whomever they could. Modern day fire fighters will just let the building burn, while trying to protect any surrounding buildings from a distance. This is not so much the fault of the fire fighter themselves, but of the political landscape which they are run by. And these are not simply my opinions, but those of actual fire fighters which I have befriended over the years.

At eighty years old, Curt's body had been through hell, literally. He had bad knees, had broken his back a few times, and had arthritis in just about every joint in his body. Our casual walk around the neighborhood was slow and difficult for Curt. All of a sudden, however, after my comment on things looking different, Curt became fully alive and energetic. His tone changed and he suddenly had a vigor in his step that I had not seen before. I could sense that something was happening, but I was not quite sure what it was.

Then Curt looks to me and says, *"Do you want to go inside?"* Curt was referring to the inside of my old house. He wanted to know if I wanted to go inside of that old house that held so many of my memories. I cocked my head back in shock and disbelief. I couldn't do that. This was not my house anymore and I surely did not want to disturb someone that I had no connection with. And I most certainly had not prepared myself for going down that road of feelings and emotions. Curt could see my hesitation and he responded by saying *"C'mon. I know Mary real well. She will have no problem letting you look around."*

The next thing I know, we are knocking on the door which is then opened by an older petite woman that Curt introduces to me as Mary. Curt explains to her that I used to live in that house some forty plus years ago. Mary's eyes opened widely, and I felt her heart and soul do the same. It was as if Mary was welcoming a long-lost friend that she had not seen in forty years. She insisted that we come in, and then told me to take a look around, anywhere that I wanted to go.

Curt and I walked into the house, with Mary following closely behind listening to my comments and stories as I recalled moments or events that had happened in my past. The house was small, much smaller than I remembered it to be, which is the case with many of the recollections of our past. We always tend to see them as bigger or make them bigger than they actually are. As I walked through the entryway and passed into the living room, I felt very uneasy and uncomfortable. I did not want to be here, and I did not want to dredge up many of the old memories that I had spent years trying to bury. I had spent a good portion of my life making every effort to stop them from coming back to haunt me again.

At that moment, Curt, who I am now convinced is not Curt anymore, puts his hand on my shoulder and begins telling me about things that he remembered of the house. The moment Curt's hand touched my shoulder, I heard a voice say, *"It is going to be okay"* and a peaceful feeling came over me. Once again, in that moment, I knew that Jesus was right there with me, leading me and guiding me through my past – through Curt.

We walked through every room of that house, stopping in each one, pausing to allow a certain event or memory to come alive. Each one I had tried so hard to never think of again. And in each one Jesus was right there with me saying *"Do you remember that...?"*

As we ended our tour my thoughts came to my wife, and I let the comment slip that I wished my wife could have been there with me and seen the house. Why? I do not know, as I have always tried to keep my past where it belonged – in the past. Mary heard my comment and quickly replied that I could bring her by anytime, and that if for some reason she was not at home, Curt had a key and could let us in.

I left that house with unexpected feelings that day. Mary reminded me of my grandma – so kind, so caring, and so genuine. I also was no longer afraid of that house and the parts of me that it held. That house, along with the neighborhood, looked completely different and updated. It looked new and fresh. I still struggle to understand how Jesus wants me to perceive this, but I saw Mary as my mother in a sense as well. She was single and it was her house, just as with my mom. She slept in the same room that my mother did. But she was new and fresh also, just like every other image Jesus showed me on that night. She was loving, caring, and had a heart that was completely open to others.

The whole experience was a lot to take in, and it took me a few days to process all that had happened. In looking back I saw that I was terrified by any thought of what that trip might reveal as well as the torment that my old wounds would force me to endure once again, so much that I was doing anything that I could to avoid it. I then saw that even while I was reliving the pain and the trauma, Jesus was standing right there with me, comforting me, telling me that I would be okay and that He was making all things new again. Jesus was telling me that this was not who I was, and that these memories had no control over me. They did not need to define who I was going forward. That He was making me new again as well.

Jesus took me to some pretty dark places in my past on that night and showed me some of the things that I had done, as well as the things that others had done to me. And at each and every one of those places Jesus was there to comfort me, not punish me or condemn me. Jesus was there to walk me through the places and things, to help me let go of them, and to show me that He loved me regardless of those things.

Jesus wanted me to face those things of my past, the things that had caused me pain and agony for years, and He wanted to do it with me. Jesus wanted to show me that with Him I have nothing to fear, and with Him these dreadful memories are not who I am. Jesus wanted to heal me, which is in fact the reason that He came to our dark world – and that is exactly what He did, in the most comforting way.

Two months later, my assignment and my time in Omaha was nearing an end. Winter would certainly arrive soon, and since I am not a fan of the cold weather, I asked to be released by the end of that month, about three weeks later. My schedule was already filled with claims for the next couple of weeks, so this meant that I would only receive new claims for about another week, which would then leave me scheduled out through the end of the month.

With my job, when we arrive on a particular assignment, we are assigned to a certain area to handle claims, most always by zip code. This is done to keep us in a tight area, allowing us to be more productive, and not having to drive very far from claim to claim. As each storm goes on some adjusters are released from that assignment as the number of new claims coming in begins to decrease. As those adjusters are then released, the area being worked by another given adjuster will increase in size, but most always will only increase in the surrounding area of where he or she was already working.

During the entire six months that I had been in Omaha, the area that I had been assigned to work was on the extreme far south side of the southern suburbs, and even into rural areas surrounding those southern suburbs. As my area expanded, it did so in areas toward the southeast, even further away from town.

During the last week that I was receiving new claims I received one claim that was smack in the middle of Omaha, or about twenty miles north of the area that I was working in. It is not unusual to receive the occasional 'mistake' assignment claim and is most always due to the computer routing system not recognizing the zip code on the policy correctly. When this does happen, most all adjusters will simply contact management and have that claim reassigned to another adjuster who is working that area. I could have done that with this claim as well, but for some unknown reason, I did not.

I recognized that the address on the claim was in the vicinity of the house where I spent my teenage years, but did not give it much further attention at the time. I figured I would just keep the claim, handle it, and it would not be much of an inconvenience. I called the Insured and scheduled the appointment to inspect their property, once again without paying much attention to the exact address.

With two days left of inspections I pulled up my claims for that day and began to prepare the paperwork that I would need for my inspections. In doing so I almost always pull up Google Streetview just to get a quick glimpse of the house that I will be inspecting - just as I did with this claim. My jaw dropped immediately, and a hundred thoughts began racing through my head once again when I saw the picture of that house.

The house – the one that I would be inspecting later that day, the one that I received completely by mistake, the one that was in an area where I had not worked one other claim the entire storm – was the old house of my buddy Steve. It was the house that I had spent many years in and out of. It was the house of the only friend that I had whose parents were still together. But I also knew that Steve, as well as his parents had long since moved away.

It is also a normal practice when receiving a new claim, and contacting the insureds to schedule the appointment, to ask them if they have any interior damage, such as water leaking into any area of the home since the storm. This lets me know if I will need them to be present or not, and if I need to go inside of the home. And when I asked this insured during my initial contact, he stated no. To be completely thorough, as well as address anything that the homeowner may have noticed since our initial phone call, I always ask them again upon my arrival for the inspection.

As I arrived for my scheduled appointment later that day, I noticed an older 1970's Chevy pickup parked out on the street. It was green and gray in color and had not been restored. It was the exact same truck, color and all, that Steve's dad used to have. This did not strike me as much at first, but later I came to realize the significance of that old truck being parked right there, at that time.

When I showed up for my inspection that day, as I always do, I again asked if they had noticed any interior damage – and now the answer was yes. The homeowners walked me through the entire house and took me upstairs to a finished attic space to show me water damage to the ceiling drywall. This finished attic space used to be Steve's bedroom – a room that I recalled oh so well.

I spent the next hour looking at every part of that home, more so for my job, and pictured the way that the home used to be as I was doing so. I finished my inspection and moved on with my day as normal, unable to get the oddities out of my head, and trying to decipher what had just happened. As is the case most all of the time, when Jesus is trying to show us something, it does not come out as clear cut and well understood as we are in a sense distracted by the experience itself. Most always we have to get out of our own way, and our own attempts to interpret these experiences, and just let Jesus do the talking to us.

I revisited that day in my head over and over again trying to understand what Jesus was trying to show me in that time, and I could derive nothing. I then explained all that had occurred to Robin, and how strange and unusual the circumstances were, and the fact that I had no clue what it all meant. Robin was also aware of the previous trips that God had taken me on in Omaha, and what they had revealed.

I believed that God had taken me to that house for a specific reason on that day, but I could not understand why. There were just too many indications that the events that had unfolded were not merely by coincidence. I was trying to ascertain the meaning of it all just as I had with the prior places which God had me revisit – with the question of *What is God trying to show me from my past that needed to be healed and addressed?*

After much discussion, both Robin and I felt that God was not trying to teach me anything on that day. We came to the conclusion that God was giving me a gift. The gift of good memories from my past, and times of joy and happiness.

God had taken me back to the other dark and hurtful places of my past, which did need to be addressed, but were difficult to get through. And in those places, I had to step in to that pain and hurt once again, which was difficult for me to do. There was a reason why I had buried those memories so deeply. However, God, being the loving, caring Father that He is, wanted to give me joy and happiness as well, and wanted that joy and happiness to be toward the end of my trip so that it would be fresh in my mind. He knew that I had to go back and face my wounds of the past to truly heal and become whole once again. And He knew that it would be painful for me, so He walked through every piece of it with me. And then to make sure that I did not stay stuck in those memories, God gave me the gift of seeing some of the good times as well to show me that I am loved and that He truly does care about my happiness.

Those good memories also included Steve's dad (hence the reasoning for that old truck that just happened to be parked out front) and the understanding of what the true family dynamic should look like. I had stated in a previous chapter that I was fearful of Steve's dad, mostly due to his size and demeanor. However, my prevailing view of his father was one of respect and admiration. Even as an outsider I was able to see that under his large, rough exterior, there was a man who truly loved and cared for his kids and family. In retrospect I can also see that maybe to some degree I was jealous of Steve, and what he had available to him every day that so many of us never get to experience or that we take for granted when we do.

Are You Open to a Change?

I know it is a difficult process to make a change in our lives. I know there is much to consider, and likely a lot of questions and doubt which may be holding you back right now. Those, again, are all the thoughts and lies being fed to you by Satan in an attempt to keep you from even considering such a choice. Let God take care of all of that – He can handle it. You only need to worry about one thing – The first step! Take the first step and let God do the rest.

A step of FAITH!

"For it is by grace you have been saved, through faith – and this is not from yourselves, it is the gift of God...." Ephesians 2:8

Once we take that first step and allow God and Jesus to come into our lives things begin to change. This does not happen overnight though, with the immediate results which we have come to expect through the world that we live in. It is a process, and for many of us it is a never-ending process in which we continue to learn and grow each and every day. Although for some, there may be a radical change, in a short period of time.

A perfect example of this radical change is the man that I have quoted numerous times thus far – the Apostle Paul. Paul's life also shows us that anyone can be saved and come to Christ, regardless of their past.

Paul, before he became Paul, was named Saul. Saul was known as 'the Pharisee of all Pharisee's', who intensely persecuted the followers of Jesus. It was Saul's mission to persecute the church of God and attempt to destroy it. Saul believed in Judaism, just as his fathers did, and was advancing quickly in status of their religious ranks. Judaism is known to be one of the oldest of religions in our world. Judaism rejects the concept of God in human form. Simply put – they do not believe that Jesus Christ is the Messiah or that He is God in any form. Judaism does not accept or acknowledge the books of the New Testament.

Several years after Jesus was crucified and rose from the tomb, Saul had heard about followers of this Jesus that may be in the synagogues of Damascus, so he went to the High Priest to basically get permission to hunt them down and imprison them. As Saul was on the road to Damascus a bright light from heaven flashed around him. Saul fell to the ground and heard a voice say *"Saul, Saul, why do you persecute me?"* Saul asked, *"Who are you, Lord?"* The voice then said *"I am Jesus, whom you are persecuting. Now get up and go into the city, and you will be told what you must do."*

Saul was blinded by the occurrence for three days until the Lord sent Ananias to him to give him his sight back. At that time Saul was baptized and filled with the Holy Spirit. Saul immediately believed and began to preach that Jesus was the Son of God. Sometime later Saul's name would be changed to Paul.

Just as with my story of being in the presence of God, Paul's life was changed as well, causing him to rethink everything that he had understood and believed in, as well as who God really was. Just as I did, Paul realized that everything that he had been taught and had come to believe was a lie.

Paul would go on to become one of the most influential Apostles with the purpose of carrying the gospel to the Gentiles. It should be noted that Paul was not one of the original Disciples either. Paul did not know Jesus when He was on Earth and only came to know Him after His resurrection when Jesus met him on the road to Damascus. Paul was specifically selected by God to be an Apostle, and to be the Apostle that would carry His word to the Gentiles. The Gentiles at that time were anyone other than the Jewish people.

So, regardless of where you come from, what your backstory may be, or what you may have done in the past – God still wants you and desires you to be with Him, and Jesus can and will wash away all of your past sins. He did it for Saul, and He will do it for each of us as well.

We do not have to do any works either or perform any tasks or deeds to receive this grace. We just need to make the first step – that move of faith that Jesus can and will take care of the rest. Jesus is already there waiting; He just wants to know that you truly want Him and desire Him as well. He wants to know that it is your hearts true desire.

"Here I am! I stand at the door and knock. If anyone hears my voice and opens the door, I will come in and eat with that person, and they with me."
Revelation 3:20

However, do not take the commitment lightly. Jesus is not a fad, or the lucky rabbit's foot that we carry around in our pocket in hopes that everything will go our way. Following Jesus is a way of life, and the way that our lives were meant to be lived. To know God and His word, and to not follow and obey, is even more harmful than if we did not know God at all.

James 1:22-24 says: *"Don't fool yourself into thinking that you are a listener when you are anything but, letting the Word go in one ear and out the other. Act on what you hear! Those who hear and don't act are like those who glance in the mirror, walk away, and two minutes later have no idea who they are, what they look like."*

Brian Anderson from TheBridgeonline.net sums it up most adequately in his study of Luke 10:1-16, and his article titled The Danger of Knowing but Not Obeying the Gospel.

"Greater Knowledge Without Obedience Brings Greater Punishment."[1]

If you are ready to take that step of faith – ready to experience life as we were truly meant to live it and ready to stop being misled by all of the lies - all you need to do is call out to Jesus and ask Him into your life by reciting the following prayer – saying it out loud, and meaning it from your heart:

Jesus – I ask you to come into my life. I accept you as my Lord and Savior. I believe with my heart that you are the Son of God, that you died for my sins, were resurrected from the dead, and are now seated at the right hand of the Father. I pray that you would forgive me of all my sins and cleanse me with the blood of your sacrifice and make me new again. I give you my life and everything in it, just as you gave your life for me. Fill me with the Holy Spirit and teach me how to live my life for you.

CONGRATULATIONS! And welcome to the Family of God. You are now a Christian, and your life will be changed forever, for the better.

You may be thinking *"That's it?"* There were no fireworks, no AHA moment, no lightning bolt out of the sky. *What a dud?* My life didn't change, and nothing seems different at all.

Well, not really. Again, your eyes and what you know are still very limited. You must remember – It is a process, and the more that you seek God and Christ, the more that will be revealed to you, and the more you will be in God and Christ.

I can assure you though, that the moment you said that prayer, Jesus, God, and all of the angels everywhere were letting out a jubilant sound like you have never heard before. God's heart was overflowing with joy saying *My son/My daughter has come home*. The moment that you said that Prayer, tears of joy and happiness were shed by God and Jesus.

This is just the beginning though. Now that you are back in 'the family', it is time to strengthen your relationships with God the Father, Jesus, the Holy Spirit and the other family members and find out exactly what it is that our Father has called you to do.

Go find a local church. Seek out other Christians and tell them that you are now a brother/sister in Christ. Don't worry – they will be open and excited to welcome you in.

I'll give you one last helpful tip – The closer you get, the more that you seek and desire, the more you will see and know!

"For God so loved the world that he gave his one and only Son, that whoever believes in him shall not perish but have eternal life. For God did not send his son into the world to condemn the world, but to save the world through him." John 3:16-17

Chapter 21

What Now?

We have covered a significant amount of information in regard to Satan, his demons, and the evil forces which are attacking us and battling against us every single day. There has also been an emphasis placed on our role as warriors, and how we are called to fight these evil forces in the ongoing war which rages on in our lives every day. However, this fight is not the reason why we are here and, therefore, should not be the main focus of our lives. It is not the rational for our existence.

Our main purpose in this life that we live, as well as our focus and priority, should be to glorify God and advance His Kingdom in everything that we do. This alone should be our daily goal and our aspiration in all that we do, which will then determine how we approach everything that encompasses our lives.

Whether you have just now accepted Jesus Christ as your Savior through the previous chapter, or you have been a Christian your entire life, the most important part of our Christianity, the unconditional foundation, is our relationship with God. And not just in having that relationship with God, but more so the quality and depth of that relationship. Christianity is following Jesus Christ and giving our lives over to Him. Simply put – Christianity is living our lives just as Christ lived His.

I think it would be fair to say that each of us would admit that it would be strange to follow someone that we did not know. However, many of us claim to

do so while having no relationship with Christ at all. We maintain that we are
followers of Christ – Christians – and at the same time, in the reality of it all we
only truly follow ourselves and our own selfish desires. We have no knowledge
of Jesus on a close, intimate, and personal level.

Being a Christian is not just a matter of going to church, nor is it our desire
to do good things, and it is most certainly not about just accepting Christ as our
Savior. It is not about going through the motions, trying to earn the good graces
of our Father through performing certain tasks or deeds, as if only to please Him.
It is not about attending seminary school or getting a job on staff at your local
church. It has no relation to how much money we may give, how many hours
of service we provide to help others, or any of the other little things that we may
do that make us feel like we are serving Christ and serving others.

Truly being a Christian is exclusively about following Christ, being one with
Him, and in complete union with Christ and God. It is about aligning our
views and beliefs with those of God and living our lives for Him and with Him
just as we were created to do. This is this reality that we all must genuinely
come to accept and believe to our inner core if we are truly Christians. And this
belief, this view, this understanding must unquestionably come from the heart.
Our heart is what God desires, and hopefully you will come to understand and
believe that our heart is the key to all things, including our lives and our life in
Christ.

Anti-Religion

This may sound a bit bizarre to many of you, and I expect that some will
immediately jump to resistance of the thought. Nonetheless – We need to
remove the religion from God and Jesus. Try that for just a moment. Getting

to know God and Jesus without all of the man-made religious expectations that have been placed upon us, and Jesus. Forget all of the church stuff that has been crammed down your throat. Forget all of the worldly views and images of God and Jesus. Forget it all and just allow the real Jesus to come into your life the way that He truly is – and not the way that we perceive Him to be, want Him to be, or have been indoctrinated in to believing.

The ways in which we have perceived Jesus in the Bible, and through many of our churches today, portrays to us the image of a stuffy, uptight, hardcore, unforgiving, black and white God and Jesus. Or opposingly, a God and Jesus that are soft, weak, and can only show love. Both lead us to see something as it is not, and as it was not meant to be. All of the images, portraits, pictures and representations that have been set forth to us since childhood are once again the interpretation of man which have been passed down through generations, only to be altered and distorted along the way allowing them to fit into the views and acceptable beliefs of a previous generation.

As time has gone on, as generations have passed, we have continually modified God and Jesus in an attempt to make them fit into our world – rather than modifying our world to fit into Theirs.

If we would truly read the Bible – and I am not implying to simply read the words through from front to back – we would see the true character and personality of Jesus, and God. I am suggesting that we take each chapter, paragraph, and verse – and stop in those passages for a moment to ascertain what was actually going on. What was Jesus actually doing at that moment? How was he actually feeling? What kind of mood was He in? When we do take time to read the Bible, we often rush through the Scripture, just as we would read through any other book, and therefore never allow time for the Word of God to come to us.

I am confident that if we were to approach God's Word in this manner, we will surely see that Jesus was a cool dude. He was the guy that everyone wanted to hang out with. He was, and still is, that guy that everyone wanted to have as a friend. Do you think that would be the case of he was an uptight, rigid jerk who was simply out to enforce the law and dish out punishment and discipline? I think not.

(Reminder - resist the temptation to form a view or belief by trying to assimilate Jesus with any of the false information that we have been fed over the course of our lives)

Jesus is easy going, laid back, and fun to be around. He is a joker, He is playful, He is energetic, He is loving, He is caring, He is compassionate and truly cares for a person's heart and soul. How many of your current friends can you say this about? These things are true about who Jesus really is, and if we actually stop to ponder the context of these verses as we are reading them, and try to understand the feelings, emotions, and intent of Jesus in these moments, we will clearly see His true character.

We need to make our first priority as Christians one of getting to know the true Jesus, and God, and getting to know them like they are our best friends. Deeply, and intimately.

Relationships

As most all of us have hopefully learned over the course of our lives, relationships are bilateral or reciprocal and require input and effort from both sides. Both parties must each give to the relationship, or add value to it. The same rules apply to our relationship with God, and Jesus. We must give to the relationship as well, and not just be consumers or users of what is being given to us.

These one-sided associations are known as unrequited relationships, where one's feelings or efforts are not reciprocated by the other. Psychologist Mark Travers states: *"At its core, unrequited love is an emotional imbalance, and the psychological toll of such one-sided relationships goes far beyond just disappointm ent.* "[1]

The Bible uses the word Yada many times when describing our relationship with God. The Hebrew word Yada means *'to know'*. It speaks to a deep intimacy that the Father longs to have with His children. A knowing, or knowledge, that brings the two together almost as one.

By now you know my wife, Robin. You know that she has long brown hair. You know that she has long legs and is very attractive. You also know that she is a Christian and that she has a deep, personal bond with Christ and is firmly rooted in her relationship with God. You know that she has four children, that she has been married for the last thirty years, and that she is married to me. You could say that you 'know' Robin.

I, on the other hand, know that look on her face when she is not feeling well. I know how soft and smooth her skin is and am familiar with every inch of it. I know that one specific spot on the back of her neck, just behind her ear, that calms her and soothes her when I rub my hand across it. I know when something is bothering her, many times even before she will admit it. I know what her passions and desires are, and what things in life she enjoys. I know when she likes to be held and when she just wants to be alone. I know the very subtle difference in her voice when she is trying to downplay or minimize something. I not only know Robin – I Yada Robin.

I also did not come to know these things, or her, just by showing up and hanging around, or by popping in and out of her life every now and then when I found it to be convenient. I truly wanted to know these things. I wanted to know her, every bit of her and every little thing about her. Why? Because I desired her. I craved her. I wanted her more than anything else in life. So, I chased after her with intention and passion and kept trying to learn more and more about her. I watched her, I listened to her, I studied her, and I involved her in every part of my day and my life. It took intention and desire, from both sides, that was truly from the heart – to not only develop that relationship, but to make it last for over thirty years now.

For many of us, our so-called relationship with God can be seen as just the opposite – we say that we know God, but we are merely just hanging around. We go to church, we pray occasionally in times of need, we do our best to be a good person and do the right things, and then we say that we know God. The reality of our relationship is that we know who God is, but we do not KNOW God! We do not have that intimate relationship with God or know Him like we are one with Him. We say and believe that we have a relationship with God and Jesus, when in truth our actions and intentions reveal that this so-called relationship only exists when it is convenient for us.

Sadly, many of us also carry this same attitude with all of our worldly relationships as well. We say that so-and-so is our friend, or that we know who this person is or that person is and claim to have a bond with them. But rarely ever do we call, text, or hang out with them and we actually know very little about their true being. We are afraid to get to close, most always due to the ways in which we view ourselves, and we then isolate ourselves in our own little bubble hoping that others will never see our flaws and inadequacies.

Even more devastatingly, we carry this behavior over into our relationships with our spouses and children as well. We make what should be a lifelong commitment to someone, drag them in to our world, and then treat them as slaves in bondage as we never fully invest ourselves into those relationships. We pull these people into our lives in an attempt to fill a void or need which we have in hopes that they will make our lives complete. In doing so we only compound our problems by adding more moving parts to them. Those relationships are never true relationships as we do not invest ourselves in them and therefore, we are not in union with the other individual.

Any and all true, lasting, and meaningful relationships take effort and investment from both sides. Without the effort and investment, one person is just using the other for a personal benefit. And lacking this effort and investment, the relationship has no value, intrinsic or perceived, and will not survive.

All of us have dependencies in our lives that we carry a great interest in, which we truly crave and desire. And if we are honest with ourselves, this interest is where we most often find ourselves focusing our time and attentions. Whether it be that attractive guy or gal at the office, that sport that we love to play, that hobby that we have, or that addiction that we just can't get enough of. We all have someone or something that we put most, if not all of our focus and attentions towards.

Our addictions, or these dependencies, signalize the fact that there is something which we do not want to face in our own lives. We most always turn to these other fixations in a hope to cover up or heal the pain or memory of something or someone that has wounded us. We are looking for a band-aid to mask that wound so that we will no longer see it and be reminded of it. The problem with these band-aids is that they only veil our pains, and the underlying issues related to them – they never really heal them. Figuratively speaking – we carelessly run through life every day breaking bones and inflicting damage upon our body and our soul. We then run down to the local pharmacy for some band-aids and gauze to fix ourselves up instead of going to see a specialist who can heal us properly – all because we are too afraid to face and deal with the real issue.

That is where Jesus Christ comes in. Not only is He our Savior and Redeemer, but He is also our Healer as well. Jesus can heal all of our wounds and pains, and He will if we simply take them to Him and allow Him into that part of our lives. We were never meant to be able to heal ourselves, and no matter what we try to put into our lives to cover up or heal our pain and issues, we will never be whole and/or complete without the healing of Jesus Christ.

Jesus also did not go through the crucifixion and resurrection just so that we may have a free pass to heaven. He came, He suffered, and He was crucified so that we may be freed from the bondage of Satan and sin, that we may be healed, and that we may be one with Him, and in Him just as He is in the Father.

Jesus tells us in John 14:20-21: *"On that day you will realize that I am in my Father, and you are in me, and I am in you. Whoever has my commands and keeps them is the one who loves me. The one who loves me will be loved by my Father, and I too will love them and show myself to them."*

Intimacy

The good news about being a Christian is that just as God has promised us, His love and grace are unconditional. We do not need to do anything other than accept Jesus Christ as our Lord and Savior to receive these. While God's love and grace affect our lives and our future – Intimacy, being in a close and personal relationship with God, directly affects the quality of our lives.

Having an intimate relationship with God brings us into union with God, as one, and we begin to know, see, feel and desire the same things that He does. We begin to experience the blessings and experiences which God has reserved only for those who are close to Him. We begin to experience life in a way that we could not have ever imagined on our own. We also begin to hear God more frequently as we are now closer to Him and in union with Him. And as we become more in union with Him, His desires become our desires, and our desires become His.

What we must fully understand and accept though, is that this complete union with God and Jesus is not something that we can make happen on our own. It is not by our efforts that we can or ever will become fully filled with Christ. It is simply through our faith, our surrender, and submitting each and every part of our lives over to Christ that we allow Him to come in and fully fill each of those parts. And once He has filled those parts, we become more like Christ as He is fully alive within us.

This complete union does take action on our part however, through the faith and surrendering, and complete openness to God and Christ. These actions are through our daily intention and commitment to spend time in that relationship with Jesus, and to strengthen that relationship. We, however, cannot make the changes or perform the healing that is needed in our lives on our own. This can only happen through the work of Christ, and by opening ourselves up to be free to allow Christ to dwell within us.

We must truly let go of everything that we know and believe, and the ways in which we perceive all things; and fully surrender our lives to Christ so that He may fill us completely with the ways in which we were created to live, which in turn offers us a life more satisfying and fulfilling than we could ever have envisioned. We must disregard the Jesus and the God that we have come to know through this world and allow both God and Jesus to come in to us, fill us, and show us who They truly are.

Going Forward

So how do we go about living our day to day lives while trying to become a better Christian? How do we grow closer to God, and become one with Him, in complete union with Him? How do we get to know what God truly has planned for us and our lives? How do we completely erase all of the lies and deceptions that we have come to believe as being the truth?

I was perplexed with these same questions as well, at my turning point. I had read the books, heard the sermons, and knew that something 'unusual' was happening in my life. I fully agreed with this new information that I had taken in and could feel God calling me to make changes. And I honestly wanted to make those changes and grow closer to God. I had become consciously aware of the 'what' that needed to be changed and was in complete understanding of 'how' to make those changes as well.

The great confusion for me came in the application. How do I apply all of these changes to the life that I am stuck right in the middle of right now? How do I gradually weave this new way of life into my current life, in a way that allows me to keep paying my bills and supporting my family? How do I transform into an entirely different person while I still have many others who are depending on the old person and his ways and routines?

I struggled with this dilemma for quite some time, trying to work bits and pieces of the new methods into my current life. I could see little improvements here and there but knew that this half-hearted attempt would never endure. I still kept trying though, to impart more of these changes into my life where I could, and where time would allow. That was the issue however – my life was already packed with non-stop chaos – and I had molded my life in a way that others were now dependent upon that chaos, and me, for their well-being and survival. I did not see how I could just walk away from this old life all at once, like flipping a switch.

Then came the best advice that I have ever received. One little phrase that suddenly made everything clear.

Stop trying to make God fit into your life and start trying to make life fit into God!

It suddenly all made sense. Initially, my life was my life, it was me, and I was just trying to add this whole God thing to it in hopes that it would make me a better person. The true breakthrough came with the realization that God is not an add-on. God is not the 'little cherry on top' of the ice cream that makes it better. God is the main course. God is IT! He is everything, all we need, and more than sufficient for any of our needs.

I began to understand that nothing in my so-called life really mattered, compared to God. It was all worthless and trivial. None of it would have any significance in the bigger picture of things. I had finally figured out that my life had to be rebuilt, completely around God, and that if I sincerely put my trust and faith in Him, God would not only take care of me but would also take care of those who depended on me.

Being one with God, and in complete union with God takes a lot of effort on our part. Remember, we are sinners by nature, and will always choose the wrong path when left to ourselves. But when we truly desire something or someone, we invest ourselves into that person or obsession. If we truly desire God, we will make the needed adjustments to make Him the priority in our lives – with a little help.

When I say effort, it is the effort in complete surrender and focus, and not an effort of works.

To help you set out on the right track, here are just a few things that will make a significant change in the way you go about your day, which will bring you closer to and more in union with God:

1 – Acknowledge

The very first thing we must do, which we must continue to do daily, is to acknowledge the fact that we are sinners and that we are in need of a Savior. We must accept the fact that we do not have control of anything, no matter how much we like to think we do. We must truly understand and believe that without Jesus Christ our lives are nothing and never will be anything. We must learn to submit ourselves and our lives to Christ and give them over to Him fully – and we must do so on a daily basis.

2 – Repentance

The next thing we must do as Christians is repent for our sins. As we have already accepted Christ as our Savior, our salvation is secured. With our salvation secured, we now turn to sanctification. Sanctification is the process in which God renews our lives and transforms our person and character. God helps us to become the person that we were meant and created to be. The sanctification process, or renewing, cannot begin until we fully admit to all of our sinful ways and desires and ask God for His forgiveness and healing. We must turn to Christ and God, acknowledge these sins, let them go, and allow Christ and God to come into our lives and begin a restorative work within us.

3 – Intention

True change will never come about in our lives without intention. We must intentionally make the commitment to seek God and grow closer to Him by changing our habits as well as the ways in which we see and do things. This will require us to rearrange our lives and schedules, as well as our priorities, making God first in everything we do.

That phrase – making God first in everything we (I) do – has become misused and generic in the ways that we describe our lives with Christ. We tend to use it in an effort to elevate our status as Christians and comfort ourselves in to believing that we are doing the right thing and making progress in our walk with Christ.

The one word that we so often overlook and negate is – *Everything*. By definition, *Everything* means - *All that exists*. Every single little thing in our lives. Every single thought, every action, every reaction, every intention, every breath, and every part of our existence. This is where it gets challenging.

Most of us who make the effort to change and attempt to make God first in everything that we do, usually start by getting up every morning and devoting time to Him in prayer and/or reading the Bible. We may set out with plans to stop a few times during our day for prayer and devotion as well. We also most always commit to attending church regularly as another outward showing of our commitment. We then throw a few Godly things in to our lives and say that we are putting God first in everything that we do.

It is a good start, but it is far from everything, or all that exists. This type of behavior again goes back to our perspective of God, our view of the world, and our beliefs of what reality actually is. The veil is still blinding us from seeing who and what God truly is, and how we were created and intended to function and live.

Remember – our perception of reality has been distorted by Satan, who wants us to focus on the world. This becomes so easy and automatic for us as it is what we can see, feel, hear, smell, and touch. It is what is right in front of us. It is what our mind can relate to and make sense of much more easily. It is what we know, and have known since our lives began, and therefore it is comfortable to us. So, we typically throw a little God in here and there and then call it 'everything' within our lives, once again, in our attempt to make God fit into our world instead of making our lives fit into God's world.

This is the point where matters become more challenging. Being able to devote and commit every single part of our lives to God, and a world that we cannot see, feel, touch, or smell. Being able to change our perspective of which world we actually live in. Being able to disassociate ourselves from this world and change our core belief that we live in and are citizens of the Kingdom of God – not of this world.

Have you ever taken a trip or vacation to some far away, unknown place that you had never been to before? Think back to what it felt like while you were there. You did not know anyone. You did not know what the culture or routines were. You did not know where things were or how to get around. You weren't comfortable there, and you most likely had your guard up at all times. You knew you did not belong there and that it was not your home.

This is the feeling and perspective that we should hold of this world – the place that we live in now. It is not our home. We should not feel comfortable. We should have our guard up at all times. And we should be anxious and excited in every moment to return home to the love and protection of our Father, and to our true family.

So how do we get to this point, the true perception and belief of what world we actually live in? With intention and faith. We intentionally make a conscious effort to place God first in every little thing that we do. We intentionally turn to God all day long for guidance, counsel and direction. We intentionally seek God out in everything that we do and ask for His view and understanding of things. We intentionally rearrange the question that we have been asking for so long – We stop asking How can I fit God into this situation? – and start asking the question How does this situation fit into my life with God?

4 - The Dailies

The dailies are exactly what they sound like – the day-to-day practices that we do which draw us closer to God and Christ to become more in union with Him. They are the little things. But it is the little things that matter the most, and those that will strengthen our relationship and union with God.

Many of us, when first becoming Christians, desire to set out to do some monumental works that will affect hundreds if not thousands of people. We have the fire and passion of the Holy Spirit alive in us, and it is something that we have never felt before. While these grand motives are all good and worthwhile, it is not the size or scale of the act that God looks at, it is the heart and faithfulness of the believer that is important to Him.

In chapter 12 of the book of Hebrews we are instructed to *"run with perse-verance the race marked out for us."*

In 1 Corinthians 9:24 Paul also states: *"Do you not know that in a race all runners run, but only one gets the prize? Run in such a way as to get the prize."*

Paul's instruction to us in these Scriptures is not about being the fastest, the biggest, or the loudest. It is about finishing. Finishing the race in order to receive the prize. It is about staying committed to Christ while persevering and enduring the daily struggles and challenges that we face. It is about keeping the faith, and doing so in whatever race God has set before us. It is about all the little things that we do daily that will allow us to eventually say *"I have fought the good fight, I have finished the race, I have kept the faith."*(2 Timothy 4:7)

It is in all of the little things that we do every single day when remaining faithful and obedient to Him that we find God, and that God presents Himself to us in our lives.

Furthermore, the dailies are so important to our lives as Christians as we are constantly being bombarded with the attacks of the enemy who is constantly trying to wound us, and turn us away from God and Christ.

Every day we lose that fire, that passion, that desire as it is stripped from us by the enemy and the world that we live in. We must continually come back to God each and every day to refill our souls, our hearts, and our minds with everything that God has to offer. That is our daily bread – the nourishment that we need to continue on.

Sin, Satan, and the world will deplete us of all that we have, every single day. We are then left feeling empty, abandoned, and hopeless. Turning to God and Christ every day, multiple times a day, refuels us for the battles that we face.

5 – We do the works that Jesus Christ has commanded us to do.

After Jesus was crucified on the cross, buried in the tomb, and had risen from the dead defeating death and sin, He appeared to the disciples once again for the last time. Jesus' last words to the disciples are what is known as *The Great Commission.*

The Great Commission is the command that Jesus gave us on what we should be doing as Christians. It is very clear, very simple, and easy to understand. Jesus commands us in Matthew 28:19-20: *"Therefore go and make disciples of all nations, baptizing them in the name of the Father and of the Son and of the Holy Spirit, and teaching them to obey everything I have commanded you...."*

The Great Commission is our purpose in this world – To share the good news of the Gospel of Christ with all people. To help them find Christ, to teach them, to train them, and baptize them in the name of the Father, the Son, and the Holy Spirit.

This is the charge and the command that has been given to us as Christians, and should be our top priority in all things that we do in this world. We need to share Jesus with everyone, everywhere, all the time.

I say that the Great Commission is our number one priority in life. However, our first and foremost priority is keeping in union with God and Christ. We cannot share the good news and advance the Kingdom of God unless we ourselves are in union with God, Christ, and the Holy Spirit. Without being in union with God, and knowing what His will and direction are, we are just acting on our own accord and desires.

6 – People. Yes, people.

One of the most important things we can do as Christians, or when becoming a Christian, is to surround ourselves with other Christians. Community. Think of it as a support group. We need the support, encouragement, and the assistance of others in the battles that we face every day. No warrior will go to fight an army on his or her own. That warrior needs an army of their own beside them.

We must fill our lives with strong, God fearing people who are desperately pursuing Christ as well. They become our brothers and sisters. They become our family. And just like any traditional family member, they will be there to help you, assist you, uplift you, and encourage you in your time of need – Just as you should be with them.

Paul tells us in 1 Thessalonians 5:11: *"Therefore encourage one another and build each other up, just as in fact you are doing."*

This step may be a challenge for many of us. Let's face it, some of us just do not like other people. This was the case with my life as well. I did not like other people, with the rare exception of a few, and always approached others with a protective shield. No one had ever cared for me in the past, or so I had come to believe, and my primary thought of others was that everyone was out to hurt me or take advantage of me. I viewed everyone as evil and as having desires and intentions of only pleasing themselves. My perspective of others was one that saw them as the problem as they were just bad people. Thanks to God, who has now shown me that it is not the people who are bad, it is the sin that they have been blinded by that makes them bad. They are people just like me, and are greatly deceived just as I once was, and can be renewed in Christ just as I have been as well.

In my past I would always see these other people and their sinful ways as attacks against me. I would immediately become defensive, and most always seek to hurt them in return. Since God has shown me the true reality of these situations – it is not the people that are attacking me, it is the sin in their lives that Satan is attacking me with – my view and compassion for others has changed greatly. I now feel saddened for these people due to the bondage that they are held captive by, and I truly feel a desire to help them or befriend them. I no longer perceive these situations as an attack against me, and when you are able to remove the personal aspect from it, you no longer perceive the situation as a threat of harm or danger and thus do not feel the need to retaliate.

Some of us have been so badly hurt in the past that we have erected impenetrable walls in an effort to keep everyone out. We simply just do not trust anyone anymore, and therefore we label everyone as being harmful and hurtful. If this is your case, I would suggest that you start by turning to Jesus with that lack of trust for others, and the wounds that you have received from others. Give it all over to Him and pray for His healing. Invite Jesus into those wounds and pain. Yes, it will take time, but Jesus will heal your pain. You must take the first step however, toward Jesus, and then He will do the rest.

A challenge for many others will be in getting rid of those people in our lives that drag us down and keep us from focusing on God. We all have them, and they have become very convenient to us. But to put it bluntly – They are holding you and I back from reaching our true potential, from becoming what we were created to become. They need to be gone, and we need to move on and find better people – Godly people.

I have had many friends like this in my life as well, and most always at my own choosing. I chose them to be in my life because they were comfortable. They allowed me to be lazy and unaccountable. They did not require me to put forth any effort. They allowed me to live in my sin, and many times even supported and encouraged it.

We will find those Godly people that we so greatly need, our brothers and sisters, everywhere we go. Many times, though, just as we do with God, we are not looking hard enough, and we fail to recognize that they are there. The easy answers of where we find these others are church, small groups, and bible studies. (This is one of the main reasons why we must attend church – not because it makes us Godly, but because it is the gathering with our family that supports us and fills us with hope and encouragement.)

However, they are people just like us, and they do the same everyday things that we do. They too are looking for other Godly people to fill their lives with as well. I found two of my closest friends and mentors on the golf course, and they have both made a significant impact on my Christian life and my pursuit of Christ. They both push me, encourage me, support me, and hold me accountable. They both make me a better me.

I heard an interesting fact the other day on the daily life and habits of Jesus Christ. Many of us believe that we must be so deeply involved in the church, or church activities, as that is where we will find, and serve Christ.

In the Gospel of Matthew, Jesus had thirty-four different personal and life changing encounters with an individual. Of the thirty-four – only one happened in a church. Jesus, as well as so many other Godly people are everywhere. We just need to open our eyes and allow ourselves to change the ways in which we see things. If we allow ourselves to remove the religious constraints and limitations that we have come to accept as being the truth, we will begin to see Jesus, as well as other Godly people, everywhere.

Jesus also tells us in Matthew 22:34-36 that the most important command that we should follow is to love the Lord your God with all of your heart, with all of your soul, and with all of your mind. He then follows that up by saying that the second greatest command is just like it – To love your neighbor as yourself.

Are we as Christians really loving God with ALL of our heart, soul, and mind? Making Him our priority and our primary focus in every single little thing that we do? I would think that even at our best, we would honestly admit that we have not even come close.

And are we as Christians really loving our neighbor as we would ourselves? Again, I would think that even at our best, we would honestly admit that we have not even come close.

Jesus was and is spiritual, not religious. We could greatly change our lives, and the lives of others, if we would be the same.

"Those who look to Him are radiant; their faces are never covered with shame."
Psalms 34:5

Chapter 22

What If?

I have always been a proponent of self-reflection. Taking the time to look back upon my life and reflect on my thoughts, my actions, my behaviors, my attitude, my goals, my desires and my direction. To look back and review what I have learned, where I am headed, and to contemplate any possible need for change.

As we near the end of the book, let us reexamine and reflect upon just a few of the facts we have discussed to see what we may have hopefully learned.

- God is present in our lives every single day; the question is do we see Him.

- God is still alive – and still speaks to us regularly, if we can put ourselves into a position to listen and allow ourselves to hear Him.

- The world that we live in is not what it appears to be on the surface. It is what Satan wants us to see and accept as being true.

- There is a constant war going on around us, and we are directly involved in that war whether we choose to admit/accept that fact or not.

- Choosing to ignore or even deny something which truly exists does not make it less of a reality, or nonexistent.

- Even though God has control over all creation, many bad things will come about every day as a result of this war which we are a part of.

- God is all powerful and has knowledge of all things. We do not and never will. There are matters which we may presume to know, but no matter how knowledgeable we may perceive ourselves to be, we really don't have a clue when it comes to the big picture of life.

- Satan has blinded us with a veil to keep us from seeing God and coming to know God. Most all of the occurrences in our lives today are a part of this veil. The distractions, the pleasures, the things that we devote most of our time too, and all of the happenings that keep us 'busy'.

- Since the creation of man, Satan and sin have attacked us with a never-ending bombardment of lies and deceptions in an effort to keep us from seeing God and seeing who we were truly created to be.

- These deceptions have plagued every person that has ever walked the earth (with the exception of Jesus, even though Satan tried to deceive Jesus as well).

- The deceptions and lies have become what we accept as normal life, and as the truth, the way things were meant to be.

- The lies and deceptions have infected every aspect of our world and have tainted the church as well, with most modern-day churches now having more of a concern for pleasing the world instead of pleasing God.

- Therefore, sadly, the deceptions have affected our views of Christianity, our views of God, and our views of what the truth really is.

- We have learned that Christianity, or being a Christian, is not about following some doctrine, or a man-made program involving a process of steps to bring us closer to God. Christianity is about God and following Jesus Christ in the model and example that He set for us.

- We have learned that Christianity is not about religion. Jesus Christ was spiritual, not religious.

- We have learned that being a Christian, and truly following Christ is about our relationship with God/Christ and being in complete union with God/Christ. That relationship and union, and that alone, is the reasoning for our creation and existence. To honor and glorify God with all of our being.

We have become so unsuspecting of the lies and deceptions and therefore have chalked them up to just being a part of our ever changing and evolving world. We then assume that we as well must evolve and change with the world or be left behind to be forgotten like yesterday's news. And before we know it, we have soon forgotten who we truly are, or were, and what we used to believe and stand for.

We have adapted. We have evolved. We have unknowingly become the poser who has modified everything about him or herself in an effort to become more appealing to others, and the world around us. Bit by bit, piece by piece, one tiny little change at a time, so that even we ourselves do not recognize what is happening to us.

Some of us, however, are fortunate. By the grace of God, and through the Holy Spirit, at some point in our lives the veil is ever so briefly pulled back, only to find ourselves horrified at where we have ended up. Completely shocked and unaware at where we have arrived, and what we have become. Those of us that do arrive at this point all have the same question – *How in the world did my life get to this point?*

These lucky few try very hard to remember who they once were, and what they once believed in and stood for. They struggle to find out where they went so terribly wrong, and what one thing led them completely astray. And while they may occasionally recall little glimpses of the person that they used to be, and the desires and passions that they once had – these things have been all but erased from our memories leaving us feeling completely lost and hopeless. Our eyes have been opened, allowing us to see that the ways in which we live life now are oh so utterly wrong, but we unable to recall any memory of what may be true or right. We are left feeling helpless with no clue how to move forward.

However, as depressing as it may be, those are the lucky ones. Lucky in the way that even if only for a brief moment, they are able to see clearly. Many others are not so fortunate. The veil is never pulled back, and they keep believing the lies and deceptions as being the truth and reality. They succumb to the ways of the world and do everything they can to fit in. They keep pushing and striving to be at the top of the pecking order, not only to gain more control, but in a belief that this elevated status will fulfill their desires and make them complete. They attempt to make their lives even more appealing to the masses, albeit in a counterfeit way, so that they may gain more 'likes' and 'followers' on social media. They quickly jump on the bandwagon of every latest-greatest thing that comes along, all while sacrificing any morals or values that they may have, just to keep up with the crowd so that they don't get left behind or become perceived as being weird or different. Or even more dreadful, they hold tightly to their dogmatic approach on who they are and what they believe, insisting that nothing could be wrong with their ways and view of life, and it is simply everyone else that is wrong.

However, even these unlucky ones will admit that deep down inside they are aware that something is missing. They know that they desire more. They know that they need more. They know and truly believe that their lives were meant for something greater. But they continually attempt to fill that need and void with artificial desires and pleasures, always ending up right back where they started

– feeling empty and incomplete. And the viscous cycle never ends. They hold tight to that feeling and belief that there is something greater out there for them, and yet again seek to fill that void with ever changing pleasures of this world in another vain attempt to be complete. Over, and over, and over again.

So now I encourage you to stop and take some time for your self-reflection. To look at your life from the outside-in, to see where it is that you may have arrived. To contemplate how you may have changed and given in to the ways of others, or the world.

Listed below are several questions to help guide you in that reflection, which will hopefully open your eyes to which reality you may be following. Ask yourself each one of the questions below, allowing yourself some time to let the answers come to you. Write your answers out in the space provided and then review them later to see where you have arrived. Don't rush it. Be open and honest. Brutally honest. After all, if we are not being honest, the only one we are lying to is ourselves and the only one that we are hurting is ourselves.

If you want to make sense of your life, you must learn to make sense of Jesus.

But first – Let us pray that the Holy Spirit would guide us through this endeavor, keeping your mind free from distractions and any evil spirits keeping you from realizing the truth. Again, it is best that you read the following prayer out loud (remember – Satan and his evil spirits cannot read your mind). If we are only reciting the prayer silently in our heads, Satan and his evil demons have no fear and will still run rampantly through your life and mind.

Lord and Savior Jesus Christ – I ask you to come into my life, my mind, my heart, and my spirit. I pray that you would guard my mind, my heart, and my spirit from any and all attacks by evil spirits as I open myself up to you. I pray,

Lord Jesus, that you would also help me to become aware of the powers that I have been given, through you, to fight and resist these evil spirits in your name.

Oh, gracious and loving Father – I pray that through your Holy Spirit you would remove the veil from my eyes and my heart and allow me to see your truths. I pray that you would expose the lies and deceptions in my life that I have come to accept as being truth and reveal to me those things in which I have made agreements with which have kept me from honoring you and being in complete union with you. I pray Father that you would convict me of these lies and agreements and forgive me for believing in something other than your true word. I hereby commit my life, my mind, my spirit and my body to you and your true word and ask that you cleanse my life, my mind, my spirit and my body with the blood of Jesus Christ and the truths of your ever living word. I ask these things in the name of my loving Savior Jesus Christ – Amen.

- What if most everything I know and believe to be true is a lie?

What if most everything that you have been taught, most everything that you have learned, most everything that you have been told, and most everything you believed was not true? How would this change your world?

- What if I was wrong about most everything that I thought I knew was the truth?

What if most all of the things we hold as actuality are really falsehoods that we have come to accept and believe as being reality? Could it be possible? If even one tiny little thing that we believe to be the truth is actually a falsehood – then it is possible that most all things we believe are falsehoods.

- What if God actually did stop trying?

What if there wasn't a God? What if God gave up on you, and us? The world that we live in is filled with so much sin and evil WITH God – how much worse off would we be if it was without God?

- What if God did not care?

What if God did just sit back and watch, without being involved? What if He did not care for us or about what happened to us? Would He have sent His son Jesus for us?

- What are some of the lies that I have accepted as being the truth?

Start with some of the easy ones – I'm not pretty. Nobody likes me. I'm not good enough. I have no value. These are all lies that we have come to accept as reality. These are not the words of our Creator and Loving Father. Now, add a few of the other lies that you have let hold you back from being the person that God created you to be.

- Do I really feel complete and whole as the person that I am?

What part of me feels empty? What is it that I am in search of, and what void is it that I am trying to fill? (Do I feel Inadequate – Abandoned – Undesirable – Unattractive – Powerless – Insecure – Afraid??)

- Is my life today what I really thought life would be like?

Have I just adapted, and tried to fit in with the ways of the world? And if so, why? Or has my life played out exactly as I had intended it too? And if so, why? What are the actions that led us down either of those paths?

- Try to remember a time in your life when you had dreams, goals, desires and ambitions.

What were they, and what was it that stopped them from happening?

- Try to remember a time in your life when everything was pure and innocent.

Where did that go, and what made things change? Do you remember the exact point in time when it did change? Every one of us had this at one point in life, and every one of us has lost it as well. When was it that things changed for you?

Best-selling author, counselor, and teacher John Eldredge states it best in his book *Waking the Dead:*

"The fact is, we are usually too close to our lives to see what's going on. Because it's our story we're trying to understand, we sometimes don't know what's true or false, what's real and imagined."[1]

Closing

Being honest with ourselves is not easy. And most times when we are, all we see is the worst in ourselves. We look for the flaws and inadequacies in an effort to self correct, simply because we do not like the feeling of the pain that they cause us. More importantly, we do so because we know that we can do better. We know, or at least want to believe, that we have the potential for much greater things.

This again is the war that we live in every day. God created us for much greater things. That is built into our DNA, our very core. That is what gives us that feeling or belief that we can do better – because deep down inside, our spirit knows what our Creator had intended us for.

Then in walks Satan and sin. Feeding us the lies and leading us to believe that we are worthless and will never amount to anything. Leading us to believe that the spirit within us cannot be trusted, therefore we push it down and ignore it at all costs. That is our battle every day – Either trusting God and the Holy Spirit to guide us to all of His promised glories - or - Believing the lies of Satan and the ways of this world.

Throughout the writing of this book, I would always pray and ask God for guidance regarding the direction that He desired the book to go, as well as to equip me with the words that would eventually fill the pages. Many times, throughout my day I would be out doing something completely different, and God would come to me with a simple direction – a word, a phrase, a verse, or a topic. I quickly learned that I needed to write these things down on sticky notes or they would slip my mind in no time at all.

As I come to the end of the book, I still have a multitude of sticky notes lying around which have not been included in the book. This troubles me greatly, and I always find myself back at the same thought – my personal desires for the outcome of this book. I truly want this book to impact the lives of many, and I truly hope and pray that in some way my story will have an impact on many others, leading them not only to come to Christ, but to have a deep, personal relationship with God.

While all of my intentions are good, and for the glory of God, they are exactly that – MY intentions and desires. They are not God's intentions or desires. I am simply a man whose heart achingly desires to please God. And even though my heart is in the right place, I am still a man, and still often fight my selfish desires and pride. I occasionally find a great desire to include all of those 'sticky notes' in this book, but then quickly come to my senses and remember that this book is not about me, and its purpose is not to glorify me.

God came to me a couple weeks ago and told me that it was time to wrap it up. That the end of the book, or my story, needed to happen soon. And while left to myself I could probably go on and on forever with many other topics and stories just hoping that it would grab someone's attention and turn them to Christ, I more importantly have to trust in God and what He will do with this book. I have to let go and give full control to God.

Many parts of this book have come fairly easy to me. The book, after all, was what God had instructed me to do. I was not a writer, let alone a reader, and writing anything was the furthest thing from my mind when He came to me with this direction. God had already taught me however, that our job is the WHAT and not the HOW. God directed me to write this book, which is WHAT I was to do. It was God's job to take care of HOW it got done and HOW it gets to where it needs to be.

I faced many challenges when putting all of these thoughts to words though. Many of which are the same that we face in our everyday lives, and ones which we have discussed in previous chapters. Almost daily, Satan would get into my head and attempt to conflict the message that God wanted me to illustrate. At one point, about halfway through the book, Satan even had me believing that I needed to scrap the whole project and start over again as it was not good enough. That thought went on for several days, tormenting me, making me question everything that I had written. The thoughts continued to tell me that my life did not matter, that nobody would care, and that there was nothing about my life that would make a difference to anyone.

However, God had already prepared me with everything that I would need to write this book, as well as this exact situation, this specific encounter, and the battle that I would be facing. God knew where He was taking me, and He also knew what weapons I would need while on that journey, so He made sure that I had them before He gave me direction and then sent me on my way. God knew the attacks would come, and He surely knew how to defeat them.

Looking back now I can clearly see that God started me on this journey long before He gave me the direction to tell my story through this book. And He did it through another Godly man that I confided in, and a book. This journey all started on one specific day when I turned to my close friend and pastor for support and advice. That friend, Pastor Brian, told me that he knew exactly what it was that I needed, and then gave me a book to read. My initial thoughts and feelings took me deeper in to despair at the time as this was not the answer that I was looking for. It was not the quick fix that I had desperately hoped he would provide. It was not the light switch that would suddenly turn everything in my world from darkness to light.

That book, however, was exactly what God knew I needed, and He also knew exactly when I would need it. As you know, I did not run home to start reading that book that Brian gave me. I threw it on the coffee table, and there it sat.

All by itself – for weeks. And then came that one day when God prompted me through the Holy Spirit to pick it up. *A few pages won't hurt that bad, let's see what it is all about.*

A few pages turned into a few chapters. Then I realized that I did not want to put it down. I breezed through that book and found myself craving more. So, I ordered more books, and then even more after that. We are only halfway through the year so far, coming to the end of June, and I have read over a dozen books this year already. Who knew I would actually enjoy reading? God knew!

I know that some will say that all of this reading is exactly what I describe in an earlier chapter – a quest for head knowledge only. I greatly disagree with that belief as I know in my heart what truly drives me to read. Yes, it is my quest for knowledge in a sense. Knowledge of the God that I love and serve. I truly want to know as much as I can about my Father and my Creator, all while trying to learn how He intended for us to live our lives. I am currently in the process of unlearning all of the ways and lies that I thought were true and right, as well as learning the truth about how and what God created us to be.

I also believe that this new reading habit is part of my initiation which God is taking me through, preparing me for other things to come. I would have never picked up a book on my own in the search for knowledge itself. We live in an era of immediate gratification. Most all of us have been taught that we can have anything that we want, and we can have it now. No waiting. No searching. And certainly without any deep thought or pondering of possibilities.

To read a book, at least for me, you need to sit down in a still, quiet place without distractions. This was a challenge for me as well. I do not like to sit still. I always have to be going and doing something. But God knew this was exactly what I needed, and He also knew that in this time there would be nothing competing for my attentions, and nothing to drown out His voice.

God took me to a place that was uncomfortable to me. A place that I had not been to before. And in that place, he began to show me how and why He created us and intended us to live our lives. He began to refine me and prepare me for what is to come.

While I was reading my seventh book, the author of that book referenced another on Spiritual Warfare. My good friend Gary had attempted on many occasions to dive into spiritual warfare with me, but it was something that was just too confusing and difficult to grasp. I always had the view that if I just ignored Satan, he wouldn't bother me. Foolish, at best.

While reading that seventh book, God would not let me get past the topic and kept sending me back to the other book that was referenced. I finally ordered a copy of it, and it would become my next big challenge. That book arrived the next day and was I in for a shocker. It was huge. That book had over six hundred pages, in very small print. My thoughts immediately went to God in saying *You want me to read this? C'mon, Gimme a break! You just got me started in reading and this thing is as big as the Bible!*

That book was *The Handbook For Spiritual Warfare* by Dr. Ed Murphy.[2] Again, God knew exactly what He was doing. I dove into it and could not put it down. I learned so much about the world that we live in and the ongoing war that we face every day. I learned that many of the struggles and challenges that we face are direct attacks from Satan, on us, God's people. I also learned how to recognize these attacks, as well as how to fight back with the weapons that God has already given us.

So, when that time came that I was being overrun with those thoughts of scrapping all of the writing that I had done and starting over, as well as the other thoughts that my life did not matter – I recognized them for what they were and fought back. I recognized that these were not the words of my loving Father, and therefore they must be from the enemy. I turned to Jesus and His word, the truths.

Take every thought captive and make it obedient to Christ. 2 Corinthians 10:5

I turned to Jesus in prayer and gave Him all of the negative thoughts that were attacking me. I then returned to the truths and direction that God had given me and got straight back to doing what I was directed to do – write the book.

I make it sound so simple and easy. In reality though, it is anything but. I have had many other struggles throughout the writing of this book as well. I still face the same challenges, frustrations, and struggles that you do – every single day. By no means do I have everything figured out. The difference now is that I am aware of what reality truly is, and I know where to turn to for my support and guidance. The difference now is that I know when my Father is speaking to me, and that I wait for and only listen to His words.

My life has changed almost completely over the past few years. However, I still find myself being able to say one thing that I had said and felt in my past – I don't have a clue how to live this life. Although I have learned much and have confidence in who I am and what I stand for, I am having to relearn how to live all over again. I am having to unlearn everything I once knew and learn the things that are true and correct.

You know just as well as I do how hard life can be in the world that we live in, and that is before we open ourselves up to the fact that there are other outside forces attacking us every day. We are in a fight my friends, a fight for our lives and our souls. A fight for our future and our destiny. A fight that we cannot simply sit back and watch. A fight that we must aggressively partake in. A fight for our families, for our freedom, and our salvation.

We must acknowledge the fight and acknowledge the simple fact that we alone do not stand a chance in this fight. Our only hope, which is guaranteed, is being in Jesus Christ and remaining in constant union with Him.

His Presence

I have put much thought and effort in to how these last paragraphs should be written. And even as I put them into words now, I have great concern that you, as the reader, will not grasp their full meaning and emotion.

I love this life, even with the challenges that it presents to me every day. I love the little things that God places into my life every day which I get to witness and marvel in. I love the experiences, each and every one of them, and so anxiously await the next and what is to come. I see God's hand at work in my life, and in the world that we live in as well.

And more than anything in this world, I love my wife, my children, and their children, and deeply desire to see the joy and experiences in their lives as they grow old. I do not want to miss any of that. I would give all that I have to be around long enough to share this with them.

Lately, however, I find myself saddened, almost to a point of depression at times. Ever since that morning in my living room and being in the presence of the Lord, I have desired nothing greater. I crave to be in His presence all of the time, and experience all of the feelings and emotions that go with that presence.

Again, being able to portray the fullness and depth of those feelings and emotions, as well as what I experienced, is something that I am just not able to put into words, or give you, the reader, a comprehension of. It is something that can only be experienced.

And as is the case with most all who have had a similar experience, I have seen/felt/experienced the 'other side', and with all of my heart I so badly want to be there and not here. I have seen and felt the wondrous indescribable life that awaits us, and I am deeply saddened by the fact that I have to remain in this world – at least for now.

Our God, our Creator, is real! He does exist and is working wonders in your life and in our world every single day. We have just become so blinded by Satan that we are unable to see and recognize these things, or the fact that God is even there.

But when we are able too, and do open our eyes to see Him, the feelings, emotions and blessings that He will pour out on to you will be indescribable as well. There is a whole 'nother world out there people, the real world, the one in which we were created to live in and one which will give us more than this world can ever offer.

"For the people's heart has become calloused; they hardly hear with their ears, and they have closed their eyes. Otherwise they might see with their eyes, hear with their ears, understand with their hearts and turn, and I would heal them."
Matthew 13:15

Lessons Learned

On the remaining pages I have composed a few short stories which highlight important lessons I have come to learn over the years which I believe are crucial in the development and growth of any Christian, or individual for that matter. I hope they are helpful for you as well, and that you are able to extrapolate God's direction from them and apply it to your life just as I did.

Chapter 23

The Kids

I have mentioned my children several times throughout this book already, and by now you have probably thought that I forgot to write about them as I said I would. This chapter will likely be the most difficult that I write in this book, as my children each hold a very special place in my heart, a place that is reserved solely for them.

I am sure that I am like most other fathers when I say that my kids mean the world to me. And not to discredit any other fathers, but mine truly do. Deep down in my heart, to my core, without hesitation, I would, without a doubt, offer my life at any moment for any one of my children. I would attempt the impossible just to see a smile on their face. And I would endure even the most painful of battles to protect them from life's struggles.

I believe that much of this conviction results from the relationship that I had with my father, or the lack of one. I once had a relationship with my father when I was young, but as I grew older, his manufactured attempts of trying to look like a 'good dad', and the counterfeit love which he displayed only when it seemed convenient became very evident. My father, once again, has recently chosen to not be a part of my life due to my faith and convictions, despite many attempts at reconciling with him, which only deepens my belief that every encounter and interaction with him was purely for his gain and satisfaction. All the while, leaving me with the perception that I never did matter to him.

As Robin and I began to build our own family, I vowed to myself and to her that our children would always know that their father loves them, cares for them, and desires them. Kids are pretty simple, right? (I can hear many of you laughing) All they really need to know, deep down inside, is that they are loved and that they are safe and secure. OK, children are much more complicated than that - but this is the basic primal desire and need for every child. If they have that, and know that, they can soar to unbelievable heights. This is what every child wants, needs, and desires – and even more significantly so from a father to his sons.

Robin and I married and began to have children fairly quickly. I was ill-equipped for fatherhood and knew very little if anything on how to be a father. I knew even less about being a dad, and still rate myself just slightly better than inadequate, many times learning the things that I should have known at the expense of my children.

There is a considerable difference between being a father and being a dad. Any man that has the ability to reproduce can be a father. This however does not make him a dad. Being a dad is what happens after you become a father. A dad is the man that is constantly there for his children to educate them, train them, discipline them, grow them, empower them, love them, nurture them, hold them, and prepare them for an adult life of their own while having the confidence and comfort of knowing that they are loved, respected, and wanted.

All of these were moments that I had never experienced in my life and therefore lacked the knowledge or ability to pass on to my children. I was, however, aware of the desires in my childhood that I did not receive, which I so badly needed, and therefore committed myself to making sure that my children would not know that pain, or that type of father.

I had also learned through my past relationship with Pam, that my choices, my decisions, and my actions, would have a direct impact on any children which I brought into this world, and the mere thought of possibly ruining another child's life would continue to haunt me for many years to come.

Joshua Allen

Our first child was Joshua. He simply goes by Josh now. Josh is almost thirty years old and now has a family of his own at this point. He married his High School sweetheart, Ryan, and they now have two little girls that Robin and I cannot get enough of. The only thing better than kids – is grand kids!

All of our children were Home Schooled, and Josh was, in a sense, the guinea pig. Robin was confident in her ability to educate the kids, but this was something unheard of and completely new to me. To say that I was a bit skeptical at first would be a huge understatement. But I did have faith in my wife and figured that we could give it a shot and see how the first couple of years went. Kids really don't learn anything in their early years anyway, right? What could be the harm?

Well, seventeen years later Josh graduated High School – Homeschool High School. We had aspirations for him to go to college, but he just was not feeling it at the time. Josh said that he wanted to wait a year or two. As parents, we all know how that works out. You guessed it – Josh never did go to college. Probably a good thing though, for Josh, and me as well, as it would have just been a waste of time and money.

Josh set out on his own and hit the ground running. He worked a few entry level jobs to start out, none of which lasted very long. And then one day he got a job with PayPal. One thing led to another, Josh switched jobs and fields a couple more times, always improving his position and salary, and he now works for a subsidiary of Microsoft and is quickly moving his way up within the company.

Josh specializes in Fraud with the corporation that he now works for. Through Josh's work in protecting the company that employs him, he recently exposed an International human trafficking scheme and has saved many victims from its potential devastation.

Josh has always been our 'easy going' kid. He never allows much to bother him and everything just seems to roll right off his back. I have always admired this about Josh, and have even envied the disposition at times, but lately it worries me. I know firsthand that life is not easy, especially with a family, and I fear at times that Josh is only masking the issues that he may be struggling with, and the difficulties that this world can offer.

When Josh set out on his own, he seemed to have everything figured out. He was a smart kid. He was outgoing. He was tackling life head on and was doing fairly well at it too. He also knew how to get a hold of me if he should have any questions or problems. I thought we had raised him pretty good and now it was time to sit back and watch him flourish. I would talk to him every now and then just to see how things were going, and I would let him know that I was always still there for him should he ever need it. I would always tell him how proud of him I was, and that he had life figured out, so I was just watching him succeed and trying not to get in the way.

Then it hit me. Like a ton of bricks. My heart broke and I gave in to tears when I suddenly realized that after twenty years of trying to raise the best son that I could – I had just FAILED!

That was MY father talking! I had become exactly what I swore I would not become. You do not stop being a dad just because they move out or now have a family of their own! You do not distance yourself just because he lives in a different place now! And you do not get to sit back and just watch! He is still my kid, and he still needs his dad!

Many times, I look at Josh and see this perfect dad, with a perfect life. His girls adore him like crazy. And as we have discussed in previous chapters, I as well try to relate to and understand that father figure that he has become based on my past experiences and understandings– and I can't. How can I, a man who did not have a father growing up, be of any guidance to someone who appears to be the perfect father? What could I possibly offer him? I always come back to the same answer – Nothing!

I have always viewed myself as a dad who was just okay. Sure, I could have done better. I could have done more. Fortunately, God has shown me that I do not have to live in this deception any longer. God has also shown me that my father does not determine what kind of father I am or should be. And, I do not have to be the perfect dad to my kids, I just need to be me and be their dad. It is a work in progress, but one that I will labor at until I depart this world.

I have since turned to Josh to apologize for, in a sense, abandoning him. I also explained the relationship that I had with my father, and the reasoning for my lack of parenting skills. I have also made Josh aware that I now realize how big of a mistake I have made, that it was never intentional, and the last thing I would ever want would be for my kids to hurt.

Josh, in the loving child that he is, forgave me quickly. Josh and I both have since committed to being there for each other and strengthening our relationship.

Kristopher Michael

Kristopher is our second child and was born about a year and a half after Josh. Kris was, and still is to some extent, a mini-me. Not only did he look just like me when he was younger (and still does), we were inseparable. Kris could not get enough of dad, and had to go everywhere that dad did, and do everything that dad did. I loved it, and I still do when the rare occasion happens.

I had a very hands-on, mechanical childhood which transferred over to Kris as he was always helping me fix things and build stuff. One year I had picked up an old run down '67 Olds 442 while I was out working a storm in south Texas. Kris and I fully restored the entire car back to its original condition, the way it looked when it came off the showroom floor. Kris and I did all of the work ourselves. I still have pictures of Kris when he was about ten years old, sitting on that concrete garage floor, scrubbing and sanding down metal brackets and mounts from the car. It is often the moments such as this which we take for granted at the time, then spend the rest of our lives desperately seeking for them to play out once again.

By the time Kris turned sixteen, he was doing brake jobs and oil changes on all of his friends' cars. I miss those days with Kris and would give anything to have just one more. Days like those are what being a dad is truly about. Those days, those moments, where the 'what' you are doing together has no real significance in the outcome of life. Those days and those moments where your son hangs on every word that you speak and looks to you as being his whole world. Those infrequent days where you pridefully allow yourself, if even only for a moment, the feeling that you have succeeded as a dad. It is those moments, those experiences, that stay with us forever.

With Kris having an older brother, everything became a competition for him. The predicament that Kris faced was that Josh was pretty darn good at everything as well. And since Josh was slightly older, and a bit bigger, Kris would many times not come out as the victor.

As Kris entered his teenage years, he began to act out with anger and violence and would often punch holes in the walls or bust items around the house. This behavior never sat well with me as a violent, chaotic home was not the environment that I desired for my family, and I surely did not want to have to shell out money to fix something that was damaged out of a temper tantrum. Outbursts of rage and anger were dealt with quickly, and most always sternly. However, this would most always fall upon Robin as I would be out of town, in another state, working another storm.

When Kris reached the age of seventeen, he could not wait to get out of our home and eagerly jumped at the chance to move in with a buddy. Despite multiple attempts from Robin and I trying to explain how this decision would adversely affect his life, he proceeded with it regardless. Shortly after moving out, he then informed Robin and I that he planned on marrying a girl that he had met at a party, who was now pregnant. Further attempts – further explanations – further predications of how his future would play out – and Kris would always do the opposite of what we suggested no matter how many times our predictions came to fruition.

I have lost many a night's sleep over Kris and his direction. Every time the phone would ring with a call from him, I would be stressfully dreading what the bad news might be this time. Kris was at one point in time someone who hung on every word that I said and could not stand to be away from me. Now our connection had diminished to the point where he would spitefully do the opposite of whatever I might suggest and no longer desired to have a relationship with me at all. Where did I go so devastatingly wrong? When did we lose what we once had? What had I done to push him so far down this road of destruction? How could I have failed so disastrously?

There were many years where the thoughts of Kris's future consumed me, and the fear of what may lie ahead for him was often too much to bear. Robin would constantly tell me – *Don't get so wrapped up in it. He is just like you were when you were young, and you turned out alright.*

Those, however, are not the words that a father wants or needs to hear when one of his children has strayed. She was right though – Kris was just like me when I was younger – and that is exactly what scared the hell out of me. I knew exactly where that road led too. And what terrified me even more was knowing that for many people who go down that road, there is no coming back. There is nothing but darkness and destruction.

Both Robin and I prayed, and we prayed hard for years. By the grace of God, I finally accepted the realization that there was nothing more that I could do to help him. Kris was going to do whatever he wanted, regardless of what I said. I had realized that the only one who could help him now was God.

From that point on, I gave my son over to God. I let go. I gave up trying to control the outcome of something which I had absolutely no control over to begin with – and gave every single thought and emotion to God to let Him handle it. At this point, God was the only one who could save him anyways.

Completely letting go was a difficult challenge for me to say the least. He was my son. My mini me. How does one sit back and just let go of someone who is more a part of them than anything else? That was the struggle for me, just totally letting go. Nevertheless, every time I would find myself struggling with the fear and worries, I would turn to God and again give them all over to Him.

After a short period of fighting with the fears, and giving them over to God, things appeared to change. I began to stop having those fears and worries. Then, about a year later, God let me in on a little secret. He came to me one day and told me that everything would be okay, and that Kristopher would be saved. God did not tell me how. God did not tell me when. God did not tell me where. I did not care about the details though, as I did not need to know. Just knowing that he would be saved was more than enough for me. My part was simply trusting and having faith in my God, and His word. It was God's promise, which I have complete trust and faith in, and I have lived in that promise every day since. After all, God loves Kristopher more than I ever could have, which again is something hard to fathom.

Giving everything over to God has removed the fears and worries which paralyzed me from being a dad to my son. I had become so consumed by the worries and stress about Kristopher's life, and all of my efforts went into trying to straighten him out or fix him. I was trying to control the life that Kris lived, and I had expected his life to fit into my preconceived box. And when it did not, I felt as though I had lost control and fear took over.

Kris now has two little boys, almost the same age as Josh's girls. These boys are another unbelievable blessing that Robin and I do not deserve. We take every chance that we can get to see them, and they know that grandma and grandpa love them dearly.

Kris and I have since had a lengthy conversation. Some talking, some yelling (which was a much-needed expression of the hurt and pain on both sides), and some crying. Both of us have gained a better understanding of how the other feels, and how we have come to reach the place we are at now. As for Kris - well, he is my boy and always will be which I am eternally grateful for. I love him more than he will ever know, and that will never change, regardless of what he may or may not do. We will go through some ups and downs as we both try to figure out how to live in this crazy world. I will not always see things from his perspective, and he will not always see things from mine. For now, I am simply enjoying being his dad once again, every chance that I can get.

Katelynn Marie

And then there was a girl! Our third child is Katelynn, and she as well came about a year and a half after her older brother. Shortly after Robin and I were married, she informed me that if we were going to have children, she would prefer it to happen sooner than later so that she could have her body back. So, boom-boom-boom. Three in a row. (I'm going to have difficulty explaining our fourth)

Katelynn was a perfect combination of both her mom and dad. She was skinny and athletic just like me but had the looks and beauty of her mother. Katelynn was a girly-girl when she was young and still is for the most part. She began taking dance classes at a very young age, learning many different styles, and continued into her late teen years. The classes, the competitions, the outfits. You name it, she did it, or had it, and tried it. Katelynn was, and still is, outgoing, energetic, charismatic, and affectionate in every sense of her being.

I treasured the bond that Katelynn and I shared when she was growing up. She was my little princess. She was always the most cheerful, smiley little ball of fire that you could imagine – well, up until the point where she would get angry. Katelynn had two older brothers who enjoyed nothing more than teasing her and getting her riled up. Little did they know that she would eventually grow up to become taller than both of them at over six feet, and more than capable of defending herself.

Katelynn loved the limelight and being on stage, which led to her choosing to attend college for an acting degree after she had graduated High School. She went, she saw, she graduated with her degree – and then returned to working normal jobs like many of us. One of the opportunities which Katelynn took after college relocated her to Oklahoma City, about three hours away from mom and dad, where she would become the manager of a newly launched location.

As previously stated, all of our children were raised in a church environment. Unfortunately for our first two boys, this unprincipled environment pushed them away from church, and from God Himself. Katelynn, however, continued to grow in her relationship with the Lord and sought out a church to attend in Oklahoma City. She stumbled upon Life Church and quickly found a home for herself at one of their campuses. Then, at the beginning of 2020, our entire existence was turned upside down resulting from something called COVID-19.

Katelynn ended up moving back home with mom and dad. The life that each of us once knew just a few short months ago was now being rewritten almost daily. People were scared and confused in their lack of knowledge concerning the pandemic, as well as the disinformation which was being spread faster than the virus itself. However, Katelynn remained grounded and never once forgot what really mattered in her life. She was insistent on continuing to attend Life Church and remaining involved with that church as much as she possibly could. Life Church had one campus in the DFW area, which was clear on the other side of town, almost sixty miles away. However, the distance did not matter to Katelynn, she was going regardless.

From time to time, Katelynn would convince Robin and I to accompany her, instead of attending our regular church. Soon after, she began to drag her little brother along with her for the Wednesday night youth group, Switch. Before Robin and I knew what was happening, Katelynn's little brother, Dylan, was waking up early on his own to go to church with Katelynn on Sundays and was actually desiring to go to the youth service on Wednesday evenings.

At that point, Robin and I realized that this church was probably something that we should be taking a closer look at, so we began attending the weekly services as well. Robin, Dylan, and I now attend the newly opened campus of Life Church McKinney and are actively involved as well. Katelynn has since married a respectable young man from Oklahoma. They currently live in his hometown and attend a Life Church campus in the OKC area.

Katelynn was, and always will be my little princess, daddy's little girl. Katelynn got married last year and is now off to start a family of her own. Katelynn and her husband come down to visit us for the weekend about twice a month which is beneficial for both Robin and me. While I will always see Katelynn as that sparkly little girl running around in tutu's, I more so see her now as the glue.

Katelynn is the glue that keeps all of our family together. She has a special bond with each of her brothers and is always reaching out to talk with them as well as their significant others. Katelynn and her mom are best friends as well. Katelynn and I, well, let's just say that nobody knows how I think better than Katelynn does. Katelynn and I have a unique bond that cannot be put into words – It is a connection that only we can understand, and one that is deeply meaningful to both of us.

Katelynn was a challenge for me when she was born. A challenge that I had allowed Satan to place upon me with the lie that I could not be a father to a little girl based on the child that I had before I met Robin. In my mind, I had failed. In my mind I could not save that little innocent girl who was hiding behind the couch. In my mind I was the one who destroyed her life. In my mind I did not believe that I had what it took to have a relationship or a bond with a daughter. And my greatest fear was possibly destroying another child's life.

And even though these lies taunted me daily for most of Katelynn's younger life, I never allowed them to push me away from her. They more than likely pushed me harder to have that connection with her, and to make sure she always knew that her dad was her biggest supporter and fan. I know that I have never been perfect with Katelynn, or any of my children for that matter, but I also know that she does not expect me to be. I know that she just expects me to be her dad, and that she will love me regardless of where that takes us.

Katelynn has a special relationship with God as well and continues to grow in this relationship every day. I see Katelynn becoming a very powerful, faithful woman just as her mother is, and a true forceful warrior for God.

Dylan Matthew

Eight years later Robin informs me that she is pregnant again! What? How can this happen? We were done! I guess not.

Along came Dylan. Dylan may have been a surprise, but by no means was he an accident. Dylan has opened our eyes to a part of this world which we had not been exposed to before, and he continues to do so every day. Dylan is our savant. He utilizes faculties of his brain that Robin and I were completely unaware of. Dylan is highly intelligent, outwardly charming, and openly affectionate – all while being 6'2 and just over two hundred pounds. Dylan has been blessed by God with numerous gifts and abilities which I am confident will have a significant impact on many others throughout his life. And as I write this chapter, he is only seventeen.

Dylan's love for sports only became evident around the ping-pong table up until roughly a year ago when Katelyn married, and her new hubby enjoyed a passion for playing golf. Dylan suddenly took an interest and now desired to take golf seriously and play more often. I have always played golf, yet Dylan never seemed to have much of a hunger for the game in my numerous attempts to teach him.

So, with his newly awakened fervor for the game we found him a set of clubs, and then another set, and then another set – all within the first year. Why? With Dylan's progressive learning abilities, an understanding of the laws of physics, as well as physical kinetics, and how they each relate to the golf swing was elementary for him. In a very short time, Dylan realized aspects of the golf swing that take most people a lifetime to recognize. I have played and taught golf at the highest levels, all across the country, at both the amateur and professional level and I have never seen anyone learn or improve at the rate which Dylan has.

Dylan is also fond of playing chess. I taught him how to play chess as well, several years ago, and then he taught himself. When Dylan and I now have the opportunity to play, the game will not likely last more than five moves – if I am lucky.

.

Dylan decided that he would like to take piano lessons a few years back. Robin located a teacher in our area and would take him in for private lessons once a week. I knew a bit about playing the piano as my grandma had taught my siblings and I how to play, and my father had played professionally.

Dylan would then order music books from Amazon and take them to his lessons to learn. After probably six months of lessons Dylan came home one day and I overheard him telling Robin that he needed more music books and then asked her if she would order more for him. At the time, I paid no attention to his request as it was nothing out of the ordinary. Roughly two weeks later I heard him make the same request - which caught my attention and made me abruptly stop what I was doing.

My initial thought was that the kid was not even trying and was just breezing through them without any attempt at actually learning. I looked at Dylan and said *"Hold on, you just bought three new books a couple weeks ago. Are you even trying? You need to go back and practice them and then work at refining the way in which you play."* Dylan looked me square in the eyes and said - *Dad, I can play all of them and they are boring me.*

The next thing I knew, he had books from Beethoven, Mozart, Bach, and Tchaikovsky. And Dylan was playing them with both hands like he had been playing for years. Dylan does not know it, but sometimes when he is upstairs playing the piano I will stand around the corner and just watch and listen – in complete admiration and joy. It is such a beautiful thing, and it is just one of the many things which he does that makes me proud to say *That is my son!*

Dylan is inherently different than I am, as well as anyone that I have ever associated with in my life. At times, I struggle with the attempt to make a connection with Dylan, just as many parents do when our children are markedly different than we are. The simple explanation for this is that I just do not know how to.

This struggle is a flaw in my being and has nothing to do with who Dylan is. My perception of Dylan is that of having superior intelligence and an understanding of matters at a level beyond my comprehension and ability. And with my long-held conviction of never wanting to fail my children, fear overcomes me with the assumption that I will only disappoint him and let him down.

The reality is that Dylan is still my child, and he is made from the attributes of me. More importantly, as a child, he still needs, craves and desires the love and attention of his dad. And as his dad, I as well, crave and desire the love and attention of my son. The cravings and desires which I do possess have thankfully continued to push me past the delusive fear of rejection that I occasionally succumb too. Dylan and I have found ways to share time together. And while I am still trying to teach him whatever I possibly can, there is equally as much that I am learning from him. Just because Dylan is my child does not mean that I cannot be the student from time to time.

No matter how different you or the child may be, you still have a common bond. Focus on that which you do have in common – start there and be willing to let things go where they may. That is how a beautiful relationship is formed – which is exactly how I would describe what Dylan and I now have.

Ownership

As a father I have always tried to teach my kids right from wrong, not only in a legal sense, but morally as well. One lesson that I had taught each of them is the act of ownership – You must take ownership, or responsibility for your actions - which means owning up to the consequences of those actions rather than attributing them to other external factors or placing the blame on other people.

The main principle of this lesson is that if you are to do something wrong, offensive, damaging or hurtful in any way; if your actions or choices have caused something negative to happen – you take responsibility, or own up to it right away, and make it right, right away.

One of the underlying factors of this principle is that of our decision-making processes. We are only able to make the decisions and choices that we do, at any given point in time, based on the information that we have available to us at that point in time. We make all of our choices and decisions based on what we know, what we believe, and how we perceive this information.

As is the case with all of us, we are continually learning new information, things we did not know in the past. We are continually growing and developing. And as we grow, and learn more, we come to understand that many of the choices, decisions or actions that we have made in the past were made with incomplete or inadequate knowledge. We have since learned more and now have a better understanding as well as a different perspective on the matter.

I have also taught my children that this is a normal and acceptable part of life as well. We cannot possibly know everything about anything, and that as we grow and increase our understanding of things, we will also realize that some of the choices, decisions and actions that we have taken in the past were just plain wrong. I have taught them that it is okay to change your perspective, your stance, or to go back and change, or correct, the choices and actions that you have taken in the past based on the new information that you now know.

When we do realize that this new information gives us reason to change our course of action, we are also then acknowledging that our initial choice or action was incorrect, or wrong. Therefore, when we go back to change the action or choice that we made in the past, we must also own up to the consequences that the inadequate information caused to happen. This usually involves swallowing our pride and admitting to others that we were wrong and then doing whatever is necessary to make things right.

I would be very hypocritical, not to mention a poor example as a father, if I did not live by the beliefs that I had taught my children. I may be a bit biased, but I believe that Robin and I have raised four pretty awesome kids. They each mean the world to me, and I always want the best in life for them, so I am always attempting to pass on my knowledge and experiences in a hope to make their lives a bit easier and much more enjoyable. And, since I have recently come to learn new information, and therefore have come to hold a more true and accurate understanding of life – GULP! (that is me swallowing my pride) ...... I must now go back and correct the wrongs which I made in the past. I must let others know that the decisions, choices and actions that I had made in the past were incorrect and were based upon inadequate or false information.

To my children......... Joshua, Kristopher, Katelynn, and Dylan – As your father I have always tried to give you the best life possible, to lead you by example, and to prepare you for a successful life of your own as responsible, loving, caring individuals. I have always believed, at least at the time, that what I was teaching you and showing you was what would be best for your life and your future. But just as I have taught you to own up to your mistakes, I am doing so now.

My views, my perspective of this world, and the ways of life which I had perceived as being true, have been terribly incorrect! My understanding of life, and the way that we are to live it, has been based upon nothing but lies. Lies that have been fed to me since my childhood, and that I had come to accept as reality and the truth. Many of these lies and deceptions I have passed on to you, whether knowingly or not.

I hope and pray that deep in your hearts you truly know that I want nothing but the best for you, and that I would never intentionally do anything to cause you harm or suffering. However, the actions that we take have the ability to cause harm to others unintentionally as well, even though they may be with good intent. This is what I have done. The fact that I have misled you with the lies that I had come to accept and believe is a pain that is almost unbearable to me, and one that will stay with me for many years to come as each of you are my most valued possession.

I am coming forward to admit that I was wrong and to ask for your forgiveness. And please understand that any misguidance was never out of carelessness or neglect, it was simply because I did not know any better myself. It was how I was raised, and the wounds that had been inflicted upon me which came to define my life with these faulty views.

These faulty views have been passed on to you, as my children. Remember, we are all products of our own environment. These perspectives and understandings have become your normal, your reality, the ways in which you see and relate to all things. And because the information that you have used to form all of your perceptions was incorrect, many of the views and beliefs that you now hold as being accurate are incorrect as well.

The sadness continues to fill my soul as I am writing this as I know that I have mentored you down a road that only takes you further away from your true self and the person that you were created to be.

But as I have taught you as well, once we become aware that we have done something wrong, we must do whatever we can to make it right and then correct those wrongs as well as the outcomes that now exist as a result of those wrongs.

So how does one go about changing and correcting almost thirty years of flawed advice and direction? Well, it is not going to be easy, but with the grace and power of God I will spend the rest of my life resolved to do so. From this day forward I commit to you, as your father......... No, as your dad, to fill your lives with the truth and to help you find your way back to that road that leads us to pure joy and happiness, and to being the person that you were created to be.

This does require some help from you though. After all, you are adults now, and are responsible for your own actions, thoughts and beliefs. As adults, we are accountable for not only our actions, but the thoughts and information that we allow in to our minds which we eventually come to accept and believe. As adults we are responsible and accountable for seeking out the truth.

It is important for you to understand one thing though. This does not make you a faulty or inadequate person. You may be reflecting on your past right now pondering what is true and what is not. And although the knowledge which I have guided you with was faulty, it does not make you faulty as a person. Each of you still are and will always be uniquely awesome. We never are and never will be perfect. And we don't have to be. For it is only through Christ that we are perfect, and only through Christ that we know and understand the truth.

"Children are a heritage from the Lord, offspring a reward from Him." Psalms 127:3

Chapter 24

The Vacation

It is now Labor Day weekend. I have spent the last four months away from home, working in Omaha. Josh and his wife Ryan have taken an extended holiday weekend from work They had initially planned to take a short vacation to our house in Texas, with their girls. However, as I was now away from home, the family gathering would require me to make the ten-hour trip for a three-day weekend which at this point was just too much. I have been running nonstop for the last four months, and twenty hours of driving over a three-day period would undoubtedly drain me more than refresh me. But the family wants to get together – and I know too well that all of us need the escape.

Our respite was adjusted and everyone agreed to meet in Bella Vista, Arkansas. If you recall, this is where my good friend Gary now lives. It just so happens that Ryan's parents had purchased a home in Bella Vista to use as a vacation rental, which Josh and Ryan have taken advantage of several times. Josh is an avid mountain biker and the mountainous terrain in northern Arkansas offers many great adventures, beautiful scenery, and mild weather; therefore, he frequents the area often.

Our initial itinerary included the use of Ryan's parents' rental house for the three-day weekend, and that our whole family would stay there allowing us to be together. I would also be able to get a round of golf in with Gary during the trip, whom I have not seen in some time.

Josh and Ryan planned to drive down and arrive on Thursday. Robin and Dylan were also planning to leave Texas and arrive on Thursday. Katelynn and her husband had to work half of a day on Friday, so they were planning their arrival for Friday evening. I had some work to finish up on Friday morning and then needed to move my RV, which I stay in when I am on the road, and assumed I would arrive mid-afternoon on Friday. Kris would not be coming, which is routinely the case with family gatherings, and something that deeply pains both Robin and me.

About a week prior to our escape, we were informed that Ryan's parents' house would not be available, causing us to desperately search for another. Despite the short notice and the holiday weekend, we managed to secure another rental home for our stay.

Josh, Ryan, and their girls arrived on Thursday just as scheduled. However, Robin and Dylan did not. Robin had several complications arise at home and was not able to leave until Friday.

I woke up Friday morning to all hell breaking loose at work, which took me the better part of the morning to straighten out. And what should have been a simple move of my RV, had now become increasingly difficult and drawn out. I finally managed to roll out of Omaha around 1pm – completely frazzled and stressed out. I would then spend the next six hours on the road trying to unwind and put myself into the right disposition for my family, which was a futile effort as the highways were packed with everyone and their brother, seeking a getaway just as I was.

As I came within an hour of our destination, my emotions began to change. I wanted.... No, I needed the break, and more so, I needed to be around people who loved me and wanted me as well. I was so looking forward to the weekend, and shaking off the chaos of everyday life, even if only for a few days.

I began to let my mind wander into the tranquility of Robin and I spending quality time together; physically, emotionally, and of course sexually. I could envision us soaking up the moments and experiences that our kids were having and appreciating every minute with our two beautiful granddaughters. I had dwindled my drive down to one final hour, but for some unknown reason, it still felt like a destination that I would never reach.

Then, the alert of a text message 'pings' on my phone. It was from Robin. She had some friends who coincidentally happened to be passing through the same area that we were staying, whom she had not seen in quite some time. Friends that our children knew as well. Her text message informed me that the family was going to meet these friends for dinner, and she wanted to know when I would be getting into town – even though I had already made it perfectly clear to her several times throughout the day as to the exact time of my arrival.

I read the text message – Almost immediately, my mind flees from the trauma and wounds of my past which have defined me as a person, seeking the safety and comfort of that hardened person that I had spawned in an attempt at self-protection. The person that I had created which was emotionless and distant, allowing me to shield myself from having to endure that pain once again. I began to shut her out and became very angry with her for yet again ruining my chance at peace, joy and relaxation. Once again, it was her that caused me pain. Once again it was her that gave me that feeling of isolation and being deserted. Once again, she has validated the fact that she is no different than everyone else.

My expectation had been that my wife, who constantly states that she loves me, misses me, and wants to be with me; along with my kids whom I love more than anything in this world, aside from my wife, would all be anxiously awaiting my arrival and welcoming me with the love and affection that I so desperately needed the moment that I arrived.

However, my expectations would be light years away from what would actually play out. An oh so familiar scene where Robin has played the primary role on many occasions before, each one pushing me deeper and deeper into the wounds of my past, without me even being aware of what the true issue was. And the ensuing outcome would always the same as well – I would retreat to safety, keeping everyone else out, and becoming even more hardened and distant than before in a hopeless attempt to not relive the pain.

Right now, you are probably thinking how childish my reaction was. Just meet them for dinner, that would be the easy answer. Of course it would, and part of me knew that as well. But that solution would defy the underlying rationale of my wounds, and what it was that I deeply desired and had sought after my entire life – again, without even being consciously aware of what that desire was.

That solution would have felt to me as giving in and giving up; therefore, just accepting the pain and living in it for the rest of my life. I would then be forced to accept as my new reality that the wounds which had tormented me for so long now had control over me and my life, and how it played out, and that I would have to forever more submit to them. That solution would require me to forever give up any hope of realizing what I so desperately desired and needed.

An hour later I arrived at the house that we had rented. No excited wife anxiously awaiting to see her husband that she had not seen in almost a month. No kids running out the door to hug the father that they admire and love. No grandkids jumping with joy as their superhero had just pulled up. No one! Not a soul in sight.

The family get away which was to bring us closer had once again left me feeling as though I was not even a part of this family. That nobody loved me, nobody wanted me, and nobody wanted to be with me. That given the chance, people would always choose to do anything else rather than be with me – even the people that say they love me the most.

This exact scenario has played out countless times over my life, and most always with Robin as the main character, tasked to remind me of the truth that I had come to believe – That no one truly loves me or wants me. And every time that it has been reenacted, I am driven down to a deeper, darker place in an effort to protect myself from that pain and suffering. And every time, that act just further validates the beliefs which I possessed, causing me to separate myself even further, not only from her, but from all people.

I walked in the door of that empty house and unloaded my belongings. I sat down in a chair with a heavy heart thinking *"Here I am again – nothing changes."* My sad, depressing life. Not even my wife and kids want to be around me.

And then it hit me like a ton of bricks. I suddenly felt so foolish and stupid. How could I not have recognized this earlier?

This is not who my wife is. This is not who my kids are. That is just not the truth! They love me, they want me, and they love having me around. So, where in the hell.......... OHHHH, that's where this is coming from! This is and has always been Satan acting through my wife to get to me. To get to me by using the person that I love the most and have the biggest weakness for, and by jabbing his arrow straight into that wound of my past which hurts me the most, the one that I still carry with me to this day.

The wound that I received in my younger years was that of not having the love and affection of my parents, or a family. No matter how much I desired it or sought it out, it would be something that I would never receive. I would also learn later in life that in all of the moments which I perceived my parents to be showing love, or at least an effort, were just merely an outward action to receive something of gain for their benefit.

I would then meander through life desperately seeking anyone or anything that would give me even the smallest piece of that love or affection. And every time a newly found relationship would fail, or something that I had ventured in to would fall apart – it only further solidified my belief that I was worthless and that no one could love me or wanted to love me. This was my life, this was the lie that I had come to accept as the truth, and my core belief.

So, when Robin came into my life and loved me for who I was, regardless of what may happen, I viewed her love as I always had with everyone else. It was just a matter of time, she would eventually see the real me and leave me as well. She really did not love me, and sooner or later I would be right back where I was before.

As I stated before, this one episode on this one trip was just a recurrence of the same experience which had played itself out so many times before. It would always be with Robin, and Robin (at least as I perceived it) would always be choosing someone or something over me. And the situation or reasoning that Robin would be utilizing was almost always meaningless as well. Nothing in and of itself that I would ever get upset about, or that would bother me, without my wound.

Just as it was on this trip when Robin wanted to see an old friend who was passing through, whom she had not seen in a long time. Most all of the other experiences were the same way – Robin would choose to do something with someone else over seeing me, and most always when we had not seen each other for some time, mostly due to my job and my travels.

I would like to think that I have never been one to hold Robin back, and that I have always encouraged her to live life to its fullest, and to have a life and friends of her own. I support this and understand the importance of this in our relationship as well.

This day was different though. While my automatic response was of self-protection, just as it had always been, I had now come to know and believe the truths and was now able to recognize the lies and the attacks and what was truly causing something to happen. I knew Robin loved me and that I was the priority in her life. I knew that what I was being led to think was not the person that she was –

It was a lie. I also knew that my kids loved me and cherished the moments that we had together.

The Holy Spirit quickly opened my eyes to see that the attack was coming from the father of lies himself. Evil spirits were using my wife to get to me in an attempt to ruin the trip that we had planned. To rob us of the joy, togetherness, and relaxation. To create division and separation. And to keep us from living out the life that God intended for us.

Those same evil spirits knew my wounds from the past and had been continually working at making them bigger and bigger only to keep me believing those lies and living in them. And they used my biggest weakness, Robin, to inflict those wounds over and over again.

Some may ask why they continually used Robin, my wife, to get to me. The simple answer is that they knew me and my tendencies very well. They knew that I, for the most part, did not care about myself. They also knew from my past that no matter how hard my life got, I would always bear down and push to get through things out of self-preservation. They knew that attacking me directly was an option that may not prove to be successful. They also knew how great my weakness for Robin was. She was my whole world. They knew that anything Robin did or said would have a direct and immediate impact upon me. With that awareness of me, the attack was simple and almost guaranteed to work. Hit me where it would hurt the most and use the person that I cared the most about as the weapon.

I quickly saw the attack for what it truly was and let go of any and all anger and frustration toward Robin – unlike I had done in the past. Again, it was not her choice or doing, and more than likely, Robin was not even aware of the effect that it was having on me, as after all, it was my wound and not hers. This is yet another attribute that evil spirits have. They have the ability to influence other people to do things which those people are not even aware they are doing. They get others to take actions against us as an attack on us. And just as in this case with Robin, the act that those people are being led to do is not who they truly are as a person.

I then turned to Jesus and asked Him to come into the situation and give me healing of those wounds. I asked Him to reassure me with His truths and His love. And I asked Him to help Robin see that she was being used and lied to as well, to hurt the one that she loved the most. I then forgave Robin, as well as my parents for the wounds that they had given me and stood up firmly against Satan declaring that his lies had been revealed and that from this point on I rescind any agreement that I may have made with those lies. I declared the truths from my true Father and declared to Satan that he has no control over me or my family.

I had turned to Jesus, my source of power, strength, and truth, when the challenges came my way. And in that moment of attack, when in the past I would always retreat in self-defense, I stood firmly and fought back against the evil that was actually inflicting the damage, with the powers and truths given to me through Jesus Christ. My perspective had become crystal clear, and I was now able to see what actually had been harming me and holding me back for all of my years.

Did everything return to a happy and relaxing weekend vacation? Not exactly. Both Robin and I were able to see the attack for what it was. However, we must also understand that even though we may fight the enemy off, the wounds still exist, and damage has still been done. We have been attacked, just as in a battle. It takes time to heal, to recover. And this healing can only come through Jesus Christ. Like many of you, I had spent a lifetime believing these lies and deceptions, and they just don't disappear the minute that we accept Christ into our lives.

It takes time. It takes Jesus Christ. And it takes our commitment and intention to remain in Christ to heal our wounds and to fully replace the lies with the Truths of our Father.

And even though Satan and his evil spirits are potent and effective, we cannot deny the fact that we hold some amount of responsibility as well. After all, it was us who allowed these thoughts and deceptions in to our minds and hearts and allowed them to come to fruition by accepting them as reality and the truth.

"Above all else, guard your heart, for everything you do flows from it." Proverbs 4:23

Chapter 25

Mid Air Collision

In the early 1990's I moved to northern Colorado to attend Flight School, with plans to eventually become an airline pilot. This new adventure was very intriguing to me as I had never before imagined the possibility of something so big or rewarding in my life. The risks, the challenges, the thrills, the exhilarating feeling of being in complete control of a man-made object that willingly disobeys the laws of gravity; all while having the potential at any moment of losing control and possibly even one's life. SIGN ME UP! I could not wait.

I was a couple years out of High School and kind of just wandering through life when my father suggested that I take up a career flying planes. My father had flown twin engine prop planes for some time in his younger days. Why he stopped flying is just one of the many things which he never took the time nor the effort to explain to me.

At this period in my life, I still perceived my father as a superhero. He could do no wrong in my eyes, in the way which so many little boys and young men crave to see their father as. In a way that so many young men need their father to be, for the necessity of their being – a true man, a leader, an example and a guide to life. Well, several years later, I would be awakened to a new reality – one where my superhero was anything but. The man that left my mother and his four young kids to fend for themselves as he chased after another woman and her children. The man who had enacted this same betrayal once before when chasing after my mother. The man that thought of nothing but his own self-satisfaction. However, that is a whole 'nother book on the issues between a son and his father, and not our point for this chapter, so we shall move on. Nonetheless, at this time in my life I was still delusional about the images of my father which I naively believed to be true.

Learning to Fly

The first goal for anyone aspiring to fly airplanes is to earn your Private Pilot's license. Much like a young teenager learning to drive a car, you must first spend numerous hours flying, or learning to fly, with an instructor. Once the student completes the required number of flight hours with the instructor, and also completes many hours of what is called 'Ground School' (the book work part of the program) where one would learn about maps, charts, meteorology, airspace and flight rules; the Flight Instructor would then 'sign off' on your skills affirming that you have been found to be competent in the ability and knowledge required to fly a plane on your own. At that point, the student would then schedule an appointment with an FAA Examiner to take what is commonly called a 'check ride'. The 'check ride' is basically the test to get your actual Pilots License. Then, if all goes well on that 'check ride', you will receive your Private Pilot's License and legally be allowed to fly anywhere you want, at any time, in your little airplane. Well......... kinda! There are some limitations and exceptions, but they are not relevant at this point.

I would like to think that I am a pretty smart guy, just as most of us do, so getting through the course and the required materials came fairly easy to me. I received my Private Pilot's License in what seemed like no time at all and was then set free to fly the world. My father and I would thereafter take the occasional random trip in a rented plane, most times just so that I could log flight hours.

On occasion we would fly up into the mountains, stopping at Steamboat Springs, just to play golf. On other outings we would fly down to the Denver metro area and do touch-and-go's at JeffCo (Jefferson County Airport), which was always a blast as the runway butts up against the foothills of the Rocky Mountains, thus creating havoc with the winds which are very gusty and change in direction every ten minutes. I became pretty skilled in an airplane, and my confidence soon grew to cockiness.

My father collected and sold antique art for his profession. He would scour the newspapers and contact many of his long-time sources to determine what items may be going up for sale on any given weekend. Again, this was the early 90's. The Internet had not yet been created, so people actually had to read newspaper ads and put in some leg work to find the information that they were seeking.

The information that we now have available to us within minutes by a simple search on the Internet, would take a person hours to obtain through the newspaper back then. If you did not have the newspaper delivered to your house, you would likely drive down to the corner store and buy one. Then you would have to scour through the ads of items listed for sale to see if anything sparked an interest. And if something did, you would then have to make a phone call to that individual who had the item for sale. No texting, no instant messaging – just the plain old landline phone.

One particular summer my father had come to learn that some particular item of value which he was highly interested in was going to be available at some type of estate sale, in some small town in the middle of Kansas, USA. That town was so small that its placename is not one that you would find worthy of remembering. That town was roughly an eight-hour drive from where we lived in Colorado, and driving to that sale would essentially involve a three-day trip (one day to drive to the town, one day at the sale awaiting the item, and then one day to drive back). In a small airplane we could be there and back, all within the same day. What a game-changer!

While it is highly debated whether Orville and Wilbur were actually the first to 'invent' flying, they were the first to create a 'flying machine' and the first to patent a so-called airplane in 1903. I find it highly improbable that the Wright Brothers ever conceived a full comprehension of exactly what their creation would lead too, as well as the extent of the impact that it would have on the world and travel as we know it today.

In our hurried day and age, with everyone and everything moving at a break-neck speed, it is of no surprise that at any given moment there are roughly ten thousand commercial planes in the air. When you include military aircraft, private planes, and cargo planes in that count, that number can easily double. All day, every day, year-round.

Aviation 101

So, my father and I made plans to make the trip to Kansas with the hopes of obtaining this sought after piece of art, and I would fly us to the destination in a smaller rented airplane. We set out early that Saturday morning of the sale, and headed down to the local airport, or what is known as the FBO (Fixed Base Operation). An FBO is not what most are familiar with in terms of an airport; where you have to check in at a counter, get a ticket, check your luggage, and go through security. An FBO is, generally speaking, a smaller type of aviation business which provides services for private pilots, or private planes. They offer services such as fuel, airplane parking, hangers, maintenance, rental cars, and most always have a pilots lounge as well. These FBO's provide services for planes, as well as their pilots, ranging anywhere in size from the smallest single engine Cessna up to the largest multi-million-dollar corporate jets. Some FBO's across the country offer Flight Schools and rent smaller planes as well, which is where I learned how to fly.

At this point in my flying career, I held only a Private Pilot's license, along with a High-Performance rating. The High-Performance rating meant that I was certified to fly an airplane rated with over two hundred horsepower, which was essential when flying in and around the Rocky Mountains.

A Private Pilot's license allows the holder to fly using a method called VFR, or Visual Flight Rules (as opposed to IFR or Instrument Flight Rules). VFR rules generally state that the pilot must have Visual clearances to be able to see where they are flying, landing and taking off from, with certain minimum clearances or distance from clouds or weather, while still maintaining the minimum required altitude above the ground or terrain that they are flying over. An Instrument rating allows a pilot to fly under almost any weather condition as they are using only their instruments for guidance and direction. Under VFR flight rules, the pilot can take-off, fly, and land whenever and wherever they may desire without having to file a flight plan or inform anyone else of what their intentions may be - generally speaking. Somewhat like driving your car – you just get in and go.

However, many areas throughout the United States are designated as Controlled Airspace, such as larger cities where the air traffic is more dense and is therefore controlled by 'Flight Controllers', or what most people know as Air Traffic Controllers. Other areas where flying a plane may be restricted, or completely prohibited, are known as Restricted Airspace and include MOA's (Military Operation Areas) and the airspace over certain government buildings. MOA's can be further broken down into different categories of access, with some being much more restrictive than others. For example – certain MOA's are used simply for the flight training of military pilots, and therefore, these types of MOA's allow general aviation pilots to pass through them without special permissions. Other MOA's include areas where the military actively engages in missile and artillery training. These areas pose an extreme danger to the general aviation pilot and are therefore highly restricted airspace.

Washington DC, being our nation's capital and the location of many prominent government buildings, has the most highly restricted airspace in our country for national security purposes.

Had I been flying into one of these areas of controlled airspace on our trip that day, I would have had to request permission to do so before entering that airspace. The airspace which we would be flying through in the Midwest of the United States, however, does have numerous MOA's and military training routes used specifically for military flight training. These MOA's are unrestricted though, and do not require special permissions to access or fly through. We would also not be flying anywhere near or around any of the other types of controlled or restricted areas on this Saturday, so there was no need for me to file a flight plan, or to notify any agency of what I was doing or where I was going.

One important lesson that I had learned early on in Flight School is that bad things can happen when you are flying an airplane, and they tend to happen very quickly. And unlike driving a car, you cannot just pull over to the side of the road, and safety, when things do go bad. Most planes that are used as rentals at most FBO's are much older airplanes which have been flown many thousands of hours. Some FBO's are also not the most solvent or well-run businesses, and many times they choose to scrimp on maintenance, even though the maintenance of an airplane has certain minimum requirements set by the FAA which must be adhered too. Therefore, I learned that it is always a good practice to have someone looking out for you, knowing where you are and where you were going, even if you do not file a flight plan.

When I fly using VFR rules, I engage in this good practice through what is called 'Flight Following'. Flight Following happens like this – A pilot takes off from whatever airport he/she is flying out of. Once that pilot reaches their cruising altitude, they would contact the Regional Center (Regional air traffic control) which in my case would have been Denver Center. The pilot would then request 'Flight Following' from that Center, and, if the Air Traffic Controller's workload allowed for it, they would follow your flight on radar and inform you of any hazards or potential issues which you may encounter, before they become an issue. The Air Traffic Controller is not required or obligated to do this; however, they most always do for pilot safety.

So, my father and I arrived at the FBO that Saturday morning, then walked through the main lobby and out the back door which led us to the tarmac and the airplane we had rented. We loaded our small amount of gear on to the plane and I commenced my pre-flight check of the airplane. This FBO had several different types and sizes of airplanes for rental, but since it was a Saturday, most all of the other planes were reserved or already being used by the time we had reserved this plane.

The plane that we rented was a Cessna 177-RG Cardinal. The Cardinal is a four-seat airplane with a cruising speed of roughly 130mph, and retractable landing gear, hence the RG. Definitely not a Cadillac, but more than sufficient for our needs on that day. Plus, I had logged many hours in this plane, and she was coming to be like a trusted friend to me. I knew the ins-and-outs of that plane, all of its components and how each one would respond, as well as every little sound that she would make allowing me the ability to quickly determine if something was worthy of concern.

I completed the pre-flight check of the plane; we jumped in and began our taxi down to the end of the runway. The airport that we flew out of was in a smaller town as well, so I did not need any clearance from a tower to take off.

The Flight

A couple minutes later we were approaching V2 (another technical flight term which signifies that you have hit the minimum speed for that aircraft to be able to become airborne) and ready to pull back on the yoke and become airborne. We climbed out of the traffic pattern and headed east toward Kansas. In a short amount of time, I had reached my cruising altitude of 7,500msl (altitude above mean sea level) and called Denver Center on the radio to request Flight Following. The controller responded and I provided him my tail number for the airplane that I was flying, my altitude, my current location and my destination, and then requested flight following. The controller then replied back and advised me to 'squawk and ident' and gave me a four-digit code. This four-digit code is four numbers which the pilot enters into the transponder on the airplane, which sends out a radio beacon signal that shows up on the controller's radar, at which point they can identify who you are and where you are at.

The 'squawk' is an aviation term for entering the code, and the 'ident' means to identify, or to push the little button on the transponder which then immediately sends out a radio signal, allowing it to 'flash' on the controller's radar screen. I 'squawked', I 'identified', and the controller came back and responded that Flight Following was in progress.

Flight Following is not to be confused with a Flight Plan, or any type of guidance or direction. It simply means that they will 'follow' me and let me know of any foreseen circumstances or issues. I am still free to fly whatever route or altitude that I want and can cancel the Flight Following at any time that I may choose to do so.

The first part of our flight was routine with no concerns and nothing unusual transpiring. We crossed over the Colorado border and into Kansas without an issue. It was a beautiful, clear, sunny day with hardly a cloud in the sky. The kind of day that pilots dream of. Smooth flying with no turbulence. Visibility for as far as you can see. And temps in the mid 70's. It doesn't get any better than this. My camaraderie with the 177 Cardinal was going well and it was proving to be a very trustworthy companion. We were on track to make it to our destination ahead of schedule, and all was looking well.

After flying over Kansas for about an hour, a call came over the radio. *Cardinal 7568Victor, Denver Center.* That was Denver Center calling out to me. The tail number on the plane that I was flying was 7568V (Victor) and was what would be used to identify my plane. I clicked the Push-to-talk button on the headset and replied. *7568Victor.*

Pilots and controllers use very limited jargon when communicating back and forth and rarely use complete sentences or words. This allows conversations to be short and precise, thus allowing more airtime for other communications with other planes and pilots.

Denver Center then responded back – *7568V, contact Kansas City Center 132.6, Good day!* to which I responded *68V, Kansas City Center 132.6.* This meant that I had reached the outer limit of the Denver Center area of coverage and that they were now handing me off to the Kansas City Center for the continuation of my flight following as I was now entering the Kansas City Center airspace. I switched the avionics radio over to the 132.6 frequency and contacted Kansas City Center.

Kansas City Center, Cardinal 7568V is with you at 7500(feet), Eastbound in route to (the name of the small town that I cannot remember). Kansas City Center then responded and asked me to squawk a new code and ident. Kansas City Center then responded that they had me on radar, to proceed as planned and the flight following would continue.

My father and I were roughly an hour out from our destination, which was in the middle of nowhere, in the middle of Kansas. At this point in the flight there was not much to do. The plane was basically flying itself as I had it set on cruise control, and on a heading that would take us to a ground radio beacon signal that was near the airport we were going to. All of my pre-flight work included charts and maps of the surrounding airspace, as well as the small airport that we were landing at, including all of the requirements and traffic patterns for that airport. All I had to do now was keep an eye out for any occasional traffic (other planes) and listen for any incoming radio calls.

As a pilot, if you have done and prepared everything as you should have, you will most always reach a point during longer flights where you are........ bored! Yep. Bored. There really is nothing to do to occupy your mind and keep you from dozing off or allowing your attention to drift to other things outside of the flight itself. I managed to get a good night's sleep the night before, so I wasn't really tired, but I was bored.

Flying thrills me and ignites a passion in me which is hard to convey to others. The freedom, the independence, the beauty of the views from high above, and yes, the feeling that at any given moment your entire existence could be brought to a tragic end without notice. I feel fully alive when I am in an airplane, and even embrace the detrimental encounters, of which I have had several. But at times like this, with the constant hum of the engine and the lack of tasks, it is very easy to let your mind wander.

Murphy's Law states Anything that can go wrong, will go wrong. Or, in other words, if everything seems to be going well, you have obviously overlooked something. This is the point in every flight where things that will go wrong, do go wrong, and always when you are least expecting it.

Pulling my wandering mind back to reality was a radio call – *Cardinal 7568V, Kansas City Center, traffic, 10 o'clock, 100 miles.* This was Kansas City Center notifying me that I had another plane heading my way, coming towards me from my 10 o'clock position, and that traffic, or plane was one hundred miles away. My response, which was a normal response acknowledging that I had received their warning was – *68V is looking.* This meant that I had not spotted the traffic yet but was looking for it.

Both my father and I began to scan the horizon for the other plane as it headed our way. As I began to do so, a very questionable alarm went off in my mind. I had been flying for some time now and had logged over five hundred hours of flight time. Having to spot other traffic, and having controllers notify me of other traffic was a common thing, especially in the fast-growing area of the Colorado front range. So why would this controller be notifying me of a plane that was one hundred miles away? That doesn't make sense! I will surely be gone and out of his way by the time the other plane gets to where I am now!

Just about the time I finished with the questions in my head, my radio goes off again - *Cardinal 7568V, Kansas City Center, traffic, 10o'clock and fifty miles.* As my head reared back in shock I responded – *68V still looking.* My father and I were still looking for the other plane, but even in the clear blue skies at 7500 feet, spotting a plane one hundred, or even fifty miles away is not likely going to be possible.

The shock that I encountered was due to the lack of time between the controllers first call of one hundred miles and his second call which seemed like only a minute later stating that the traffic was now at fifty miles. Simple math would tell you that since the traffic was at my 10o'clock, the ground that he was gaining on me was almost solely due to HIS speed, and not mine, or me approaching him head on. My shock then turned to a near state of panic as my mind began to calculate possible scenarios. I knew right away that this had to be a jet; a very, very fast jet. Several other thoughts came to mind quickly as when you have a frightful or near-death experience. Many things flash before your eyes very quickly and your 'supercomputer' brain kicks in to overdrive with thoughts and contemplations.

My first thought was that the other plane had to be a commercial airliner, which was ruled out quickly as there was no logical reason that a commercial plane would be flying at 7500 feet out in the middle of Kansas with no larger airports in the vicinity. This thought was coupled with the thought and the image of a small bug being splattered against the windshield of a large semi-truck. And I would be the bug.

As if the Air Traffic Controller knew the thoughts I was having and was trying to save me from my own harmful deductions, the radio went off again. We still had not spotted the oncoming plane. This time, however, the call was no longer a cautionary warning. In a very stressed, quick and commanding voice, the controller came over the radio – *ALL OTHER TRAFFIC ON THIS FREQUENCY STAND BY – CARDINAL 68V, TURN RIGHT, HEADING 170 IMMEDIATELY. TRAFFIC AT 10 O'OCLOCK IS AN F4 FIGHTER JET DESCENDING FROM 12,000 FEET FOR A MILITARY TRAINING ROUTE.*

I quickly turned to the heading of 170 as directed by the controller and began a more southerly direction. Just as I did, I glanced out my side window, and the F4 fighter jet came zooming through the space which I had just occupied at a speed which was likely well in excess of Mach1. Mach1 is equivalent to the speed of sound, or roughly 767mph.

My heart was now probably beating faster than he was flying. I then responded to the controller that we were clear, and had the traffic in sight, which he already knew by now, as he had an eye on the situation long before I even knew that there may be a potential problem. I captured my breath and settled back into my previous state within a few minutes. My father and I then safely continued on to our destination, with no further issues or concerns.

I never really gave that day or incident much thought until recently, after God had brought many things to my attention. God has shown me many situations and encounters which have happened throughout my life, and how He was there with me the entire time, even though I had chosen to ignore Him.

Isaiah 35:8 says: *"Then will the eyes of the blind be opened and the ears of the deaf be unstopped".*

The main point that I learned from this experience is that we all need someone watching out for us. Someone guiding or leading us down the path which is best for us. Someone who truly cares about us and has the best intentions for us. God created each and every one of us, in His likeness. He put us in this world with one main purpose for our lives – To honor, obey and glorify Him, and Him alone. God wants the best for us and wants us to fully enjoy the lives that we have. God also knows the bigger picture, things that we do not know and cannot see, and He wants to protect us and guide us away from those things that do not lead us to that life full of joy.

Unfortunately, over time, the world that we live in has become so detached from God that He is not the main focal point in the lives of people in modern generations. We have been taught and raised to live a life dependent upon ourselves, and a life that is self-fulfilling and satisfying. This is also known as the Self-Life. Placing ourselves, our self-satisfaction, and other gods above the one true God – The Creator of All Things.

God truly desires to provide us with and lead us to that better life. However, as we separate ourselves from God, and do not have that constant contact and communication with God, we are unable to receive these gifts and promises that He so badly wants to bestow upon us.

God showed me that things could have been much different on that day, in that plane, had I not had someone watching over me. Someone giving me guidance and direction to the path which was best for me to get where I needed to go. On that day the Air Traffic Controller was watching over me. Seeing things and knowing things which I had no comprehension or understanding of. I had to trust in the ability and the guidance of that controller, and that he had my best interest in mind. I also had to be the one to go to the Air Traffic Controller and ask for the flight following. I had to seek out and establish the communication and relationship. He was there the whole time, just waiting for me to reach out and ask.

When we choose to walk separately from God, without His guidance and direction, we do not have the ability to see the things that God wants us to see or know. He reveals many things to us when we turn to Him and draw closer to Him seeking to do His will, and not our own. When we turn to God and acknowledge that we do not have all of the answers, and ask for His guidance and help, He will provide us with the answers and the direction to lead us where we need to go, and through The Holy Spirit, help to keep us from becoming that bug on a windshield. God wants this more than anything, and He has been wanting you since He created you.

But...... He wants you to want Him as well. That is the free will that God gave us – the free will to choose and decide what we want and whom we want to serve. And when you choose to serve the one and only true God, you will begin to see clearly the many things that have been right in front of your face for years, but were unable to see as you were blinded by the darkness of sin and Satan who does not want you to see the blessings and wonderful things that God has planned for you.

"Trust in the Lord with all of your heart and lean not on your own understanding; in all your ways submit to Him, and He will make your paths straight." Proverbs
3:5-6

Chapter 26

The Accident

September 23rd, 2022 – A day that I will never forget, for more reasons than one.

We had just begun the escape from the hot summer months in north Texas, but for us, summer was long from over. It had been one of the hottest and driest summers in many years. Most, if not all, of the south-central U.S. was experiencing extreme drought conditions. Temperatures had been in excess of one hundred degrees for what seemed like months now, and it felt like we had not had a drop of rain since Noah built the ark. The ground had become so dry that any grass which may have once existed on my acreage had withered away some time ago, and the now exposed dirt had fissures, or openings, so big that you could literally put your whole foot down inside them. Our town, as well as many other surrounding towns, had been placed on water restrictions several months ago, and there was no end in sight.

Our property is surround on three sides by a large farm field. Three hundred and sixty-four acres of farmland that is actively used to grow corn during the summer months. This is just one of the benefits that we love about our new home, nothing around us but peace and quiet.

A few weeks prior, the farmer was working in his field, harvesting his crop with a large tractor. About the time he had made it halfway through the field, friction created by the metal blades grinding against the dry crop had caused the field to catch fire. We did not have much wind that day, fortunately, but what wind we did have was blowing straight towards our property, and our house.

I just happened to be up in town that morning and was headed back home. As I started to head down the road to our home I could see the smoke, and the fire. There are not many other houses around ours, and from the distance that I was it appeared that our house was what was burning. I hit the accelerator to get home as fast as I could. As I approached our house, I realized that it was the field that was burning and not our home. This was a short-lived relief, however, as I then recognized that the blaze was headed our way with nothing to stop it.

We live in rural Texas. Nothing but volunteer fire departments. Don't get me wrong, these guys and gals are great, but they are not just sitting around at some fire station waiting for your call. It usually takes a bit longer for them to respond, quite a bit longer. And time was not something we had on our side that day.

Dylan and I jumped into action and did the only thing that we could do. Our home has a water spigot at the front and back corner of the house, so we each grabbed a hose and began drenching the edge of the field closest to our home in hopes that it would be too wet to burn. We hoped to create a fire block in some sense.

One thing which shocked me initially when I first saw the fire, but did not give much further thought too as I was busy trying to do whatever we could to save our house, was that the farmer driving the tractor had just completely disappeared. He had driven off towards the front of his property, and did not appear to be returning.

As Dylan and I are doing our best with two garden hoses, I see a large pickup truck pulling a flatbed trailer come racing through the field. The truck then began to make circles around the fire, over and over again. Fortunately for us, the farmer was prepared. He knew the potential risk that day, and he had what was probably a thousand-gallon tank of water on that flatbed trailer. Just as the farmer got control of the blaze, the fire department showed up.

About a week later, one little thunderstorm popped up just to the west of us. Finally, we were going to get some relief. The storm moved closer to us, and then suddenly veered to the south, giving us no rain or relief at all. What we did get was the outflow on the back side of the storm, with strong gusty winds for about ten minutes. Strong enough to cause more friction on the already parched fields and igniting another fire. A phenomenon that Californians are oh so familiar with during the Santa Ana winds.

This time the fire was in the neighbor's field across the street from us. And with the winds coming out of the south, it was all being blown our way once again. By the time I had made it outside of our house I was unable to see the street as the air was completely filled with smoke. My initial reaction again was to go for the hose; however, it is two hundred and twenty-five feet from the front of my house to the street. Most garden hoses are only fifty feet long, and that is if you buy a good one.

Fortunately, we were prepared. I had several hoses, and a few of them were one hundred feet long. I would just need to go get them, hook them up, and hopefully make it to the fence line in time before the inferno jumped the street and into our yard. I had no clue how far the fire had spread as I still could not see to the fence line, but I had to at least try.

By the time I had multiple hoses hooked up and had made it to the street, a couple of our other neighbors were out doing whatever they could with shovels and buckets. We managed to get another hose from another property and attacked the fire from two sides and were able to get it under control......... just as the fire department showed up.

Two close calls in just a week or so. However, those were just the events leading up to September 23rd.

That Day

I remember the day so clearly. It was a Friday, and it was another scorcher. September can also be an active month with my job. September 10th is the peak of Hurricane season, and almost every year in the past has had some type of hurricane or tropical storm develop during the time from the end of August to the end of September. This year would be no exception. There was a major hurricane which had formed off the east coast and was heading towards the U.S., and I just knew that I would be getting deployed soon.

At about 9am that morning I got a text message on my phone from my employer that I was being put on 'stand-by'. That just meant that I had better start getting ready, as more than likely the phone call would be coming soon. I began to start taking care of some things around the house to prepare for my departure, which would hopefully make Robin's life a bit easier should I be gone for the next couple months.

Dylan had piano lessons every Friday in the town just north of ours. Dylan had just turned sixteen the month before but did not have his driver's license yet. He was still driving on his learners permit due to the fact that since COVID, you were now required to schedule an appointment to get your license, and the first available appointment was most always several months out. This, however, was not a problem for us as it would give him more time to build up experience with another licensed driver in the car. That other licensed driver would almost always be Robin.

At about 2:30pm, Dylan and Robin left our house to head north for his piano lesson. Dylan was driving the car and Robin was in the passenger seat. I happened to be outside doing some work in the yard, exactly what I was doing I can't quite remember. I do recall that I had our John Deere tractor/mower out and had been riding around on that.

Dylan has always been what I would consider a good driver. He is not like your typical teenage boy, being carefree and reckless. He is cautious, but not to a dangerous extent. At this point he had been driving for almost a year now, and was comfortable with the vehicle, as well as knowledgeable of the laws and what he should expect from other drivers.

One point which I have always tried to get my kids to understand when it comes to my concern for their safety is that my apprehension is not due to a lack of trust in them or their ability – it is simply that I do not trust all of the other drivers on the road. I have tried to get them to have this viewpoint and mentality as well, that they always have to be aware of what everyone else is doing and be prepared to react accordingly. And, that they have to expect the other driver to do the unexpected.

Another safety tip that I have prepared my kids with is that the best way to remove yourself from a dangerous situation is to not put yourself into that situation to begin with. One simple example would be if you were driving down the interstate and both lanes were filled with traffic. There is no way that you can get around the traffic, so there is no point in flying up on the traffic and then riding someone's rear end with impatience. If something bad were to happen with one of those cars in front of you, you are now stuck right in the middle of it with no way out. Hang back a bit and give yourself some room to react and essentially remove yourself from the situation.

Tragedy

Dylan and Robin left the house for his piano lesson, and I watched them drive down the road as I was riding around on the tractor. About five to ten minutes later, for some unknown reason, I just happened to stop and get off the tractor. I was walking around and then heard my phone ring. I went to answer it and saw that the call was coming from Robin's phone. Had I still been driving the tractor I would not have been able to hear the phone ringing.

I answered the phone, and the call got cut off. The phone then rings again. Again, from Robin's phone – and again it gets cut off once I answer it. At this point I am figuring that Robin had just forgot something or was wanting me to do something while she was gone. The phone rings again – and again the call gets cut off. This happens several more times and by now I am beginning to get frustrated with the interruptions.

About the seventh time, I answer the call from Robin's phone again, and I hear Dylan's voice. The call is breaking up and is still not very clear, and I can only make out a few words here and there. However, I can distinctly hear screaming and sirens in the background – and then I hear Dylan say: *"Accident.......... North...... town"*, and the call is then cut off once again. I immediately dropped whatever I had and ran to my truck. I was not even sure if I left the tractor running or not, but at that moment I did not care.

We live roughly three miles south of the small town which we call home, and the town that Dylan was referring to. I ran and jumped into my truck and must have been doing 90mph as I flew towards town. As I approached town from the south side, a large cloud of black smoke off in the distance to the north came into view. My heart sank to the bottom of my chest with a heavy pain, and I immediately began to pray. My mind flashed depressing cogitations and I could see my whole world changing in an instant and could hardly bear the images of what it may look like without them.

The only road north out of our little town is a small county highway. The speed limit is 55, and that highway funnels traffic directly on to State Highway 75, about two miles north of town. There are a few crossing roads that this small county highway encounters, all of which have a flashing red light or stop sign for the oncoming traffic on those roads. The largest, and busiest of those crossroads is just prior to reaching State Highway 75, and the point at which you would be merged onto State Highway 75.

This last cross street has the city High School on the east side and then an overpass to the west. The overpass allows access to the smaller county highway for any traffic that has exited State Highway 75 on the southbound side. Once these vehicles cross over the overpass and to the smaller county highway, they are met with three different warnings respective to the traffic on the smaller county highway – The first being a flashing red light, indicating that they must make a complete stop and yield to any oncoming traffic – The second being a Stop Sign – and the third being a large yellow warning sign that reads 'Caution – Cross traffic does not stop'.

As I made my way north, out of our little town, and approached that intersection the blazing fire and thick, black smoke became very evident. My eyes were constantly scanning the surroundings for my wife and son, nowhere to be seen. I pulled my truck off to the side of the road where a large dirt cutout had been formed over the years by other vehicles. I quickly jumped out of my truck and began to look for any sign of my wife or son. To my right I could see Robin's car at the bottom of the roadside embankment, flipped on its side, completely ablaze as the fire department attempted to stop the inferno from spreading into the adjoining field.

To my left I can see another fire truck and an ambulance. Patiently sitting in the middle of the road I see a tow truck waiting for the firefighters to finish so that he can clear the wreckage. There are a few Police Officers pacing around, but no one has a sense of urgency. I cannot see my wife and son, anywhere. I loudly cry out - *"Please God, No, not them!"*

I then rushed closer to the scene, occasionally being opposed by a Police Officer, who stood no chance at stopping me as I barreled my way through. My eyes still scanning every possible place for any sign of my wife and son. As I get to the middle of the intersection, I can now get a full view of the mangled and charred wreckage laying at the bottom of the hill, and the visual confirmation that it is Robin's car. My mental capacities do not allow me to conceive a way that anyone could survive such an event, and my heart sinks even deeper.

I continue to search frantically around the area with little to no hope. No one is interacting with or confronting me either. It is as if they know something that I don't, something that for one reason or another they are reluctant to share. My head and my emotions are spinning out of control at this point. I am unable to comprehend how to go on from here, or how to even leave this scene, if they are not leaving with me. I do not know of and have never imagined a life without them in it.

As the last bit of hope begins to fade from my soul, I made one final turn around another fire truck that was sitting off to the other side of the highway. Right away I caught Dylan out of the corner of my eye, and could not hold my emotions in. I still could not see Robin, but as I rush over to Dylan, I see a man holding up a blanket, shielding my wife from the hot summer sun. They were both alive! They were both conscious! I honestly did not care what injuries they may have, or if this would change our lives forever. I just knew that God had heard me, and that God chose to pour His love out on me greatly by giving me many more days with them. Nothing else mattered. I truly did not care about anything else at that point.

The How

Dylan and Robin had made their way north that day. As they approached that last intersection before getting on to Highway 75, a minivan decided to suddenly proceed through the three warning signs just as Dylan was going through the intersection. The minivan clipped the back end of Robin's car causing it to spin out, slam into a pole, and then flip and role three times as it went down the embankment. Robin's car came to a stop at the bottom of a ditch and was lying on its passenger side. The lady driving the minivan proceeded through the intersection and then pulled over to the side of the street and waited, doing nothing further until the Police arrived. She just sat there, in her vehicle, and waited while the rest of the incident played out.

If you recall the first part of this chapter, we were experiencing an extreme drought. Fields and crops were catching on fire with just the slightest bit of friction or spark. I am unsure if it was due to the car sliding down the embankment, or if it was an electrical spark from the car, but almost immediately a fire had started near the front end of Robin's car. Robin and Dylan were still inside the car, and Robin was trapped on the passenger side, unable to get out.

At some point after the impact, Robin's right arm was smashed against the door or the dash and was completely severed in two about halfway down her forearm. Her left ankle had become jammed up underneath the dash which had torn one of the ligaments that connects her ankle and foot. Dylan was moving but was in complete shock. They both noticed the fire that was growing larger by the second but were not sure what to do. Being on the driver's side, and up in the air, Dylan could get out of the car and to safety, but he could not get his mom out of the car.

What would happen next told me more about my son than I had ever come to realize through his entire life. Dylan knew he could get out and to safety. He also knew that the fire was growing very quickly, and that it would not be long before the entire car was in flames. But Dylan also knew that he was not going to leave his mother, no matter what the cost may be. He knew that he would fight with every last breath to do anything that he could to try and save her. So, Dylan stayed, he kept trying, and the fire kept growing.

I find myself continually thinking back to that moment, trying to comprehend what my son must have gone through. I try to understand what it must have been like, and I am sure that any comprehension that I may have is nowhere close to what the reality of the situation was. I cannot even begin to grasp the thoughts and fears that must have been going through his mind in that moment. And then I question - would I have done the same thing at his age? I am not sure that I can say that I would have, and I don't think many others would have either.

Then I reflect even deeper – Where did he get that ability, that strength, that courage, that love from? And the questions become even more puzzling from there. My youngest son, our so called 'baby', had more courage and resilience than I had ever been witness to in my life. To say that I was proud of him would be a dramatic understatement. Awe and admiration would be more fitting. The young boy teaching the father what it is to be man.

Dylan stayed in that car struggling to get his mother free. The fire continued to grow and spread. Then, out of what seemed to be nowhere, appears a man. A man from several towns over who really had no purpose for being at that intersection, on that day, and at that time. A man that I truly believe was sent to be there, by God. He was a man of courage and strength as well. A man with morals and values. And a man that cared for others without any forethought of what the cost may be to himself.

That man immediately, without hesitation, ran into the fire and was able to get both Robin and Dylan out of the car and across the highway, to safety. Two minutes later the entire car was engulfed in flames. That man then stayed there with my wife and son and continued to hold that blanket up behind Robin to protect her from the scorching sun – even long after the fire department and paramedics showed up. That man was one of the last to leave the scene that day. That man was the protective, comforting, loving hand of God on that day. I wholeheartedly believe that he was put there at that moment by God and did the things that he did through the power of God and the Holy Spirit.

Robin and Dylan were taken by ambulance to the Emergency Room at the hospital in a town about ten miles to north of us. I followed behind and arrived shortly after they did. Robin received the majority of the attention, and the hospital paged the on-call Orthopedic Surgeon prior to her arrival. Soon after, she was being rolled out of the ER and rushed upstairs for emergency surgery. I was then told that the surgery would take several hours, if not most of the night, and the surgical nurse gave instructions on where we could wait for her as she came out of surgery.

All of my focus was on Dylan now, who had been poked, prodded, scanned and x-rayed by just about every team in the hospital. I have a nickname for Dylan that I gave him back when he was just a toddler. Dink. As in dinky, or small. It is a contrarian nickname that is completely opposite in describing who and what he is. At sixteen years old, Dylan was 6 foot 2 and weighed about two hundred pounds. He was a big boy! Neither Robin nor I are big people, however, Dylan, as well as his sister, were both well in excess of six feet tall.

After several hours of being checked over from head to toe, the ER nurse informed me that Dylan was fine and that he could go home. He had bumps and bruises all over his body, and numerous places where he had been cut and scraped and even had a few pieces of glass still stuck into his skin, but no broken bones and no internal injuries. An unexplainable sense of relief poured over me knowing that his injuries would quickly heal.

Dylan had been through a lot that day and making him sit in a waiting room for several hours until Robin came out of surgery did not seem like the smart choice. I figured that I would take Dylan to get some food, and then take him home where he could relax and get some sleep. After all, I needed to shower and change my clothes as I had been out working in the yard all day prior to the accident. (Hmmmm, I again wonder if the tractor is still running or not?)

Dylan and I returned home, and I made sure he was comfortable before I would head back up to the hospital. While Dylan did not have any significant physical injuries, the shock, the stress, and the trauma that he had been through would start a downward spiral for his mental state that we were ill-equipped to deal with. Leaving him home alone, after such a traumatic event, was probably the worst thing I could have done. Despite my insistence that he stay home and rest, Dylan wanted to go with me to be there for his mom -which kept me from making a stupid decision which I would later only regret.

We both headed back up to the hospital, and soon after, my daughter Kate-lynn arrived as well. I called my two oldest boys, who still lived in Nebraska, to make them aware of the situation. They too wanted to immediately come down, but I told them that at this point there was no need or reasoning for that.

Several hours later Robin came out of surgery and was being wheeled up to a hospital room where she would spend the next four days. I distinctly remember the surgeon coming in the next day to check on her arm and see how she was doing. I would later come to learn that he was highly skilled and one of the best in his field. You don't have much of a choice in the matter though when you are rushed to the ER on a Friday night. I guess we were lucky – again.

Robin was a bit groggy that next morning, and I'm not sure she realized who the doctor actually was. There had been so many nurses, doctors, and hospital workers in and out of her room that morning that it was a bit confusing as to exactly what his role was. The surgeon introduced himself and then explained to Robin and I what had taken place. Two steel plates and seventeen screws had been set to the bones in her arm to tie them back together. And then there was all of the nerve and tissue damage. Robin's right forearm had been completely snapped in two during the accident, to the point that she had to carry a good portion of her right arm out of the car with her left hand.

As the surgeon was discussing the surgery with Robin, he came to a pause. His head cocked downward and to the side a bit as if in shame. He then looked at Robin and said: *"I'm sorry dear, I did the best I could with what I had to work with."* Robin's arm was wrapped in a brace and thick gauze from the tip of her fingers to a point just past her elbow and would remain this way until our follow up visit with that surgeon. Until then, we would have no clue what it would look like.

It would take six months for Dylan to get back into a car again, let alone drive one. He would heal rather quickly from the physical damages, but the mental anguish would carry on for some time. He became withdrawn and began to isolate himself. Robin and I were trying to do everything we could to be supportive, and soon realized that even with our best intentions, this was something which we were unequipped to adequately handle on our own.

Through our church, and my friend Pastor Brian, we were able to find a good Christian youth counselor who specialized in the areas of teen trauma. We set an appointment, and soon after Dylan began seeing this counselor on a regular basis. I do not know the specifics of every conversation that they had, or what was discussed, but I have come to understand many things that transpired during their sessions.

I have never been an advocate of counseling, or therapy in the past. C'mon, are you surprised? Look at my past. I have always been a take charge, 'I have control of everything' kind of guy. I had always believed that if you needed counseling or therapy, you were weak or had a flaw. The truth is that I was the one with the flaw. I realize now that I was the hypocrite. As said before, I would always tell my kids to become an expert in one area and then go seek out an expert on things that you know little about. But me, in my inner core, still held the belief that I did not need anyone's help. I was smart. I knew enough. I could figure anything out. WRONG!

Dylan's counseling sessions did not seem to be making a whole lot of progress at first. I began to question the whole process, and the counselor. What I was not accepting was that it was a process. We were dealing with the human mind, and that is something that you just cannot heal in one session. After several months the moment came when I knew there had been a breakthrough. I remember that day vividly as my whole outlook and attitude changed for the better. I was suddenly filled with hope again, that my boy would be okay.

Dylan came home from his counseling session that day, and as usual, I would ask him how it went and if he wanted to talk about it. He began to detail what had transpired throughout the session, and then it came out. He told me that they played Chess. He then told me that the counselor did not know how to play Chess, so he had to teach her.

Dylan loves Chess. He has multiple different boards, as well as books on strategy. I taught Dylan how to play Chess and have considered myself to be a better than average Chess player. I could give most people a run for their money or at least drag the game out till there were only a few pieces left. Soon after Dylan got 'the bug' for the game, I would realize that I no longer stood a chance against him. He was now at a completely different level. The last time we played he ended the game in four moves. And I didn't even see it coming.

When Dylan told me that he had played Chess with his counselor, and had taught her how to play, I knew right away that we had him back. Playing the game required him to be involved in a process with someone else. To open up. Teaching the game required him to give care and thought toward others. He had come out of seclusion and was allowing himself to venture back out into this scary world.

Through his counseling, Dylan was taught to understand and accept the fact that trauma happens. It is inevitable and there is nothing that we can do to change that. What is important is how we respond to and frame that traumatic event. Do we let it define us and who we become, or do we define it? Dylan learned many different ways of coping with, or responding to the traumatic event, and learned that this event is just one brief moment in his life. It is NOT who he is or what he will become.

It has been two years now since that traumatic day. Dylan got his driver's license a few months ago and now has a truck of his own. He is back to his normal, outgoing and bubbly, loving self – for the most part. However, I have lived many years in this dark evil world and while I know that he is back to what we would call normal, I also know that he still carries that event with him and evil will continually try to use it against him.

Robin's arm has healed nicely, and the surgeon was pleased with the way that her bones had begun to grow back together. She has a very large and deep scar in the shape of an X that runs from her wrist almost all the way down to the bend in her arm. She despises it and cannot stand the sight of it. The woman who has been anti-tattoo her entire life is now considering the possibility of getting one to cover up the scar.

I have a different perspective of that scar though. I see it as a reminder to us, daily, of what God did for us on that day. The amazing grace, love, and care that He had for us, His children, and how He was right there with us the entire way making sure that we were protected and taken care of. I see it as God's reminder to us, and His way of saying - *"Ya, bad things are going to happen, but I am going to be right there with you and see you through all of it."*

Robin's ankle still has the torn ligament which makes it hard and painful for her to do things that she routinely did in the past. We are down to surgery being the final option, one which the doctor uses as a last resort. Several months after the accident we also became aware that Robin was still suffering from a concussion. This was not evident at first due to her other injuries and the medication that she was on. Her two biggest issues with this are her memory and her focus. She consistently forgets even the simplest routine things.

The struggle is further compounded as she has now become aware that it is happening, and it has become so frustrating to her that at times it sends her in to a depressive state. She knows she is not remembering things, but she cannot do anything about it on her own. She has tried everything from sticky notes to reminders on her phone – but she just forgets those are even there as well.

God gave me a gift on that day of the accident – a gift that I did not deserve, nor ever will. When it seemed that death and destruction were certain to be the only outcome, He gave me more time with my wife and son. He gave me hope, He gave me perspective. I no longer cared about anything else at that point, and certainly did not care what kind of physical condition they would be in. I just wanted them to be alive.

I also do not care if my wife has long lasting injuries which may alter the way she looks, or if her mental capacity has now changed to the point that we have to modify our lives. These things do not change my view of that woman at all. What absolutely tortures me is seeing her go through the pain and sadness that they cause her. She is my partner and my best friend, and what I want most is to see my friend enjoying her life to the fullest.

While many things have changed in our lives since that accident, we still have each other. I think that in some ways the whole experience has strengthened us all and brought us even closer to God. And while we still face many challenges as a result of the accident, I know one thing for sure – God was there with us in every step through the accident, the surgeries, and the counseling. I know who my God is, my Father, and I know that He was not just there to see us through that traumatic event. He is still with us and is seeing us through all of the other trials, and the rest of our lives. He has promised us that He will not forsake us, and I see that promise every day.

Many other issues are still unfolding as a result of the accident, even two plus years later. The lady that hit our car carried only State Minimums for insurance coverage. In the State of Texas that is a limit of $30,000 that her insurance company would be obligated to pay out for any injuries to Robin and Dylan each. Dylan, who only spent a few hours in the ER, easily surpassed that amount in medical bills alone. This lady was severely under-insured.

The simple answer, which I can see swimming in your mind right now, is to take her to court and sue her for the differences. That thought came to our minds as well. However, we have come to find out through our lawyer that she is living on bare minimums and there is no acceptance of responsibility in any aspect of her being. She currently has seven other judgments against her, and we would basically be standing in line to hopefully get something that will never come.

So, what did I learn from all of this. First and foremost, I learned that I was making progress in my faith, and my transformation from my past life. My immediate response in the past would have been to let my mind run wild with the thoughts of everything that I had lost and what the entire situation would cost me. It would have been filled with negativity on how everything is working against me, and how I can never seem to get ahead. I would have focused on the car that was burning at the bottom of the hill, the medical bills that continued to pile up, and the fact that my wife and son were not the same anymore.

My newly found faith in God, and all of His promises and truths, kept me focused on what really mattered. On what was important - my wife and son. It also gave me a new perspective. One in which I was now able to see all of the good things that God was doing for us, and how He was right there with us the entire time. And one in which I could now see that I did not have to carry the burden of all these things, as He would carry them for me.

I was overjoyed with the change that I had made, and that by the grace of God the veil of sin and darkness had been lifted from my eyes, and I was able to now truly see what had been right in front of me for most all of my life. The things that Satan and evil did not want me to see – the Glory of our Heavenly Father!

As Dylan learned in counseling – the trauma, the violence, the negativity, the hatred, the crime, the evil will always be there and there is nothing that you or I can do to stop it from happening. It is how we frame it that matters. How are we painting that picture in to our minds? It is how we perceive it, and what we are actually seeing that shapes and molds our future and our life!

"..... Don't slip back into your old ways of living to satisfy your own desires. You didn't know any better then. But now you must be holy in everything you do, just as God who chose you is holy. For the Scriptures say, "You must be holy because I am holy."" *1 Peter 1:14-16 NLT*

References

Chapter 2 - In the Beginning

1 – W. Clement Stone (1902-2002) – American businessman and philanthropist.

2 – Frampton Comes Alive! – 1976 – Released by A&M Records. Produced by Peter Frampton.

3 – Rolling Stone magazine – rollingstone.com – November 21st, 2012. https://www.rollingstone.com/music/music-lists/readers-poll-the-10-best-live-albums-of-all-time-18920/3-peter-frampton-frampton-comes-alive-131998/

4 -Wild At Heart Expanded Edition- John Eldredge. Copyright © 2001, 2010, 2021 by John Eldredge. Published by Nelson Books.

5 - Wild At Heart Expanded Edition - John Eldredge. Copyright© 2001, 2010, 2021 by John Eldredge. Published by Nelson Books. – Quote from Chapter 4, pg 58

Chapter 3 – The Fallout

1 – National Center for Family and Marriage Research - Bowling Green State University study on Divorce rates.

https://www.bgsu.edu/ncfmr/resources/data/family-profiles/loo-divorce-rate-US-geographic-variation-2022-fp-23-24.html

Chapter 4 – The 1980's

1 – Rebel Yell – Billy Idol, 1983. Chrysalis Records. Produced by Keith Forsey.

2 – Fight Club – 1999 film starring Brad Pitt and Edward Norton. 20th Century Studios. Directed by David Fincher. Produced by Fox 2000 Pictures.

Chapter 6 – The Child That Saved My Life

1 – Merriam-Webster dictionary – Deception

https://www.merriam-webster.com/dictionary/deception

Chapter 7 - A Better Man, A Better Person

1 – Dracula, 1897 Novel written by Bram Stoker. Published by Archibald Constable and Company (UK).

2 – Albert Einstein quote – BrainyQuote.com

https://www.brainyquote.com/quotes/albert_einstein_109012

3 – How to Win Friends and Influence People – written by Dale Carnegie. 1936. Published by Simon & Schuster.

Chapter 10 – Mr. G

1 – Hurricane Andrew – 1992 – Category 5. Wikipedia.

https://en.wikipedia.org/wiki/Hurricane_Andrew

Chapter 11 – The Beginning of The End

1 – Financial Peace University – Dave Ramsey.

https://www.ramseysolutions.com/ramseyplus/financial-peace?snid=products.pay-off-debt-and-build-wealth.financial-peace-university

2 – Dave Ramsey quote – https://www.instagram.com/daveramsey/reel/Csv_4_NgFr9/

3 – Dave Ramsey quote – https://x.com/DaveRamsey/status/1218179165943476224?mx=2

Chapter 13 – The Lies

1 – The Handbook for Spiritual Warfare – Dr. Ed Murphy. Copyright©1992, 1996, 2003 by Edward F. Murphy. Published by Thomas Nelson, Inc.

2 – The Bondage Breaker – Dr. Neil T. Anderson. Copyright © 2000 Neil T. Anderson. Published by Monarch Books.

3 – The Handbook for Spiritual Warfare – Dr. Ed Murphy. Copyright©1992, 1996, 2003 by Edward F. Murphy. Published by Thomas Nelson, Inc.

4 – Quote from Craig Groeschel – Senior Pastor Life Church, during weekly church sermon

Chapter 14 – Perception

1 – Merriam-Webster dictionary – definition of Perception
https://www.merriam-webster.com/dictionary/perception
2 – Wikipedia – definition of Perception
https://en.wikipedia.org/wiki/Perception

Chapter 15 – The Christian Life

1 – Merriam-Webster dictionary – definition of Believer
https://www.merriam-webster.com/dictionary/believe
2 – Inclusive New Testament INT version of the Bible – © Altamira Press 2004
3 – Merriam-Webster dictionary – definition of Things
https://www.merriam-webster.com/dictionary/things
4 – Merriam-Webster dictionary – definition of This
https://www.merriam-webster.com/dictionary/this
5 – Beautiful Outlaw – John Eldredge. Copyright© 2011 by John Eldredge. FaithWords Publishing.
6-8 – quotes from Beautiful Outlaw – John Eldredge. Copyright© 2011 by John Eldredge. FaithWords Publishing.
9 – George McDonald - quoted from Beautiful Outlaw – Copyright© 2011 by John Eldredge. FaithWords Publishing.
10 – Sacred Romance – Written by Brent Curtis and John Eldredge. Copyright© 1997. Published by Thomas Nelson.

11 – The Spirit of The Disciplines – Dallas Willard quote. Copyright© 1988 by Dallas Willard. HarperCollins Publishers.

12 – The Spirit of The Disciplines – Dallas Willard. Copyright© 1988 by Dallas Willard. HarperCollins Publishers. quote from pg. 5

13 – Merriam-Webster dictionary – https://www.merriam-webster.com/dictionary/salvation

14 – In Touch Ministries – Dr. Charles Stanley. Radio sermon *Waiting on God's Timing*. February 17, 2025.

https://www.intouch.org/listen/radio/waiting-on-gods-timing-part-1

15 – The Spirit of The Disciplines – Dallas Willard. Copyright© 1988 by Dallas Willard. HarperCollins Publishers. quote from pg. 210

Chapter 16 – The Battles That We Face

1 – Definition of War – Cambridge dictionary
https://dictionary.cambridge.org/dictionary/english/war

Chapter 17 – The Warrior in You

1 – Triumph – Fight the Good Fight – From the album Allied Forces 1981 – Produced by Triumph. Attic Records.

2 – YouVersion Bible Plan – The Heart of a Warrior (quote from day 1 of plan) https://www.bible.com/reading-plans/3871-the-heart-of-the-warrior/day/1

Chapter 18 – Prayers

1- El Reno largest tornado – https://en.wikipedia.org/wiki/List_of_tornadoes_by_width

Moore-Norman fastest windspeed – https://en.wikipedia.org/wiki/1999_Bridge_Creek%E2%80%93Moore_tornado

2 – Moving Mountains – Praying with Passion, Confidence and Authority – John Eldredge. Copyright© 2016 by John Eldredge. Published by Nelson Books.

Chapter 19 – Answers

1 – Craig Groeschel – Senior Pastor Life Church – self-reflective questions taken from church sermons personally attended.

2 – Get Your Life Back – John Eldredge. Copyright© 2020 by John Eldredge. Published by Nelson Books.

3 – The One Minute Pause App – created by John Eldredge and WildatH eart.org

4 – The Power to Change - Craig Groeschel. Copyright© 2023 by Craig Groeschel. Zondervan Books.

Chapter 20 – What Are You Waiting For?

1 – Brian Anderson – TheBridgeonline.net – The Danger of Knowing but Not Obeying the Gospel. Used with free permissions as listed on webpage.

https://thebridgeonline.net/sermons/the-danger-of-knowing-but-not-obe ying-the-gospel/

Chapter 21 – What Now?

1 – Quote from Psychologist Mark Travers – https://www.forbes.com/sites/traversmark/2024/09/16/a-psychologist-sha res-5-types-of-unrequited-love-and-which-is-worst/

Chapter 22 - What If?

1 - Waking The Dead – John Eldredge. Copyright© 2003, 2016 by John Eldredge. Published by Nelson Books.

2 – The Handbook for Spiritual Warfare – Dr. Ed Murphy. Copyright©1992, 1996, 2003 by Edward F. Murphy. Published by Thomas Nelson, Inc.

Discover the path to understanding the real truth and unlock a wealth of resources by visiting our website at DontHaveAClue.org. Empower yourself today!

Enhance your upcoming event by booking Ken Jones as a speaker! For inquiries and scheduling, please visit our website at DontHaveAClue.org. Don't miss the chance to motivate your audience!

Additional books by Ken Jones, including his new release, *The Poser*, can be found at most outlets, including Amazon.

Join thousands of others who now have a clue and know the truths. Become part of the movement and unlock true insight and knowledge today!
www.DontHaveAClue.org

 DontHaveAClue_thebook

 /Ken Jones

 @AuthorKenJones